Harvard English Studies 19

# The Black Columbiad

Harvard English Studies 19

# the Black Columbiad

## Defining Moments in African American Literature and Culture

edited by

# Werner Sollors
# Maria Diedrich

Harvard University Press
Cambridge, Massachusetts
London, England 1994

*Library of Congress Cataloging-in-Publication Data*

The Black Columbiad : defining moments in African American
literature and culture / edited by Werner Sollors, Maria Diedrich.
    p.   cm. — (Harvard English studies ; 19)
Includes bibliographical references.
ISBN 0-674-07617-6 (alk. paper).
ISBN 0-674-07618-4 (pbk. : alk. paper)
1. American literature — Afro-American authors — History and
criticism.   2. Afro-Americans — Cultural assimilation.   3. Afro-
Americans — Civilization.   4. Afro-Americans in literature.
I. Sollors, Werner.   II. Diedrich, Maria.   III. Series.
PS153.N5B553   1994
810.9'896073 — dc20        94-19727
CIP

Designed by Gwen Frankfeldt

# Acknowledgments

Some of the essays in this collection were first presented at the crowded workshop sessions on the Black Columbiad at the American Studies conference in Seville, Spain, organized by the European Association of American Studies with the participation of the American Studies Association; it was on that occasion that the possibility of the present volume first suggested itself. Now, with enthusiastic encouragement and support from Leo Damrosch and Lindsay Waters and the endorsement of Derek Pearsall, Larry Benson, and the Rollins Fund of Harvard University, this volume has become a reality as part of the Harvard English Studies series. We wish to thank them and the anonymous reader as well as Lauren Gwin, Alison Kent, Amanda Heller, and Minh-Trang Dang for their careful readings, helpful suggestions, and editorial assistance. We also wish to thank Berndt Ostendorf, one of the Seville participants whose work could not be included in the present volume, for contributing the Flip Wilson epigraph from his lecture "The Black Columbiad according to Moms Mabley and Flip Wilson." Thanks also to Brown,

Kraft & Co. and Triad Artists for permission to include the Flip Wilson piece in this book.

The contributors come from many different countries, and their approaches have been shaped by heterogeneous contexts. By and large, Maria Diedrich was responsible for selecting the Europeans and Werner Sollors for inviting the Americans. As a result, the present volume may be the most international and transnational collection to date dedicated to African American literature and culture. It is hoped that its publication will stimulate further comparative work, inspire more international cooperation, and thus contribute to the ongoing internationalization of American Studies.

# Contents

WERNER SOLLORS
MARIA DIEDRICH
  Introduction                                                          *1*

## Conceiving Blackness

ISIDORE OKPEWHO
  The Cousins of Uncle Remus                                            *15*

ANN DUCILLE
  Postcolonialism and Afrocentricity: Discourse and Dat Course         *28*

CARL PEDERSEN
  Sea Change: The Middle Passage and the Transatlantic
  Imagination                                                          *42*

GENEVIÈVE FABRE
  Festive Moments in Antebellum African American Culture               *52*

WILSON J. MOSES
  Sex, Salem, and Slave Trials: Ritual Drama and Ceremony of
  Innocence                                                            *64*

ANNALUCIA ACCARDO
ALESSANDRO PORTELLI
  A Spy in the Enemy's Country: Domestic Slaves as Internal Foes       *77*

STEFANIA PICCINATO
  The Slave Narrative and the Picaresque Novel                         *88*

CHRISTOPHER MULVEY
  The Fugitive Self and the New World of the North:
  William Wells Brown's Discovery of America                           *99*

Rosemary F. Crockett
 Frank J. Webb: The Shift to Color Discrimination                    112

Michel Fabre
 Paris as a Moment in African American Consciousness                123

## Sources of Modern African American Cultural Authority

Shamoon Zamir
 "The Sorrow Songs"/"Song of Myself": Du Bois, the Crisis of
 Leadership, and Prophetic Imagination                              145

Josef Jařab
 Black Stars, the Red Star, and the Blues                           167

Małgorzata Irek
 From Berlin to Harlem: Felix von Luschan, Alain Locke, and
 the New Negro                                                      174

Friederike Hajek
 The Change of Literary Authority in the Harlem Renaissance:
 Jean Toomer's *Cane*                                               185

Paola Boi
 Zora Neale Hurston's *Autobiographie Fictive:* Dark Tracks on the
 Canon of a Female Writer                                           191

Robert Gooding-Williams
 Black Cupids, White Desires: Reading the Recoding of Racial
 Difference in *Casablanca*                                         201

M. Lynn Weiss
 *Para Usted:* Richard Wright's *Pagan Spain*                       212

Sigmund Ro
 Coming of Age: The Modernity of Postwar Black American Writing     226

Gerald Early
 "Black Herman Comes Through Only Once Every Seven Years":
 Black Magic, White Magic, and American Culture                     234

## Defining Moments since the 1960s

David Lionel Smith
 Chicago Poets, OBAC, and the Black Arts Movement                   253

PHILLIP BRIAN HARPER
    Around 1969: Televisual Representation and the Complication
    of the Black Subject    *265*

UGO RUBEO
    Voice as Lifesaver: Defining the Function of Orality in Etheridge
    Knight's Poetry    *275*

FRITZ GYSIN
    Predicaments of Skin: Boundaries in Recent African American
    Fiction    *286*

JEFFREY MELNICK
    "What You Lookin' At?" Ishmael Reed's *Reckless Eyeballing*    *298*

KATRIN SCHWENK
    Lynching and Rape: Border Cases in African American History
    and Fiction    *312*

SÄMI LUDWIG
    Dialogic Possession in Ishmael Reed's *Mumbo Jumbo:* Bakhtin,
    Voodoo, and the Materiality of Multicultural Discourse    *325*

SYLVIA MAYER
    "You Like Huckleberries?" Toni Morrison's *Beloved* and Mark
    Twain's *Adventures of Huckleberry Finn*    *337*

HÉLÈNE CHRISTOL
    Reconstructing American History: Land and Genealogy in
    Gloria Naylor's *Mama Day*    *347*

JUSTINE TALLY
    History, Fiction, and Community in the Work of Black
    American Women Writers from the Ends of Two Centuries    *357*

ABBY ARTHUR JOHNSON
RONALD JOHNSON
    Charting a New Course: African American Literary Politics
    since 1976    *369*

## Prospects?

ADRIENNE KENNEDY
    Motherhood 2000    *385*

EVERYONE has idols, right. People who inspired them and drove them on to greater horizons. As a kid my idol—and he is still my idol—of all the great American heroes, my idol is Christopher Columbus. What a great thing that was, discovering America. I wouldn't have found it. I don't know where you people would have been. I wouldn't have found it. You know, discovering America wasn't a thing Columbus had gotten wrapped up in after getting older. As a kid this was all he talked about. He lived in a little town with his mother and father, their names were Mr. and Mrs. Columbus. Everybody thought Chris was off his cookie. Like the neighbors would be teasing, would come over, lean over the fence and be there in the yard and they'd say, "Christopher Columbus, what you gonna do when you grow up?" And he'd say, "I'm gon' discover America." They'd say, "You better cut that out. You know there isn't any America. You know the world is square." And Chris would say, "They sure are."

At thirty-five, he'd gotten out of grammar school. He arranged an audience with the queen, Queen Isabel. Isabel Johnson, that was the queen's name. She asked him about this America project. And Chris tells her, "If I don't discover America there's not gonna be a Benjamin Franklin, or a Star-Spangled Banner, no land of the free, and the home of the brave, and no Ray Charles." When the queen heard "no Ray Charles" she panicked. The queen said, "Ray Charles? You gonna find Ray Charles? He in America?" Chris said, "Damned right, that's where all the records come from." So the queen's running through the halls of the castle screaming, "Chris gon' fine Ray Charles. He goin' to America on that boat. What you say."

She wrote him out a traveler check. Chris ran to the local Army and Navy Store. He bought three used ships, two pair of fatigues, and some shades, and then he got supplies for the ships: two chicken sandwiches, three cans of Vienna sausage, five cases of scotch, and a small Seven-Up. Then he got a new rag to tie his head with, too. He's ready to leave. All of the photographers and reporters are at the pier to see him off. All the girls are there. They are all screaming. "Goodbye, Columbus, he's goin' on that boat. He's goin' to America."

Queen Isabel is there, and she's had a few. "Chris gon' find Ray Charles." Chris says, "Be cool, Isabel, be cool."

He turns to the first mate. "Weigh anchor." About ten minutes later the guy goes, "7,482 pounds." Chris says, "Put the anchor in the boat. Don't weigh it. You don't even know how to weigh anchor."

When they gotten out of the harbor the first mate asks, "Chris, which way is America?" Chris says, "I don't know. We better sail around until we bump into it. So we better go this way. If we go that way we'll sail off the edge like them other guys." A hundred days later the men are ready to mutiny. Chris has been goofing. He has been going through a bit like, "Back up, make a right, watch out for the edge."

First mate says, "Come here Chris. Chris, the men are ready to mutiny. The cabin boy said if you don't find America in two days he's going to smack you in the mouth." Right then a piece of wood floats by the ship. Chris said, "There is a piece of wood. So we are not far from America. That's American wood. I know American wood when I see it."

The first mate says, "Why don't you cut that out, it's a piece of the ship. They are breaking up on us." Right then the guy in the mast yells, "Land ho." Chris says, "What does that mean?" "It means he sees land." Chris says, "PULL OVER. Maybe that's America. You gonna pass right by it. You guys don't even know America when you see it. And that IS America: look at all those spacious skies, those amber waves of grain, dig that purple mountains' majesty. I bet there is fruit out there on the plain."

It's a big holiday in America that day, a big holiday called "Not-Having-Been-Discovered-Yet-Day." All the Indians on the beach, they are celebrating. They got sandwiches, sixpacks, three or four bags of whatever it is they putting in the pipe. Chris leans over the rail of the ship, he says, "Hey y'all. Y'all. Where is this?"

Fine little Indian girl, fine little Ind . . . fine little West Indian girl standing there on the beach. "Why, what's yo' name? What the hell you want, comin' round here in dem ships?" "My name is Christopher Columbus. I'm a discoverer. I'm gonna discover America. I'm going to discover y'all." Little Indian girl says, "We don't want to be discovered. You can't discover nobody if they don't want to be discovered. You better discover your ass away from here."

The first mate says, "Chris, they are hostile." Chris says, "Yeah, and they are mad too. We're going in there, anyway. That's America. They can't keep us out. America belongs to everybody. Let down the long boat." And they let down the long boat. This is really the short boat on the side of the big boat. They call it the long boat because they had a PeeWee boat, but they weren't going to use that.

They are piling into the shore and the men are laying down in the boat because the Indians are throwing rocks, spears, flaming arrows, tree trunks . . . yelling out a bunch of profanities about Chris's mother and everything.

The first mate says, "Chris, we better not go in there. Those Indians are crazy."

Chris says, "Turn the boat around, we'll leave. We'll make a map and give it to the pilgrims. The pilgrims'll fix their ass."

—FLIP WILSON, "Christopher Columbus" (1967)

# The Black Columbiad

Werner Sollors
Maria Diedrich

# Introduction

W hen the Pilgrims finally reached the North American continent after their perilous transatlantic passage, they fell on their knees to thank their god, "who had brought them over ye vast & furious ocean, and delivered them from all ye periles & miseries therof, againe to set their feete on ye firme and stable earth, their proper elemente," as William Bradford, one of their leaders, informs us in his *History of Plimouth Plantation.* But the land they saw once they allowed their eyes to rove over the new territory offered little reason for triumph and relief. They had arrived in a wilderness in which nothing familiar welcomed them. Bradford illustrated their sense of loss by refraining from describing what they saw; instead, he focused on their deprivation, listing only the things they missed: "Being thus passed ye vast ocean . . . they had now no freinds to wellcome them, nor inns to entertaine or refresh their weatherbeaten bodies, no houses or much less townes to repaire too, to seeke for succoure." The Pilgrims whom Bradford portrayed encountered a place which, for them, was without history, "a hidious & desolate wildernes, full of wild beasts & willd men," a place which had to be conquered and subdued before it could be integrated into God's kingdom.[1] Bradford's wife, Elizabeth, unable to bear the shock of the unfamiliar, apparently committed suicide by drowning herself in the Atlantic. By the end of the first harsh New England winter, a large percentage of the Pilgrims had fallen victim to cold, starvation, and sickness—and yet the letters the survivors sent back to the Old World abound with variations on Columbus's famous words, "I have discovered Paradise."

1. William Bradford, *Of Plimouth Plantation* (Boston: Wright & Potter, 1928), pp. 94–95.

Just as the utopian dreams of the ancient Greeks were transformed by their first encounter with India, the "discovery" of America made Europeans dream. In Thomas More's *Utopia* of 1516, in William Shakespeare's *Tempest* of 1611, in the poetry of Andrew Marvell, Michael Drayton, George Herbert, Jonathan Swift, and William Blake, we find images of a Golden Age and a Golden World which had lost the element of the purely speculative or escapist because they could be associated with a clearly defined geographic locale. Medieval Christian Europe had replaced the ancient concept of worldly happiness as the ultimate end of human endeavors with its exclusive concentration on life after death, but the awareness of a New World somewhere in the West rekindled in many Europeans the belief that happiness could be achieved in the here and now. Europe invented, spelled, and deciphered America as a social laboratory of human happiness, as a symbol of human aspirations. The New World made the Old World dream again.

The African American historian Nathan I. Huggins was among the first American scholars who, by rewriting this encounter between the Old World and the New from the black perspective, reminded us that this dream was not representative for all those human beings who were of central importance to the transformation of the dream into at least a semblance of reality—not representative because a large percentage of these people were not white. Huggins discarded Benjamin Franklin's "American destiny is white" approach to American history and associated instead with a tradition of African American representations of this history, from Olaudah Equiano's account of New World slavery and William Wells Brown's powerful metaphor of the three ships that created America (Columbus's *Santa Maria*, the *Mayflower*, and the slave ship in the James River), to W. E. B. Du Bois's concept of double consciousness, to contemporary rewritings of the African diaspora. Huggins's rewriting of history from the bottom up opened our eyes to the fact that slavery and racism, far from being "aberrant and marginal to the main story of American history," are in fact definers of that history.[2] His conviction "that there can be no white history or black history, nor can there be an integrated history that does not begin to comprehend that slavery and freedom, white and black, are joined at the hip"[3] did not merely challenge the conventional master narrative; it taught us that the New World became

2. Nathan I. Huggins, *Black Odyssey: The African-American Ordeal in Slavery* (New York: Vintage, 1990), p. xxxiii.
3. Ibid., p. xliv.

truly new only when the European Columbiad was redefined by the African diaspora, when the European inventions of America encountered the inventions of America that were manufactured by the involuntary African pioneers.

In his study *Landscape and Written Expression in Revolutionary America* the British scholar Robert Lawson-Peebles insists that "before America existed on the map, it existed in the imagination," and he documents how the preconceptions of the explorers, conquistadors, and settlers influenced their perception of the New World.[4] Richard Gray confirms this argument in his analysis of the southern myth, *Writing the South:* the early American colonizers, determined to overcome their sense of displacement, "figured the wilderness in terms that would not only help them to appropriate and subdue it but [that] would also enable them to see it as redemptive."[5] In their struggle to claim a land that appeared hostile in its defiance of their projective faculties, they imposed their vocabulary on it in terms of a meaningful system, so that the geographic place became one with the landscape of the mind—a mind in search of the earthly paradise which Christopher Columbus as well as the British adventurer Captain John Smith and the Puritan settler John Winthrop claimed to have found. Their fantasy thus represented what Annette Kolodny calls "symbolic forms . . . that clarify, codify, organize [and] explain . . . the raw data of experience."[6] For the early "explorers" America was a metaphor they constructed to support and authenticate their sense of identity, an attempt "to name and codify reality as a means of self-expression and self-knowledge."[7] Submitting to what Lawson-Peebles calls the "imperialism of the mind,"[8] their projections shaped the territory they entered.

If the images which the Europeans imported shaped the territory they entered, if they reconstructed the New World, we have to ask ourselves how the "discovery" and appropriation of this unfamiliar continent could be

---

4. Robert Lawson-Peebles, *Landscape and Written Expression in Revolutionary America: The World Turned Upside Down* (Cambridge: Cambridge University Press, 1988). p. 7.

5. Richard Gray, *Writing the South: Ideas of an American Region* (Cambridge: Cambridge University Press, 1986), p. xii.

6. Annette Kolodny, *The Land before Her: Fantasy and Experience of the American Frontier, 1630–1860* (Chapel Hill: University of North Carolina Press, 1984), p. 10.

7. Wayne Franklin, "The Literature of Discovery and Exploration," in *Columbia History of the United States,* ed. Emory Elliott (New York: Columbia University Press, 1989), p. 16.

8. Lawson-Peebles, *Landscape,* p. 9.

achieved by those who had never asked to participate in this encounter between the Old World and the New—African slaves and their descendants. What was their situation? While they were still living in their African societies, the New World had been outside their perceptive realm. Before their kidnapping they had no incentive, and after it no chance, to prepare constructively for their confrontation with the unfamiliar, to invent a transatlantic New World, or even to anticipate the New World in terms of its promise. America as both locale and dream was nonexistent in the African cosmology. Violently torn from their communities, with their cyclical concept of history, and dragged across the continent in chains, the African prisoners were herded together on slave vessels by beings whom they could only perceive as evil spirits, skinless and savage creatures, as early slave narratives relate.

Olaudah Equiano's narrative of 1789 documents this process of violent departure and loss of orientation in a paradigmatic way. Nothing in the life of this black child prepared him for his Columbiad. He grew up in a society that taught him with great care to become a useful member of a community which perceived itself in terms of repetition and continuity, but which did not know the words *future* and *progress* and which provided no vocabulary for the confrontation with the nonfamiliar, with the deindividualization and fragmentation that were to characterize his biography. After an endless odyssey through West Africa, during which he was denied explanations about his destiny and destination, he reached the coast and encountered his first white men. The boy, as a consequence of his upbringing, was unable to perceive them as human beings; he could only associate them with the evil spirits which threatened the lives of men in his native cosmology: "I was now persuaded that I had gotten into a world of bad spirits, and that they were going to kill me. Their complexions too differing so much from ours, their long hair, and the language they spoke, (which was very different from any I had ever heard), united to confirm me in this belief." The narrator dramatizes the quality of the child's perceptual paralysis by having his protagonist lose consciousness: "and, quite overpowered with horror and anguish, I fell motionless on the deck and fainted."[9] Equiano experienced his loss of identity, his banishment as a slave from the community of human beings, his transformation into a piece of property, and, finally, his symbolic

9. Paul Edwards, ed. *The Interesting Narrative of the Life of Olaudah Equiano, or Gustavus Vassa, the African: Written by Himself* (1789; rpt., London: Dawsons, 1969), pp. 70–71.

death as a social being immediately after he was carried on board: "I was immediately handled and tossed up to see if I were sound, by some of the crew."[10] That is, the storability, stability, quality, and, finally, the potential market value of the product were tested. Only articles in perfect condition were taken aboard; damaged goods were rejected, discarded.

After a long and painful transatlantic passage, to where they did not know, the African travelers reached a continent of whose very existence they had not even been aware. They were purchased by whites whom they feared as cannibals because the whites handled them like slaughter cattle, and whom they despised as savages because they defied all laws of civilization, all African notions of morality and decency, by raping, mutilating, and killing those over whom they had acquired power. The slaves were driven across a land which contained no recognizable landmarks for them, and they ended up on plantations which they could not define in terms of a geographic locale. There they lived among whites they had already learned to fear as devils, and among blacks with whom they could not communicate. Their masters increased their inner paralysis not only by depriving them of the power of the word, but also by denying them any information about the location of the plantation, the surrounding countryside, or the geography of the country. For if you don't know where you are, you don't know where to run.

Whereas Columbus conquered "new" lands for Europeans, thus increasing their mobility and freedom and providing them with new perspectives, the African diaspora stands for the end of freedom, for the loss of perspective; for the European the encounter with America represented human progress in history, but for the slaves it meant their expulsion from history; whites celebrated the New World as their potential paradise, while the Africans drifted in a world of evil spirits which threatened them with social and physical annihilation—in hell: "The shrieks of the women, and the groans of the dying rendered the whole scene of horror almost inconceivable," Equiano writes.[11] Finally, unlike the white settlers, who explored and subdued the new territory by using their cultural skills, the slaves came unprepared to a hostile world, and those who imprisoned them denied them the information they needed to cope. "Only myself was left," Equiano writes, remembering those first months of linguistic and social isolation and loss of orientation.

10. Ibid., p. 70.
11. Ibid., p. 79.

"I was now exceedingly miserable . . . I had no person to speak to that I could understand. In this state I was constantly grieving and pining, and wishing for death rather than anything else."[12] Houston A. Baker, Jr., refers us to the Heideggerian concept of nothingness as an adequate equivalent to this experience: "Man is in this world, a world limited by death and experienced in anguish; is aware of himself as essentially anxious; is burdened by his solitude within the horizon of his temporality."[13]

And yet, when in 1816 prominent American slaveholders such as James Madison, James Monroe, Andrew Jackson, Henry Clay, and John Marshall founded the American Colonization Society to rid the New World of the involuntary black "explorers" by shipping them back to Africa, the free African Americans of Philadelphia protested against their expulsion from a continent which they had come to consider as their homeland. In an open letter of 1817 they wrote: "Whereas our ancestors (not of choice) were the first successful cultivators of the wilds of America, we their descendants feel ourselves entitled to participate in the blessings of her luxuriant soil, which their blood and sweat manured; and that any measure or system of measures, having a tendency to banish us from her bosom, would not only be cruel, but in direct violation of those principles, which have been the boast of this republic."[14] This statement is one of the defining moments in African American history and culture. As Malcolm X's quip "We didn't land on Plymouth Rock, my brothers and sisters, Plymouth Rock landed on us"[15] declares, the ancestors of contemporary African Americans had not asked to participate in the encounter between the Old World and the New. But this open letter also reveals that the appropriation of the unfamiliar and hostile continent by men and women who had come without images of America and in chains had taken place against all odds. Yet how do we define this process of "discovery," invention, and appropriation? What were the values, the images, and the vocabulary which accompanied our African "explorers" on their terrifying Columbiad? And what were the values, the images, and the vocabulary these people developed in their survivalist endeavors to familiarize themselves with the unfamiliar—to reinvent, rediscover,

12. Ibid., pp. 90–91.

13. Jean Wahl quoted in Houston Baker, Jr., "Autobiographical Acts and the Voice of the Southern Slave," in *The Slave's Narrative*, ed. Charles T. Davis and Henry Louis Gates, Jr. (New York: Oxford University Press, 1985), p. 245.

14. "By the 'Free People of Color' of Philadelphia," in *Chronicles of Black Protest*, ed. Bradford Chambers (New York: Mentor, 1968), p. 52.

15. Malcolm X, *Autobiography of Malcolm X* (New York: Grove Press, 1965), p. 201.

and redefine America from a black perspective, to endure in and to accommodate themselves to this appalling and attractive New World? How did the extremely heterogeneous group of African pioneers manufacture themselves into African Americans?

No single answer is given to this question in the following pages. Instead, what many of the contributors to this volume propose is that a great variety of at times quite unpredictable elements has informed or has given special meaning to African American literature and culture. Instead of attempting to "canonize" a limited repertoire of such moments—be they tied to social history, political orientation, rhetorical figures, gender, or intraethnic literary influences—this volume takes some steps toward a fuller exploration of themes that have been central as well as those that have been marginal or invisible in past approaches. The essays focus on diverse moments such as slavery, the transatlantic tradition, urbanization, rape and lynching, gender, Paris, periodicals, festive moments, a Berlin ethnologist, Afrocentrism, Mark Twain, Spain, *Casablanca*, orality, the 1960s, black-Jewish relations, television images, comedy, magic, and boundaries. Among the authors discussed in some detail are William Wells Brown, Frank Webb, W. E. B. Du Bois, Alain Locke, Zora Neale Hurston, Richard Wright, Etheridge Knight, Ishmael Reed, Toni Morrison, Gloria Naylor, and Charles Johnson; they appear here, side by side, with the trickster in the Middle Passage, "postcolonial" practice, John Canoe, domestic slaves as foes, expatriates, blues and jazz in the United States and eastern Europe, Benin art, the magician Black Herman, the Emmett Till case, the television series *Room 222* and *Julia,* the Black Arts movement, the albino motif, Bakhtin, voodoo, genealogy, and recent black journals.

This procedure may help to call attention to the vast areas of cultural interplay that were not always emphasized by approaches that silently proclaimed a single element or a select number of moments as the truly defining ones. By contrast, the catalogue emerging here is meant to be open-ended, as the collection is intended to expand—not limit—the discussion of the ways in which the study of African American cultural expression has at times been framed. Now that African American literature and culture are being taught much more widely than in the past, both in the United States and abroad, it may be useful to explore wider contexts that do justice to the great and often unpredictable variety of complex cultural forces that have been at work in black America.

In order to serve this function best, this volume presents only new, previously unpublished essays which are somewhat shorter than usual in order to permit the inclusion of more work. Many of the contributions are excerpted from fresh research, thus giving the reader glimpses of work in progress and suggesting some of the directions into which Afro-Americanists are currently moving. The ongoing scholarship sampled here ranges from dissertations that are being completed by young Americanists to recent research findings by senior scholars. And although most contributions are from literary and cultural critics, some historians, philosophers, independent scholars, and writers are also represented here. The pieces are arranged in three larger sections, "Conceiving Blackness," "Sources of Modern African American Cultural Authority," and "Defining Moments since the 1960s." The collection concludes with a not altogether optimistic view of the future: Adrienne Kennedy, the Obie Award–winning playwright best known for *Funnyhouse of a Negro* and *The Owl Answers,* the author of the postmodern autobiography *People Who Led to My Plays,* and a Lila Wallace Fellow, contributed the prophetic piece "Motherhood 2000."

Although the arrangement loosely follows a chronological order from distant past to recent past to present and future, this does not, of course, imply any attempt at achieving comprehensive historical representativeness. The purpose is always to provide suggestive provocations for future scholarship and to make facile generalizations more questionable. To "round up the usual suspects" (in the famous line spoken by Claude Rains in *Casablanca,* the cult film also subjected to a novel scrutiny in these pages) will be harder than ever now that so much new and exciting scholarship, inside and outside this volume, is emerging.

# Conceiving Blackness

*O*RIGINS—departure—passage—arrival. This terminology is associated with human progress when related to the conventional understanding of the concept of the Columbiad. Yet it acquires a radically different meaning, a tragic quality in reference to an analysis of that transatlantic odyssey suffered by those millions of Africans who encountered the New World not as voluntary pioneers but as captives and slaves of the European explorers. The essays in the first section of this volume focus on the complex and often contradictory processes of transmission that characterized and still characterize the perennial struggle for inventing African Americanness or blackness out of interactions with disrupted forms of Africanness.

The genius and imaginative courage of New World black cultures are lost and the scarring quality of the African diaspora is denied in romantic or sentimental readings of these cultures that insist on African survivalism, on an uninterrupted continuity of the African and African American experience. In reality the relationship is much more complex, and involves appropriations, retrievals, inventions, and discontinuous, fragmented memories. Isidore Okpewho—whose *Epic of Africa* remains the standard treatment of its subject—challenges contemporary approaches to African American folklore in the volume's opening essay, "The Cousins of Uncle Remus." The relation of the black diaspora to Africa is neither a shameful disremembering of the African past nor a proud replication of African traditions.

In "Postcolonialism and Afrocentricity: Discourse and Dat Course" Ann duCille—the author of *The Coupling Convention: Sex, Text, and Tradition in Black Women's Fiction*—positions herself in the current debate on the invention of ethnic identities by suggesting that "for every Other constructed by the academy, there is a self attempting to assert its subjectivity." The result of what Robert Farris Thompson and Paul Gilroy have studied as the Black Atlantic tradition, the Black Columbiad is for duCille a perennial colonial contradiction. It generates the argumentative dilemma of an academic discourse that theorizes a postcolonial condition while implicitly establishing a precolonial connection. The complex and interlocking phenomena characteristic of the diasporic experience are suppressed in favor of a "would-be familiar" which is inherently incompatible with the postcolonial self.

The discourse of the single voice which celebrates the master's movement westward toward emancipation while suppressing the experience of those forced to travel in chains in the ship's hold has failed to do justice to the multifarious dimensions of the Middle Passage. So argues Carl Pedersen in "Sea Change: The Middle Passage and the Transatlantic Imagination." His analysis of selected works from African American and Afro-Caribbean literatures, using the limbo gateway as its metaphor, documents the need for an open-ended dialogism, for "between the fixed points of Europe, Africa, and the Americas, dialogic discourse in its many forms subverts colonial domination by becoming part of its consciousness."

Geneviève Fabre's "Festive Moments in Antebellum African American Culture" describes and interprets the diverse functions of the Jonkonnu or John Canoe festivals, the equally playful and resistant festive events of the American slave communities. By insisting on the "complex web of meaning" which these festivities acquired in a large variety of settings and in different historical situations, by rediscovering and relocating them in time and place among a vast field of histories and geographies, Fabre—the author of the classic study of modern African American drama *Le théâtre noir aux États-Unis*, published in a shortened English version as *Drumbeats, Masks, and Metaphors*, and many other works—delineates a plea for a creative defiance of closure, for dialogic open-endedness in the methodology of African American scholarship.

Stressing the common origin of trial and drama in primal ritual, Wilson J. Moses's comparison of the Salem witch trials of the seventeenth century and the New York conspiracy trials of the eighteenth in "Sex, Salem, and

Slave Trials: Ritual Drama and Ceremony of Innocence" goes beyond the interpretation of "civil libertarians" who see these events as paradigms of the paranoic style of persecution suffered by women, nonconformists, and minorities in the course of American legal history. By rereading these events as epic trials that rely on the "primal rites and dramatic ceremonies of fertility, innocence, and guilt" with the intention of controlling through ritual, Moses—the author of *The Golden Age of Black Nationalism, Alexander Crummell,* and other books—insists that their function was not to prove the innocence or guilt of the accused individuals "but to ceremonize and regulate the innocence of societies."

Alessandro Portelli, who has published numerous books, including *Bianchi e neri nella letteratura americana* (Blacks and Whites in American Literature) and, more recently, *The Text and the Voice: Writing, Speaking, and Democracy in American Literature,* and Annalucia Accardo, a co-editor of an essay collection on American autobiography, collaborated on "A Spy in the Enemy's Country: Domestic Slaves as Internal Foes." Covering a wide and heterogeneous range of texts on slavery, from the antebellum slave narrative and Mary Chesnut's diary to Ralph Ellison's *Invisible Man* to Malcolm X's *Autobiography,* Accardo and Portelli's essay takes on one of the most piously held assumptions of black-white relations under the "peculiar institution." Reductionist inventions of the domestic slave as the treacherous "house nigger" are challenged in a sophisticated analysis of the slaves' emotional relationship to whites, as well as the whites' feelings and attitudes toward their slaves, that visualizes and illuminates the painfully confusing entanglements of the color line.

Adopting the binary structure of rhetoric that characterizes the abolitionist discourse of William Wells Brown as a model for his own analysis, Christopher Mulvey, in "The Fugitive Self and the New World of the North: William Wells Brown's Discovery of America," focuses on those paradoxes of the American political creed which dominated nineteenth-century black antislavery writing. Mulvey, a specialist in the field of Anglo-American travel literature and the author of *Transatlantic Manners,* perceives Brown's *Fugitive Self* as a classic statement of the reinvented self. Brown's flight from slavery becomes a powerful rewriting of Columbus's journey from a black perspective, since Brown had to discover America from within and to make himself over by gaining his own self-possession, as much literally as figuratively.

Stefania Piccinato, who has published numerous works, including *Testo e contesto della poesia di Langston Hughes* (Text and Context in Langston Hughes's Poetry), takes a new look in her essay, "The Slave Narrative and the Picaresque Novel," at the antebellum slave narratives and their relation to *Lazarillo de Tormes* and the European picaresque tradition. She offers a detailed examination of the two genres and depicts them as foundational examples of a literary tradition. The interaction between past and present, the concept of exemplarity, and the communal discourse are discussed as connecting links between African American and European texts.

Rosemary F. Crockett's "Frank J. Webb: The Shift to Color Discrimination" is an impressive piece of African American archaeology. Part of a larger work in progress on the little-known but fascinating mid–nineteenth-century novelist Frank J. Webb, the essay provides some newly found biographical information, and thus renders visible the challenges a biographer faces in snatching from oblivion and reconstructing the life of an African American in an antebellum America that denied free African Americans political and social participation, and consequently failed to record the black contribution to the shaping of American history.

The beauty of the city, its racial liberalism, its sophistication and refinement, its respect for difference, in short, what James Baldwin called its "fine, old air of freedom," has given Paris a special place in the African American mind, according to Michel Fabre—internationally known as the critical biographer of Richard Wright and the author of the study *La Rive Noire* (published in English as *From Harlem to Paris*)—in "Paris as a Moment in African American Consciousness." He describes the elation of African American visitors at the freedom they experienced in Paris. The complex process of redefing their relationship to the United States and to their own work as well as to their African Americanness which these intellectuals underwent as a result of their European encounter is carefully explored in this account of generations of African American travelers and expatriates sojourning in the City of Light.

*Isidore Okpewho*

# The Cousins of Uncle Remus

*O*n Christmas night, 1977, in the village of Ibusa in southwestern Nigeria, I was the guest of my old elementary school headmaster, Chief S. O. Aniemeka, at a banquet featuring oral performances organized for my benefit. The audience was made up of Aniemeka's extended family and neighbors—mostly peasant men, with their wives and children clustering around my recording tackle. Also present was Ojiudu Okeze, the best-known narrator in the village, some of whose tales I had recorded the previous night.

Most of the event was, understandably, turned over to Ojiudu Okeze, who told his stories in the loose, colloquial, but colorful diction that characterizes his style. Ojiudu recorded several stories for me, to the accompaniment of various percussion instruments struck by two members of the audience to supplement the music of his thumb piano; the rest of the audience, myself included, participated actively in the performances with gasps, applause, laughter, comments, questions, and other forms of response.

One of Ojiudu's stories was about a stalwart loafer, Opia Nwammemee, short-tempered and antisocial, who thought nothing of dispossessing friend and foe alike of their wives. Although the wives in the audience were just as affected as anyone else by the humor of the tale and participated in singing the accompanying songs, they blushed quite visibly at the hero's machismo and, for the benefit of their husbands, condemned the ease with which the hero's victims seemed to yield to his rapture. Another tale was about the forest-dwelling ogre Nwankebeli, a staple of nighttime performances which scared smaller children but amused the adolescents who had learned to take the mythical character somewhat less seriously.

Chief Aniemeka also encouraged anyone in the audience who had a story to tell or a song to sing to come forward. I was particularly struck by the performance of Adaeze Nwajei, a young woman of about thirty. She prefaced her tale by leading the rest of us in a nationalistic chant—an anthem, as it were—glorifying her village, Ibusa, over the neighboring towns and villages; her derogatory reference to Asaba was made with an apologetic smile in my direction, for she knew Asaba was my (maternal) hometown.

She then told a tale which folklorists would readily identify as an explanation of the origin of death. Briefly, mankind, distressed by the persistent loss of its members through death, addressed a plea for immortality to God through the dog. God granted the plea and sped the dog on its way home. But the dog had spent so much time peeing on one spot or object after another on its way, and sniffing each on its return, that mankind became worried about the fate of its plea. So it addressed a similar plea through the chameleon, a slower but more diligent animal. On receiving the same message from a different envoy, God was offended that mankind was trifling with him and withdrew his offer; every human being would die in due course.

In my investigations of the kinship between African and Afro-American traditions, I have found the constituent motifs of this tale refracted in two New World variants. The first is a tale from Guadeloupe.[1] Briefly, Cat and Dog had an argument: Cat held that once a person died, that should be the end of the matter, but Dog contended that when people died, they should rise again. They decided to approach God to settle the issue. While Dog schemed to slow down Cat's progress by placing bits of butter along his way, Cat conceived a similar scheme by placing bones along Dog's path. Cat studiously avoided the decoys laid for him by Dog, but Dog could hardly resist the temptation to eat the bones. So Cat got to God first and received an assent to his case; when Dog finally reached God, he found he was too late.

The second variant is an Afro-American tale reported by Langston Hughes and Arna Bontemps about a father dog who took his puppy on a walk to help him learn his way in the world:

---

1. Harold Courlander, *A Treasury of Afro-American Folklore* (New York: Crown Publishers, 1976), pp. 90–91.

They walked from place to place, and at each stop the old dog smelled an object (a garbage can, a fireplug, and so on), and the young one followed suit. Finally, they encountered a "she-dog," which the old one smelled, nuzzled, and "jumped up on her and knocked himself off a piece." So the young one did the same. Later, when the old dog was quizzing the young one on what he had learned, the latter admitted he was a little perplexed about things. "What's the idea of being out in the world? I don't see any rhyme or reason to it." To which the old one replied, "Well son, my only advice is anything in this world you can't smell, eat, or make love to, piss on it."[2]

Now, how do we treat the relationship of these New World tales to the African one? Even more broadly, how do we view those tales from the African diaspora as bearing any resemblance to tales recorded from African societies?

A contribution to this old debate[3] has been made by John Roberts. Reacting against a prevailing Eurocentric trend in the study of the Afro-American folk heroic narrative, Roberts adopts an "Afrocentric" approach which "emphasizes a profound and enduring relationship between African and African American cultures and oral traditions." Roberts traces the genealogy of Afro-American folk heroes from the "trickster hero" of slave tales. This, for him, derives from an African trickster-tale tradition that reflects the vicissitudes of a hostile ecology (drought, famine, and the like) and the conflicts engendered by "a rigid, hierarchical social structure," and provides for the slaves the only available model of behavior in a repressive system where they are forced to depend on their wits for survival.[4]

In time, Roberts tells us, social and power relations within the slave system were altered with the entry of the black slave driver appointed by the master to enforce his control over the slaves. There was some ambivalence in the

2. Roger D. Abrahams, ed., *Afro-American Folktales* (New York: Pantheon, 1985), p. 7.

3. For arguments about African survivals in New World traditions, see the debate on the black family between E. Franklin Frazier, "The Negro in Bahia," *American Sociological Review*, 7 (1942): 465–478, and Melville Herskovits, "The Negro in Bahia," *American Sociological Review*, 8 (1943): 394–402, On oral narratives, William R. Bascom and Richard Dorson have led two opposing armies of folklorists arguing, respectively, for and against African origins; see Richard Dorson, *American Negro Folktales* (Greenwich, Conn.: Fawcett Publications, 1967), for the casus belli; Daniel Crowley, ed., *African Folklore in the New World* (Austin: University of Texas Press, 1977), and (posthumously) William R. Bascom, *African Folktales in the New World* (Bloomington: Indiana University Press, 1992), for the major salvos.

4. John Roberts, *From Trickster to Badman: The Black Folk Hero in Slavery and Freedom* (Philadelphia: University of Pennsylvania Press, 1989), p. 11; subsequently cited in the text.

driver's position. On the one hand, to the extent that he represented the authority of the master, he was distrusted by the slaves. On the other hand, as a black man he was one of them and could be counted on to shield them from the excesses of the system. Both sides of the driver were inevitably reflected in the next stage of development of the Afro-American heroic tradition, the "John and Old Master" cycle of tales, in which the driver responds sometimes with trickery, sometimes with bravado in his confrontation with the slave system.

The next stage of growth of the heroic tradition brought to the fore "conjure-men," mystics professing skills in healing, fortune-telling, and other forms of ministration the slaves had known in Africa. They were often distrusted and feared by the slaves, and were considered by the whites a menace to both the Christian ministry and the authority of the masters. At any rate, the slaves saw the conjure-man as an ally in their relations with the system, and several "conjure tales" portrayed the conjurer as a hero in using his mystical resources to thwart the power of the enslaver.

The slaves did yield in large numbers to Christianity, embracing it with the ecstasy they had felt toward the divinities of their traditional religions. Still, in their surrender they found material within the new faith to sustain their psychological need for allies to combat the evil system. Here, an array of figures who had faced various forms of repressive authority—Moses, Joshua, Joseph, Daniel, even Jesus—became for the slaves a pantheon of heroes whose virtues they sought, through their spiritual songs, to internalize in their confrontation with the system. Indeed, many notable leaders of slave revolts—Nat Turner, the Prosser brothers, Denmark Vesey, and others—were men inspired by biblical precepts.

The genealogy of heroes ends with the outlaw, the last in the long line of figures enshrined in the folk narrative imagination as defenders of the black community's well-being and traditional values. In the Reconstruction that followed the Civil War two character types emerged. The first was dubbed the "bad nigger," a "neighborhood bully" who made life difficult for fellow blacks and "threatened their abilities to maintain the value that they placed on harmony and solidarity as a form of protection against the law" (Roberts, 179). The second was the "badman," who, operating as a law unto himself, proved a menace both to the "bad nigger" and to the machinery of the law whereby the whites continued their repression of black people.

The Afro-American heroic tradition was thus adjusted to accommodate the legends of notable outlaws—Stagger Lee, Railroad Bill, John Handy, Devil Winston, Batson, and others—who epitomized the people's struggle to protect their material and spiritual welfare in a post-emancipation era of free enterprise in which " 'bad niggers' and the law posed serious problems for African Americans with upper-class pretensions" (Roberts, 213). True, these heroes inspired as much fear as respect in the black psyche, which is why their careers often landed them in hell or in soul-searing penitence. But for Afro-Americans they fit well with a "tradition of folk heroic creation based on values traditionally recognized as the most advantageous for protecting their identity and well-being as African people from both external and internal threats" (Roberts, 215).

Roberts's book deserves to be taken seriously as an analysis of the conditions that made possible the transformation of an oral tradition as it moved across time and space. He is convinced that "the expressive forms that emerge as a result of cultural transformation . . . may be conceptualized as 'new wine in old bottles' " (Roberts, 12), and sees his study as an Afrocentric project designed to locate this folk tradition within a long history of culture building among African peoples.

The links with Africa are indeed recognizable enough for the wine to be just as familiar as the bottles. For instance, an Akan-Ashanti tale—about how Ananse the Spider acquired his treasury of tales from the Sky God[5]— strikingly parallels another from the Sea Islands off South Carolina, about how Rabbit acquired enhanced power from God.[6] Also from the Sea Islanders comes a dilemma tale of three fellows, Trackwell, Divewell, and Breathewell, each of whom plays a significant role in rescuing a drowned girl and claims her for himself.[7] This is clearly a variant of a dilemma tale, recorded from the Loma of Liberia, of three hunters who perform equivalent feats in the killing, dressing, and packaging of an elephant.[8]

The performance techniques of African and Afro-American raconteurs also amply demonstrate the kinship of the traditions. Observing black narra-

5. Paul Radin, *African Folktales* (Princeton: Bollingen Press, 1970), pp. 25–27.

6. Abigail Christensen, *Afro-American Folklore Told around Cabin Fires* (New York: Negro Universities Press, 1892), pp. 36–41.

7. Elsie Clews Parsons, *Folklore of the Sea Islands, South Carolina* (New York: American Folklore Society, 1923), p. 41–42.

8. William Bascom, "African Dilemma Tales: An Introduction," in *African Folklore*, ed. Richard Dorson (Bloomington: Indiana University Press, 1972), p. 153.

tors in Michigan, Richard Dorson remarks on the energy with which they simulate the movements and speech habits of human and nonhuman characters in their tales[9]—which reminds me of the hilarious exertions of one of my narrators, Odogwu Okwuashi of Onicha-Ugbo, as he mimicked the seductive movements and speech of women in his tales. Afro-American narrative performances are just as marked by unrestrained audience participation—in the form of laughter, exclamations, comments, and the like—as are African ones.

Finally, if the informal apprenticeship of storytellers is anything to go by, then the homely setting of the cotton field has proved as effective a nursery as the African subsistence farm. When in 1981 I asked Charles Simayi of Ubulu-Uno how he had learned the tales he told me, he said he had picked them up simply by listening to his father and his fellow farmers as they exchanged yarns during intervals of farm work.[10] Ralph Ellison makes a similar point about schoolmates back in Oklahoma, who would skip school every fall in the cotton picking season just to listen to their fathers exchanging stories about ghosts and outlaws in the cotton patch, then return to charm him and others with these stories.[11]

And yet, however enlightening the connections Roberts makes, one is left with the sense of a hermeneutical gap and is forced to ask of the transformations for which he argues, how new is the wine, and how old the bottles? The problem arises because, although Roberts endeavors to locate the two traditions within their respective historical and sociological contexts, he does not venture to identify the ethical and other factors that sustained heroic creation in Africa and whose disappearance during the Middle Passage forced changes on it in the New World.

Indeed, Roberts's problem may be traced to his reading of the trickster tales. On the whole, he sees the trickster of the Afro-American oral tradition as a role model. So convinced is he of this figure's African ancestry that he exaggerates "the prominent position that [Africans] gave animal trickster tales in their performances" (Roberts, 29).[12] Universally popular they cer-

---

9. Richard Dorson, *Negro Folktales in Michigan* (Cambridge, Mass.: Harvard University Press, 1956), p. 24.

10. Isidore Okpewho, *African Oral Literature* (Bloomington: Indiana University Press, 1992), p. 21.

11. Ralph Ellison, *Shadow and Act* (New York: Vintage Books, 1964), pp. 7–8, 157.

12. I believe I have said enough in my study *Myth in Africa* (Cambridge: Cambridge University Press, 1983), p. 68, to indicate where trickster tales belong on the spectrum of African narrative performances.

tainly are; even children tell them. But they are mostly lighthearted fare, and although symbolic analysis has often interpreted them as reifications of problems in social relations, they occupy a far lower position in a people's hierarchy of conventional wisdom than those stories in which they record the traces of their emergence as a nation or a culture.

Roberts is no doubt right in the development that he so carefully traces for the Afro-American narrative tradition—trickster tales to heroic narratives—but such a progression can hardly be claimed for Africa, where the two kinds have long existed side by side. Nonetheless, although they frequently share characteristics such as performance techniques and (at a general level) content, they exist in different sectors of the generic spectrum because they serve somewhat different needs in the tradition.

Now, if we really want to query those needs, we ultimately have to answer the question Roberts's discussion raises but hardly tackles: How was it that the enslaved Africans brought with them such a superabundance of trickster tales but almost no heroic tales or epics? Why was it that, in Roger Abrahams's words, "the grand bardic forms of epic and other kinds of praise singing, the elaborate recitations of genealogies, and . . . most of the political and philosophical dimensions of African story were lost to us in the Middle Passage"?[13] We know that, whereas trickster tales are told by all and sundry, epics and the more complex forms are narrated by artists with a long and intensive apprenticeship and, in some cases, a privileged attachment to certain circles. Could it be that all such artists died in the Middle Passage, to a person?

Roberts rightly provides the sociological background to the entrenchment of the trickster model in the Afro-American narrative psyche, but he ignores the ecological considerations. Surely conditions such as drought, which Roberts identifies as a factor in the growth of the African trickster tradition, were just as endemic in the New World,[14] and may be considered just as effective an aid to cultural memory as the counterpoise (real and symbolic) between all creatures great and small. More seriously, however, Roberts fails even to suggest the cultural conditions—"the political and philosophical dimensions," to cite Abrahams again—that permitted the growth of the heroic

13. Abrahams, *Afro-American Folktales*, p. 18.

14. See Herbert Aptheker, "Maroons within the Present Limits of the United States," in *Maroon Societies*, ed. Richard Price (Baltimore: Johns Hopkins University Press, 1979), p. 160, for references to "drought" and "uncommon dryness" in 1827 in New Orleans.

tradition in Africa but whose absence severely postponed its emergence in America for some three hundred years. Even the likes of Nat Turner and Denmark Vesey failed to make a lasting impression on the oral narrative memory. Although they enjoyed a guarded apotheosis in the eyes of their fellows, they provided no more inspiration to heroic song than the post-emancipation outlaw because they invariably lost their campaigns.

But African heroic epics were built around figures who won their campaigns. Even when one historical tradition records that a figure lost a war, a different tradition (especially from the figure's ethnic group or community) may reverse the evidence, a phenomenon I captured in my recording of the account of the Benin-Ubulu war from Charles Simayi on October 12, 1980. And even when the hero loses his life in the campaign, like Kelefa Saane among the Senegambian Mandinka, he is presented as a winner precisely because he has lived up to a long-cherished ideal best enshrined in the Mandinka saying "A *kooring*'s white bones, but not a *kooring*'s white hair,"[15] for death was eagerly embraced as the occupational hazard of that warrior class.

What were the foundations of the heroic ethos—Abrahams's "philosophical dimensions"—in traditional African society? We could go back to the nativity rites for the newborn child, but it is more fruitful to start with the initiation rites for teenage youths, which included sequestration and circumcision. These ceremonies often concluded with the youngsters emerging from the grove, boasting how bravely they had withstood the circumciser's knife, never shaming their family or their age set, and proceeding to assume personal praise names signifying their eagerness to cross the boundary separating them from the next age set in the traditional gerontocracy, the warrior class (ages about twenty-two to fifty). All this was done because warfare—and similar perils to the individual spirit—was seen in most traditional African societies as the ideal of the honorable life, one that wins a man true regard and glory in the eyes of his fellows. Hence Kunta Kinte, enslaved not long after his initiation, would continue to brag that he was a Mandinka warrior even though he had not actually fought in a war; nor could he ever have seen himself losing one![16]

15. Gordon Innes, *Kaabu and Fuladu* (London: School of Oriental and African Studies, London University, 1976), p. 57.

16. For a discussion of the age set system in Bendel State, Nigeria, see Isidore Okpewho, " 'Once upon a Kingdom . . .': Benin in the Heroic Tradition of Subject Peoples," in *The Heroic Process*, ed. Bo Almqist et al. (Dublin: Glendale Press, 1987), pp. 619–620. For a sample initiation song of self-glorification, see Francis Mading Deng, *The Dinka and Their Songs* (Oxford: Clarendon Press, 1973),

The appeal of glorification, of self as well as others, continues well into the adult life. In several societies of western Africa hunters and warriors were often accompanied by appointed praise singers whose duty it was to fire the master's spirit before the encounter and afterwards incorporate the feat into his growing list of praises. The careers of legendary southern African warriors such as Moshoeshoe and Shaka have also been encapsulated in highly metaphorical praise poetry. Even the warriors themselves sometimes composed their own praises; thus we learn that the Susu leader Sumanguru had a harp-lute to which "after each victory he would come and sing his own praises."[17] As in war, so in peace. Even today among the Igbo of Nigeria those who have made a mark in various fields of endeavor—business, education, politics, sports, public service—come home to the community to be honored with a chieftaincy title; and part of the ritual involves the chanting in masquerades of praise titles carefully chosen to portray their subject as the best there ever could be in his or her field.[18]

The conventions surrounding heroic praises and narratives of figures such as Shaka and Sunjata provide one more explanation for the absence of these forms in the Americas before emancipation. Some of the major epics we have today were originally composed by praise singers attached to rulers on a regular basis—the *griot* among the Mandinka and the *imbongi* among the Zulu—and charged with recording the rulers' (and their forebears') achievements in praises and narratives on special occasions such as the performance of periodic rites, the reception of important guests, even the death of the ruler. The body of narrative is frequently punctuated with chanted passages whose meanings are so condensed as to elude the comprehension of those whose are ignorant of the events alluded to, especially since they go back a considerable way to the layered ancestry of the community. In his study of Gambian Mandinka epics Gordon Innes has suggested that such passages are really the pivot of the text—the narrative sequences being merely the connecting links—and the moments which have the greatest emotional impact on their audience.

The epics also have a personal interest for various members of the audience. The story of Sunjata, for instance, records the names of some of the

---

p. 192. See also Henry F. Morris, *Heroic Recitations* (Oxford: Clarendon Press, 1964), for the epitome of self-praise among the Bahima of Ankole (Uganda).

17. Djibril Tamsir Niane, *Sundiata* (London: Longmans Green, 1965), p. 39.

18. For a sample text, see Romanus N. Egudu and Donatus I. Nwoga, *Poetic Heritage* (Enugu, Nigeria: Nwankwo-Ifejika Publishers, 1971), p. 37.

generals who played key roles in their leader's campaigns and then went on to push the frontiers of the Mandinka empire further west of Mali. The recitation of the names of these ancestors must therefore instill some pride in their descendants among the audience. So when, during the *griot* Bamba Suso's performance of the Sunjata epic, his accompanist Amadu Jebate tells him, "Make clear to us which families, with which surnames / Trace their descent from Tira Makhang,"[19] he must know how deeply his master would touch the hearts of those in the audience whose families trace their lineage from that legendary ancestor. Also, in the performance of *The Ozidi Saga*,[20] some of the comments from the Ijo-speaking audience may suggest a nationalistic empathy with a tale that enshrines the triumph of their ancestors over the monstrous powers of ancient Benin.

The implications of my arguments should be clear. The heroic tradition thrives essentially in an atmosphere where people are sufficiently in control of their destinies, are free to dream dreams, to have an exaggerated notion of their worth, and to see themselves as winners at anything they may dare. It is nourished by certain institutions—initiation rites and title-taking ceremonies, among others—that enshrine the heroic ethos or that sense of an insuperable self which seeks due recognition in the eyes of the community. And it holds a cherished place in the hearts of the people because it inscribes within their collective memory the feats of hallowed ancestors who continually remind them what endless possibilities await anyone who defies the limitations of mortal life.

The only black societies in the New World that had a chance of reenacting such a scenario were the maroon communities in the Americas and the Caribbean; for in these isolated enclaves the escaped slaves had removed themselves from the culture of the enslaver and could carry on their traditional African folkways. But even here there were essentially two problems. First, these societies lived under the perpetual threat and even reality of reprisals; they hardly had enough peace to consolidate their traditions or memorialize their heroes in a lasting oral record.[21] The second problem is revealed by the situation of the Saramaka of Surinam. Although they were much like other

19. Gordon Innes, ed., *Sunjata* (London: School of Oriental and African Studies, London University, 1974), p. 69.

20. John Pepper Clark-Bekederemo, ed., *The Ozidi Saga* (Washington, D.C.: Howard University Press, 1991).

21. Orlando Patterson, *The Sociology of Slavery* (Rutherford, N.J.: Fairleigh Dickinson University Press, 1967); Price, *Maroon Societies*.

maroons in having a culture "forged in an inhospitable rain forest by people under constant threat of annihilation,"[22] they nevertheless enjoyed a much longer respite from harassment which enabled them to develop institutions—kinship, ritual and religion, oral and plastic arts, and others—that recalled the African traditions from which they had been torn, to experience a continuity of ties that could translate as an ancestry, and even to forge a language that bore the formal marks of their respective African sources. What the Saramaka had achieved, however, was a syncretization of diverse strands and layers, but without the benefit of a "history and genealogy . . . particularized in specific pieces of ground."[23] Within their layers of growth the Saramaka must have received Africans who had told heroic tales in their original communities. But, alas, where now were the kings and clansmen to whom they might continue to sing, and for whom the recondite idioms of the texts would duly resonate?

In conjuring an image of shared cultural wisdom I do not wish to imply a community of undifferentiated interests. This brings me to a final problem raised by Roberts's discussion. Throughout the study he continually evokes a sense of communal harmony and an outlook on life uniting the slaves right up to emancipation. I have no wish to do battle here with an old myth enunciated by Emile Durkheim in his characterization of "primitive" society, for I concede that in their peculiar circumstances the slaves must have felt a greater need for cohesion than any group of Africans may have shown in their homeland. I would simply like to provide evidence from my own fieldwork that might persuade Roberts to be less confident in "extrapolating backward to Africa."[24]

I have recorded most of my heroic narratives from Charles Simayi of Ubulu-Uno, Ojiudu Okeze of Ibusa, and Odogwu Okwuashi Nwaniani of Onicha-Ugbo, all from the Anioma Igbo of Nigeria. In surveying their material I have observed that, although there is a general sense in which we can identify heroic conduct, there is a discernible ethical line separating one class of heroes from another, which suggests two distinct levels of interest within the narrators' society. Simayi has long been a member of the village council

22. Sally Price and Richard Price, *Afro-American Arts of the Surinam Rain Forest* (Berkeley: University of California Press, 1980), p. 215.

23. Sidney Mintz and Richard Price, *The Birth of African-American Culture* (Boston: Beacon Press, 1992), p. 66.

24. Ibid., p 54.

of Ubulu-Uno. Most of the tales he has told me concern characters operating in courtly or conciliar circumstances and who, despite their superior power, do not upset the system of authority or rulership with which they contend. Thus, in the story of Meeme Odogwu of Ogwashi, who goes to Abba to rescue the ravished wife of a townsman and fellow privy councillor, Meeme storms into the village council of Abba and seizes the culprit but does not sack the council.[25] Even in the story of Ezemu, the war between the Ubulu and the Bini ends in a civilized demarcation of boundaries between the two peoples; although the Oba of Benin is humbled in the war, his rulership is not violated.[26] It is reasonable to suggest that in these stories Simayi is inclined to respect the sanctity of traditional authority in which he has a vested interest.

But the two other narrators are ordinary citizens with no such obligations, and so they have no hesitation in celebrating heroes who have little regard for sanction. Earlier I cited Ojiudu's story of the stalwart Opia Nwammemee, who dispossessed other men of their wives and belongings at will. An even more relevant story by Ojiudu is of a misogynist hunter finally subdued by a woman who bears him twins. Later in his life the hunter becomes the victim of a periodic order by the Oba of Benin to give him a tooth. The twins have now grown prodigiously and, outraged by the Oba's order, not only kill the emissaries sent to pluck their father's tooth and destroy the entire punitive force sent against them but go on to behead the Oba and set their father on the foreign throne of Benin![27] Odogwu Okwuashi's stories of the intractable outlaw Omezi reveal an equivalent antipathy.[28]

The difference, then, between Simayi on the one hand and Ojiudu and Odogwu on the other is suggestive. There is one segment of society which has a stake in keeping alive the machinery of political control, and so tailors the heroic tradition to enshrine its interests. Then there is another which is bent on giving full rein to the libertarian spirit, even at the risk of upsetting established authority. Whatever may be the implications of this model—of a social fabric straining at its seams—it certainly offers little comfort to that easy view of communal harmony by which Roberts sets so much store in his cultural history.

•     •     •

25. Isidore Okpewho, ed., *The Oral Performance in Africa* (Ibadan, Nigeria: Spectrum Books, 1990), pp. 127–135.

26. Okpewho, *African Oral Literature*, pp. 192–201.

27. Okpewho, "The Hunter Who Became an Oba."

28. Ibid.

It would be fair to say that Roberts has made a notable contribution to the study of the Afro-American oral tradition by setting it within the context of its African relations. In foregrounding an Afrocentric ideology, however, he has problematized his cultural history and, more seriously, weakened the promise of that sociology whereby he has situated the growth of the tradition within an American environment.

Let us return, for one final moment, to that African story of the pissing dog and its two New World variants. In the African tale the motif lends itself to a plain, naturalistic inquiry into a common human fate. In the Guadeloupean tale the inquiry endures, but it is now set within a contest that transforms what was a troubled plea into a frenzied game of one-upmanship. In the Afro-American tale, however, we are down to the naked motif which lends a rebel spirit the cutting edge of sass; here, the tale helps the enslaved Africans to take some sort of moral revenge on a system with which they have a score to settle. Whereas, therefore, in the African tale we have a humble dialogue with nature, in the New World variants we see reflected not so much the background of a tradition as the dynamics of a confrontation. So what grounds do we have for privileging cultural history over present imperatives?

Let me hasten to stress that an exploration of the kinship between African and Afro-American traditions is in itself a worthwhile enterprise; there is everything to be said for a program aimed at meeting "the demands of Afro-Americans for a cultural history that is relevant to Black people."[29] The problem with Roberts's approach is that in its archival shuttling it compromises the duty to expose the sheer creativity of the Afro-American tradition. The novelty of the wine is just as deserving of our interest as the antiquity of the bottle, and there is hardly need to scramble the evidence or romanticize the past just to stress the ancestry of the tradition.

The point I am making is that we do not give proper credit to the Afro-American genius if we put all our investigative energy into tracing to African sources every cultural achievement it has recorded. Certainly the African and Afro-American oral narrative traditions derive from the same ancestry, but they have followed different lines of development. A study such as Roberts's should be devoted more to celebrating the achievement of Uncle Remus and other bearers of the New World tradition. Their African cousins should be invited to the banquet but need not sit at the head of the table.

29. Roger Abrahams and John Szwed, "After the Myth: Studying Afro-American Cultural Patterns in the Plantation Literatur," in Crowley, ed., *African Folklore*, p. 82.

*Ann duCille*

# Postcolonialism and Afrocentricity:
# Discourse and Dat Course

After the Egyptian and Indian, the Greek and Roman, the Teuton and Mongolian, the Negro is a sort of seventh son, born with a veil, and gifted with second-sight in this American world—a world which yields him no true self-consciousness, but only lets him see himself through the revelation of the other world. It is a peculiar sensation, this double-consciousness, this sense of always looking at one's self through the eyes of others, of measuring one's soul by the tape of a world that looks on in amused contempt and pity.

—W. E. B. DU BOIS, *The Souls of Black Folk,* 1903

*f*or every action there is an equal and opposite reaction. For every doubly conscious racial or ethnic Other constructed by the academy, there is a self attempting to assert its subjectivity. For many black and postcolonial intellectuals, asserting a racial and/or national self has meant claiming as "familiar" everything African, Indian, or Caribbean and expelling as "foreign" all things British, French, Spanish, or even Anglo-American. Ironically, however, centuries of cross-cultural close encounters of the Columbian kind have produced a world out of joint in which it is often actually the would-be familiar that is foreign, and the self who is alien. Black Americans, many of whom will never see Dakar or Lagos, choose "African" names from books (most likely published in the United States or Britain) in unwitting contradiction of the very cultural traditions they wish to celebrate.

In many traditional West African societies—among the Yoruba of Nigeria, for instance—naming is an essential postnatal ritual, a communal cultural event that generally takes place after birth, after a child has presented himself or herself to a waiting, watching extended family, which only then christens the infant in ceremonial splendor and cultural specificity. For Africans whose names were so chosen the would-be Afrocentric African American tradition of christening a child *in utero*—with the aid of a book of "African" names—is something akin to a sacrilege. Much the same is true for the Afrocentric practice whereby black adults rename themselves. Ghanaian names are particularly popular among African Americans seeking to reclaim what slavery stripped them of, but for many Ghanaians the idea of an adult male born on a Monday inadvertently naming himself Kofi (Friday) rather than Kojo (Monday) is at once laughable and deeply lamentable.

This (mis)naming and other similar efforts to reclaim home and nation often only reinscribe our cultural dislocation. Even the language in which we write at once underscores our alienation from "home" and our arrival within the academy, for it is not in Hindi or Yoruba that we contemplate our postcoloniality and Afrocentricity but in the fine and proper English of the colonizer. What we seek is a precolonial connection; what we theorize is a postcolonial condition; what we're stuck with is a perennial colonial contradiction. Made illiterate in the language(s) of the homeland, we must use the master's tongue to talk our way out of his house—even when that house is on our land. Even as we labor to expel the alien within, our acts of intellectual exorcism, however culturally empowering, often produce blind spots and black "wholes" that misshape, color-code, and monolithize our postcolonial conditions and our Afrocentric ideas.

In this essay I explore what seems to me the increasingly fraught (but rarely discussed) relationship between postcoloniality and Afrocentricity as popular and not so popular intellectual perspectives—as acclaimed and disclaimed discourses, respectively. Translating Newton's law into the grammar of contemporary cultural studies, I hope to begin a kind of cause-and-effect analysis of these two discourses within the context of what might be called academic imperialism. My goal, however, is not to rid first world academia of its imperious assumptions about Afrocentricity and postcoloniality, but to point out some of the presumptions and oversimplifications, the slippages and displacements that underpin the academy's varied responses to these two discourses.

I should acknowledge from the start, I suppose, that my ruminations here turn on an implicit distinction between African American and postcolonial studies as institutionally validated disciplines and Afrocentricity as an academically disparaged political perspective, which, according to Molefi Kete Asante, who coined the term, seeks to place Africa and African ideals at the center of all analyses of Afro-diasporic cultures.[1] Although I refer briefly to

---

1. Molefi Kete Asante, *The Afrocentric Idea* (Philadelphia: Temple University Press, 1987), p. 6.

the status of black studies in the U.S. academy, my focus in this essay is not on African American discourse per se but on the state and the fate of its "poor relation" Afrocentricity in the age of postcoloniality. Juxtaposing postcolonial studies and Afrocentric politics is an admittedly slippery move on my part. It allows me, from the somewhat institutionally valorized position of an African Americanist, to cast my stones both globally and locally—to critique at once the academy's newly arrived favorite son and my own poor relation, the "black sheep" of academe.

While I make no overt claims of neutrality, I do want to establish that I am neither a proponent of Afrocentricity nor an opponent of postcoloniality. I come neither to praise nor to bury. Rather, I hope first to demonstrate some of what these two discourses have in common as therapeutic antidotes to the imposed alterity of imperialism and second to explore what their different deployments within academia suggest. Whereas Afrocentricity is often dismissed as methodologically sloppy anti-intellectual identity politics, postcoloniality is affirmed as theoretically sophisticated oppositional discourse. It seems to me, however, that the most critical factor in the current reception of these two resistance narratives may have more to do with market than with methodology—that is, with the academic merchandising of *different* difference.

If postcoloniality is discourse—an exotic, foreign field whose time has come within the U.S. academy—Afrocentricity is "dat course"—local color (homeboys and girls) whose foreignness has become all too familiar. What Richard Wright said about the American Negro may now apply to Afrocentricity: it is "America's metaphor" whose day has come and gone, if indeed it ever was here. In cultural studies within the U.S. academy, the enslavement and breeding of African women is yesterday's news like the Doberman biting the mailman. Widow burning, however, is not simply history; it is story.

In a special issue of *Social Text* which, among other things, problematizes the use of phrases such as "third world" and "postcolonial," Ella Shohat defines the latter term as "a new designation for critical discourses which thematize issues emerging from colonial relations and their aftermath."[2] Indira Karamcheti, like Shohat, has taken note of the increasing popularity of

2. Ella Shohat, "Notes on the 'Post-Colonial,'" *Social Text,* 31/32 (1992): 99–113. The quotation appears on p. 101.

these discourses, of all things "postcolonial": postcolonial theory, postcolonial studies, and particularly postcolonial literature. "The stars of postcolonial literary studies shine brightly in the dim skies of academe," Karamcheti writes, citing names such as Edward Said, Gayatri Chakravorty Spivak, Kwame Anthony Appiah, Gauri Viswanathan, Sara Suleri, R. Radhakrishnan, Abdul JanMohamed, and Rey Chow.[3]

Like the presence and preeminence of these luminary scholars, evidence of interest in the emergent discipline of postcoloniality is everywhere in the academy: in numerous journal articles, including several "special issues" devoted entirely to postcolonial themes (in *Representations, PMLA, Calalloo,* and *Social Text,* among others); at university presses, which now boast special series on postcolonial discourses; in MLA and other job announcements calling for specialists in postcolonial literary, theoretical, and cultural studies; and in learned societies whose annual meetings for the past few years have sponsored a full complement of panels devoted to postcolonial themes. For many of us who regularly read such publications and attend such conferences, these times have felt more and more like the dawning of the age of postcoloniality.

But while the designation "postcolonial" may be new, the thematizing of relations of power between colonizer and colonized is not. In the U.S. black intellectuals such as W. E. B. Du Bois, Alexander Crummell, Pauline Hopkins, and Anna Julia Cooper engaged in such thematizing in the late nineteenth and early twentieth centuries. More recently, but still years—even decades—before the rise of postcoloniality as an academic discipline, black activists, scholars, writers, and theorists such as Marcus Garvey, C. L. R. James, Frantz Fanon, and Aimé Césaire explored and exploded colonial and postcolonial power relations. In current academic theaters Stuart Hall, Sylvia Wynter, Selwyn Cudjoe, Paget Henry, Paul Gilroy, Hazel Carby, and Cheikh Anta Diop are among the many African, African American, Afro-Caribbean, and other scholars of African descent who continue to problematize and critique the relationship between Prospero and Caliban, metropole and province.

The difference between my list of black scholars engaged in anti-colonialist or postcolonial studies and the earlier inventory of primarily Indian and

---

3. Indira Karamcheti, "Disciplining Postcoloniality: or, Taking Liberties with Countee Cullen," paper presented at Johns Hopkins University, Baltimore, April 30, 1993.

Middle Eastern postcolonial theorists is a distinction that has inspired at least two kinds of charges from some Afrocentric circles: (1) that once again foreigners have entered *our* field and taken it over; and (2) that it takes the interest and theorizing of outsiders to legitimize and glamorize a discourse of which the academy took little note when it was dominated by diasporic blacks. Athough these charges are not without a degree of historical resonance in the realm of black studies (white scholars who have turned to African American studies frequently have achieved greater academic and commercial success than the black scholars who pioneered the field), they may not be pertinent to the rise of postcolonial studies. There is at least one other causal relation that Afrocentrism has all but ignored—one not of appropriation and cooptation but of spontaneous generation; one in which postcoloniality (like Afrocentricity) developed as an equal and opposite reaction to the action of imperialism. In this configuration postcoloniality is not so much the heir apparent to and beneficiary of African and African American resistance narratives as their coincidence—an oppositional discourse with its own distinguished history of what Paget Henry calls "discursive insurrection" played out in the texts of native writers throughout the subaltern.[4]

Were I as well versed in other "minority literatures" as I am in African and African American studies, I could no doubt rattle off a list of nineteenth- and twentieth-century Indian, Chinese, or Middle Eastern textual insurrectionists with the same facility and sense of history with which I cite the names of black writers and intellectuals. The first world academy in which so many of us are trained, however, has rarely fostered or encouraged such knowledge of either the non-European self or the "foreign" Other. In attending so narrowly to its own racial and cultural self, Afrocentrism, it seems to me, perpetuates the same divide-and-conquer ignorance on which imperialism has depended.

But if Afrocentricity errs in its cultural monocentrism, postcoloniality, precisely because it is taken so much more seriously by the academy, potentially has an even more dangerously myopic relation to the company it keeps

---

4. See Paget Henry and Paul Buhle, "Caliban as Deconstructionist: C. L. R. James and Post-Colonial Discourse," in *C. L. R. James's Caribbean*, ed. Paget Henry and Paul Buhle (Durham: Duke University Press, 1992), pp. 111–142; see also Edward Said, *Culture and Imperialism* (New York: Knopf, 1993). Said traces the history of textual or "discursive insurrection"—what he calls an "oppositional strain"—in the works of a variety of writers who, in one way or another and often in the "master's" own tongue, challenged the colonial order.

and the company that keeps it. Like Afrocentricity, it suffers from a limited, often binary insight that sees primarily its own colonized body in relation to that of a particular imperial force, even as it claims a global perspective. Moreover, the academy to which it has become attached has a vested interest in promoting the illusions, if not delusions, of grandeur that the very term *postcolonial* suggests. From the ivory tower, conceptualizing a politically correct postcolonial globe makes it easier to ignore the fact that much of the world's population encompassed within the designation "postcolonial" lives in conditions which are hardly that. This is particularly true cross-culturally of women, who, as Anne McClintock notes, "do ⅔ of the world's work, earn 10% of the world's income, and own less than 1% of the world's property."[5] False universals such as "the postcolonial woman," "the postcolonial Other," "the postcolonial condition," and even "the postcolonial critic" camouflage the variety of neocolonial circumstances in which masses of people live, work, and theorize. Although Afrocentricity has, if anything, an overly determined (and some say grossly exaggerated) sense of its own glorious past, the false universals with which postcoloniality is invested often obscure both its lineage and its connectedness to other narratives of marginality such as African American studies.

According to Indira Karamcheti, postcolonial discourse arises today in the U.S. academy as the "far more glamorous offspring" of what previously has been called world literature, third world literature, Commonwealth studies, or similar contemplations of the exotic, foreign Other. As an academic discipline postcoloniality takes its present preeminence not only from the traditional, often orientalist, and remarkably well funded area studies it has somewhat eclipsed but also from the very resistance narratives its current favor within the academy seems to some to threaten—African American studies and women's studies, for example. Unlike African American and other local narratives of marginality, Karamcheti argues, postcoloniality is being figured as a "universal" master narrative that contains all difference. "If it continues to be developed as a totalizing narrative cut off from a local place," she warns, "it can be used within academia to displace those minority groups whose social struggles for inclusion, empowerment, and representation cleared the space within which post-coloniality operates."[6] Put another way,

---

5. Anne McClintock, "The Angel of Progress: Pitfalls of the Term 'Post-Colonialism,'" *Social Text*, 31/32 (1992): 91–92.

6. Karamcheti, "Disciplining Postcoloniality," pp. 2–3, 4–5.

its ties to poststructuralism and the dissolution of the very subjectivities so essential to many minority discourses make postcoloniality not simply a resistance narrative but (potentially) a containment strategy.

Karamcheti is not alone in sounding a warning bell about the uses and potential abuses of academic postcoloniality. Noting that some ethnic studies scholars feel set adrift by the rising tide of postcolonial studies in North American English departments, Ella Shohat suggests that the term *postcolonial* has received such ready institutional endorsement in part because it enables a "partial containment of the POCs (people of color)." In the North American context, she adds, "one has the impression that the 'post-colonial' is privileged precisely because it seems safely distant from 'the belly of the beast,' the United States."[7] Whereas the critique posed by African American studies and the alternative (non-Eurocentric) worldview asserted by Afrocentricity cut uncomfortably close to home, postcoloniality seems to offer its opposition from a distance—as Gayatri Spivak might say, "in other worlds."

But postcoloniality is a discourse still very much in the process of locating itself. It has been taken up by an academy that does not necessarily know what this so readily institutionalized discourse actually is. Afrocentricity, by contrast, has been dismissed and disdained by the same academy that knows only too well what it is. Despite the current breath of life given it by Molefi Asante, the Afrocentric idea is hardly a new one. Speaking perhaps a bit reductively, one could say that this effort to read Afro-diasporic experiences through reconstituted African ideals, belief systems, and cultural traditions has led other lives as black nationalism, as Pan-Africanism, as Garveyism and back-to-Africa-ism, as Negritude in the 1930s, and as the Black Arts, black-is-beautiful movement of the 1960s.

However culturally empowering it may be for *some* black scholars, Afrocentricity has been spurned not only by the white European and Anglo-American academy but also by premier black intellectuals such as Henry Louis Gates, Jr., Clarence Walker, and Cornel West. West, for example, defines Afrocentrism as a contemporary brand of black nationalism that represents a "gallant yet misguided attempt to define an African identity in a white society perceived to be hostile." The effort is gallant, West argues, because it centers on "black doings and sufferings" rather than white anxi-

---

7. Shohat, "Notes on the 'Post-Colonial,' " p. 108.

eties and fears, and misguided because, "out of fear of cultural hybridization and through silence on the issues of class, retrograde views on black women, gay men, and lesbians, and a reluctance to link race to the common good—it reinforces the narrow discussions about race."[8] Rejected, or at least severely critiqued, even by what it would take to be "its own," Afrocentricity is a kind of "bad kid" ideology within first world academia, a "thankless child" anti-intellectualism that denies Daddy, that resists paternity, that refuses to acknowledge Europe as its great white father. As its very name implies, *post*coloniality, by contrast, *seems* to be a properly indebted, if resistant, intellectual offspring. Its name announces its relation not to Mother Africa or India or China but to Father Europe, the colonizer without whose intervention there would be neither colonial nor postcolonial. Where Afrocentricity is culturally exclusive and self-centered, postcoloniality is intellectually elastic and decentered. Where the former disdains theory, the latter thrives on it. Where the one is "unembarrassingly black," in the words of the black feminist critic Joyce Joyce, the other is "black" only by default—de fault of being nonwhite.

The nonwhite, no-fault "blackness" of Indian, Bengali, Asian, Arab, Egyptian, and other "brown" postcolonial scholars has proven a boon for the U.S. academy. For one thing, affirmative action need no longer be an act of contrition. The displacement of cultural and geopolitical difference and its simultaneous replacement with blackness have made possible an easy diversity, a "black" presence without the problematic historical and political particularities of what Spivak has called "black blacks." The academy, in effect, gets to eat its chocolate cake and have it too (mocha as opposed to devil's food). Among the ingredients it leaves undigested, however, are racial identity, geopolitical ethnicity, and cultural specificity.

In academic circles both Afrocentricity and postcoloniality have their origins in such undigested, hard-to-swallow difference—in an alterity that is at once institutionally produced and promoted and intellectually erased and denied. By this I mean that, on the one hand, the academy fosters a kind of skin trade that has made alterity the hottest commodity in the intellectual marketplace. On the other hand, it theorizes racial difference in solipsisms that obscure color, class, caste, culture, gender, sexuality, and place. In this skin trade blackness is the metonymic expression of race, and the rainbow

8. Cornel West, *Race Matters* (Boston: Beacon Press, 1993), p. 4.

coalition is viewed through a monochromatic or, rather, dichromatic scale that really only sees black and white. Put another way, although race may be, as Gates has argued, a sign of reducible difference, it also may be, in the context of the academy, a sign of irreducible sameness—of a homogenization that, as Sneja Gunew suggests, refuses specificity.[9] Let me try to purge my own prose a bit and clarify the point I'm trying to make by returning to the example of "the Indian."

I am working on an series of articles on black and other would-be multicultural Barbie dolls. As part of my research I am in hot pursuit of Indian Barbie. The dealers, collectors, and sales clerks I talk to understand readily enough what I mean when I ask for Eskimo Barbie or Spanish Barbie or Malaysian Barbie or Jamaican Barbie, but when I say I'm looking for Indian Barbie, the response is invariably either a question—"American or East Indian?"—or the assumption that of course I mean the doll Mattel markets as Native American Barbie.

In America (which really means the continental United States), "Indians" have red skin and live on reservations, where they play bingo and plot to take white people's land away from them. Columbus discovered and named them five hundred years ago. Marlon Brando rediscovered them in the 1960s, as did Kevin Costner in the 1990s. Even though it repeats and institutionalizes Columbus's blunder, we continue to call these people "Indians." Our current use of "Indian" as a synonym both for native and for Native American replicates the fifteenth- and sixteenth-century usage of the term as the generic designation for "nonwhite"—a (mis)nomenclature which, through the centuries, has given the world Chinese, African, Australian, Mexican, Caribbean, Hawaiian, as well as many varieties of North and South American "Indians." What does this nomenclature mean for natives of the Indian subcontinent—for people of the Indus—whose own cultural, racial, and geopolitical specificity is denied by this generic use of the name they would call themselves?

For the postcolonial from the jewel in the crown of the British Raj, claiming self—claiming "Indianness"—in America begins not only with the assertion of India, the land Columbus did not discover, but with the unnaming

9. Henry Louis Gates, Jr., "Writing 'Race' and the Difference It Makes," in *"Race," Writing, and Difference,* ed. Henry Louis Gates, Jr. (Chicago: University of Chicago Press, 1985), p. 5; Gayatri Chakravorty Spivak, "Interview with Sneja Gunew," in *The Post-Colonial Critic: Interviews, Strategies, Dialogues,* ed. Sarah Harasym, (New York: Routledge, 1990), p. 64.

of the "Indians," the people he supposedly did. Then, too, there are the multiracial, ethnically variegated inhabitants of the Caribbean—what the world (or part of it anyway) calls the "West Indians." What are we to make of them? Contemplating all these Indians (something I think we rarely do in the academy) has recalled the racist song I was taught in elementary school: "One little, two little, three little Indians." Even if some of them appear without war paint and tomahawks, three little "Indians" are at least two too many for intellectual ease and theoretical comfort. First world academia has gotten around this problem, it seems to me, by erasing "Indianness" from its lexicon, if not from its cultural consciousness. It has largely ignored Columbus's misnamed "Indian," except where the discourse of political correctness and romantic notions of native spirituality have necessitated a kind of lip service attention to the "Native American."[10] It has translated the multivocality, racial diversity, and ethnic variety of what it calls the "West Indian" into a monochromatic scale of ubiquitous blackness, ignoring both Indians from India and the native Caribs and Arawaks. The "one little, two little, three little Indians" have disappeared and have been replaced by "the black" or, more recently, "the postcolonial"; that is to say, the same academy that has embraced and rushed to validate postcoloniality has elided Indianness. The alterity of the Indian as postcolonial is generic, categorical, locational, but, interestingly enough, not racial, or at least not racially specific. Race, it seems, is the proper attribute (if not the private territory) of black or African people.

In Britain Indians are "black," along with Africans, Afro-Caribbeans, and African Americans. In the United States the racial status of Indians and several other "minorities" has varied with the political, social, cultural, and/or economic agenda of the historical moment. Anthropologically, Indians had been classified as Caucasians, but when migration from India to the United States began in the early 1900s, that designation did not necessarily entitle them to the rights and privileges of other white immigrants, particularly naturalization, land ownership, and citizenship. In fact in 1922 the Supreme Court case of *U.S. v. Thind* ruled that Bhagat Singh Thind, a high-caste Punjabi, was not eligible for U.S. citizenship because he was not "white" in the sense intended by the original framers of the Constitution. Academi-

10. There is, of course, considerable irony in this nomenclature as well, since "Native American" also invokes the colonizer—the Italian explorer Amerigo Vespucci, for whom the Americas are named.

cally—that is to say, within the U.S. academy—the racial status of Indians has been even more ambiguous or fluid. Forgive me for not naming names—citing sources—but I know of more than one institution of higher learning that either by accident, ignorance, or design has augmented its statistics on the recruitment and retention of black professors by counting Indians and other "brown" scholars among its black faculty.

On both sides of the Atlantic a Eurocentric vision that actually sees only white and nonwhite translates the object of its intellectual gaze into white and black, where black is the metonym for all racial alterity. Within the U.S. academy in particular, then, it is blackness, not Indianness, that has racial and cultural currency. Ironically, however, it is postcoloniality and not Afrocentricity that has intellectual currency.

Yet, returning to physics, it seems to me that the joke may yet be on the academy. I began this essay by invoking Newton's laws of motion to suggest that, for every Other constructed by the academy, there is a self attempting to assert its subjectivity. Afrocentricity is, in some measure, such a reaction—an attempt to assert a distinctly African racial and cultural subjectivity, a "truly black consciousness," or, as Joyce Joyce has suggested, an "unembarrassingly black" identity. Unfortunately, this particular effort to assert a black self denies cultural specificity and geopolitical ethnicity and reproduces racial hierarchies (who's blacker than whom?) in much the same way as the academy. The vitriolic exchange in the pages of *New Literary History* (Winter 1987) between Joyce Joyce, on the one hand, and Henry Louis Gates, Jr., and Houston Baker, Jr., on the other, is a glaring case in point. Arguing from an Afrocentric perspective which necessarily decries what it sees as the European incursions of contemporary critical theory, Joyce in effect accuses Gates and Baker of not being black enough, even as they charge her with being too black.

While the empowering premise of an "unembarrassingly black" Afrocentric methodology offers an essential challenge to the assumed universality of European paradigms, it does not, to my mind, sufficiently address the question of cultural mediation that is the consequence of centuries of appropriation and cross-fertilization. Although it acknowledges blacks in the Americas as an African-derived people with a cultural legacy different from that of Euro-Americans, it does not adequately consider the degree to which that culture is necessarily intertwined with others around it. Nor does it consider the global implications and ramifications of the imperialist agenda or what Spivak and others refer to as the colonial object.

"Cultures are not containable," the white deconstructionist Barbara Johnson tells us, in words that serve to authorize her own readings of African American texts. Even the terms *black* and *white* are fallacious, she argues. They "imply a relation of mutual exclusion"—a binarism based on the notion of "pure, unified, and separate traditions"[11]—in the face of what are, I would add, complex and interlocking cultural and linguistic phenomena. But in Afrocentric theaters my own acknowledgment of cultural symbiosis is a kind of heresy likely to place my blackness (like Gates's and Baker's) under suspicion. Many Afrocentrists, perhaps at least in part in reaction against such notions and the appropriations and encroachments that come with them, have taken physic in an attempt to purge themselves and African diasporic discourses of what Larry Neal called the "white thing" within. If my appropriation of Newton's ("white thing") theory holds, I wonder what the consequences will be when the postcolonial Other "takes physic(s)." Will the action of cultural erasure and racial transfiguration I have outlined cause a reaction of intensified ethnic identification, sectarian struggles, and geopolitical contestation?

In part because of its engagement with theory, postcoloniality as a discipline has the potential to present, in global proportions, the kind of finely honed critique of Western hegemonic systems that Afrocentricity as a perspective—as a therapeutic essentialism—has restricted to the confines of its own local politics. I haven't taken a head count, but it seems to me that, at the moment, the majority of scholars actively engaged in carving out the contours of what the academy calls postcolonial discourse are Indians. Speaking through the authority of African American academic experience, I predict that the more currency postcoloniality gains within the academy, the less this will be true. The almost inevitable turn away from the "authentic" Indian postcolonial to the intellectually produced postcolonialist is presaged by a number of events in and around the university, including the birth of a new generation of graduate students seeking training not in British, American, or even African American literature but in postcolonial studies. Another sign of this turning tide is the diminished presence of Indian contributors to any of a number of recent journal issues devoted to postcoloniality. The contents of many of these special issues suggest that there is a thin

---

11. Barbara E. Johnson, response to an essay by Henry Louis Gates, Jr., "Canon-Formation and the Afro-American Tradition," in *Afro-American Literary Studies in the 1990s,* ed. Houston A. Baker, Jr. and Patricia Redmond (Chicago: University of Chicago Press, 1989), p. 42.

line between postcolonial and neocolonialist discourse. Will Indian scholars fight to hold that line, perhaps theorizing an "Indocentricity"?

As a recast, reconstituted cultural/historical narrative Afrocentricity serves a therapeutic function not unlike that served by other sacred texts, including the Bible and the Koran. Like the Old Testament, it is a kind of creation myth that gives a displaced and diasporized people a home and a history, even as it denies the hybridity which has become a part of that history. My playful speculation about an Indocentricity notwithstanding, I would not wish the denials and blind spots of Afrocentricity on another discourse. What I would wish for postcoloniality—as self-congratulating as it may seem— is not the therapeutic essentialism of Afrocentricity but the strategic essentialism of African American studies. As an African Americanist I know its faults and fractures too well to hold up my own discipline as a perfect model to be emulated. Rather, I mean only to suggest that as a politicized discourse African American studies falls somewhere between the hyperlocalization and nativism of Afrocentricity and the global or universal delocalization of postcoloniality. Among other things, in its absolute insistence on a local place black studies implicates the same United States that postcoloniality, for the most part, lets off the imperialist hook.

I began by using as an epigraph Du Bois's famous ruminations about what he called double-consciousness. I want to close my own ruminations by drawing on Edward Said:

> No one today is purely *one* thing. Labels like Indian, or woman, or Muslim, or American are not more than starting-points, which if followed into actual experience for only a moment are quickly left behind. Imperialism consolidated the mixture of cultures and identities on a global scale. But its worst and most paradoxical gift was to allow people to believe that they were only, mainly, exclusively, white, or Black, or Western, or Oriental.[12]

Despite the decades and the racial and cultural differences that separate them, the visions of Du Bois and Said are remarkably similar. Both passages suggest the extent to which imperialism and colonization have given us a world out of joint, have turned the planet and its peoples upside down and inside out so that indeed no one is purely or simply any one thing. But what

---

12. Said, *Culture and Imperialism*, p. 336.

do we do with this knowledge? To what use do we put this sense of our two-ness, our multiplicity, our interrelatedness, and our interdependence?

It is no accident, I suppose, that as I contemplate these questions, I am drawn to both Du Bois and Said—to African American discourse and to postcolonial theory. But what of Afrocentricity? By now I see what my readers no doubt have seen all along: more than poor relation or black sheep, Afrocentricity is a kind of straw man in this discussion. Yet, beyond the tufts of straw and the feet of clay, I wonder what these three discourses—African American studies, postcoloniality, and Afrocentricity—might learn from one another, and in particular they might teach one another about the first world academy that both claims and disclaims them. As they do their work and launch their critiques, these disciplines would do well, I think, to be less suspicious of one another and more suspicious of the academy that keeps them, promotes them, and even (re)produces them. For if the world is out of joint, as Du Bois and Said maintain, the university—as an ideological apparatus of imperial states—is a perilous place in which to try to put it right.

*Carl Pedersen*

# Sea Change: The Middle Passage and the Transatlantic Imagination

*I*n his 1862 essay "Walking" Henry David Thoreau, taking a page from Greek mythology, views the gap between Europe and America as a sea of oblivion that demarcates the restricted space of the Old World from the boundless space of the New: "The Atlantic is a Lethean stream, in our passage over which we have had an opportunity to forget the Old World and its institutions."[1] Yet ironically, in constructing this ideology of unremembering, Thoreau is nonetheless compelled to draw on a particularly European frame of reference, familiar to most educated European Americans of his day. Furthermore, he demonstrates, in Wayne Franklin's phrase, the ability of European language to plot New World experience in advance. The course of Thoreau's walking headed away from Europe: "Eastward I go only by force; but westward I go free."[2] Thoreau's formulation of the trajectory of American cultural development is linear and unproblematic: the movement westward is unmitigated by burdensome memories that would slow the settler on the journey to spiritual regeneration. In this paradigm the sea has washed away the past.

According to legend, retold in Paule Marshall's *Praisesong for the Widow* and Julie Dash's film *Daughters of the Dust,* Ibo warriors, transported to the shores of the Carolinas by the slave ships, took one look at this new world and turned their gaze eastward. They decided to return home: "Chains didn't

---

1. Henry David Thoreau, "Walking," in *The Portable Thoreau,* ed. Carl Bode (New York: Viking, 1947), p. 604.

2. Wayne Franklin, *Discoverers, Explorers, Settlers* (Chicago: University of Chicago Press, 1979), p. 5. Thoreau, "Walking," p. 603.

stop those Ibo. They just kept on walking, like the water was solid ground."[3] For African Americans the Atlantic was a different kind of space. Instead of a breach separating past from present, it constituted a transformative Middle Passage where an African past and the American future, one in danger of fading from memory, the other imposing its hegemonic will, were constantly in conflict over contested spheres of power. If, following the Thoreauvian paradigm, slave owners and slave traders had willingly severed their bonds with the past, they seemed determined to expunge forcibly the African past among their captives, sensing, perhaps unconsciously, that memory could be a means of resistance and liberation. Breaking free of these ideological fetters, the slave imagination was articulating an alternative discourse rooted in memory and yearning for a return.

Thoreau notwithstanding, the African Middle Passage haunted the white imagination. "Poised against the *Mayflower* is the slave ship," as William Carlos Williams would have it,[4] and this juxtaposition is evident in Herman Melville's "Benito Cereno," and even invades the aesthetic consciousness of non-American representations of the slave ships, such as Prosper Merimée's "Tamango," and J. W. F. Turner's painting *Slavers Throwing Overboard the Dead and Dying.* Writing at about the same time as Thoreau, Martin Delany hinted at the existence of an Atlantic world that provided a way out of physical and cultural bondage in the Americas: "Africa is our fatherland and we its legitimate descendents . . . I have outgrown, long since, the boundaries of North America, and with them have also outgrown the boundaries of their claims."[5] A little more than a century after Delany the Barbadian poet Edward Kamau Brathwaite would declare that only by returning to Africa could he discover his native Caribbean.[6] Brathwaite's journey to Ghana confirmed his belief that Caribbean culture had a strong African undercurrent which had been suppressed by the European colonizing powers. Thus the Middle Passage emerges as more of a bridge than a breach, a space-in-between where memory entails reconstructing the horrors of the voyage westward and retracing the journey of Africans to the Americas.

3. Julie Dash, *"Daughters of the Dust": The Making of an African American Woman's Film* (New York: New Press, 1992), p. 142. Paule Marshall, *Praisesong for the Widow* (New York: Plume, 1983), pp. 38–39. Another version of this story, repeated in folktales and rearticulated in Toni Morrison's *Song of Solomon,* has the Africans flying back to their homeland.

4. William Carlos Williams, *In the American Grain* (New York: New Directions, 1956), p. 208.

5. Martin Delany, *Official Report of the Niger Valley Exploring Party* (1859), quoted in Paul Gilroy, *The Black Atlantic: Modernity and Double Consciousness* (London: Verso, 1993), p. 26.

6. Edward Kamau Brathwaite, "Timehri," *Savacou,* 2 (September 1970): 38.

Since Fernand Braudel's pathbreaking study *The Mediterranean and the Mediterranean World* (1949), in which history is integrated by the sea, it has become a commonplace in historical and geographical studies to investigate the slave trade in terms of interconnected Atlantic zones. More recently John Thornton and D. W. Meinig have mapped out an Atlantic space of political, economic, and cultural interdependence that bears little resemblance to Thoreau's Lethean stream.[7] In part inspired by these reconceptualizations of the Atlantic world, I am concerned with charting a complementary literary geography of an African American transatlantic imagination. Following Delany's notion of expanding boundaries, I intend to examine selected works from African American and Afro-Caribbean literatures that engage in an exploration of an Atlantic world which can ultimately widen the symbolic dimensions of the Middle Passage. For, to dwell for one final moment on Thoreau's imagery, if the Atlantic is seen as a Lethean stream for European voyagers to the Americas, it has subsequently in slave historiography, at least up to Stanley Elkins in the 1950s, also been thought of as a Lethean stream for enslaved African Americans. If there was an African past, it had been left behind, and slaves were held in bondage by European representations. Because Africa, as Hegel would have it, stood outside of history, enslaved Africans in the Americas could enter history only by blindly replicating European culture. In this view Africans were culturally malleable, veritable putty in the hands of their owners. If, by contrast, they were deemed incapable of attaining this culture, they would be forever consigned to the dark realm of savagery.

The contribution of Afro-Caribbean critical writing has been largely ignored in the recent literature of slavery and the literary imagination. With C. L. R. James as an intellectual trailblazer, writers such as Edward Kamau Brathwaite, George Lamming, Wilson Harris, Edouard Glissant, Derek Walcott, and others have produced a sizable body of critical work that either implicitly or explicitly addresses the idea of a Middle Passage. Taken together, this work furthermore offers an eloquent refutation of the notorious claim by V. S. Naipaul that "nothing was created in the West Indies."[8] One

7. Fernand Braudel, *The Mediterranean and the Mediterranean World* (London: Collins, 1972–73). John Thornton, *Africa and Africans in the Making of the Atlantic World, 1400–1680* (New York: Cambridge University Press, 1992). D. W. Meinig, *The Shaping of America*, vol. 1 (New Haven: Yale University Press, 1986).

8. V. S. Naipaul, *The Middle Passage* (New York: Macmillan, 1963), p. 28.

early assessment of the meaning of the Middle Passage in the transatlantic imagination is the Guyanese novelist Wilson Harris's little-known essay from 1970 "History, Fable, and Myth in the Caribbean and Guianas." Pointing to what he calls a "cleavage . . . between historical convention . . . and the arts of the imagination," Harris focuses on a particular cultural practice which explains the larger significance of the Middle Passage experience: the limbo. This dance, according to Harris, was born on the slave ships because of the lack of space. From an environment of coercion, which would seemingly allow no cultural room to move, a new configuration emerges in the form of the slave contorted into a human spider, provoking a "dislocation of a chain of miles" which opens up space not for a replication of the African past, but rather for "the renascence of a new corpus of sensibility that could translate and accommodate African and other legacies within a new architecture of cultures." Connecting limbo with the Jamaican spider figure Anancy and Haitian vodun, Harris emphasizes the dynamism of reconfiguration and transformation, not the stasis of essentialism or emasculation. Paradoxically, the cramped figure of the slave dancing the limbo heralds a "re-assembly" that promotes "a new growth." The new kind of space that was constituted during the Middle Passage is constantly rearticulated and points "to the necessity for a new kind of drama, novel, and poem."[9] Harris's concept of reassembly is echoed in Derek Walcott's 1992 Nobel lecture, in which he counters Naipaul's negative view with an alternative vision: "Break a vase, and the love that reassembles the fragments is stronger than that love which took its symmetry for granted when it was whole. The glue that fits the pieces is the sealing of its original shape. It is such a love that reassembles our African and Asiatic fragments, the cracked heirlooms whose restoration shows its white scars."[10] The geography of Walcott's polyglot Antilles contains an African memory of the Middle Passage and of slavery that defies attempts to deny its existence. This memory provides a rich source for the imagination, for, as Walcott has declared elsewhere, "every event becomes an exertion of memory and is thus subject to invention."[11]

9. Wilson Harris, "History, Fable, and Myth in the Caribbean and Guianas" (Georgetown, Guyana: The National History and Arts Council, Ministry of Information and Culture, 1970), pp. 8, 9, 10, 11.

10. Derek Walcott, *The Antilles: Fragments of Epic Memory* (New York: Farrar, Straus, and Giroux, 1993), unpaginated.

11. Derek Walcott, "The Muse of History," in *Is Massa Day Dead? Black Moods in the Caribbean,* ed. Orde Coombs (Garden City, N.Y.: Anchor, 1974), p. 2.

An early narrative anticipating Harris's new kind of writing, and one that can be claimed as part of the African, Caribbean, American, and British literary traditions, thereby touching all four Atlantic zones as defined by Thornton and Meinig, is *The Interesting Narrative of the Life of Olaudah Equiano,* first published in 1789. Incorporating many key elements of Atlantic history and culture, Equiano's narrative is one of the first examples of Harris's limbo gateway joining the African past with the African American present. Equiano's journey takes him from the interior of Africa to the coast, across the Atlantic to Barbados, then to a Virginia plantation, and finally to England. The many Middle Passages that propel his story are part of a narrative strategy that hovers between the demands of his audience and his sponsors and his own writerly ambitions which subvert these demands. In this sense the text itself replicates and reacts to constrictions of space, both physical and mental, imposed by economic imperatives and dominant discourse. The authority which Equiano acquires in the course of his many voyages functions as a narrative representation of his growing confidence as a writer.

By contrasting Africa with Europe, Equiano forces his readers to encounter culture from a multiple perspective. From the time of his childhood in an Ibo village to the moment when he distills his experiences in his *Narrative,* Equiano's life is one of Middle Passages. Each stage of his account underscores the tension between firsthand memory and mediated reconstruction. Thus, for example, his recollection of his Ibo childhood is informed by his reading of the works of the Quaker antislavery writer Anthony Benezet. In the opening passages dealing with Africa, images of social harmony and cooperative labor clash with the slave division of labor and the insatiable avarice which characterize English society.

During the journey to the Americas Equiano finds himself caught between the horror of the Middle Passage and a sense of wonder at European technology that made it seem as if he were "in another world." So intense is this conflict between unreality and abject terror that Equiano longs for death. Nonetheless, embarking on a later voyage across the Atlantic eastward from Virginia to England, Equiano recounts how fear and trepidation gave way to empowerment and resistance: "When I got on board this large ship, I was indeed amazed to see the quantity of men and guns. However my surprise began to diminish, as my knowledge increased; and I ceased to feel those apprehensions and alarms which took such strong possession of me when I came first among the Europeans, and for some time after. I began

now to pass to an opposite extreme; and was so far from being afraid of any
thing new which I saw, that after I had been some time in this ship, I even
began to long for an engagement."[12] Equiano, of course, was not alone in
undergoing such a transformation. An earlier allusion to Greek mythology,
employed by slaveholders and prevalent at the time that Equiano was writing
his autobiography, referred to the potential for rebellion in the Atlantic
world as a many-headed Hydra that linked black and white laborers, both
slave and free.[13] The Atlantic system was creating connections that its design-
ers had not foreseen.

During the nineteenth century the widespread fear of slave rebellion in
the Americas was an unconscious acknowledgment from the slaveholders
that the Middle Passage was not an end but rather the beginning of a new
cultural configuration formulated by resistance. Resistance took many forms:
dance, folktales, or religion, as Harris stresses, the development of nation-
language, defined by Brathwaite as "the *submerged* area of that dialect which
is much more closely allied to the African aspect of existence in the Caribbean,"[14] and slave revolts on land and at sea. Equiano's empowerment is
echoed in two narratives of the transatlantic imagination in the nineteenth
century, Frederick Douglass's short novel *The Heroic Slave*, (1853) and Martin Robison Delany's novel *Blake; or, The Huts of America* (1859–1862).

Douglass's only work of fiction recounts a Middle Passage not from Africa
to the Americas but from the United States to the Caribbean in his reconstruction of the revolt on the brig the *Creole* in 1841. The leader of the
revolt, Madison Washington, recognizes, as did Equiano, that the ship at
sea represents not only oppression but the possibility of emancipation, for
"you cannot write the bloody laws of slavery on those restless billows. The
ocean, if not the land, is free."[15] Even the failed revolt on board the *Vulture*
in Delany's novel has the rebellious blacks and an Atlantic storm joined in
opposition to the crew of the slave ship: "The black and frowning skies and
raging hurricane above; the black and frowning slaves with raging passions

12. Olaudah Equiano, *The Interesting Narrative of the Life of Olaudah Equiano,* in *The Classic Slave Narratives,* ed. Henry Louis Gates, Jr. (New York: New American Library, 1987), pp. 36, 45.

13. Peter Linebaugh and Marcus Rediker, "The Many-Headed Hydra: Sailors, Slaves, and the Atlantic Working Class in the Eighteenth Century," *Journal of Historical Sociology,* 3, no. 3 (September 1990): 225–252.

14. Edward Kamau Brathwaite, *History of the Voice* (London: New Beacon, 1984), p. 13.

15. Frederick Douglass, "The Heroic Slave," in *The Negro Carvan,* ed. Sterling A. Brown, Arthur P. Davis, and Ulysses Lee (New York: Dryden Press, 1943), p. 26.

below, rendered it dreadful without, fearful within, and terrible all around."[16] In these narratives the sea functions as a trope marking the unruly space between the past memory of Africa and the present reality of slavery in terms of active resistance.

In *Being and Race,* a book of literary criticism, Charles Johnson observes that much contemporary African American writing is "a meditation on re-membrance." Citing David Bradley's *Chaneysville Incident* as a prime exam-ple of this obsession with memory, Johnson notes how in Bradley's novel "the racial past begins to appear . . . as partly a product of imagination, a plastic and malleable thing freighted with ambiguity."[17] In line with Harris and Walcott, facts for Johnson can yield meaning only by a conscious effort of the imagination. His 1990 novel, *Middle Passage,* displays the effort of a transatlantic imagination transforming the Middle Passage experience into a microcosm of Atlantic history and an allegory of growing self-awareness. Structured as a series of entries into a ship's log over a period of a little more than two months in 1830, *Middle Passage* recounts the exploits of Rutherford Calhoun, a free black and petty thief from Illinois. In New Orleans he stows away on the *Republic* only to discover that it is a slave ship under the com-mand of Ebenezer Falcon, whom Calhoun equates with the young nation: "He, like the fledgling republic itself, felt expansive, eager to push back fron-tiers, even to slide betimes into bullying others and taking, if need be, what was not offered."[18] For Calhoun as well the sea represents a reaffirmation of the frontier spirit of the settlers, an escape from the oppressiveness of eastern culture. In the course of the *Republic's* voyage to Africa and back to New Orleans, Calhoun realizes that he is caught in the economic and cultural web of the slave trade. Commercial interests make the crew of the *Republic* no freer than their African captives, the Allmuseri and their god. Drawing a parallel between the physical contortions and mental transformations of the Africans, Calhoun observes that they are "no longer Africans, yet not Americans either."[19] Representing an alternative history ultimately un-dermining Calhoun's confidence in frontier ideology, the rebellion of the Allmuseri and the sinking of the *Republic* during a storm transform him into a "cultural mongrel." The Middle Passage is not confined to the hold

16. Martin Delany, *Blake, or The Huts of America* (Boston: Beacon Press, 1970), p. 234.
17. Charles Johnson, *Being and Race* (Bloomington: Indiana University Press, 1988), pp. 74, 79.
18. Charles Johnson, *Middle Passage* (New York: Atheneum, 1990), p. 50.
19. Ibid., p. 125.

of the slave ship; it invades the consciousness of all who enter the Atlantic zone.

The prerogatives of empire supposedly enabled dominant cultures to block out alternative histories and narratives. A central point of the Middle Passage, however, is that it effectively transformed the cultures of Europeans and Africans alike, binding them in an uneven yet symbiotic relationship. In his novel *Natives of My Person* (1971) George Lamming describes a voyage that would attempt to deny that relationship. In his allegorical explora- tion of the meaning of the slave trade, Lamming attempts to penetrate the seventeenth-century mind in order to arrive at an understanding of the root causes of the European urge for colonization and slavery. As early as 1960 he had offered one possible explanation: "The slave whose skin suggests the savaged deformity of his nature becomes identical with the Carib Indian who feeds on human flesh. Carib Indian and African slave, both seen as the wild fruits of Nature, share equally that spirit of revolt which Prospero by sword or Language is determined to conquer."[20]

What the commandant of the *Reconnaissance* proposes on this new voyage is nothing less than to undo the past by undertaking a mission that will "reverse all previous philosophies."[21] Like Ebenezer Falcon, the commandant has been on numerous voyages to capture slaves on the African coast and to exterminate the indigenous peoples of the Caribbean. He now plans to undertake an unauthorized voyage to establish an ideal community on the imaginary island of San Cristobal, one of the places he had ravished. Mem- ory, however, thwarts the realization of the commandant's vision of a future with no past. Using journal entries and flashbacks Lamming records how the officers of the ship, like the commandant, have committed atrocities against their captives which affect their present actions.

In Lamming's view all human relationships are haunted by the memory of the slave trade. He continually draws parallels between the officers' ruthless treatment of slaves and of women. Colonization possesses a logic that ex- tends from white over black, to the masculine over the feminine, and finally to the mind over the self. Even without the physical presence of slaves, the mission of the *Reconnaissance* is doomed.

Paule Marshall once observed that her first three novels "constitute a tril-

20. George Lamming, *The Pleasures of Exile* (London: Allison & Busby, 1984), p. 13.
21. George Lamming, *Natives of My Person* (London: Allison & Busby, 1986), p. 250.

ogy, describing, in reverse, the slave trade's triangular route back to the motherland, the source."[22] The difference between Marshall's effort of the transatlantic imagination and the futility of the mission of the *Reconnaissance* is obvious. The former eagerly encourages memory, the latter militantly seeks to deny it. Yet the longing for a physical or imaginative return can ultimately succumb to the same essentialist propensities as the officers of the *Reconnaissance*. Richard Wright and, more recently, Eddy Harris returned from their reverse Middle Passages to Africa with any racial fantasies about the continent largely dispelled. As Harris concluded at the end of his journey of self-discovery: "Africa is the birth of mankind. Africa is the land of my ancestors. But Africa is not home. I hardly know this place at all."[23] Yet Afrocentrists such as Molefi Kete Asante tend to downplay if not entirely ignore African complicity in the slave trade, are keen to register "pure," unmitigated African retentions in the Americas, and seek to introduce a coherent African worldview into the school curriculum. The virtue of Wilson Harris's model of a transatlantic imagination is that it celebrates hybridity. Instead of refuting the history of the slave trade, he seeks to incorporate this experience in charting the development of a new African diasporic culture. In this conception the Middle Passage extends from the sands of the Sahara to the rivers of the Americas, from the Sudan to the Cunje and the Mississippi. Memory opens Harris's limbo gateway to the exploration of the space-in-between and its many tributaries.

The implications of the limbo gateway are wide-ranging. It eliminates the fixed boundaries between the literary and the extraliterary as it engages historical events in narrative terms. A parallel can be drawn between Harris's fusion of history and literature into a notion of cultural syncretism and Bakhtin's dialogism. Seen in linguistic terms, efforts to possess meaning as a fixed entity in the discourse of a single voice divorced from social interaction are doomed to failure. Similarly, in terms of the development of the Atlantic world, efforts to suppress the voices of the hold result in incomplete, monologic history. Between the fixed points of Europe, Africa, and the Americas, dialogic discourse in its many forms subverts colonial domination by becoming part of its consciousness.

22. Paule Marshall, "Shaping the World of My Art," quoted in Gay Wilentz, *Black Women Writers in Africa and the Diaspora* (Bloomington: Indiana University Press, 1992), p. 100.
23. Eddy L. Harris, *Native Stranger: A Black American's Journey into the Heart of Africa* (New York: Simon & Schuster, 1992), p. 312.

Toni Morrison has mapped out a critical geography expressing the dialogic relationship between the Africanist presence in the United States and
the white imagination in her book of literary criticism, *Playing in the Dark*.
In her own work, and in the work of many African Americans and African
Caribbeans, it is the effort of memory that confirms the resilience of an
Africanist presence, not essentialized but the creation of a Middle Passage
experience. In an interview with Paul Gilroy, Morrison provides an acute
description of the Lethean currents of Americanist thought: "We live in a
land where the past is always erased and America is the innocent future in
which immigrants can come and start over, where the slate is clean. The
past is absent or it's romanticized. This culture doesn't encourage dwelling
on, let alone coming to terms with, the truth about the past. That memory
is much more in danger now than it was thirty years ago."[24] In contrast, the
transatlantic imagination sees the Middle Passage as a transformative process
that bridges the geographical space from East to West and from West to
East, fills the space between memory and history, reconstructs the space left
by historiographical omission, and negotiates the space between colonizer
and colonized. By reassembling the fragments of history and restoring the
writing on the slate, memory comes to terms with a troubled past.

24. "Living Memory: Meeting Toni Morrison," quoted in Gilroy, *Black Atlantic*, p. 222.

Geneviève Fabre

# Festive Moments in Antebellum African American Culture

*f*estivities and carnivals were special moments in the life of the African American community in antebellum times. Not only did they bring a welcome break from the usual toil which allowed for some license, but they also offered spaces where freedom could be reinvented. Infused with memories of the past and intimations of the future, they could become utopian and prophetic, performing the collective desire for a better existence. These events had many functions. They were times of intense communal life and socialization which often established a network of communication stronger than the written word. They were acts of assertion—of forgotten rights and usurped prerogatives, of a culture whose codes had to be constantly reconstructed. Intermittently disruptive and subversive, they were challenges to the established order, forms of resistance to the pattern of domination, and an idiom of experimentation. They contained suggestions of unruliness which could lead to outbreaks of revolt; but simultaneously they helped to master violence.

Mostly festivities and carnivals introduced new modes in the lives of slaves and freemen. The "politics of mirth"—the deployment of festive misrule—was allied with the tradition of the jeremiad. A form of game playing, they put to use many cultural resources, which evolved into strategies of manipulation and resistance. Lastly, as moments of performance, stylization, and ritualization, they held particular symbolic significance. Performance was not simply an outlet for repressed creativity and the expression of skills in oratory, costuming, dance, and music; it became a cultural pattern encapsulating many styles and experiences. It had a purpose and a direction, and often these rituals of social existence had, despite their crude practicality, a moral meaning which invested certain details of the festivity with a sacred character. Festive performances thus became a matrix for the "invention of culture" where traditions from many regions merged.

Centering mostly on a unique festival, that of Jonkonnu—an originally Afro-Jamaican celebration recreated in North Carolina—this essay examines the many levels of significance of festive moments in the culture of slavery. First recorded in 1688 in Jamaica by a British traveler, Sir Hans Sloane, Jonkonnu was a Christmas celebration which spread from the Caribbean. It was witnessed among the slaves of eastern North Carolina, where by the 1820s, it had become a very popular festival. Combining music, dance, and song, it was known mostly for its use of unusual instruments, some stringed and banjolike, others imitating the forbidden drums, as well as cowbells and rattles tied to the legs and wrists of dancers; for its "sinful tunes" and loud shouting; for its extravagant costumes usually made of rags and tatters, the fanciful headdresses and gruesome masks worn by celebrants, and the use of cowhides and feathers; for its noisy crowd of followers; for its style of performance, both grotesque and majestic; for its processions and parades, its special dance steps, its rituals of visiting wealthy people's houses and requesting gifts.

Many travelers' accounts include vivid descriptions of the festivities, which were very different from the usual Christmas celebrations and other "big times." These reports are strewn with epithets expressing a whole range of feelings from admiration, surprise, or dismay to harsh disparagement. They often reinterpret the event in terms of more familiar European and Christian customs, some perceiving it as mere harmless frolic, others condemning it as dangerous revelry. Observers may have failed to catch the true spirit and meaning of the feast, misread its signs and codes, showed their inability to capture the complexities of a cultural manifestation foreign to their culture; they nevertheless voice their fascination with the Kooners, or celebrants, and feel privileged to have been able to witness performances which stand as crucial moments in their visit. Their testimonies span more than three centuries of Jonkonnu festivals in the African American diaspora; they constitute a valuable body of material on slave culture and its evolving forms, and build evidence on the importance of celebratory rites which have often been overlooked.

Geography and history combine to make of Jonkonnu a singular occurrence in the panoply of African American festive events. Space and time, and the subtle ways in which they interact, assume symbolic significance. The site becomes resonant with the memory of many places and events associated with its genesis and development.

Because the first known description of a Jonkonnu celebration was recorded in Jamaica,[1] and because the festival as it was performed in the 1750s received further attention in Edward Long's *History of Jamaica* in 1774,[2] Jonkonnu is usually identified as initially Afro-Jamaican. It was maintained in the island throughout the eighteenth century and had its heyday then, but is still observed today. Its transformations can be followed through reports found in accounts by William Beckford (1790) and Matthew Gregory Lewis (1845).[3] We thus learn that women, who had not been prominent in the festivities, began to appear around 1790 in teams dressed in blue and red. From Jamaica Jonkonnu spread to St. Vincent (1819), then to Belize, where black Caribs migrated in the first quarter of the nineteenth century, then to the Bahamas, Bermuda, where it became the basis of the Gombay festivals,[4] and the Florida Keys.[5]

Migration was probably a key factor in this dissemination. The way Jonkonnu reached isolated spaces on the North American continent is more mysterious. (One would not have expected it to be celebrated at Key West, where it is still observed today). It became really notable in North Carolina, whereas it remained practically unknown in the neighboring states. It had a brief existence in the town of Suffolk, Virginia, as well as in South Carolina, but was censored after the Nat Turner rebellion in 1831. Jonkonnu was observed in small towns along the North Carolina coast: at Edenton, where it was a "common sport with slaves" in 1824, according to the State Archives; at New Bern, Hilton, Hillsbury, Southport, and Fayetteville; but mostly in Wilmington (where it was outlawed after the riots of 1898). It also took

1. Hans Sloane, *A Voyage to the Islands of Madeira, Barbados, Nieves, St. Christopher, and Jamaica* (London, 1707), 1:xlix.

2. Edward Long, *History of Jamaica* (London, 1774), 2:423–426.

3. William Beckford, *Descriptive Account of the Island of Jamaica* (London: Egerton, 1790), 1:389–390. Matthew G. Lewis, *Journal of a Residence among the Negroes in the West Indies* (London: John Murray, 1845), pp. 23–29.

4. H. Carrington Bolton, "Gombay, A Festal Rite of Bermudian Negroes," *Journal of American Folklore*, 3 (July–September 1990): 222–226.

5. Virginia Kerns and Robert Dirks, "John Canoe," *National Studies*, 3 (November 1975): 5–6; Judith Bettelheim, "Jonkonnu and Other Christmas Masquerades," in *Caribbean Festival Arts*, ed. John W. Nunley and Judith Bettelheim (Seattle: University of Washington Press, 1988), pp. 39–84.

place on plantations: at Somerset Place, where one of the most impressive annual festivals was held; at a plantation near Bertie County; on a family estate near Durham; in the Cape Fear region;[6] and in Chowan County, as reported in Harriet Jacobs's *Incidents in the Life of a Slave Girl*.[7]

If the festival spread mostly through migratory flux from the islands to the continent,[8] Somerset Place presents a different story, one through which the origins of Jonkonnu can be traced back directly to "Affrica."[9] Some of the slaves brought on the brig *Camden* directly from the Guinea coast in 1786 were still living on the Somerset Place plantation in 1829.[10] The tradition of observing Jonkonnu would have been passed on from there to other slaves in Edenton. This exceptional itinerary supports the theory according to which the ceremony had originated in West Africa—the Guinea coast, Senegambia and Sierra Leone—where a similar festival, the Lantern Festival, was observed. From Guinea Jonkonnu would have spread to the American continent by way of the Caribbean, or, more rarely, would have migrated directly there.

This geographic route and the many connections and ramifications it established in the African diaspora in the New World account for the singularity of Jonkonnu. With only a few variations the festival was performed in many places, rural and urban, and in island and mainland settings, but yet managed to preserve the features that set it off from other Christmas or New Year celebrations. In that respect Jonkonnu indicates the way culture circulated between continents, and represents a significant moment in the invention of slave culture. Placed at the center of much scholarly interest, this unusual performance can be approached as a rich site in both African American historiography and history, the study of which may highlight important unheeded aspects of cultural processes.

The origin of the term is a matter of speculation. The spelling varies from the one adopted here to John Konnu, John Cooner, John Conny, John Ca-

---

6. Louis T. Moore, *Stories Old and New of the Cape Fear Region* (Wilmington, NC: Louis T. Moore, 1956).

7. Harriet A. Jacobs, *Incidents in the Life of a Slave Girl, Written Herself* ed. Jean Fagan Yellin (Cambridge, Mass.: Harvard University Press, 1987), pp. 118–120.

8. Jeffrey J. A. Crow and Flora J. Atley, eds., *Black Americans in North Carolina and the South* (Chapel Hill: University of North Carolina Press, 1984), pp. 85–86.

9. Ira De A. Reid, "John Canoe Festival: A New World Africanism," *Phylon*, 3 (1942): 349–369.

10. Edward Warren, *A Doctor's Experience in Three Continents* (Baltimore: Cushings and Bailey, 1885), pp. 200–202.

noe, and others. The term is mostly used in the singular, thus emphasizing the importance of a central figure who is the main celebrant but also the object of celebrations, the chief actor and also the emblematic leader toward whom all signs converge. In some accounts the verbal form "coonering" and the plural substantive "Kooners" are used, referring to a collective style of performance or masquerade and to the performers, their costumes, instruments, and dance. By homology JonKooners has been likened to the French words *gens inconnus*, stressing the wearing of masks and the necessity of hiding one's identity, or *jongleurs*, medieval jesters, or again to *jeunes caneurs*, young canefield laborers, thus bringing attention to specific skills or to homely occupations and background. These meanings were often suggested for the Caribbean festival, in a cultural area where one was more aware of plurilinguistic settings and reciprocal influences. Furthermore, the use of these terms emphasizes similarities with European feasts rather than African ones. Another interpretation focuses on "canoe," a word that becomes figuratively and historically suggestive, referring to the boatlike headdresses worn by the early John Canoes, the long narrow boats built by the Arawak Indians, or the English tradition of Christmas "mumming," to which Jonkonnu, with its fantastic headcovers, masks, and parades, has often been compared.

The multiplicity of terms and spellings attests to the indeterminacy of the festival's origin but also to the plurality of the site and its many layers of significance. We may note that whereas one set of names brings out the exoticism—the most intrinsically singular or even the weird—and suggests evidence of Africanisms, the other focuses on reproductions of more familiar European customs in the New World. In the latter frame Jonkonnu becomes a less exceptional occurrence. In order to get a full picture, all these semantic possibilities and ethnographic roots should be considered. Name and naming may well be one of the central metaphors.

It is worth looking more closely at one of the alleged origins of the name, which sends us back less to an African rite than to a historical moment pregnant with elements which give further resonance to such a carnivalesque event as Jonkonnu. The festival is said to honor a certain John Conny, who became quite prominent in Guinea in the early eighteenth century at a historical point when roles were shifting or even being reversed;[11] then, power

---

11. John Atkins, *A Voyage to Guinea, Brazil, and the West Indies* (1735; rpt. North Brook, Ill.: Metro Books, 1972), pp. 75–88; Beverly Robinson, "The Jonkonnu Festival," paper presented at the Paris Conference on Feasts and Celebrations, December 1990.

moved from hand to hand and, from nation to nation, rulers appeared and withdrew, alliances were broken or sealed, and the African slave trade became institutionalized. An unexpected convergence of factors led an African chief, who subsequently won the title of "Last Prussian Negro King," to perform different functions in the confrontation between English, Prussian, and Dutch powers and to play a crucial part in the development of the slave trade.[12] The story starts at a strategic point, in the Gold Coast near Axim, when, in 1711, John Coony (or Konny) ruled over a Prussian fort, Fort Brandeburgh, also called Fredericksburgh, built by the Brandeburghers. Konny, who defended the fort against British and Dutch attacks, was left in charge of the place when the Prussians, worried by the decline of the trade, sold their interests in the Gold Coast to the Dutch West Indian Company. When the Dutch came to claim the fort, Konny declared it his land and property. Taking advantage of the Prussian-African alliance, he assumed the full title of "Negro King" and, as sole ruler of the fort rebaptized "Konny's Castle," became a powerful military leader. He was able to withstand the Dutch assault for seven years, and won a great reputation among slave traders. His real allies, according to the legend, were supernatural forces (Jannanin) and Canno, the supreme being. Jonkonnu is supposedly the African name of John Conny, or a combination of the names of the spirits who helped install his power.

This episode suggests the complexities, oddities, and ironies of history. The fort and the chief played a role in funneling slaves to the New World. Conny, the intermediary between Africans and European, then New World, slave traders, was strangely enough perceived not as a betrayer but as a man of great character, an image of authority and power. He was a mediator between two eras and three continents at a crucial moment when the slave trading system changed. Whether or not the link between this figure and the Jonkonnu of the New World festival is supported by sufficient historical evidence, the symbolic connection is there. Many descriptions of the festival insist on the centrality of Jonkonnu, on his awesome presence, on his kingly stature, majestic demeanor, and menacing looks which seemed to hold everyone at bay. What is of interest here is that the feast continued to bear the name of a character who remained its main figure, symbol, and emblem; who set the pattern for the whole ceremony, its costumes, movements,

12. Kwame Yeboa Daaku, *Trade and Politics in the Gold Coast, 1600–1720* (Oxford: Clarendon Press, 1970).

rhythms, forms, colors, and mood; who directed the feast but also performed; and whose name echoed through many shouts and songs announcing or celebrating his coming. The name that has traveled across continents and centuries and found its place in different cultures is at the same time familiar and mysterious, and resonant with many images which blend authority with danger, security with threat. Jonkonnu, the festive event, the place and time of its celebration, and its central figure and hero are thus set in a complex web of meaning connecting diverse cultural spaces and eras.

If one considers these intricate configurations, the conjunction of place and time, history and myth, and their implications, Christmas seems a very unlikely moment for a Jonkonnu festival. Yet Jonkonnu was always associated with the Christmas and New Year period, not only because it was celebrated then (it was more rarely observed on the Fourth of July or Halloween) but because this season of relative freedom and mobility, of hope and change, proved to be appropriate to the festival. It enabled the slaves to stage their own ways of celebrating Christmas, to give it special and secret meaning, to blend Christian and conventional traditions with elements derived from their own collective imagination and memory, to combine religious with secular rituals, the sacred and the carnivalesque. Jonkonnu and Christmas stood in sharp contrast to each other in a way that was parodic and derisive; yet, simultaneously, each infused the other with its mood.

Because Jonkonnu took place at Christmastime, after the planting season in the South, when slaves were granted some rest from daily toil, routine, and constraints, its celebration came to seem legal and legitimized. Since "big times" were so rare, it was important to make the most of them. Many festivities were packed into these few days and carefully distributed between night and day, between secret hidden places near the quarters and more public areas near the big house or in the streets of the cities. Christmas was a much-anticipated season of family reunions, mobility, and gatherings, and Jonkonnu intensified these movements. Encouraged to participate in the general festive atmosphere, slaves were determined to use the occasion to their own ends, to reap whatever privileges and rewards they could get.

They appropriated the mumming tradition of visiting wealthy people's houses, setting themselves on an equal footing with their masters or white neighbors, demanding gifts as a just retribution, deriding in their songs those not generous enough to accede to their requests. By visiting white people's houses not as servants but as neighbors, they trespassed on unauthorized ground and changed the etiquette of southern customs. They reaffirmed principles—of hospitality, generosity, and reciprocity—that must prevail on festive occasions, showed the implications these principles could have in master-slave and white-black relations, and pointed out the contradictions inherent in their situation. They allowed themselves a familiarity not meant to be overtly acknowledged. They presented themselves in the assigned role of entertainers (in keeping with the tradition) but simultaneously asserted their right to be *entertained* with proper decorum. They claimed that the privilege of ostentatious luxury should be extended to them, but they demonstrated through the magnificence of their own performance that they were perhaps better equipped than their white hosts to sustain a tradition of festivity and mirth.

This reinterpretation of mumming, of the Roman Saturnalia custom of masters serving their slaves during the festival, and of the visiting and gift-giving rituals enabled the slaves to make statements on their condition as well as claims to greater social justice. Festive time with its role reversal offered an opportunity to assert certain privileges as legitimate rights. The Kooners emphasized reciprocity, the give-and-take process, with an implicit criticism of what was considered the normal state of affairs: the usages seen as exceptional on this holiday (the right to move freely, to visit, to receive gifts) should be adopted permanently. The feast set the mood for a revolution in attitudes and feelings.

At the eve of the New Year, slaves who dreaded the coming of another year of toil and deprivation called attention to the permanence of their fate as opposed to the impermanence of the feast. They showed what could happen if the transgressive reordering of social etiquette, obligations, and privileges were to be extended to the rest of the year. Jonkonnu was a reminder that the social system entrenched in so many codes and rules could be turned topsy-turvy, that this "day of absence" could become common practice and herald radical changes. All these potentialities were presented as a jest which nonetheless had to be taken seriously. The mixture of attitudes accounts for the ambiguity of Jonkonnu. On the one hand, slaves overacted their roles as servants by asking for patronage and seemingly paying tribute to authority; on the other hand, they made exorbitant claims far beyond their condition and jestingly gave a serious warning: any refusal to comply could lead to trouble.

Observers have stressed the menacing character of Jonkonnu, the irreverence and defiance; there was much threat behind the playfulness. Costuming in mock imitation of the European masquerading tradition, the rags reminiscent of jesters' garments, the animal heads, the cowtails and boar tusks, the "hideous" and disquieting masks surmounted by enormous headdresses (ship, house, or animal shapes), the wooden sword ferociously brandished by the Jonkonnu figure, the whip wielded ominously by his escort cavorting in wild dance, the rattling of bones, the ruffian ways, the fierceness of the performers, the deafening din of the parade, the exuberance of gestures and movements, the deliberate impinging on the senses: everything was scary (and was meant to be). Jonkonnu spelled danger and betrayed the devilish presence of otherwordly and vengeful powers who could wreak havoc. Even the least superstitious minds were inclined to dread this devilment. The sacred significance of the feast as a ritual of appeasement of the angry dead, the presence of the Jannanin, the voodoolike atmosphere lingered behind many performances and gave them an uncanny character.

The combination of guise and disguise so characteristic of this carnival further enhanced the mystery and the threat. The more indeterminate the meaning of the feast, the more fearsome the blurring of identities. If Jonkonnu was tolerated, it was for fear that its interdiction might bring greater disturbances. The intrusion of the "rowdy" Kooners into the white world was disruptive, and those whites who were ready to put up with the inconvenience or were not too ill disposed toward those "weird antics" did not know what to make of this black mumming or saturnalia. The prolongation of the feast late into the night, out of their gaze and control of the whites, was perceived as a challenge to their authority. It was a sign of irreverence on the part of the revellers, who allowed themselves more license than had been tacitly granted. The transgression seemed to announce the possibility of further disorder.

The more gruesome aspects of Jonkonnu connect it to another tradition attached to the Christmas season: it was a time propitious to plots, when insurrections were planned, when one could take advantage of the bustle and agitation that prevailed in large meetings and days of festivities. The whites were very much aware of the danger and increased their surveillance; they occasionally summoned their militia. This insurrectionary potential, enhanced by some elements of the ceremony, may explain the alliance that was formed in the last years of the nineteenth century in North Carolina after the rioting. Marching in the streets was forbidden; stringent vagrancy laws were enacted; mayors and officials outlawed the feast. Significantly, the reasons given were not political but moral, and the newly rising black middle class and educated black elite joined the whites in condemning Jonkonnu for encouraging drunkenness and misbehavior and for lowering their status. The feast was associated with the least reputable section of the population and disapproved of at a time when "Progress" and "advancement of the race" had become a major preoccupation. The formerly enthusiastic followers "got dicty," and the church preached Jonkonnu out of existence.

Yet this controversial ceremony, which, like most feasts was more recently revived in modern commercial form (thus bringing more attention to the extravagant styles of performance than to their meaning), rightly belongs to an important tradition in African American culture. Jonkonnu is part of an ensemble of celebrations to be found throughout the diaspora: the Kings' Elections in New England; the Pinkster festival in New Jersey; a Christmas festival observed in colonial Boston;[13] the Black Indians parade during Mardi Gras in New Orleans; the Yula tradition in Jamaica (of which Jonkonnu was part); El Día de Los Reyes, the Afro-Cuban feast famous in Havana in the mid-1850s, with its John Crayfish leader, akin to Jonkonnu; the Cuban Day of the Epiphany and other such fiestas in other Spanish islands. Jonkonnu has many counterparts in the Caribbean and in South America from Guyana to Brazil. Scholars have also found other connections with diverse West African (Yoruba or Ashanti) cultures.[14]

My purpose here is not to analyze the similarities and differences between these manifestations but to probe into the significance such festivities might have held for African Americans. At a time when blacks, free and slave, were denied participation in the politics of the country and, in many cases, access to instruction, festive celebrations offered a possibility of engagement in public life, of deploying authority in their own affairs as well as in those of the wider world. It was also a means of establishing communication with their rulers, of airing their grievances, of reaching out to their brothers and sisters. Feasts therefore became crucial and memorable moments when an impressive arsenal of devices and traditional forms was used to express knowledge, savoir faire, and opinion without taking risks. Whereas in the North free blacks had slowly developed rhetorical strategies for direct verbal

---

13. James Newhall, *History of Lynn, Massachusetts, 1864–92* (Lynn, Mass., 1896), p. 236.
14. Sterling Stuckey, *Slave Culture* (Oxford: Oxford University Press, 1987).

expression of their political thinking through speeches, sermons, and orations, southern blacks used carnivalesque performance for the same purpose. The physicality of the festive crowd intensified the sense of collective identity, the possibilities for interacting and formulating common goals and desires.

If carnivals offered an implicit critique of an unjust society, there is more than parodic intent in the use of travesty and the derisive misuse of masks. The ceremonial procession, its orderliness and deceptive disarray, the princely figure of Jonkonnu in borrowed plumage, his court and followers, the magnificence and the grotesque inappropriateness of the costumes—the powerful ambivalence of it all emphasizes the presence of authority. The festive liberty, which is the occasion for many transgressions, sets forth an alternative view of society and the right to be visible and different. All the devices belonging to the carnivalesque tradition—guise and disguise, rule and misrule, crowning and uncrowning—and the combination of homely objects with awe-inspiring symbols[15] are given a particular resonance in this African American festival. The whip, for example, which is handled by one of the performers is both a magical instrument and, in mock imitation of the driver's lash, a tool to chastise and enforce order; in the procession it was also wielded to keep onlookers at a respectful distance. The presence of the whip, used to increase production and to discipline the laborers in the "normal" setting of slave existence, becomes more ominous here: the smashing and thrashing (an essential element in carnival) could be turned against other objects. And since disguise becomes the rule and everything can be changed into something else, carnival abuse could lead to violence, displacing well-established privilege.

The irreverent festival actualizes the utopian desire for freedom, coupled with a sense of historical injustice, and legitimizes certain hopes and expectations. In jest and earnest it stages its strategies of emancipation. Jonkonnu as a Lord of Misrule is both object and agent of derision. He is the instrument by which arbitrary authority can be challenged and uncrowned. He is also the emancipatory figure, identified with some distant image of African power but coming unexpectedly at that moment from the lowest stratum of society, who can challenge his rulers. Furthermore, the time of the festival is emphatically collective, and Jonkonnu offers a comprehensive art and ethos of col-

---

15. Natalie Zemon Davis, *Society and Culture in Early Modern France* (Stanford: Stanford University Press, 1975).

lective life. Its wide array of resources may be seen as instruments through which the community demonstrates its will and ability to sustain itself and to propose critical representations of the existing order as well as experimentations with another form of society. Like many festive moments Jonkonnu was a privileged site in which African Americans could engage in the invention of a second culture.

*Wilson J. Moses*

# Sex, Salem, and Slave Trials: Ritual Drama and Ceremony of Innocence

Ach! You young gods have trampled on the laws
Of elder times. Stripped justice from my hands.
I, naked, suffering, pregnant with abuse,
Shall void upon the land vindictive poison
Dread discharge of my womb, pour on the ground.

—AESCHYLUS, *The Eumenides*

We see a small percentage of the world's populace feeling happy and contented with this civilization that man has evolved and we see the masses of the human race on the other hand dissatisfied and *discontented with the civilization* of today—the arrangement of human society. Those masses are determined to destroy the systems that hold up such a society and prop such a civilization.

—MARCUS GARVEY, *Philosophy and Opinions*

*T*he term "witch hunt" has become the standard accusation hurled by partisans of the left and of the right whenever an American show trial is enacted in the government or in the press or in the arts. The Salem witch trials of 1692 became the liberal metaphor for political persecution in the early 1950s, and Arthur Miller's play *The Crucible* was the most celebrated artistic commentary on McCarthyism. In the early 1970s the metaphor was revitalized by political conservatives in the context of the Watergate hearings. More recently the same trope has influenced discussions of the Iran-contra investigation and the Clarence Thomas confirmation hearings. The ritual function of a witch trial is not to prove an actual wrongdoing but publicly to defile and morally incapacitate the accused, regardless of the trial's ultimate verdict. The witch trial also serves the function of ritually cleansing a society and fixing guilt on a limited number of individuals so that others may be confirmed in their righteousness.

The New York Slave Conspiracy trials were spatially, temporally, and culturally proximate to the Salem witch trials. The trial of 1712 was enacted only twenty years after the Salem drama, but was easily within the memory of many persons involved in the earlier judicial ritual. The conspiracy trial of 1742 was performed fifty years after the Salem witch trials, but still within the lifetime of some observers and participants. These public ceremonies were associated by contemporaries with rites of propitiation to an easily offended God. Codes of gender, images of sexuality, and preoccupations with fertility obsessed both the law and its victims.[1] Both sets of trials illustrated the ability of authorized elites to give aesthetic discipline to the blood lust of majorities, using the state's Kafkaesque machinery of ritualized torture. Both sets of trials demonstrated the solemn innocence with which a chosen people could participate in the oppression of designated victims. Both illustrated the true devotion, the sense of duty, the simple righteousness of the "public intellectuals" among us, worldly priests who have convinced themselves that they are prophets.

The conspiracy of 1712 began in New York on April 6 between twelve and one in the morning, when a group of around twenty-three slaves gathered in an orchard in the middle of town, armed with firearms, swords, knives, and hatchets. Their leader was a man named Coffee (Kofi or Cuffee) who set fire to one of his master's outbuildings, then called up his fellows from the orchard to the scene of the fire. In the meantime the white people of the town were drawn to the excitement, and the slaves, who were lying in wait, fired on the crowd. The noise of the shooting soon spread the alarm, and the whites who escaped quickly spread the word of the fire's cause. This, according to one report, was the reason why "not above nine Christians were killed, and about five or six wounded."[2]

The militia were roused, and they pursued the slaves into the woods to the north, where most of them were captured, although six had quickly committed suicide, thus depriving the society of its ceremony of innocence. Although, according to the report of Governor Robert Hunter to the Lords of

---

1. Carol Karlsen, *The Devil in the Shape of a Woman: Witchcraft in Colonial New England* (New York: W. W. Norton, 1987), has indicated the defining nature of gender in the Salem proceedings. For an alternative view on gender and empowerment in the practice of witchcraft, see Sheila S. Walker, *Ceremonial Spirit Possession in Africa and Afro-America* (Leiden: E. J. Brill, 1972).

2. Edmund Bailey O'Callaghan, ed., *Documents Relative to the Colonial History of the State of New York*, 15 vols. (Albany: Weed, Parsons, & Co.), 5:341–342.

Trade, there had been around twenty-three participants in the disorder, of whom six were dead, the court condemned some twenty-seven individuals, "whereof twenty one were executed, one being a woman with child, her execution by that meanes suspended, some were burnt others hanged, one broke on the wheele, and one hung a live in chains in the town, so that there has been the most exemplary punishment inflicted that could be possibly thought of." Among the accused was a man named Mars, who was first acquitted, then retried, and found guilty, but the governor felt that this last was due to a personal grudge that Attorney General Bickley held against a Mr. Regnier, the owner of Mars. Governor Hunter, believing that the evidence against Mars was defective, and noting that no one had testified against him "thought fit to reprieve him till Her Majesties pleasure be known therein."

Governor Hunter also petitioned on behalf of two men who were prisoners "taken in a Spanish prize this war and brought into this Port by a Privateer, about six or seven years agoe and by reason of their colour which is swarthy, they were said to be slaves and as such were sold, among many others of the same colour and country." Hunter "secretly pittyed" these two men, named John and Husea, and reprieved them because prior to the conspiracy he had received petitions from several of these "Spanish Indians," as they were called in the colony. He does not give his full reason for granting this reprieve, but apparently he believed their story that they were "free men subjects to the King of Spain." It is a matter of some interest that these "Spanish Indians" should have been objects of the governor's pity simply because they were believed to be free men rather than slaves. As we shall see, another magistrate might have very likely considered Spanish subjects instigators or participants in a slave insurrection. The fact that John and Husea were swarthy rather than black may have been the ultimate reason for Hunter's inclination to pity.

The purpose of Hunter's letter to the Lords of Trade is obvious: he was unhappy with what he saw as excessive retribution and an abuse of justice, but it was not in his power to stem the abuse. He reminded the Lords of Trade that "in the West Indies where their laws against their slaves are most severe, that in case of a conspiracy in which many are engaged a few only are executed for an example." At the time of Hunter's report to the king, six others had been executed and six had "done that justice on themselves, [so that] more have suffered than we can find were active in this bloody affair." Governor Hunter's letter did not account for the appearance of the ten additional conspirators who were tried and convicted after the apprehension of the sixteen living insurrectionists. Nor does he tell us what happened to the seven persons convicted of conspiracy who were not put to death. He is also unclear with respect to the fate of the woman with child, whose execution was suspended, although it is possible that Hunter desired her reprieve along with those of the others who were waiting in prison on Her Majesty's pleasure.

So far we see a number of interesting issues in connection with these formalities. First of all, we note the lack of precision in counting the number of conspirators involved. We note, nonetheless, the insistence of the community on performing its ceremony of guilt and innocence, despite the deaths of six conspirators. We note that the colonial magistrates were not inclined to be guided by the West Indian precedents, which would have insisted only on making examples of the most dangerous participants; the magistrates insisted on executing at least as many as were involved. The matter of whether or not those executed were actually involved was clearly less important to some of the officials than making certain that ceremonial retribution would not be thwarted by the suicides.

Similar patterns of ceremonial retribution appeared in the conspiracy trials occasioned by a series of fires in New York beginning on March 18, 1741. On that date a fire mysteriously started in the governor's house and spread throughout the fort in which it was located. It spread to the King's Chapel, the secretary's house, the barracks, and the stables, all part of the fortress complex. This led to the explosion of a minor store of ammunition, which caused great consternation in the community, although the main powder stores were not affected. Within the next few days there were several other fires around the city, and the rumor spread that these were the work of arsonists. Two weeks later a Mrs. Earle reported that while looking out her window on a Sunday morning, she saw three Negroes coming up Broadway, and overheard one of them say to his companions, "with a vaporing sort of an air, '*Fire, Fire. Scorch, Scorch,* A LITTLE, damn it, BY-AND-BY,' and then threw up his hands and laughed." The following morning Mrs. Earle informed her alderman of what she had heard, and that same day more fires broke out. Rumors spread that the arson was the work of a group of Spanish Negroes, crewmen on a captured ship, who had been brought to New York as prizes of war and sold into slavery. Others felt that this was a plot of the entire black population, bent on destroying the city. Witnesses had seen a black man running from the scene of one of the fires. He had been captured and carried off to jail by a mob of pursuers.

People remembered that it was just a few days short of the anniversary of the insurrection of 1712. And even as the magistrates sat in session discussing the new alarm, another fire broke out. In the words of one historian, "The ringing of the alarm bell had become almost as terrifying as the sound of the last trumpet, and the panic became general." The town was thoroughly searched, and sentries were posted throughout the community with orders to stop all suspicious persons carrying bags or bundles. Many townspeople packed up their possessions and fled into the countryside. Africans regardless of age and sex were indiscriminately arrested and summarily jailed. But frustrated in their attempts to detect any evidence of a conspiracy, the authorities offered a reward of $100 and full pardon to anyone who would testify as to the leaders of the supposed ring. Finally a witness was found in the person of one Mary Burton, a sixteen-year-old indentured servant employed in a tavern owned by John Hughson where African slaves of the criminal class were served, and where they often came to fence the articles that they acquired by theft around the town.

At first Mary Burton refused to testify, but in the face of alternate cajolery and threats, and when faced with imprisonment, she reported that she had seen three Negroes meet often in the tavern, and that they had discussed burning the fort and the city and murdering the inhabitants. Three white persons were involved in the conspiracy, according to her original report, including her master, her mistress, and a young Irishwoman known as Peggy, "the Newfoundland Irish Beauty." Peggy was known under several aliases, and was thought to be kept as the mistress of a "bold, desperate Negro named Caesar."

Peggy was sent for, and she made what she claimed was a full confession, but she pointed the accusing finger at one John Romme, a relative of the alderman William Romme. John Romme had met with ten or eleven Africans and fed their resentment against the white populace, especially against those who were well-to-do. Peggy's testimony aroused the imaginations of her inquisitors and reminded them of the 1712 conspiracy. On May 11, ten days after the court proceedings had begun, Peggy's consort, Caesar, was hanged, along with another African named Prince. It is interesting to note that Caesar and Prince were executed not for conspiracy but for robbery.

As Daniel Horsmanden, one of the judges, reported in a four hundred–page document:

> They died very stubbornly, without confessing anything about the conspiracy; and denied they knew anything of it to the last . . . These two Negroes bore the character of very wicked idle fellows; had before been detected in some robberies for which they had been publickly chastised at the whipping-post, and were persons of most obstinate and intractable tempers; so that there was no expectation of drawing anything from them, which would make for the discovery of the conspiracy, though there seemed good reason to conclude, as well from their characters as what had been charged upon them by information from others, that they were two principal ring leaders in it amongst the blacks. It was thought proper to execute them for the robbery, and not wait for the bringing them to trial for the conspiracy, though the proof against them was strong and clear concerning their guilt as to that also; and it was imagined, that . . . stealing and plundering was a principal part of the hellish scheme in agitation.[3]

The lieutenant governor of New York proclaimed "a day of public fasting and humiliation, [which] was reverently and decently observed . . . by persons of all persuasions." The populace was overwhelmed with a sense of calamity brought on by a declaration of war with Spain, the aftereffects of an extremely severe winter during which many cattle had been lost, and now the conflagration of the town fortress and several other houses, without any definite revelations as to a conspiracy. "All these distresses, succeeding upon the heels of each other, were surely most likely to awaken us to our duty, and a sense of our demerits," wrote Judge Horsmanden.

On Mary Burton's further testimony Peggy was condemned next, along with John Hughson and his wife. Peggy, on learning that her cooperation with the court would not secure her pardon, retracted her entire confession before she was led "pale and weeping" to the gallows. Other Africans soon were condemned to more imaginative forms of execution. Quack and Cuffee were condemned to be burned at the stake in the public square, where a great crowd turned out to witness the unusual punishment. As they were brought to the stake, Quack and Cuffee, stricken with terror, claimed that

---

3. Daniel Horsmanden, *A Journal of the Proceedings in the Detection of the Conspiracy formed by some White People, in Connection with the Negro and other Slaves for burning the city of New York in America and Murdering the Inhabitants* (New York, 1744). Reprinted as *The New York Conspiracy,* ed. and with an introduction by Thomas J. Davis (Boston: Beacon, 1971), p. 66.

the Hughsons were responsible for the plot but that Mary Burton could name many more conspirators. They died screaming for mercy as the fires shriveled up their forms. Their confessions, extracted by torture, led to further revelations by Mary Burton, grown big with her newfound importance. She now remembered, after a three-month lapse, that the real instigator of the conspiracy was one John Ury, a schoolmaster. It somehow became important to the prosecutors to prove that Ury was a Catholic, and not only a Catholic, but a priest. The attorney general opened Ury's trial by reminding the jury of all the crimes of the papacy against the Protestant faith. England was at war with Spain, and it was rumored that the Spanish priests of Florida were conspiring to murder all English colonists. Together these matters lent credence to the accusations of a sixteen-year-old indentured servant—accusations extracted with open threats of imprisonment and unspoken threats of torture. John Ury was hanged, despite his continuing protestations of innocence, but the magistrates eventually lost faith in Mary Burton, not because of the increasing extravagance of her claims but because the persons she eventually began to finger came from the higher strata of society.

In the Anglo-Saxon tradition every trial is a trial by ordeal. Guilt and innocence are judged on the basis of the demeanor of the accused under torture. In the twentieth century we no longer allow physical torture; we now rely on psychological torture, intimidation, character assassination, browbeating, defamation by the press. A good cross-examiner is an expert at the art of personality destruction. In fact, a good cross-examiner may leave an individual an emotional cripple for the rest of his or her life. And the process of being indicted, either by the press or by the courts, may render the accused, whether innocent or guilty, emotionally and economically devastated. Most Americans are perfectly willing to accept and defend this process of intimidation and harassment when the accused is someone who does not share their political views. Various factions feel that public figures such as Eugene V. Debs, Owen Lattimore, and Richard Nixon have been victims of this process.

One recalls, too, the harassment, imprisonment, and breaking of Marcus Garvey, convicted in 1925 of using the mails to defraud: Marcus Garvey, a stout black man in costume reminiscent of an Austrian archduke or perhaps some dignitary of the Knights of Columbus, his eyes glaring from the shadows beneath a plumed hat. He declared himself "Provisional President of Africa," and from the speaker's rostrum his voice resonated in a deep baritone, "There are 400 million Africans in the world, who have Negro blood coursing through their veins, and we believe that the time has come to unite these 400 million people for the one common purpose of bettering their condition." His goal was "Africa for the Africans," and a Black Star Line of steamships to carry his millions on their mission of destiny. The decrepit hulk of a paddle wheel excursion craft foundered hopelessly on the murky waters of the Hudson River, leading to his economic defeat and conviction for fraud. But ranks of stern-faced black men and women marched under his banner of red, black, and green, inspired by his call: "Up you mighty race! You can accomplish what you will!"[4]

Theatrical? Yes. The words "visionary" and "megalomaniac" are associated with the name of Marcus Garvey. Often he is accused of simply assuming the tired costumes and rhetoric of European imperialism. But Garvey, like many of his contemporaries in the years following the First World War, was more critical than approving of modern civilization. Before the vogue of Sigmund Freud or Frantz Fanon, it was Garvey who linked the idea of modern civilization with existential discontent, observing that most of the human race is "discontented with the civilization of today."[5] Garvey was the founder of a utopian political movement; some have called it a religious movement. He provided his crowds with a ceremonial embodiment of their discontent and their aspirations. If flamboyance and religious rhetoric in the cause of business enterprise were crimes, then Billy Sunday, Aimee Semple McPherson, and Father Charles Coughlin were all criminals. They too deserved to be broken and imprisoned.

Sexual themes clearly provide the most interesting trials, as anyone can deduce from the programming on the American cable channel Court TV. Consider the televised trial of Amy Fisher, a teenager accused of attempting to murder her middle-aged lover's wife. The court channel seems successful

4. Sources include *Philosophy and Opinions of Marcus Garvey*, ed. Amy Jacques (1925), reprinted with a new introduction by Robert A. Hill (New York: Atheneum, 1993); Tony Martin, *Race First: The Ideological and Organizational Struggles of Marcus Garvey and the Universal Negro Improvement Association* (Westport, Conn.: Greenwood Press, 1976); and John Henrik Clarke, ed., *Marcus Garvey and the Vision of Africa* (New York: Vintage, 1974).

5. The phrase "discontent with the civilization" was employed by Garvey six years before Sigmund Freud published *Das Unbehagen in der Kultur*, translated in 1930 as *Civilization and Its Discontents*, although Freud's suggestion for the English translation was *Man's Discomfort in Civilization*. See James Strachey's introduction to *Civilization and Its Discontents* (New York: W. W. Norton, 1961), pp. 3–4.

in maintaining the interest of its viewers, even against the competition of soap operas and daytime talk shows, whose obsessions tend toward incest, rape, and pornography. Trials, especially when they have to do with sex, can be entertainingly profitable, as Hollywood learned a half century ago. Court TV has now discovered that it can reliably deliver television audiences to commercial sponsors. Televised prurience nurtures the everlasting bonfire of sexual hysteria.

Sex has replaced anticommunism as an important ingredient of "the paranoid style in American politics."[6] With the decline of the "communist threat," the accusation that one is a communist has lost much of its force. Our tradition of mass hysteria, which thrives on the ritualized torture of human beings, must feed on something else. Sexual misconduct has replaced communism as the unforgivable sin in American public life. The common causes of the periodic waves of hysteria that sweep this country are in no way an instance of American exceptionalism. Nor are they rooted solely in the Puritan tradition or the excesses of the so-called religious right. They are part of a tradition that is more ancient, more powerful, and more frightening than the supposed rigidity of repressive Christianity.

Every trial is a trial by ordeal, and the hidden text in every trial is its inevitable linkage to mass hysteria, social paranoia, and intolerance. Courts still subject their victims to Kafkaesque tortures designed to strip away the dignity of their victims and, by the highest technology available to the society, to leave them turning slowly in the wind. If one can choke back one's pity and terror at what happens to the victims, one must view with admiration the ritual majesty of the processes that ceremonialize the innocence of the courts as they perform their acts of oppression.

The great issue in both the Salem and the New York trials was more than the failure of self-conscious Enlightenment rationalism in the face of mob delusion. The trials in both instances represented the necessity of controlling through ritual, a force more ancient than Puritan rationalism, a power that is mythic and chthonic, the Dionysian frenzy, the Orphic terror, in the face of screaming Erinyes. Far from failing to accomplish the purposes of trials, the Salem and New York courts accomplished their purposes all too well. For the function of epic trials, like the function of epic drama, is not to discover the guilt or the innocence of individuals but to ceremonialize and

---

6. Richard Hofstadter, *The Paranoid Style in American Politics* (New York: Knopf, 1965).

regulate the innocence of societies. Trials justify the destruction of victims whom society has already convicted in its collective consciousness.

The issue in trials is never the actual guilt or innocence of the accused. Far more important to any civilized person is the power of the state to rationalize and justify the arbitrary and sporadic nature of law enforcement. This it does with primal rites and dramatic ceremonies of fertility, innocence, and guilt. Trial and drama, as is well known, have a common origin in Western civilization. It is from fertility ritual that the pre-Homeric drama arises, and the mutual regeneration of drama and trial is like the worm Ouroboros which feeds itself and for cycles without end reproduces both trial and drama. When Aeschylus created his dramas, he heard the echoes of prehistoric shrieks from beyond the grove of the Eumenides.

Trials generate drama, and drama informs the process of the trial. Both reach their most extreme expressions when they are related either consciously or subconsciously to fertility rituals, reminiscent of ancient days when dance and song guaranteed vegetative, animal, and human fertility. It should not be surprising that the "trial" of Clarence Thomas originated in laws having to do with fertility, and expanded to include questions of women's rights and priapic symbolism. Judge Thomas's hyperbolic metaphor of "high-tech lynching," was perhaps more apt than he realized, for lynching was the punishment for the "unnamable crime" in the South of his boyhood. Some feminists immediately countercharged the Senate Judiciary Committee, along with Clarence Thomas, with the crime of "high-tech rape." The sexual metaphors were appropriate, given the agenda of reproductive rights and sexual harrassment. What was essentially a discourse of fertility and fecundity centered appropriately on pubic and phallic references. George Bush had loosed forces of Dionysian magnitude. Anita Hill was never lying; she and her supporters were possessed. Their goal was not to lynch Clarence Thomas but to defile him publicly, and they succeeded. He became the spoiled offering by which the priest-kingship of George Bush was destroyed.

Lynching and disorganized violence may provide some gratification to the lewd and boorish, but for persons of refined sensibility trials are more satisfying than lynchings. Sporadic violence ignores the formal and stately rituals that appeal to society's more solid elements and that ceremonialize the community's innocence as well as the victim's guilt. Thus, mob violence against black folk resembles witchcraft persecutions only on the superficial level of violence and victimization. At Salem there was a controlled flow of emotion between public sentiment and judicial proceedings. The issue that excites interest is the putatively rational trial process and the relationship of this process to the American paranoid style. There is a controlled flow of emotion and rationality in such quasi-judicial proceedings as the Army-McCarthy hearings and the Watergate proceedings, as well as the trial of the police officers in the Rodney King beating, and the trial following the brutal lynching of Yankel Rosenbaum in the streets of New York. All have illustrated the power of public outcry to introduce paranoia into the justice system. In fact, despite our attempts to maintain an illusion that the courts are not influenced by politicians or by the press, it is very difficult for the courts to preserve such innocence. It is this problem that is really at issue when we reflect on the Salem witch trials.

The reader may be familiar with a story by Shirley Jackson titled "The Lottery." The plot, which is a simple one, depicts a strangely familiar community, somewhere in a timeless Middle America, where a small town's inhabitants have gathered in the square on a clear, sunny, perfect full-summer day to enact a process that involves drawing lots from an old black box. Only at the end of the story do we discover the purpose of the lottery in which every citizen but one is a winner. The loser of the lottery becomes the victim of a stoning. One never forgets the shock of recognition when Shirley Jackson makes one of her wry observations toward the end of the story: "Although the villagers had forgotten the ritual and lost the original black box, they still remembered to use stones."

The poet X. J. Kennedy suggests some questions for discussion about the story, among them whether "Jackson takes a primitive fertility rite and playfully transfers it to a small town in North America." One does not have to be a trained anthropologist to catch the allusion when a character called Old Man Warner shares with us a bit of homely folk wisdom: "Lottery in June, corn be heavy soon." The relationship between witchcraft, drama, fertility rite, human sacrifice, and trial by ordeal is as ancient as human society. Arthur Miller's play *The Crucible,* based on the Salem witch trials of 1692, simply reenacts and restages relationships between literature and art which were observed by the Greek dramatists Aeschylus and Sophocles. Greek drama grew out of ancient fertility rituals that are closely related to witchcraft in anthropological terms. Through the medium of drama the Greeks transformed folk rituals into classical art. Interestingly enough, these dramas often dealt with the relationship of the judicial process to more archaic institutions of justice and ritual cleansing.

Why do I choose to call a story about the stoning of a guiltless victim a ceremony of innocence? Because the ritual serves to preserve the innocence of a society. The ceremony of innocence as described in Sir James Frazier's *Golden Bough* is concerned with the selection of a victim—perhaps a king, perhaps a slave, perhaps a peasant youth—a person who must simultaneously serve society's need for a symbol of innocence and of guilt, and whose sacrifice will take away the sins of the world. The victim may become in the eyes of society either a scapegoat from the devil's flock or a lamb of God. Without ceremonies of innocence the land is smeared with blood, stricken with pestilence, slaughter, famine, and death. When Jackson's crusty old codger observes, "Lottery in June, corn be heavy soon," he reminds us that either coincidentally or by the will of God ceremonies of innocence select a victim or martyr for a ritual cleansing to secure the prosperity of a society. The ritual stoning enacted in Jackson's unnamed town is expedient and noncorrupting because the citizens are not guilty of hypocritical justifications and juridical rationalizations. The ritual is simple; there are no lawyers' sophistries, no bribed witnesses, no intimidated judges. The town takes care of business cleanly, innocently, and with very little fuss. Judgment is passed in the clear, clean light of day, not in some murky Kafkaesque courtroom or Senate chamber.

One begins to suspect that it is impossible to have a rational judicial process, even when aided by modern tools of science and technology. In the case of the Los Angeles police officers tried twice for beating Rodney King, we see how frail are our abilities to justify in rational terms our ceremonies of innocence. Material evidence, regardless of technological sophistication, does not seem to have the power to endow a judicial process with rationality. The report of the Kennedy assassination commission headed by Chief Justice Earl Warren, despite the scientific and technological skills at its disposal, was unable to allay the fears and suspicions of mass society. The rituals of American judges and juries are ultimately concerned with justifying distinctions between faith and knowledge. What did the president know and when did he know it? What did the American public know and when did we know it? Was there a conspiracy? Was there a coverup of the conspiracy? Did we actually read all those Watergate transcripts? What was Angela Davis accused of? What did we see in the Rodney King videotape? Why did Anita Hill "come forward"? Do we follow the dictates of our senses and our own common sense when judging evidence, or do we follow the instructions of the judge? Is the prosecutor guilty of intimidation and psychological terrorism, or is she or he simply rigorous in getting at the truth?

Justice, religion, theater, fertility rite, phallic symbolism, belief system, guilt, retribution: is it any wonder that trials inspire drama and that dramatic techniques rather than rational discourses dominate all juridical processes? Aeschylus and Sophocles perceived, with the uncanny second sight that good dramatists always possess, that all the ingredients of drama have existed from prehistoric times, when primitive peoples chanted and sang while tilling their fields and harvesting their crops. Witches, as Cotton Mather and the New York magistrates well knew, damage fertility by spoiling the increase of nature and of human societies. The Salem rite of purification, with its chorus of furies, is not far removed in spirit or in subject from the New York conspiracy trials, with their religious overtones, accompanied by public fasting and penance. The forces at work in a trial proceeding are more primitive, more mythic, than we care to admit.

Aeschylus's drama *The Eumenedes,* performed in 458 b.c., revealed a knowledge of the relationship between superstition and justice far more sophisticated than anything we dare to teach in a modern law school. There is more at work than a lively sense of the metaphorical when Arthur Miller shows us drama in a seventeenth-century courtroom. The issues of religious bias and sexual obsession which so obviously motivated the proceedings against African Caesar and Irish Peggy in New York were not far removed in time or spirit from the drama of Salem fifty years earlier. Even today the survival of primal rites, based in sexual obsession and religious fervor, cannot be rationally excluded from the discourses surrounding crime and punishment in American courtrooms or congressional hearings. We are far more primitive than we think, and the ceremonies of innocence that we shroud in the technical intricacies of our American judicial system barely conceal the savage chanting of the barbaric pagan rituals from which they evolved.

*Annalucia Accardo*
*Alessandro Portelli*

# A Spy in the Enemy's Country: Domestic Slaves as Internal Foes

In 1822 Charleston, South Carolina, witnessed one of the most important attempted rebellions of slaves and free blacks in American history, led by Denmark Vesey. One of the leaders of the rebellion, Peter Poyas, warned his partners not to reveal their plans to those domestic slaves who received gifts of castoff clothes from their masters lest they betray the plot.[1] Peter Poyas had good reasons to be suspicious. As the Charleston judges later wrote, "Few if any domestic servants were spoken to as they were distrusted." Peter Devany, who denounced the plot to the authorities, was in fact a "house slave."[2] And yet so were some of the "principal officers" of the rebellion. Ned Bennett was "a confidential servant, and his general good conduct was commendable"; Rolla Bennett "was the confidential servant of his master; so much so that when his master's public duties required his absence from his family, they were left under the protection of that slave."[3] "Indeed," one slave owner wrote, "it is now well ascertained that most of the coachmen & favorite servants in the City knew of it [the rebellion] even if they had not participated in the intentions and plans proposed."[4] Another commented that the success of servile conspiracies depends mostly on the participation of this class of slaves, who are in a position to murder their masters in their sleep at night.[5]

1. John Oliver Killens, ed., *The Trial Record of Denmark Vesey* (Boston: Beacon Press, 1970), p. 52.

2. Ibid., p. 17; Robert S. Starobin, ed., *Denmark Vesey: The Slave Conspiracy of 1822* (Englewood Cliffs, N.J.: Prentice-Hall, 1970), pp. 4–5.

3. Killens, *Trial Record,* p. 23.

4. John Potter to Langdon Cheves, July 10, 1822, in Starobin, *Denmark Vesey,* p. 77.

5. Achates [Thomas Pinckney], *Reflections Occasioned by the Late Disturbances in Charleston, in Slave Insurrections. Selected Documents* (Westport, Conn.: Negro Universities Press, 1970), p. 14.

This double image of visible subordination and secret subversion makes the domestic slave a disturbing figure in the historical and literary imagination. The house slave is both a member of the slave population and a part of the master's household, yet is an outsider to both. He is suspect to the other slaves because he is too near the master; but this very intimacy fills the master with fear. Thus, the domestic slave is a potential traitor both to fellow slaves, as was Peter Devany, and to the masters, as were Ned and Rolla Bennett.

This ambiguity is highlighted if we compare two classic texts of modern African American culture. In one of his most famous speeches Malcolm X contrasted the domesticated "house slave" who "lived near the master [and] loved the master more than the master loved himself" to the "field slave" who "lived in a shack" and "hated his master."[6] Malcolm had in mind mainly two polarized psychological attitudes, yet his allegory identifies them with two distinct social figures (or perhaps stereotypes). By contrast, Ralph Ellison in *Invisible Man* offers a glimpse of ambiguity and dissimulation in the intriguing last words of the narrator's grandfather. An ex-slave who had been "the meekest of men" and "never made any trouble," he reveals to his descendants that "our life is a war and I have been a traitor all my born days, a spy in the enemy's country." He explains how this invisible war is to be fought: "I want you to overcome 'em with yesses, undermine 'em with grins, agree 'em to death and destruction, let 'em swoller you till they vomit or bust wide open."[7]

A "traitor" and a "spy," once again, but this time "in the enemy's country"; not a spy for the master against insurgent slaves but a lone guerrilla infiltrating the master's own space, so clandestine that he is invisible to his own neighbors and relatives. The tranquillized mask of subordination not only hides an untamed anger but turns his very "meekness" into a "dangerous activity." Yet, had he died in silence as he had lived, this secret rebel would have gone down in history and memory as a specimen of slave docility, a testimony to the "human" aspect of the system. By trial and error the hero of *Invisible Man* interprets and applies this ambiguous message and becomes "acquainted with ambivalence." The inner duplicity and the visible mask under which he conducts his "good fight" become a metaphor for

6. Malcolm X, "Message to the Grassroots," in *Malcolm X Speaks* (New York: Grove Press, 1965), pp. 10–11.

7. Ralph Ellison, *Invisible Man* (1952; rpt. Harmondsworth: Penguin Books, 1978), p. 17.

everyone's double-edged invisibility. As a planter's daughter noted in her post–Civil War diary: "Every black man is a possible spy."[8]

During the War of 1812 the Virginian statesman John Randolph observed that the dangers of an English invasion from outside were accentuated in the South by "the danger from an internal foe," the slave.[9] "Internal foe" is a fascinating and revealing oxymoron. Usually the fear implicit in "foe" is mitigated by the sense that the threat is relegated to an external otherness, one that becomes real only in times of crisis and war. But an internal foe is constantly near at hand: there are no crises because there can be no peace, only a normal condition of impending fear. All slaves are internal foes, and many owners "would never go to sleep without one or two pistols under their pillow."[10]

But the sense of being constantly surrounded by enemies can be too terrible to be countenanced; hence, the masters' need to cultivate a "psychologically comforting denial" of the slaves' hostility.[11] In her diary of plantation life Frances Anne Kemble described the southern ambivalence of fear and self-deception: "I know that the southern men are apt to deny that they do live under an habitual sense of danger, but a slave population, coerced into obedience though unarmed and half-fed, is a threatening source of constant insecurity, and every southern woman to whom I have spoken on the subject has admitted to me that they live in terror of their slaves."[12] This attitude requires both external and internal controls—military and political vigilance and psychological reassurance. Both are implicit in the formula used by an anonymous Virginian: "If we will keep a ferocious monster in our country," he wrote, "we must keep him in chains."[13] The "chains" embody the physical form of control, the label "monster," which relegates the foe to a space outside humanity, the psychological one.

8. Donald A. Petesch, *A Spy in the Enemy's Country: The Emergence of Modern Black Literature* (Iowa City: University of Iowa Press, 1989), p. 73.

9. Quoted in Herbert Aptheker, *American Negro Slave Revolts* (New York: International Publishers, 1978), p. 25.

10. E. P. Burke, *Reminiscences of Georgia,* quoted ibid., p. 51. see also p. 143 on the frequency of poisoning.

11. Catherine Clinton, *The Plantation Mistress: Woman's World in the Old South* (New York: Pantheon Books, 1982), p. 195.

12. Quoted in Aptheker, *Revolts,* p. 50.

13. Quoted ibid., p. 65.

The distinction between "field slaves" and domestics is another way of breaking up the oxymoron of the internal foe by grouping the slaves into two categories relegated to distinct spaces: the hostile ones outside the house, the faithful ones inside. This dichotomy disrupts the unity of the slave community and, more important, allows the masters to believe that they can trust at least those of their slaves with whom they are in most intimate contact. This reassurance is of the essence to the everyday viability of the system.

The spatial opposition between domestics and field slaves is completed by another important distinction in the masters' minds, between their own (internal) slaves and all the other (external) ones. Even after one of her cousins had been murdered by his own slaves, Mary Boykin Chesnut, a planter's wife, insisted that "nobody is afraid of their own negroes." The monsters always belong to someone else: "They are horrid brutes—savages, monsters—but I find everyone . . . ready to trust their own yard."[14]

As Antonio Gramsci has shown, coercion alone is not enough to sustain a hegemonic relationship. Consent is also necessary—that of the ruled, of course, but also, more secretly and deeply, that of the rulers themselves. The slaves' consent is needed both as a prevention of rebellion and as a cure for the masters' guilt, which is the foundation of the masters' "consent" to themselves. Thus, Harriet Jacobs's master, wishing to possess her sexually, is not satisfied with forcing her but must attempt to seduce her. Beyond the specific sexual aspect, seduction is a metaphor for the masters' wish to believe that the slaves will do by consent what they could be forced to do by coercion.

The illusion of consent is filtered first through the belief that the masters' "kindness" is automatically reciprocated by the slaves' affection and gratitude. Mary Chesnut writes: "Hitherto, I have never thought of being afraid of negroes. I have never injured any of them; why should they want to hurt me?"[15] Another pillar of this ideology is to persuade oneself that blacks, intrinsically inferior, take their servile condition for granted. But as Herman Melville's Benito Cereno learns from experience (and as Charles Chesnutt confirms in the story "The Doll"), the barber dutifully shaving his master is in fact holding a blade at his throat.

In every moment of their lives, indeed, the masters have their slaves' blades

---

14. C. Vann Woodward, ed., *Mary Chesnut's Civil War* (New Haven: Yale University Press, 1981), p. 212.

15. Ibid., p. 211.

at their throats. They can be slaughtered while being shaved, burned in the arson of their houses, suffocated in their beds by the servants who sleep on the floor at their feet, poisoned by the food prepared by their good "mammies." In the wake of the Denmark Vesey plot there was a rumor that domestic slaves had been given the task of poisoning the town's wells; indeed, as early as 1751 South Carolina law prohibited slaves from passing on to their fellows knowledge about "any poisonous root, plant, herb," and druggists and physicians were forbidden to allow slaves near drugs of any kind.[16]

After the Vesey plot many masters were shocked at the collapse of their hegemonic illusions, as they mirrored themselves in the slaves' revealing eyes:

> When the constables went into Mr. Horry's yard to take up his waiting man— he assured them they were mistaken—he could answer for his innocence— he would as soon suspect himself—he accompanied him on his trial convinced still he could not be guilty—on hearing the evidence—he turned round to his man—tell me, are you guilty? for I cannot believe unless I hear you say so— yes replied the negro—what were your intentions?—to kill you, rip open your belly & throw your guts in your face.[17]

In the prologue to *Invisible Man,* in a trance induced by music and smoke the narrator evokes an old woman slave who sings a spiritual and tells him her story.

> "I dearly loved my master, son," she said. "You should have hated him," I said. "He gave me several sons," she said, "and because I loved my sons I learned to love their father though I hate him too."
> "I too have become acquainted with ambivalence," I said.[18]

This is a fantastic, stylized tale; but the confrontation with ambivalence is intrinsic to the African American experience, and the encounter of slave and master is one of its topoi. Louise Piquet, bought as a concubine by a man with whom she subsequently had three children, revealed in her autobiography a state of mind not unlike that described by Ellison.

16. R. S. Starobin, "Introduction," in *Denmark Vesey,* p. 5; Clinton, *Plantation Mistress,* p. 194; Deborah Gray White, *Ar'n't I a Woman? Female Slaves in the Plantation South* (New York: W. W. Norton 1985), p. 79; Elizabeth Fox Genovese, *Within the Plantation Household: Black and White Women in the Old South* (Chapel Hill: University of North Carolina Press, 1988), pp. 306–307, 315–316.

17. Mrs. Martha Proctor Richardson to her nephew, Charleston, S.C., August 7, 1822, in Starobin, *Denmark Vesey,* p. 83.

18. Ellison, *Invisible Man,* p. 13.

I begin then to pray that he might die, so that I might get religion; and then I promised the Lord one night, faithful, in prayer, if he would just take him out of the way, I'd get religion and be true to Him as long as I lived . . . Then, when I saw that he was sufferin' so, I begin to get sorry, and begin to pray that he might get religion first before he died. I felt sorry to see him die in his sins. I prayed for him to have religion when I did not have it myself.[19]

Just as it was impossible for the masters to recognize fully the hostility of the slaves among whom they spent their lives, it was also very difficult for the slaves to live in the masters' house without investing some human affection in them. This did not necessarily imply an acceptance of slavery: "A slave could wish to be free without hating the man who kept him in chains." A woman who had run away from the plantation could, years later, retain "fond memories of her master and other whites."[20]

Though logically distinct, personal affections and the rejection of slavery could be emotionally and politically confused. The material privileges of domestic slaves might have been slight, yet they were tangible and desirable; the psychological ones, by contrast, might be even more important. In a system that did not recognize their full personal identity or grant them distinct social roles, for some slaves obtaining the master's trust became a path to achieving self-esteem and a limited but real visibility and presence.

"Pride and approbation were as native in my soul as probably they ever were in that of the greatest soldier or statesman,"[21] writes Josiah Henson. "Julius Caesar never aspired and plotted for the imperial crown more ambitiously than did I to out-hoe, out-reap, out-husk, out-dance, out-everything every competitor; and from all I can learn he never enjoyed his triumph half as much." This attitude allowed Henson to rise to the role of his master's familiar slave and accomplice: "For many years I was his factotum and supplied him with all his means for all his purposes whether good or bad." He proved his worth and his loyalty by driving his master's slaves through the free state of Ohio back to slavery in Kentucky. These servile attitudes, however, were motivated less by consent to the system than by the quest for a personal pride ultimately inadmissible in a slave ("My vanity had been flat-

19. Louise Piquet, *The Octoroon: A Tale of Southern Slave Life* (1861), ed. Rev. H. Mattison, in *Collected Black Women's Narratives*, ed. Anthony G. Berthelemy, (New York: Oxford University Press, 1988), p. 22.

20. Kenneth B. Stampp, *The Peculiar Institution: Slavery in the Ante-Bellum South* (New York: Vintage Books, 1956), p. 379.

21. Josiah Henson, *Life of Josiah Henson, Formerly a Slave* (Boston: Arthur D. Phelps, 1849), p. 8.

tered all around the road by hearing myself praised," writes Henson).[22] In this view, we must not underestimate the meaning of Henson's comparison between his ambition and Julius Caesar's. Slave owners used to pile ridicule on their slaves by bestowing on them names of great men of classic or biblical antiquity (Pompey, Cato, Josiah). But what the master meant as a joke the slaves may have taken seriously. The desire to be praised by the master over-lapped with the need to be respected as a capable and reliable person. There is no reason to doubt that, say, Rolla Bennett was indeed proud of and pleased by the fact that the master trusted him with the safety of his family. And yet this responsible role may have contributed to preparing him for leadership in the Vesey rebellion.

The slave's ambivalence as well as the master's pivots on the idea of reci-procity: as Eugene Genovese writes, slaves take to be rights what masters consider only benevolent unilateral concessions.[23] The need for recognition and self-respect becomes antagonistic when the slave realizes that these do not derive automatically from good behavior. When this illusion breaks down, the basis of identification and consent also fails.

"The honor of a slaveholder to a slave!" writes Harriet Jacobs, recalling how her grandmother was cheated by the benevolent mistress to whom she had lent her savings. "Notwithstanding my grandmother's long and faithful service to her owners," she concludes, "not one of her children escaped the auction block."[24] Even the trustworthy Josiah Henson was sorely disillu-sioned, and took off for Canada when the master tried to sell him "down the river" and stole his dearly bought freedom papers. In most cases the emotional and behavioral strategy consisted of a complex, mutable negotia-tion between the necessity of survival and the awareness of injustice. Even among the most faithful slaves there was a limit to obedience: when Henson was ordered by his master to whip his fellow slaves, he only pretended to do so, and his dissimulation mingled with that of the supposed "victims" who pretended to scream in pain.

Under normal conditions, however, compliance is the only option, mate-

22. Josiah Henson, *Truth Stranger Than Fiction: Father Henson's Story of His Own Life* (1858), quoted in Charles H. Nichols, *Many Thousand Gone: The Ex-Slaves' Account of their Bondage and Freedom* (Bloomington: Indiana University Press, 1963), p. 77.

23. Eugene D. Genovese, *Roll, Jordan, Roll: The World the Slaves Made* (New York: Pantheon Books, 1974).

24. Harriet A. Jacobs, *Incidents in the Life of a Slave Girl, Written by Herself,* ed. Jean Fagan Yellin (Cambridge, Mass.: Harvard University Press, 1987), pp. 7–8.

rially but in part also emotionally. When all alternatives seem out of reach, it is easiest simply to forget—at least at the most immediate level of consciousness—any other ideas or fantasies. After all, it is impossible to live forever only in dissimulation: in order to survive, a degree of identification is necessary. In order to dissimulate most effectively, slaves must not only pretend to be faithful and obedient but, provisionally and partially, actually be so. When an opportunity arises, however, things change; indeed, often opportunity alone makes the difference between the docile slave and the rebel. After the Denmark Vesey plot, for instance, a slave owner wrote: "I have no reason to suppose any of my house servants were guilty, but [had the plot been] anyway successfull even for a moment all or nearly all, would have joined!"[25]

"Mrs. Flint," writes Harriet Jacobs, "like many Southern women, was totally deficient in energy. She had not strength to superintend her household affairs."[26] The antebellum ideal of "true womanhood," especially in the South, required women to be frail, sexless, disembodied. The strong physical and sexual presence of black women's bodies was an unacceptable yet inescapable shadow which undermined the hegemonic ideal, "the dark side of a repressed self," inseparable from the mistress's image of herself, necessary and "intolerable." The threatening, intimate nearness of black women's bodies in their own households drew out the hostility in the white mistresses. With all of Mrs. Flint's frailty, Jacobs continues, "her nerves were so strong, that she could sit in her easy chair and see a woman whipped, till the blood trickled from every stroke of the lash."[27]

The ideal of domesticity also implies a division of space, between the public male sphere of production and business and the private female sphere of feeling and reproduction. In slavery this partition is repeated by the separation between the field and the house: the field is the external male territory, ruled by the violent law of coercion; the house is the inner female territory, where affection and consent supposedly rule. The relationship between the mistress and her female domestics was at the apex of the reciprocal ambiguities of slavery.

25. Starobin, *Denmark Vesey,* p. 79.

26. Jacobs, *Incidents,* p. 12.

27. Minrose C. Guin, *Black and White Women of the Old South* (Knoxville: University of Tennessee Press, 1985), p. 49; Jacobs, *Incidents,* p. 32 ("my presence was intolerable to Mrs. Flint," p. 12).

When Harriet Jacobs's Aunt Nancy died, her mistress Mrs. Flint, in an apparent demonstration of affection, offered to have her buried in the white cemetery, at the foot of her own grave. But Jacobs wryly notes that the mistress was so used to "sleep[ing] with her lying near [her] on the entry floor" that "it was painful to her to have Nancy buried away from her."[28] An ambiguous attachment indeed: the display of affection continues possession and dependency even in the grave.

The figure of the slave girl sleeping on the entry floor of the mistress's bedroom represents the elusive and dangerous presence of the slave's body as extension of and substitute for the mistress's negated one. In Willa Cather's *Sapphira and the Slave Girl* the mistress believes that her slave Nancy is carrying on a relationship with her husband with the complicity of the other slaves, and contrives the idea of having her seduced by another man. As Toni Morrison notes, Sapphira thus "escapes the necessity of inhabiting her own body by dwelling on the young, healthy, and sexually appetizing Nancy," for "it is after all hers, this slave woman's body, in a way that her own invalid flesh is not."[29] In an even more extreme version of this vicarious sexuality, the slave girl in Gayl Jones's *Corregidora* shares both her master's and her mistress's beds and caters to the sexual cravings and frustrations of both.[30]

No longer does the slave lie at the bedroom door or at the foot of the bed watching over the mistress's sleep; rather, the mistress anxiously watches the slave's still body, so near and yet so mysterious. Just as Sapphira feverishly watches Nancy, Harriet Jacobs's mistress likewise "spent many a sleepless night to watch over me." Sometimes, she recalls, "I woke up, and found her bending over me. At other times she whispered in my ear, as though it was her husband who was speaking to me, and listened to hear what I would answer . . . At last, I began to be fearful of my life."[31]

In theory the slave might be tempted to seek from her mistress a woman's understanding and solidarity. "Sometimes," Elizabeth Fox Genovese notes, "the master's severity threw slave woman and mistress into each other's arms."[32] "One word of kindness from her would have brought me to her

28. Jacobs, *Incidents*, p. 46.

29. Toni Morrison, *Playing in the Dark: Whiteness and the Literary Imagination* (Cambridge, Mass.: Harvard University Press, 1992), pp. 23, 26.

30. Gayl Jones, *Corregidora* (1975; rpt. Boston: Beacon Press, 1992), p. 23.

31. Jacobs, *Incidents*, p. 34.

32. Genovese, *Plantation Household*, p. 313.

feet," writes Harriet Jacobs; most often, however, "the mistress who ought to protect the helpless victim, has no other feelings toward her but those of jealousy and rage."[33] When this expectation of reciprocity also fails, the slave returns the mistress's obsessed gaze with a lucid eye which sees clearly through her. While Mrs. Flint watches her at night, thinking she is asleep, Jacobs is awake and aware of what she is doing. This crossing of gazes—one unseeing, the other unseen—allows Jacobs to see through the fiction of genteel womanhood which imprisons her mistress, and through the institution of slavery which imprisons them both.

"Now, I am a black woman and I am not free and I don't know any black woman that is, nor any black man, either," says Mrs. Nancy White, a descendant of slaves and a domestic worker all her life in a 1980 interview. "White women," she goes on, "are not free, either, but most of them think they are."[34]

The relationship of mistress and domestic perpetuates its ambiguities beyond the demise of slavery. Mrs. White describes the subordination and self-deception of her white employers in the same terms used by Malcolm X for house slaves:

> My mother used to say that the black woman is the white man's mule and the white woman is his dog. Now she said that to say this: we do the heavy work and get beat whether we do it well or not. But the white woman is closer to the master and he pats them on the head and lets them sleep in the house, but he ain' gon' treat neither one like he was dealing with a person. Now if you was to tell a white woman that, the first thing she would do is to call you a nigger and then she'd be real nice to her husband so he would come out here and beat you for telling his wife the truth.[35]

Like Malcolm's house slave, then, the white woman exchanges her dignity and humanity for the superficial privileges she derives from proximity to a master who treats her with the same paternalistic benevolence intended for lower beings. Both prefer to play the role of the spy and the traitor rather than listen to the truth about themselves and join their natural allies. At least, this is what the black domestic thinks she sees. But, just as the field

33. Jacobs, *Incidents*, pp. 27, 32.

34. John Langston Gwaltney, *Drylongso: A Self-Portrait of Black America* (New York: Random House, 1980), p. 143.

35. Ibid., p. 148.

slave does not always know what is in the house slave's mind, perhaps what is in the mind of the house-confined white woman is hidden from both her servant and her master. Could they have read not the minds but at least the diaries of some of their mistresses, the domestic slaves might have been intrigued. Though still mired in "an inability to recognize their black sisters' individuality and humanity,"[36] plantation wives such as Mary Chesnut were still able to see the discrepancy between illusion and reality in their own homes, and to describe it in unforgettable words: "God forgive us, but ours is a monstrous system, a wrong and iniquity."[37]

36. Guin, *Black and White Women,* p. 112.
37. Quoted in Clinton, *Plantation Mistress,* p. 199.

*Stefania Piccinato*

# The Slave Narrative and the Picaresque Novel

*A*s many an essay has explored, the slave narrative is strictly related to the picaresque literary tradition,[1] as well as in some cases showing influences derived from the eighteenth-century sentimental novel. Here I discuss the mode of antebellum slave narratives and their governing structure, from the 1830s to the late 1850s, taking into account their relation to the picaresque, including *Lazarillo de Tormes* and the European tradition (mainly English) inaugurated by *Lazarillo* through Alain-René Lesage's work. This relationship actually reveals a strong methodological and structural similarity from the narratological point of view. Moreover, the early picaresque as is universally acknowledged, is as it were a master mode, a source of many of the narrative techniques and choices that characterize much of western literature in its ironic shaping of the classical antihero.

In the first place, both modes of narration are retrospective. The narrator, looking back from the perspective of having acquired his freedom (the ex-slave) or of assessing a society that formerly rejected him (the picaro), selects the episodes and the circumstances of his or her prior brutalized life to be written down and made known. The episodes thus form a progressive series, each one shaping itself predominantly as a sort of trial in which the hero at

---

1. See, for instance, Henry Louis Gates, Jr., "Binary Oppositions in Chapter One of 'Narrative of the Life of Frederick Douglass, Written by Himself,'" in *Afro-American Literature,* ed. Dexter Fisher and Robert B. Stepto (New York: Modern Language Association of America, 1979), pp. 212–232; Raymond Hedin, "The American Slave Narrative: The Justification of the Picaro," *American Literature,* 53 (1982): 630–645; Charles H. Nichols, "The Slave Narrators and the Picaresque Mode: Archetypes for Modern Black Personae," in *The Slave's Narrative,* ed. Charles T. Davis and Henry Louis Gates, Jr. (Oxford: Oxford University Press, 1985), pp. 283–298. See also William L. Andrews, *To Tell a Free Story* (Urbana University of Illinois Press, 1986).

the same time sustains a growing consciousness of the harsh and contradictory reality surrounding him. Lazarillo's trials, to quote Charles Nichols, "create in him a personality ruled by selfishness, deceit, and trickery. The desperate jeopardy of his condition forces upon the servant-slave-picaro the urgency of his search for an identity, for survival."[2] And so, consequently, the hero is forced into deception and trickery, drawing on his or her ingenuity and skill, a situation Henry Bibb, William Wells Brown, Josiah Henson, Frederick Douglass, and others describe and comment on. This use of deception, apparently negative at first sight, is in reality an authentic victory of the mind, a sort of mental conquest that can be traced back to the Homeric Ulysses as a demonstration of intelligence winning over force. While we curiously find explicit references to Defoe in William Wells Brown (twice) and in Harriet Jacobs, we must not forget the connection, in both modes of narration, with folk and oral tradition. Furthermore, in both the picaresque and the slave narrative the pattern of narration, while recalled at the height of success, is characterized by an upward movement: from inhuman conditions to a status of freedom (the slave) or integration into society and freedom from want (the picaro)—for both a condition of fulfillment.

The picaresque novel, especially in its early versions, can certainly be seen as an intentionally ironic reversal of the heroic chivalric ideal, whereas the slave narrative—very often itself enriched by rhetorical turns of speech based on subtle forms of irony and parody—in its crude disclosure of the world of fear, aggression, and moral deprivation undoubtedly performs a similar function vis-à-vis the southern romantic tradition. As far as religion is concerned, both modes of narration reveal a formal acceptance of the prevailing forms and rites while intimately recognizing and deprecating the inherent contradictions and hypocrisy: the slave silently embracing the God of Israel, the picaro consciously adapting himself to the standards of worship of his environment.

Now, having outlined parallels that shape the two modes of narration, I move on to a more detailed inspection of the two genres, one that should lead us to recognize them as founding examples of a literary tradition.

## Past and Present Tense: A Functional Interaction

In considering these narratives a point of departure could properly be Emile Benveniste's distinction between "time of discourse" and "time of the

---

2. Nichols, "The Slave Narrators and the Picaresque Mode," p. 284.

story,"[3] that is, the present of narration versus the past of narrated events. I do not intend to offer here a definition of the autobiographical genre (definition of which is rather complex and sometimes controversial), but one point is firm and certain: the author-subject of the narration begins his or her recording of events from the standpoint of a newly acquired and apparently final status of freedom. This is very significant—so much so that, to underline the initial distance between the two moments, it might be convenient to recall the title of an important Italian autobiographical novel of the mid-nineteenth century, Ippolito Nievo's, *Confessions of an Octogenarian,*[4] in which the author uses the device of narrating the events of part of the protagonist's life at the end of it, when he is eighty years old. Such a choice stresses the importance of distancing the time of the story from the present of narration in order both to give the recording of events the gloss of an objective tale and to insist on the quality of a "final moment" inherent in the very act of writing.

The peculiarity of the slave's act of narration is, in my opinion, that of showing—in many cases at least—a supplementary "time" to be added to Benveniste's distinction: a "time of the future," strictly connected with the concept of exemplarity which pervades the narratives in question. That is to say, the slave narrative offers itself as a testimony of the "peculiar institution" and the individual story or adventure toward freedom but also as an "exemplum" of a very special kind of hero who, while attesting to the full right of the black man or woman to enter the community of the equal and the free, offers himself or herself to an implicit addressee—his or her companion in bonds—as a model, an example to be followed. This aspect of future time is asserted in Jean Starobinski's "Style of Autobiography" where he speaks of style as a qualifying element of autobiography, which assumes "the dual function of establishing the relation between the 'author' and his own past; but also, in its orientation toward the future, of revealing the author to his future readers."[5]

In considering the interaction of the different levels of "story" and "discourse," we notice, as I have mentioned, that they are intended to give a double testimony: of the personal history of the ex-slave, on the one hand,

---

3. Emile Benveniste, *Problèmes de linguistique générale* (Paris: Gallimard, 1966).

4. Ippolito Nievo, *Confessions di un ottuagenario* (Florence: Le Monnier, 1867).

5. Jean Starobinski, "The Style of Autobiography," in *Autobiography: Essays Theoretical and Critical,* ed. James Olney (Princeton: Princeton University Press, 1980), p. 74.

and, on the other, of the reality of the institution of slavery, of the horrors of slave life. To take an example from Frederick Douglass's *Narrative* [6]—let us, in this context, refer to it as a master narrative—the beginning of the first chapter gives us a signifying specimen: "I was born [past] in Tuckahoe, near Hillsborough, and about twelve miles from Easton in Talbot County, Maryland. I have [present] no accurate knowledge of my age, never having seen any authentic record containing it. By far the larger part of the slaves know [present] as little of their ages as horses know of theirs, and it is [present] the wish of most masters within my knowledge to keep their slaves thus ignorant." At its outset the text thus discloses at once the three dimensions that constitute it. First, the past (subjective: "I was born"), followed by detailed information (on places, locations, and names) intended to authenticate it: it is the *truth*. Second, the present (subjective) of discourse, of attained awareness ("I have no accurate knowledge"), a sentence in which the affirmation implying knowledge immediately introduces, at the very beginning, the sustaining element of the text itself in its own functional performance: knowledge (and from it therefore consciousness) as a primary and absolute tool, the first necessary step in the passage from "unconscious non-identity" to "conscious non-identity, vulnerable to the assaults of knowledge," as Angela Davis says à propos of Douglass.[7] Third, and last, the collective present ("the larger part of the slaves know as little"), which relates the individual "I" of the narrator to the collective reality of race, to the institution of slavery, to the oppression which is still perpetrated and against which the struggle is to be led.

As far as the structure of slave narratives is concerned, many are the patterns singled out by critics as bearing common traits.[8] If we carefully consider Frederick Douglass's work, however, we might be able to single out a perhaps more schematic, but also paradigmatic pattern coinciding with the different

6. *Narrative of the Life of Frederick Douglass, an American Slave. Written by Himself* (1845; rpt. Garden City, N. Y.: Doubleday, 1963).

7. *Angela Davis parle* (Paris: Editions Sociales 1971). The quotation is from the text of Davis's introductory lectures to her first course at UCLA in 1969, which focused on Douglass's autobiography and the process of his self-consciousness and liberation viewed as exemplary in contemporary society. For Davis the shift from the (negative) moment of the opposition slavery/death (suicide in order to overcome slavery) to the (positive) moment of the opposition slavery/struggle (even at the cost of death) is highly significant.

8. See Jean Fagan Yellin, *The Intricate Knot: Black Figures in American Literature, 1776–1863* (New York: New York University Press, 1972); and Frances Smith Foster, *Witnessing Slavery: The Development of Ante-Bellum Slave Narratives* (Westport, Conn.: Greenwood Press, 1979).

phases of the growth of consciousness and the liberation of the narrating "I." Furthermore, such a narrative pattern is common to several other slave accounts, and is present in Afro-American literary productions up to recent times, in addition to its parallels in the picaresque tradition.

What I am actually proposing is a three-fold scheme. A first nucleus of the narrative centers on the organization of the system of slavery described by means of emblematic experiences of the slave child. In the interaction of past and present a strict relationship between the life of the individual and the authenticating comment is constructed. From the standpoint of discourse the narrator looks back at himself as a gear within a system. He or she is just one among many, and the annulment taking place in the writing corresponds to the annihilation of the individual's identity brought forth by slavery. A second nucleus registers the growth of consciousness: the awareness of the "mental darkness" conditioning the life of the protagonist, the awareness of the importance of knowledge as a means of deliverance. It is now that escape is envisaged as an active form of struggle and redemption through the investigation of the mutual behavior of master and slave and, above all, through the new awareness of the refusal of slavery. The third nucleus, with the ultimate choice of escape, registers the appropriation of one's story as an individual even more than the growth of a decision-making consciousness. The object becomes subject in his or her relation to reality, and rebellion is seen both as an individual act and a shared communal event: solidarity on the one hand and on the other the protagonist's representation of the "collective individuality" of the race. It is at this third stage, furthermore, that the addressee is most often called upon, not only as a witness ("you have seen") but also as someone who must receive and take heed of the message.

Indeed, the achievement of literacy (the word)—and of the name[9] signi-

---

9. We may recall the important decision, in Douglass's narration, to acquire a specific name after many compulsory changes: "I gave Mr. Johnson the privilege of choosing me a name, but told him he must not take from me the name of 'Frederick.' I must hold on to that, to preserve a sense of my identity." And so Frederick was named Douglass after, he says, Scott's *Lady of the Lake:* "From that time until now I have been called 'Frederick Douglass'; and . . . I shall continue to use it as my own" (*Narrative*, pp. 109–110). And a solemn baptism, as it were, takes place in the life (the free life) of William Wells Brown. "I told him [the good Quaker friend] . . . I would give him the privilege of naming me . . . 'But,' said I, 'I am not willing to lose my name of William' . . . 'Then,' said he, 'I will call thee William Wells Brown.'" *Narrative of William Wells Brown, A Fugitive Slave, Written by Himself* (Boston, 1847); quotations are from Gilbert Osofsky, ed., *Puttin' on Ole Massa* (New York: Harper & Row, Evanston: 1969), p. 221.

fying it—is generally the central point of the victory of manhood in the journey from slavery to freedom. If the word exists—following Mikhail Bakhtin—only in the reality of the Other, its appropriation becomes the moment of the building up of communication, of the discovery of the interlocutor, of the destination of one's message. We find different modes of asserting this fact in the various narratives, but it becomes a symbolic act full of metaphorical resonances. Through the decoding of one's past and the mastery of tools suited to interpreting the world, the protagonist becomes a subject of that world and of its culture: the political act (the testimony) coincides with a cultural act. The author's identity, differentiated in the narrative by temporal distance, thus becomes the object of narration (as protagonist of the past) as well as the subject (in the present of writing)—an exemplary mimesis, on the level of discourse, of the passage from slavery to freedom which has taken place in the story.

A threefold scheme is also discernible in the structure of *Lazarillo*. The first part of the narration focuses on the description of the child's surroundings, the poverty and misery of family life, the disruption of social values which not only are personal but also affect the whole community. Moreover, according to the critical heritage ranging from Bataillon to Guillén, to Gilman, Rico, Carreter, and the Italians Puccini and Battaglia, "the picaresque is the first representation of society in explicitly critical terms . . . The protagonist . . . besides posing himself as spectator of his own life, becomes an active witness of society."[10] The individual's story is in fact always placed in contrast with a new way—as compared with the former literary tradition—of registering elements that concern external and collective social conditions. And if we do not find a shift from the level of the "story" to the level of "discourse" in *Lazarillo*, we certainly can ascertain such a shift in *Guzmán de Alfarache* and in *Moll Flanders*, for instance, where comments on the "present" social condition follow the description of personal situations viewed as typical of a community. As for *Lazarillo*, the episode of the blind master who bumps the simpleminded boy's head against the stone bull marks the passage to a second nucleus of the narrative, where the picaro's new awareness sustains his own struggle for survival. The third phase of the

10. "Il picarismo costituisce . . . la prima rappresentazione della società in termini esplicitamente critici . . . Il protagonista . . . oltre a porsi come spettatore della propria vita, si fa solerte testimone della società." Salvatore Battaglia, "L'ironia del picarismo," in *Mitografia del personaggio* (Naples: Liguori, 1991), p. 179.

narrative is pervaded by the picaro's consciousness of the need for emancipation and a final assessment. So Lazarillo, like Frederick Douglass and his freed brethren, at the apex of his experience conquers the "word" and tells his own story.

## Exemplarity

It now becomes relevant to return the discussion to the fundamental concept of exemplarity which sustains the primary model of picaresque narration. To be sure, *Lazarillo* and its ilk are to be inscribed in the tradition of medieval "exempla" and didactic literature. The "exemplum," according to the Latin writer Festus, "is what we follow or avoid,"[11] and as such becomes the core or nucleus of more articulate narrative solutions and eventully of the novel form. In fact, exemplarity is an inalienable prerogative of the tradition of the medieval *novella;* in particular, it works as such in that it performs the function of "history," where every event is a source of wisdom. Each *novella* (I am again paraphrasing the great scholar of medieval romance narrative tradition, Salvatore Battaglia) is but a "report" of life, a fragment of daily chronicle raised to the order of "history," of "ideal precept." So *Lazarillo* (and some picaresque novels) is the proposal of an example, the display of a case to be pointed out as "exemplary" because it is embodied by someone who has been able to coerce Fortune's plans. But, it must be added, with respect to the medieval scheme, the "historical" weight and the intentionality which the author ascribes to that performance of exemplarity have changed. Thus, *Lazarillo* offers itself as a record of an exemplary life in whose serial phases or trials (threefold, following the tradition of folk narrative, according to Vladimir Propp) we can find the embryo from which the modern novel developed.

The picaro, through his trials, each leading to a new awareness and, consequently, to recourse to ingenuity and trickery, finally overcomes all obstacles and assesses himself or herself "honorably"[12] in a world that had formerly rejected him or her. Lazarillo, who has finally reached his "buen puerto,"

11. "Est quod sequamur aut vitemus." Quoted in Salvatore Battaglia, *La coscienza letteraria del Medioevo* (Naples: Liguori, 1965), p. 476.

12. We might note that the concept of honor in *Lazarillo* and the picaresque tradition—where honor is a displaced concept for riches as source of honor—is ironically similar to the misguided (and superficial) concept of honor pertaining to the southern plantation tradition.

or safe harbor,[13] is content (and so, for instance, is Moll Flanders) cynically accepting the contradictions of society and reality, enjoying the place and role assigned him in that same society—and in that same reality—and from that condition of fulfillment writes his own story and describes his own "heroic" (that is, mock-heroic) exploits. It must be added that Lazarillo confesses in the prologue the necessity of relating his own history "del principio" (from the beginning),[14] thus revealing an additional similarity to the slave narratives and what we might call the formula of their incipit: "I was born." Furthermore, such a choice implies the will to submit the organization of the narrative to a project—the project of displaying the personality of the author-protagonist in its wholeness. The selection of events related to his material, psychological, and inner life, to his growth of consciousness, gives birth to a new mode of narration, to a new shaping of the individual and his relation to society, thus implying, in short, the germ of a bildungsroman.

Finally, the end of the story's coinciding with the beginning (the prologue) assigns to the project a further aim disclosed by the very first words of the text, where the author-protagonist asserts his willingness to be read: "I believe it a good that such remarkable things . . . come to be known by many."[15] And, it must be added, the text—the narration—has been requested by the prologue's addressee and written accordingly: "Since your Lordship writes me to write you and to relate extensively my story."[16] This necessity also has something in common with the slave narration's declared or implicit purpose.

## The Word as Social Commitment: A Communal Discourse

As for the ex-slave, the end of the story also coincides with the beginning if—beyond the present time of recording the experiences of the past—we take into account the authors' prefaces (Henry Bibb's, for instance, or James W. C. Pennington's, among many others), or William Wells Brown's dedicatory letter, Frederick Douglass's appended letters by William Lloyd Garrison and Wendell Phillips referring to the text, and so on. The "final moment"

---

13. These are the final words of the prologue. See R. O. Jones, ed., *La vida de Lazarillo de Tormes y de sus fortunas y adversidades* (Manchester: Manchester University Press, 1963), p. 4.

14. Ibid., p. 4.

15. "Yo por bien tengo que cosas tan señaladas . . . vengan a noticia de muchos." Ibid., p. 3.

16. "Y pues V.M. escribe se le escriba y relate el caso muy por extenso." Ibid., p. 4.

of the ex-slave undoubtedly is a moment of fulfillment: it is the moment of liberation, of the acquisition of freedom, from whose heights he or she can look back and tell the story of his or her trials. But the great freedom is also precisely this one: the freedom to write, to communicate. The act of writing is therefore an act of consciousness, of perspective; the more conscious the ex-slave is, the freer he or she is, and the more pressing becomes the need to write. And let us not forget that the autobiographical choice, the choice of a specific point of view—that is, first-person narration—all the more bears the exalted weight of testimony.

The act of writing, though, is not only the response to the necessity of telling one's own story of liberation; it is consistently also the response to the urge to project that story onto a collective concept of freedom. Thus, the "final moment" is not final. The world the ex-slave has entered is far from being satisfactory, and his responsibility—because he is responsible— is to fight for a better one.[17] A world that tolerates a system as evil as slavery has to be modified, in accordance with the reformistic aspirations of the time, to bring forth the achievement of a utopian society. Hence the commitment, the active participation in the antislavery movement. The antebellum narrative is not an individual representative story, as most frequently was the case with eighteenth-century slave narratives, which often exemplified salvation through God's benevolence, but rather an emblematic "collective" story aimed at a collective goal. I do not intend here to deny the project and act of deliberate involvement in antislavery activities of, say, a Gustavus Vassa. I simply want to stress the collective dimension inherent in the antebellum narratives. The point of view from which the story is narrated— freedom—becomes a "modern" value; and the resort to the Holy Scriptures we often find in these works is itself a "modern" value in that, by attesting to the narrator's right to call himself or herself God's creature, he or she is freed of theology as the sanction of "the one chosen by God," and claims everyone's right to be considered God's creature. And this right, like freedom, is collective.

Freedom, I want to stress, is not an individual ideal or conquest. In fact, many are the references to be found in the narratives to the collective value of freedom and, implicitly, to the individual act as representative of a com-

17. Referring to the picaresque mode, Charles H. Nichols asserts that it "is the achievement of a necessarily devious and subtle consciousness . . . and nothing in [the picaro's] experience creates in him a sense of responsibility." Nichols, "The Slave Narrators and the Picaresque Mode," p. 284.

munal goal thus emphasizing the exemplary force of the text. In Henry Bibb's preface to his *Narrative* he exclaims: "To be changed from a chattel to a human being, is no light matter, though the process with myself practically was very simple. And if I could reach the ears of every slave to-day, throughout the whole continent of America, I would teach the same lesson, I would sound it in the ears of every hereditary bondman, 'break your chains and fly for freedom!' "[18] While Mary Prince asserts that "to be free is very sweet," she adds, referring to the free servants in England: "They have their liberty. That's just what *we* want."[19] Finally, Solomon Northup remarks: "Let them [men who may write fictions portraying lowly life as it is] know the *heart* of the poor slave—learn his secret thoughts . . . and they will find that ninety-nine out of every hundred are intelligent enough to understand their situation, and to cherish in their bosoms the love of freedom, as passionately as themselves."[20] The same character of collective voice is assigned to the slave narratives by Henry Louis Gates Jr., when he writes: "In this process of imitation and repetition, the black slave's narrative came to be a communal utterance, a collective tale rather than merely an individual's autobiography. Each slave author . . . wrote on behalf of the millions of silent slaves still held captive throughout the South."[21] And, finally, a collective project is certainly implicit in the picaro's narration, where, as Lázaro Carreter among other scholars observes, "The author, writing in the first person, proposes himself as a triumphant model for the underprivileged."[22]

If we can inscribe some of the narratives in the general American pattern of the testimonial "self-made man" autobiography (Josiah Henson, James W. C. Pennington, Frederick Douglass in certain respects, and many others), attesting the Puritan values of individual enterprise and honest industry,[23]

18. *Narrative of the Life and Adventures of Henry Bibb, An American Slave, Written by Himself* (New York, 1849), quoted in Osofsky, *Puttin' on Ole Massa*, p. 63.

19. *History of Mary Prince, A West Indian Slave. Related by Herself* (London, 1831), in *The Classic Slave Narratives*, ed. Henry Louis Gates, Jr. (New York: Penguin Books, 1987), pp. 214–215.

20. *Twelve Years a Slave: Narrative of Solomon Northup* (1853), quoted in *Twelve Years a Slave*, ed. Sue Eakin and Joseph Logsdon (Baton Rouge: Louisiana University Press, 1968), p. 158.

21. Henry Louis Gates, Jr., "Introduction," in *The Classic Slave Narratives*, p. x.

22. "El autor, escribiendo en primera persona, so propone como modelo triunfante para los desheredados." Fernando Lázaro Carreter, *"Lazarillo de Tormes" en la picaresca* (Barcelona: Ariel, 1972), p. 39.

23. A great help in the reading and visualizing the influences of Puritan ideology on the slave narratives are Sacvan Bercovitch, *The Puritan Origins of the American Self* (New Haven: Yale University Press, 1975), and in particular *The American Jeremiad* (Madison: University of Wisconsin Press, 1978), as well as Andrews, *To Tell a Free Story*.

most of them, as well as *Lazarillo* for that matter, anticipate the modern hero we subsequently find in Afro-American literature, and in literature toutcourt, from the first years of the twentieth century onward: a relativistic hero, freed from the grip of scholasticism and transcendence. Even if set in a perspective conditioned by a specific human state, the ex-slave frees himself and discovers freedom as its own reward, as a value in itself.

Writing emerges from this awareness, and it is precisely in this collective perspective that our hero-writer can and must offer himself or herself as an example. Stephen Butterfield chooses, for his chapter on Frederick Douglass,[24] the title "Language as Weapon." He asserts: "One of the most important critical lessons of the slave narratives is that the literary achievement proceeds *through* and *from* the political involvement of the writer." Furthermore, in the introduction to the volume he writes: "The 'self' of black autobiography . . . is not an individual with a private career . . . The self is conceived as a member of an oppressed social group, with ties and responsibilities to the other members. It is a conscious political identity, drawing sustenance from the past experience of the group, giving back the iron of its endurance fashioned into armor and weapons for the use of the next generation of fighters."[25]

Thus freedom, having progressed from individual achievement, to a collective goal, through the word (through writing), ultimately becomes power.

24. Stephen Butterfield, *Black Autobiography in America* (Amherst: University of Massachusetts Press, 1974).
25. Ibid., pp. 88, 2–3.

Christopher Mulvey

# The Fugitive Self and the New World of the North: William Wells Brown's Discovery of America

Columbia is the poetical name for America, and the Columbiad is the poetical name for the journey to the New World. This journey is a quest, but it is a quest for special prizes, special riches which represent both the idea of a New World and the idea that that New World should be one distinct from a world known, explored, and exhausted. For the inhabitants of the New World that is Columbia, the Old World that is Europe is a place of tyranny and imprisonment, a world that denies to all but kings, emperors, and popes expression of self and ambition. The air of the New World is believed to be fuller, richer, cleaner, more exhilarating than the air of the Old World. Breathing that air makes possible the realization of dreams—dreams most powerful when they have been expressed as dreams of liberty.

Columbia is also that name for America which refers to the image of the continent as a land discovered by a European. Christopher Columbus is more present in the name Columbia than is Amerigo Vespucci in the name America. America has overwhelmed Amerigo, but Columbia has not overwhelmed Columbus. He remains the great figure, the great father, the great author. There is a tension between the image of the authoritative father figure, giving the law and siring the children, and the image of the land possessed by those children, the daughters and the sons of Columbia, a land of American freedoms and American dreams. A dilemma confronts anyone approaching Christopher Columbus and his particular discovery of America because it is plain that the Columbiad of Christopher Columbus was a journey not of dreaming and freedom but of calculation and enslavement. Knowing this seems to make little difference to the magical quality of the words Columbia and Columbiad. They resist their historical interpretations and insist on their mythological, mythopoeic meanings, which associate them with the human spirit. These conflicts of language and symbols, the paradox of Columbus, are felt everywhere through what has often been called the first black American novel, *Clotel*[1] by William Wells Brown, published in London in 1853.

William Wells Brown was born in Lexington, Kentucky, about the year 1816, and he died in Chelsea, Massachusetts, in 1884. He is described in the *Concise Dictionary of American Biography* as a "negro reformer," as a man who "escaped from slavery," and as one "celebrated in his own time as a lecturer and a historian of his race." Like other artists of his time, William Wells Brown used the name Columbia to represent a poetical America, and his America was discovered, like the traditional Columbia, by three ships; but William Wells Brown's three ships are not the *Santa Maria,* the *Nina,* and the *Pinta,* commanded by Christopher Columbus. For Brown, Columbus discovers the continent, but it is two later ships that discover America. In chapter 21 of *Clotel* Brown describes these three ships. First, there is the *Santa Maria,* Columbus's ship, a ship of "moral grandeur." Second is the *Mayflower:* "Next in moral grandeur, was this ship to the great discoverer's: Columbus found a continent: the *Mayflower* brought the seed-wheat of states and empire" (*Clotel,* 183). The third ship is the first Jamestown slaver, which in Brown's historical vision made land on the same day as the *Mayflower:* "But look far in the Southeast and you behold, on the same day, in 1620, a low rakish ship hastening from the tropics, solitary and alone, to the New World. What is she? She is freighted with the elements of unmixed evil . . . Listen to those shocking oaths, the crack of the flesh-cutting whip. Ah! it is the first cargo of slaves on their way to Jamestown, Virginia" (*Clotel,* 184). Brown did not call these slaves "Pilgrim Fathers," but this is the term which suggests itself from the moral construct that evolves in his vision of the *Santa Maria,* the *Mayflower* and the slaver, the founding ships of the land that was to become the United States of America. Brown makes no reference at all to the thousand intervening landings between 1492 and 1620 which created the cultures of South, Catholic, and Latin America. Brown was an American

1. William Wells Brown, *Clotel; or the President's Daughter: A Narrative of Slave Life in the United States* (London: Partridge & Oakey, 1853). All further references will be cited by page in the text.

Protestant and he wrote like one, but he was also a black American Protestant. He matched the moral event which founded white America with the moral event which founded black America.

"Behold the Mayflower anchored at Plymouth Rock, the slave-ship in James River. Each a parent" (*Clotel*, 184). Brown saw in these two ships two Americas which would attempt to occupy the mythical space of Columbia. This vision presented American history as tragic from its outset, a history leading directly from the landings of 1620 to the struggles of the 1850s which consumed Brown's life and writing. "These ships are the representation of good and evil in the New World, even to our day," he wrote in *Clotel*. "When shall one of those parallel lines come to an end?" (*Clotel*, 184). In 1853, when he published *Clotel*, he was of the opinion that the United States was moving, by way of the Fugitive Slave Act and the increasing violence against the antislavery movement, more toward the parentage of the slaver than of the *Mayflower*. William Wells Brown himself had had to compromise his resolution not to traffic in his own "body and soul." He had had to agree to his American freedom being bought from the man who claimed to own him.[2] Had he not done so, he would have returned as a slave in 1854 to the land that he had left as a freeman in 1849.

The historical vision of *Clotel* looked at both the white *Mayflower* and the black slave ship and saw "each a parent" (*Clotel*, 184). Brown's father was a white man and his mother was a slave, and he could see in each of the ships an ancestor. Here was a conflict and a union for William Wells Brown more primary even than that of the United States itself. It generated a pattern of contradictions and affirmations that created the central story of his fictions as much as it created the actual fact of his life. The most complete working out of this theme was in the first version of *Clotel* and was made clear by the subtitle of the 1853 London edition of the novel, *Clotel; or the President's Daughter*. The president was Thomas Jefferson, and his role in the novel is to father the heroine and her sister before removing to Washington to take up office. Jefferson becomes in Brown's fiction the author of the Declaration of Independence and Clotel.

The epigraph on the title page of *Clotel* reads: "We hold these truths to be self-evident: that all men are created equal; that they are endowed by

---

2. William Wells Brown, *Three Years in Europe; or, Places I Have Seen and People I Have Met* (London: C. Gilpin, 1853), p. 297. All further references will be cited by page in the text.

their Creator with certain inalienable rights, and that among these are LIFE, LIBERTY, and the PURSUIT OF HAPPINESS." Thomas Jefferson's language promised a universal meaning for the Declaration of American Independence. But for William Wells Brown that meaning had been canceled. He puts it simply in the first sentences of his autobiography: "Chapter 1. I was born in Lexington, Ky. The man who stole me as soon as I was born, recorded the birth of all infants which he claimed to be born his property, in a book which he kept for that purpose."[3] The ledger recorded an original act of theft; the Declaration recorded the original act of liberty. The Declaration of American Independence might have taken moral precedence over the plantation ledger, but the Declaration did not protect William Wells Brown the man when he was William the slave. The text quoted on the title page of *Clotel* had to be denied as often as it was affirmed. William Wells Brown's life and writings contained a continuing but quite unresolved confrontation with the fact that the Declaration of Independence was written by a slave owner. The moral authority and the human author could not be brought into the same focus. It was as if a Zionist had to look to a Nazi philosopher for the highest statement of Jewish aspiration.

In the opening chapter of the novel William Wells Brown quotes John Randolph. Randolph had represented Virginia in Congress almost continuously from 1799 to 1829, and he was remarkable for, among many other things, declaring that "the blood of the first American statesmen coursed through the veins of the slave of the South" (*Clotel*, 55). This fantastical piece of southern rhetoric contained as a boast one of Brown's main indictments of the South and one of the major elements of the American paradox: American fathers were using and selling their own children as slaves. This was not only an actual fact, it was an attested and unashamed fact. From Brown's point of view the case against men like Randolph was so well made by men like Randolph that moral indignation and action were all but nonplussed. The result was Brown's constant re-presentation of the American paradox and the constant disintegration of his argument. He was appealing for moral outrage but could not establish the moral indictment.

The Fugitive Slave Act of 1850 made the paradox "more perfect" because it explicitly involved the North in the Jeffersonian contradiction of a consti-

---

3. William Wells Brown, *Narrative of William Wells Brown, an American Slave. Written by Himself. With Additions by the Rev. Samuel Green*, (London: W. Tegg & Co., 1853), p. 13. All further references will be cited by page in the text.

tution designed for freedom being used to enslave people. "On every foot of soil, over which Stars and Stripes wave," Brown wrote in the preface to *Clotel*, "the negro is considered common property, on which any white man may lay his hand with perfect impunity. The entire white population of the United States, North and South, are bound by their oath to the Constitution, and their adhesion to the Fugitive Slave Law, to hunt down the runaway slave and return him to his claimant, and to suppress any effort that may be made by the slaves to gain their freedom by physical force" (*Clotel*, iii–iv). This insistence reinforced a further point, one central to the moral action of the novel: the whole South was to be held accountable for the worst excesses of any one part of the South. "It does the cause of emancipation but little good," Brown wrote, "to cry out in tones of execration against the traders, the kidnappers, the hireling overseers, and brutal drivers, so long as nothing is said to fasten the guilt on those who move in the higher circle" (*Clotel*, iv). The Fugitive Slave Act had extended that higher circle effectively to the whole people of the United States of America.

In the Fugitive Slave Act, William Wells Brown had a symbol for the constitutional outrage of the American paradox; in his own person he had a more immediate symbol for the human outrage of the American paradox. In the "Memoir of the Author," which William Wells Brown attached to his work *The Black Man*, he says: "My fair complexion was a great obstacle to my unhappiness both with whites and blacks, in and about the great house."[4] The great house was the home of Dr. and Mrs. Young, and since Brown was the son of a close relative of the doctor, there were occasions when visitors to the house took him to be Mrs. Young's child. For this Mrs. Young had him whipped. His fellow slaves mocked him.[5] The vulnerability of the fair-skinned Negro in the slave world is central to the tragedy of *Clotel*. In chapter 15, "To Day a Mistress, to Morrow a Slave," Brown gives an account of Clotel's fate when her owner-lover and sham husband, Mr. Horatio Green, takes a legal wife, Gertrude, a blond-haired but less beautiful woman than Clotel. The new and legal Mrs. Green makes it her business to end her husband's bachelor arrangements and insists on the sale of Clotel and Mary, Clotel's daughter by Mr. Green.

---

4. William Wells Brown, *The Black Man: His Antecedents, His Genius, and His Achievements* (Boston: James Redpath, 1863), pp. 18–19. All further references will be cited by page in the text.

5. William Edward Farrison, *William Wells Brown: Author and Reformer* (Chicago: University of Chicago Press, 1969), p. 14.

The dynamics of Brown's novel required continuous intensification of the American paradox so that the dual authorities of Thomas Jefferson could be seen to be more and more in profound self-contradiction. The moral authority of the Declaration of Independence had to be defied in the case of a woman who not only was Jefferson's daughter but was to all appearances white. If Brown was not certainly saying that it was better to enslave one of another race than to enslave one of your own, he was certainly saying that it was morally more abhorrent to enslave your own child than to enslave another's. "Nature abhors it; the age repels it; and Christianity needs all her meekness to forgive it," he wrote (*Clotel*, 61), but southern custom had so altered values that the sale of an American president's daughter did not excite those reactions. "The appearance of Clotel on the auction block created a deep sensation amongst the crowd. There she stood, with a complexion as white as most of those who were waiting with a wish to become her purchasers; her features as finely defined as any of her sex of pure Anglo-Saxon; her long black hair done up in the neatest manner; her form tall and graceful, and her whole appearance indicating one superior to her position" (*Clotel*, 62–63).

The full-length description of the heroine of this Victorian novel, seen in as vulnerable a posture as Hester Prynne or Tess of the D'Urbervilles, enables Brown to confront his white Anglo-Saxon and Protestant readers with the fact that, like the purchasers at the auction, they are dealing with one of their own kind as well as one of Brown's kind. The auctioneer's cry emphasises the point: "How much, gentlemen? Real Albino, fit for a fancy girl for any one" (*Clotel*, 63). William Wells Brown matches the bidding to her attributes, and the price rises as the auctioneer draws attention to her health, her looks, her education, her Christianity, her virginity. "This," says Brown in summary, "was a Southern auction, at which the bones, muscles, sinews, blood and nerves of a young lady of sixteen were sold for five hundred dollars; her moral character for two hundred; her improved intellect for one hundred; her Christianity for three hundred; and her chastity and virtue for four hundred dollars" (*Clotel*, 63–64). William Wells Brown had now established his main charge against America, and it led him once again to restate the American paradox: "Thus closed a negro sale, at which two daughters of Thomas Jefferson, the writer of the Declaration of Independence and one of the presidents of the great republic, were disposed of to the highest bidder" (*Clotel*, 64).

With her dark hair and fine eyes, Clotel is no albino. When Brown carries Clotel's romance with her purchaser to its next stage, she reappears in chapter 4 living in an idyllic rural cottage, in an idyllic "outward marriage," blessed with a daughter yet more white than Clotel herself. This is the daughter Mary, of whom Brown says only her eyes were African: "The iris of her large dark eyes had the melting mezzotinto, which remains the last vestige of African ancestry, and gives that plaintive expression, so often observed, and so appropriate to that docile and injured race" (*Clotel*, 80). Mary's whiteness eventually enables her to live happily ever after in England. The effect of the final twist of the paradox leaves the heroines of this black drama effectively white. Indeed, William Wells Brown makes them appear to be white, in part because his plot requires it. Clotel is able to make her escape from New Orleans to the North and then return to Richmond because she can pass as white. Althesa, Clotel's sister, must be able to pass as white if she is to take advantage of the protection offered by the moral sensitivity of her husband. Mary similarly needs to be able to pass if she is to live in England as a white woman. Nonetheless, alternative plot devices were available, and Brown had an unusually rich knowledge of the ways in which fugitives escaped from the South, a knowledge gained from his own work: "In one year alone, I assisted sixty fugitives in crossing to the British queen's dominions" (*Black Man*, 25). In choosing to have Clotel's escape depend on her fair skin, Brown was as much emphasizing Clotel's mulatto state as he was obliged to make her mulatto in order to have her escape.

In *The Black Man: His Antecedents, His Genius, and His Achievements,* his biographies of fifty-seven black men and women, Brown speaks with pride about his African heritage and its claim to a culture antecedent to that of the Anglo-Saxon. "I admit," he wrote in the introductory essay, "that the condition of my race, whether considered in a mental, moral, or intellectual point of view, at the present time cannot compare favorably with the Anglo-Saxon. But it does not become the whites to point a finger of scorn at the blacks, when they have so long been degrading them. The negro has not always been considered the inferior race. The time was when he stood at the head of science and literature. Let us see" (*Man,* 32). He gave a history of the Ethiopians and the Egyptians, assuming it "as a settled point that the Egyptians were black" (*Black Man,* 32). He quoted with pleasure a comment by Cicero, writing to his friend Atticus, advising "him not to buy slaves from England, 'because,' said he, 'they cannot be taught to read, and are the ugliest and most stupid race I ever saw' " (*Black Man*, 34). William Wells Brown did not distinguish between the Anglo-Saxons and the ancient Britons, but the point was a good one.

Brown's history showed that racial prejudice varied the object of its contempt, but not the grounds of the contempt so that now one race and then another would become despised and persecuted. A race that had been up at one point in history would be down in another. The Anglo-Saxons had once been considered contemptible barbarians but were now considered the most civilized of people; the Africans had once led civilization and were now considered contemptible. Of his collection of black biographies Brown wrote: "If this work shall aid in vindicating the Negro's character, and show that he is endowed with those intellectual and amiable qualities which adorn and dignify human nature, it will meet the most sanguine hopes of the writer" (*Black Man*, 6). Although Brown spoke of the amiable qualities of human nature, he did not mean to stress the docility of the black man. Several of his portraits celebrate militant and military black heroes. He concludes his account of Nat Turner with the remark that "every eye is now turned towards the south, looking for another Nat Turner" (*Black Man*, 75). Brown admired the slave-insurgent, and in addition to Nat Turner, he included lives of Toussaint L'Ouverture, Denmark Vesey, Madison Washington, and others. This was a theme that he included in *Clotel*.

Chapter 24 of the novel, titled "The Escape," deals not with the escape of Clotel but with the story of George, the house slave who is the lover of her daughter, Mary. George has been imprisoned for taking part in Nat Turner's rebellion. He had done so because he "had heard his master and visitors speak of the down-trodden and oppressed Poles; he heard them talk of going to Greece to fight for Grecian liberty." Inspired by this dinner table conversation, George joined the slave revolt (*Clotel*, 222). For this he is eventually condemned to death but is given the freedom of the court to speak after he has heard his sentence. Brown uses this as an opportunity to state again the central paradox of American liberty. "I will tell you why I joined the revolted negroes," says George. "I have heard my master read in the Declaration of Independence 'that all men are created free and equal,' and this caused me to inquire of myself why I was a slave" (*Clotel*, 224). George goes on to say that if he and his companions had succeeded in establishing their liberty, they "would have been patriots too," and he asks the court to think about the meaning of Independence Day celebrations in a slave state: "You make merry on the 4th of July. Yet one sixth of the people of this land are in chains and slavery" (*Clotel*, 225).

George moves his listeners to tears, but he does not move the law to compassion. His sentence is not commuted, and he escapes death only by the intervention of his lover, Mary, who sets in train a pattern of events that lead to life and freedom in England. In due course, and several years later Mary too escapes and makes her way to England. By complete coincidence the lovers unite, embrace, marry, and live happily ever after. George, says Brown, "being somewhat ashamed of his African descent" (*Clotel*, 231), has told no one that he is a fugitive, and so the couple are able to disappear into the English crowd and escape the persecution of their race. But they escape only through the fantasies of fairy-tale and romance fiction and through George's denial of a self which had led him earlier to speak as powerfully at the bar of history as any European freedom fighter.

For the climactic chapter of *Clotel*, in which the heroine takes her own life rather than return to slavery, the moral and topographical scene has been fully set. Clotel is imprisoned, says Brown, "midway between the capitol at Washington and the president's house" (*Clotel*, 215). When she jumps to her death from the Long Bridge over the Potomac, this formula is repeated. Clotel hopes to escape: "But God by his Providence had otherwise determined. He had determined that an appalling tragedy should be enacted that night, within plain sight of the President's house and the capitol of the Union" (*Clotel*, 217). Clotel is midway between the president's house, where once her father had lived, and the Capitol, which gives expression in stone and mortar to the Declaration of Independence. This irony leads William Wells Brown to repeat once again, as he never tires of doing, the American paradox: "Thus died Clotel, the daughter of Thomas Jefferson, a president of the United States; a man distinguished as the author of the Declaration of American Independence" (*Clotel*, 218).

Brown's anger and frustration spill over once he has killed his heroine. He takes up the theme that Americans have the greatest admiration for all the world's freedom fighters, except for black American freedom fighters. "Had Clotel escaped from oppression in any other land, in the disguise in which she fled from the Mississippi to Richmond, and reached the United States, no honour within the gift of the American people would have been good enough to have been heaped upon the heroic woman," he writes (*Clotel*, 218). He is angry that having no tears for Clotel, the American people "have tears to shed over Greece and Poland; they have an abundance of sympathy for 'poor Ireland'; they can furnish a ship of war to convey the Hungarian refugees from a Turkish prison to the 'land of the free and the home of the brave'" (*Clotel,* 218). His heroine is buried in a riverbank without inquest or religious service; and yet, he says, she is a woman who, "if she had been born in any other land but that of slavery, would have been honoured and loved" (*Clotel,* 218–219).

The energy Brown brought to the expression of this paradox arose from the moral contexts which conditioned his own narrative and life. These can now themselves be seen to be paradoxical. He had learned his ideals within the world of the plantation and of hired service, where he found these ideals systematically violated; but having adopted them under such adverse conditions, he would not abandon his ideals about the nature of men and women, about heroes and heroines, about the virtues of love, loyalty, generosity, and sacrifice, about the life well led. When in 1834 the man escaped from the morally bleak world of the slave owner, William Wells Brown carried with him little more than this orthodox moral freight, which endorsed a traditional right and wrong, a traditional virtue and vice. The Declaration of American Independence remained his statement of the politically ideal. Brown quoted Jefferson against Jefferson, but Brown did not propose to devalue the language of the American creed he was resolved by insistent use to defend the right of force against American violations of the creed, to give the creed its full meanings, and to make its language include black as well as white.

Perhaps William Wells Brown should have resisted these meanings and this language and worked with a mythology that did not lead him constantly to contradiction and paradox. But his writings insist that he was an American, and he would not forgo that rich poetry, language, and rhetoric which any American could and can adopt. The language went before him and made him what he was. He could no more remake the language than any other user could remake the language. More important, he did not *want* to remake the language. He wanted to talk about America in America's language, and he did so always with a sense of how it mocked him even as it spoke. One hundred and fifty years later the language has been remade by history and by politics and by the accumulation of personal interventions. These amount to little on their own, but in time and with sufficient number they can reshape the moral dialect of a language. The twentieth-century reader can then see the limitations that the language had for Brown perhaps more clearly than he could himself. What today's reader cannot see are limitations of contemporary language which will no doubt be obvious to readers in another one hundred and fifty years' time.

For students of American studies, the American paradox is so familiar that it has become a truism, and no student is without a ready explanation of how Jefferson could say one thing and live another. But William Wells Brown did not work out any solution to the paradox, nor did he seem to want to. Rather he seemed to wish to exist at the center of the contradiction, to continue to experience its anger, grief, and frustration, and constantly to expose his white readership to this moral anguish. Perhaps he believed that this witness to suffering should, would, must bring about the conversion of his readers. In the preface to *Clotel* Brown pitted one set of white readers against another, hoping that British readers would be so moved by the moral paradox of their former colony that British public opinion would move to influence American public opinion. Brown believed the English to be free of racial prejudice. "Hatred to oppression is so instilled into the minds of the people in Great Britain," he wrote in *Three Years in Europe*, "that it needs little to arouse their enthusiasm to its highest point; yet they can scarcely comprehend the real condition of the slaves of the United States." (*Europe*, 247).

But there was a lesson here that Brown was not learning, both about the British and to some extent about the Americans. His inference that the British were not racists in the 1850s was not borne out by their behavior in India and Africa. William Wells Brown's was a strong test, and the willingness of the British to shake his hand, welcome him to their homes, and have him at their tables could not be denied, but it was at the same time a partial test. It might mean that the British were free of racial prejudice, but it might also mean that the British rarely met cultivated Americans of African descent, that they did not feel any immediate interest threatened by Brown's presence, and that they could gain considerably in moral and political capital by investing in his friendship. This is not to say a lot about the British or any other people. It has the perhaps unpalatable consequence that the Americans are to be judged as no better and no worse than the British in general, though they were far worse to William Wells Brown in particular.

He was angered on the one hand by the American celebration of European liberationists such as John Mitchel of Ireland and Louis Kossuth of Hungary and on the other hand by American persecution of fugitive liberationists such as himself and Frederick Douglass. Yet William Wells Brown appeared to share the prejudice of the English against Disraeli, whom he called, as they did, "the Jew," and of whom, in *Three Years in Europe,* he gave a pointed present-tense description in a midnight sitting of the House of Commons: "There sits Disraeli, amongst the tories. Look at the Jewish face, those dark ringlets hanging round that marble brow. When on his feet, he has a cat-like, stealthy step; always looks on the ground when walking . . . is believed to be willing to support any measures, however sweeping and democratical, if by doing so he could gratify his ambition" (*Europe,* 288, 292). Brown's hostility can be accounted for on political grounds, but his expression of it resorted to stereotypical comments on Jewish looks and behavior. The admiration for liberty expressed by those who gave receptions for Louis Kossuth in 1851 were less abstract celebrations of political ideals than Americans celebrating what they thought were mirror images of themselves, so that they could once again celebrate their own worth and history. It was the establishment of their own republic and the overthrowing of their own tyrannt that made them wild for Louis Kossuth, though neither they nor he would have been too conscious of this.

By 1854 William Wells Brown had been five years in England. Of this exile he wrote: "I had become so well acquainted with the British people and their history, that I had begun to fancy myself an Englishman by habit, if not by birth" (*Europe,* 303). Brown was becoming an Englishman by self-adoption, and in so doing he was repeating a process of self-discovery, self-creation, and self-invention that had been a vital part of his life as a slave and as an American. Identification with his native land was always one that he made with difficulty. "I recommenced," he wrote of that period when he was steeling himself to cross the Atlantic, "with palpitating heart the preparation to return to my nativeland. Nativeland! How harshly that word sounds to my ears" (*Europe,* 303). Indeed, earlier in this book he had begun to refer to England as his "father-land," exactly as many a white New Englander or Virginian did. (*Europe,* 161). William Wells Brown identified nationally with the English because they did not reject him racially. Brown had a white father and English ancestors, and there was no reason why he should not claim the link, along with New Englanders, with what Nathaniel Hawthorne called their "Old Home."

On his arrival in Philadelphia after his return from London in 1854, he

was told that he could not board the omnibus with his two white companions when they left the ship. "Had I been an escaped felon, like John Mitchel,
no one would have questioned my right to a seat in a Philadelphia omnibus,"
he wrote (*Europe,* 312). John Mitchel, the Irish agitator and the author of
*Jail Journal,* a text beloved of Irish freedom fighters, had just escaped to the
United States, where he was eventually to buy a farm and slaves in the South
and settle down to a more prosperous and less arduous life than the English
had allowed him in his native land. Almost from the day of his arrival in
the United States, Mitchel declared himself a strenuous opponent of abolition. One country's freedom fighter was another's tyrant. Brown constantly
pointed up the paradox that men and women are inconsistent in their hero-
ism. It troubled him deeply, as it troubles all idealists who want to make
out of single human beings consistent persons to admire consistently. It
remains a fact that in 1834 William Wells Brown's Black Columbiad into
the New World of the northern United States brought him from the moral
clarities of slavedom and into the moral contradictions of freedom. It still
remains a fact that in 1776 it was a slave owner who wrote the Declaration
of Independence. And it still remains a fact that in 1492 Columbus did not
know where he had arrived and was forever to believe that he had found
the edge and the boundary of Asia, the continent of tyranny, whereas in fact
he had stumbled upon the edge and the boundary of America, the continent
of liberty.

*Rosemary F. Crockett*

# Frank J. Webb: The Shift to Color Discrimination

*T*he *Garies and Their Friends* was the first African American novel to explore the problem of color discrimination. Writing in the 1850s, a decade that witnessed a flowering of American literary talent, Frank J. Webb seized on his personal experience as a free northern black and defined the topic of African American literature for the next century. But since his 1857 debut Webb has slipped into almost total literary obscurity. The purpose of this essay is to explore the reasons for Webb's fall into oblivion, to recover the basic outline of his life, and to acknowledge his rightful place in the African American literary tradition.

Webb has been neglected for two major reasons. First, his treatment of slavery ran counter to the literary mainstream. The focus of the slave narratives and the two other African American novels published during the 1850s is the horror of slavery. By setting his novel in a free colored community in the northern city of Philadelphia, Webb shifted the literary focus from slavery to color discrimination.

The charge made by Arthur P. Davis, Addison Gayle, James H. DeVries, and others that Webb was soft on slavery is basically unfounded. In his 1980 doctoral dissertation Richard Yarborough noted that "in setting up a contrast between the bucolic pastoral life on the Garie plantation and the brutal racism awaiting the couple in Philadelphia, Webb takes the sentimentalist's view of the South . . . This treatment of slavery may have suited the structural needs of his plot; but, like Stowe before him, Webb thereby stumbles into the trap of indirectly justifying the existence of slavery."[1] Webb is obviously

1. Richard Alan Yarborough, "The Depiction of Blacks in the Early Afro-American Novel" (Ph.D. diss., Stanford University, 1980), pp. 118–119.

establishing a parallel between the ease and comfort of life for the white plantation owner Clarence Garie, his mulatto "wife" Emily, and their children in the South, despite the shadow of slavery and their isolation from friends and neighbors, with the destruction that color discrimination wreaks on their lives in the North. Ultimately four of the five Garie family members die as a result of color discrimination. In *The Garies and Their Friends* Webb's major plot revolves around color discrimination. Slavery plays only a minor supporting role.

But even the idyllic description of slavery on the Garie plantation is not a stamp of approval for the institution. Webb presents the Garie plantation as the best of all possible worlds within the acknowledged confines of slavery: there are no beatings; slaves are well fed, housed, and clothed; the plantation is run by the elderly slave Ephraim, without interference from Clarence Garie; and Emily is treated as Garie's legal wife. Yet Webb makes perfectly clear that this is not the rule but the exception. Through the stories of Emily, Celeste, and George Winston, as well as Garie's neighbors, Webb shows the slave on the auction block, the separation of families, the uncertain fate of slaves upon the death of a master, the disastrous fate of the slave mistress upon the legal marriage of the master, physical abuse of slaves, and the generally malevolent character of the overseers and plantation owners. Webb does not ignore or diminish the horrors of slavery, but he makes slavery a minor rather than a major focus.

A second possible reason why *The Garies* and Frank Webb have languished in obscurity for more than a century is the mystery that has surrounded the life of Webb himself. Most reference works state that Webb must have been raised in Philadelphia, where much of *The Garies* is set. They note his obvious acquaintance with Harriet Beecher Stowe and British antislavery activists, but can add little else to the story. Although a lack of biographical information has not impeded study of the works of William Shakespeare, it has perhaps had an adverse effect on studies of Frank Webb. Some biographical facts have been recovered and should assist in raising Webb from literary oblivion.[2]

Frank Johnson Webb was born in Philadelphia on March 21, 1828. Little else has been discovered of Webb's early life. The 1850 U.S. Census lists Frank Webb, aged twenty-two, and his wife Mary, aged twenty-one, both mulattoes, living in Ward 1, North Mulberry, Philadelphia. Webb's occupa-

2. Several scholars are currently working on the biography of Frank J. Webb, notably Roy E. Finkenbine and Allan Austin.

tion appears to be cited as "Clothing Store," although in a 1991 article Phil Lapsansky notes that "city directories for 1851 through 1854 list Frank J. Webb as a designer, or commercial artist in the printing trade." Lapsansky suggests that Webb may have been the son of an earlier Frank Webb, who was active in the First African Presbyterian Church and the Augustinian Society. This "elder Webb is listed in city directories as a China packer living on Relief Alley, a small South Philadelphia back street similar to the location of the Ellis family, the colored family that serves as a foil to the Garies."[3]

Documentation becomes more abundant after Mary and Frank Webb's departure for England in 1856. Mary had achieved moderate success as a dramatic reader in the northeastern coastal states. Harriet Beecher Stowe had in fact adapted a portion of *Uncle Tom's Cabin* expressly for Mary's presentation. Frank Webb wrote the biographical sketch of Mary which accompanied this adaptation. Mary's mother, he states, was "a woman of full African blood," while her father was "a Spanish gentleman of wealth." Just three weeks prior to Mary's birth her mother succeeded in escaping from slavery in Virginia to the protection of a family in New Bedford, Massachusetts. After experiencing both luxury and hardship in her youth, at the age of seventeen Mary wed Frank, "who engaged in business in Philadelphia, where they enjoyed the regard of a large circle of friends." No clue was given about how or why they met. But, Webb goes on to note dryly, "Mr. Webb's failure in business led Mrs. Webb to reflect upon the possibility of turning her marked elocutionary powers to some practical account." Mary was obviously attempting to keep the couple afloat financially. She made her dramatic debut in Philadelphia in 1855, then toured New England, "where she was warmly received," before deciding to try her luck in England.[4]

On May 24, 1856, Harriet Beecher Stowe wrote a letter to Mr. and Mrs. Edward Baines in England introducing the Webbs. Most of this letter focuses on Mary. Stowe mentions Frank only briefly: "Mr. Webb you will find a gentleman of superior cultivation and refinement and any kindness you may bestow upon them will be well bestowed and I shall consider it a personal

---

3. Phil Lapsansky, "Afro-Americana: Frank J. Webb and His Friends," in *The Annual Report of the Library Company of Philadelphia for the Year 1990* (Philadelphia: Library Company of Philadelphia, 1991), p. 35. Lapsansky, curator of the Afro-Americana collection, has also gathered information on Mary Webb as well as other family members.

4. "The Christian Slave: A Drama, Founded on a Portion of *Uncle Tom's Cabin*, Dramatised by Harriet Beecher Stowe, Expressly for the Readings of Mrs. Mary E. Webb. Arranged with a Short Biographical Sketch of the Reader, by F. J. Webb" (London: Sampson, Low, Son, & Co., 1856).

favor as I take the greatest interest in their success both from personal friendship and the influence it will have upon the opinion which is generally held respecting the ability of her race." Mary Webb achieved some success on this tour, receiving at least one favorable review, in the *Illustrated London News* of August 2, 1856, which heartily commended her performance.

While she was reading, was Frank writing? The precise development of the novel remains obscure. Perhaps Frank wrote the novel both in the United States and in England. What is known is that on August 12, 1857, Webb sold the English copyright to *The Garies* to George Routledge & Co., a well-known English publishing house, for £75. Routledge published two thousand copies of a deluxe edition as well as twelve thousand copies in their "Cheap Series." The latter sold for eighteen pence per copy.

The *Sunday Times* of London reviewed *The Garies,* but 80 percent of the review consists of an excerpt of the most dramatic incident in the novel—the attack by the white mob on the house of the wealthy Walters. In a single paragraph of actual commentary the *Times* review covers the popularity of the novel, the right and ability of "colored" people to attain emancipation, and the abilities of the race. It comments rather disdainfully that the introductions to the novel by both Harriet Beecher Stowe and the English anti-slavery activist Lord Brougham would ensure its "world-wide popularity." It continues: "It will be read with more than ordinary interest, even without its high introduction, on account both of its being the production of a man of colour and of the fashion which since the presentation of *Uncle Tom's Cabin,* prevails, for looking upon every heart-rending fiction as a fact, if it have but a negro for its hero." Additional reviews and personal comments are needed to confirm or contradict this presumption of predestined popularity.

The unnamed reviewer, having dealt with "negro" heroes, turns to the abilities of the race. The commentary ends on a positive though not totally unambiguous note, stating, "Of the capabilities of the race, the manner in which Mr. Webb wields his pen sufficiently testifies." This could be interpreted as high praise for the race, based on Webb's superior skills, or it could mean that the limited capabilities of the race are demonstrated by the limited literary abilities of Webb. The reader is left to decide. On the question of emancipation of the slaves, however, the reviewer is quite clear: Webb should have provided a successful solution to this vexing problem. The "negro's" right to emancipation is no longer questioned, the review continues, but "the means by which it is to be effected, without as much injury to slave as to slaveowner, is the question that is untouched by the author." The focus of the review is on slavery. Webb is criticized for not providing a formula for the emancipation of the slaves, even though he is writing not about slavery but about the discrimination that "coloreds" such as himself were experiencing in the urban North.[5]

The *Athenaeum* of London describes *The Garies* as imitative and lacking in originality. If Harriet Beecher Stowe hoped to arouse the sympathies of the English through this tale of oppression, success was certainly not achieved with this reviewer. Coupling *The Garies* with another American book, *Mabel Vaughan*, the review notes that neither Lord Brougham nor Mrs. Gaskell, who commented on the latter novel, had stated anything concerning the texts they introduced.[6] It continued: "Clearly enough, these literary sponsors have no faith in their own office, and little enough in the capability of their 'proteges' to run alone. We agree with them in thinking that to put good names as a guarantee to second-rate books is not a pleasant position for the owners of the said names, although it may give an emphasis to the advertisements. The publishers are the only parties who take anything by the device." Unlike the *Sunday Times*, which equated the abilities of colored people with the capabilities of Frank Webb, this reviewer attributes any achievements to "European blood." Describing the free colored people, the reviewer says:

> Most of them have an admixture of European blood in them; so that the question intended to be at once raised and answered by this work—whether slaves are capable of self-government—is not fairly stated. There is no doubt that the mixture of race gives to the original slave stock capacities for civilization and moral qualities of self-control which render them capable of achieving freedom and undertaking all its responsibilities, which in their original state they were *not*—and, when the majority are capable of being free, they will no more remain slaves than the Britons . . . but *till then* all the amiable intentions in the world will not make them free or give them the souls of freemen.

"European" and "freemen" are equated and confused here just as "African" and "slave" are. Slaves were not self-governing because of their social-

---

5. Review in *Sunday Times* (London), September 27, 1857, p. 2.

6. The *Athenaeum* review may be quite accurate on this point. A September 1857 letter from Webb to Lord Brougham seems to indicate that Brougham had not yet read *The Garies* when he wrote the preface. In this letter Webb thanks Lord Brougham for writing the preface and forwards him a copy of the novel, which he says "may merit your perusal."

political status as slaves. Their African "blood" was not the cause of their enslavement. The reviewer reveals no awareness that most Africans were free and self-governing people before they were forcibly enslaved by the Europeans to whom the review attributes the "capacities for civilization and moral qualities of self-control."

Yet again the focus reverts to slavery and not to the discrimination that capable colored people such as Mr. Walters, Charlie Ellis, and Clarence Garie were confronting in the cities of the North. But the reviewer goes on to deal with that very point, evidently believing that antipathy of white for black is natural and inevitable:

> The intense abhorrence of the Free States for their coloured brethren is an antipathy stronger than institutions . . . Black remains black, unpleasant to white. We may read a story that shall give us intense sorrow and sympathy with negroes; but the negro speciality is always kept out of sight; and Uncle Tom himself—the type and model of chivalrous and faithful slaves—would not have excited the enthusiasm in bodily reality that he does in Mrs. Stowe's description of him.

This five-paragraph review in the *Athenaeum* also ends on an ambiguous note, stating, "Taken as a tale of a pariah and oppressed class, 'The Garies and their Friends' is interesting, and well written." This is surely damning with faint praise! Although Harriet Beecher Stowe and Frank Webb did not achieve their goal of changing the hearts and minds of men in this particular case, this review was certainly provocative enough that it should have attracted readers to the book.[7]

The Webbs left England shortly after the publication of *The Garies*. According to Lapsansky they spent the winter of 1857–58 in southern France owing to Mary's frail health. They then returned briefly to Philadelphia en route to Jamaica, where the duke of Argyle had secured a post office position for Webb. The May 7, 1858, *Falmouth Post* hailed the arrival of both Mary and Frank in Jamaica:

> Mr. Webb is a colored gentleman of dark complexion, but by no means "Unknown to Fame." He has figured in the literary world as the author of the

7. Review in *Athenaeum* (London), no. 1565, October 24, 1857, p. 1320; advertisement p. 1315. Much work remains to be done on the reception of *The Garies* in England and in the United States. An editorial comment in the January 1, 1870, *New Era* (Washington, D.C.) states that the book was "extensively read in England and this country," but few reviews or comments have been located to date.

Anti-Slavery novel, "The Garies and their Friends" . . . Mrs. Webb is celebrated for her public readings of Shakspeare and of "Uncle Tom's Cabin" dramatised . . . We are happy for the acquisition of these two distinguished persons to our community, and trust our genial climate will be the means of restoring Mrs. Webb to health. Mr. Webb has already taken out letters of naturalization—he is a very gentlemanly person, and we are sure will be much esteemed by those who may make his acquaintance.[8]

Mary began to offer dramatic readings almost immediately. The May 15 *Daily Advertiser* gave mixed reviews to her first public performance, in which she presented works by Shakespeare, Stowe, Longfellow, and Monk Lewis for the benefit of the juvenile reformatories of Kingston. From April 1858 until 1864, Webb worked as a clerk in the General Post Office in Kingston, with salary increases from £180 to £250. According to Kingston baptismal records, he later became a planter on the island. Four of the six Webb children were born in Jamaica: Frank Rodgers, Evangeline Maria Louisa, Ruth Mary Rosabelle, and Clarrie Madeline Olive. The general outline of the Webbs' life in Jamaica is clear, yet many questions remain to be answered. Did reasons other than Mary's health lead the Webbs to emigrate to Jamaica? Mary's birthplace was sometimes given as Massachusetts and in other instances as the West Indies. Did she have relatives in Jamaica? When and how did Webb become a planter? The Jamaica story begs for further exploration.[9]

Frank next surfaced in Washington, D.C., without Mary. In January 1870 the *New Era*, a weekly newspaper edited by Sella Martin and Frederick Douglass, published Webb's short fiction "Two Wolves and a Lamb," as well as one poem and two articles. The short story is a gothic tale of love, death, and revenge that makes no reference to people of color. It takes place in France among the leisured upper class and is far removed from the situations presented in *The Garies*. The February editions of the *New Era* carried another journalistic article as well as a poem. Another short fiction piece, "Marvin Hayle," was serialized in the March and April issues.[10]

8. *Anti-Slavery Advocate* (London), March 1858, p. 120. *Falmouth Post & Jamaica General Advertiser* (Falmouth, Jamaica), May 7, 1858, p. 1.

9. *The Daily Advertiser & Lawton's Commercial Gazette* (Kingston), May 15, 1858, p. 2. *Blue Book—Island of Jamaica*, 1859, 1862, 1864. Register of Baptisms, Kingston, 1855–1867; 1868–1870.

10. On January 13, 1870, *New Era* published the poem "None Spoke a Single Word to Me" by F. J. W. On February 24 it published "Waiting" by F. J. W.—To M. R. W. I attribute both to Frank J. Webb. Webb used several different signatures: Frank J. Webb, F. J. Webb, and F. J. W. He used the last at the end of the biographical sketch of Mary in "The Christian Slave."

The rapidity with which these pieces appeared indicates that many were probably written prior to 1870. Both "Marvin Hayle" and "Two Wolves and a Lamb" are tales that Webb could have created based on his European experiences. Marvin Hayle, a poor but principled artist, is an outsider in the upper-class circles in which he socializes because of his impecunious condition. The rules of society separate him from his wealthy love interest, Ella, despite their mutual devotion. This situation immediately invites comparison with that of Clarence Garie, the son in *The Garies and Their Friends*. Clarence and Birdy are separated by the rules of society which dictate that no one with any African ancestry can marry a person without African ancestry. The principled Marvin Hayle obeys his pride and the rules of society. He abandons Ella to her wealthy merchant father, only to be rewarded in the end when the father becomes bankrupt and dies, leaving Ella and Hayle in a position of financial equality and therefore free to marry. Clarence, by contrast, is unprincipled. He cannot bring himself to reveal his African ancestry to Birdy or to her family. He is exposed by an enemy, and both he and Birdy die estranged and broken-hearted.

While Webb's writings were appearing in the *New Era*, he was leading another life as a student at Howard University Law School and as a part-time clerk at the Bureau of Refugees, Freedmen, and Abandoned Lands. Students were first accepted at the law school in 1869. An article dated July 7, 1870, on "the second annual examination of the Law Department of Howard University" in the *New Era*, lists "Frank J. Webb, Philadelphia" as having participated in the exercises, delivering a paper titled "Slander and Libel." Most of the law students could not afford to pay their university fees while also supporting themselves and perhaps a family. So employment was arranged for them in various offices of the executive branch of the federal government, often at the Freedmen's Bureau. Webb was appointed to a part-time (three hours per day) clerk position there effective January 24, 1870. A letter of recommendation from Massachusetts Governor William Claflin to the secretary of war, General W. W. Belknap, was written on Webb's behalf four days later. Webb probably studied and worked during the day, since law classes were held from five to nine three evenings per week.[11]

11. On the Howard University Law School, see Maxwell Bloomfield, "John Mercer Langston and the Rise of Howard Law School" (pamphlet); William F. Cheek, "Forgotten Prophet: The Life of John Mercer Langston" (Ph. D., University of Virginia, 1961); and John Mercer Langston, *From the*

While writing, working, and studying law, Webb boarded at 1153 17th Street, N.W., according to *Boyd's Directory of Washington, Georgetown, and Alexandria.* He was also engaged at least occasionally in the social whirl of Washington's colored society. The *New Era* of February 3 mentions "Mr Webb, of Jamaica" among the guests at a soiree given by George T. Downing, also a frequent contributor to the *New Era,* in honor of Mississippi Senator Hiriam Revels. Webb was obviously leading a full life in Washington. But where was Mary? Where were the children? What caused Webb to leave Jamaica? And how did he support a wife and four children on his part-time clerk's salary of $600 per year? In any case the job was short-lived. The Freedmen's Bureau was being phased out. Employees were being released, and Webb's own appointment was revoked effective October 1870. Howard University's first law school class graduated in 1871; Webb was not among the graduates.

Unemployed, without a law degree, and apparently alone, Webb migrated westward. On January 17, 1871, the Freedmen's Bureau received a letter from Frank J. Webb posted from Galveston, Texas. According to the correspondence log Webb "forwards copy of resolutions adopted by Republican Association at that place condemning the course of the A.M.A. in allowing no colored teachers in Barnes School." Webb had not only relocated but had become actively involved in the colored community and in local politics. He was employed as a clerk by the U.S. Post Office in Galveston as early as 1872 at an annual salary of $1,000. Webb was earning $1,200 when he left his postal position in 1877 or 1878.[12]

He left the job, but not the Galveston area. The 1880 federal census shows Webb, his wife, two sons, four daughters, a married sister-in-law, and a widowed brother-in-law all living on Crockett Street in Columbus, Texas. Columbus was the capital of Colorado County, just two counties west of

---

*Virginia Plantation to the National Capitol* (Hartford: American Publishing Company, 1894). Howard University Law School reports no record of Webb as a student there. Bureau of Refugees, Freedmen, and Abandoned Lands records are available at the National Archives, Record Group 105. For the Claflin-Belknap letter, see Record Group 107, Records of the Office of the Secretary of War, National Archives.

12. "Registers & Letters Received by the Commissioner, Bureau of Refugees Freedmen and Abandoned Lands, 1865–1872," M752, Roll 12. See *Register of Officers and Agents, Civil, Military, and Naval, in the Service of the United States, on the Thirtieth of September, 1873 . . .,* (Washington, D.C.: Government Printing Office, 1874), p. 378; (1875), p. 472; (1877), p. 374.

Galveston. The two youngest Webb children, Thomas and Ethelvid, were born in Texas.[13]

Sometime around 1881 Webb changed careers from postal clerk to educator. The city directory for Galveston for 1882–83 lists Frank J. Webb as the principal of the Third District colored public school, which was also known as the Barnes Institute. Webb served as principal there for thirteen years, although the name of the school was changed to West District School. Under his stewardship the school evidently flourished, more than doubling its 1882 staff of four teachers to nine, plus one night-school teacher, by 1894.

Domestically Webb led a peripatetic existence. After boarding with Maggie Burney during 1882–83, he boarded with a merchant, Robert Mills. Then he and his daughter Eva (Evangeline) boarded with C. J. Waring, principal of Central Public School (colored), where Eva taught. By 1890–91 Webb had secured his own residence, which Eva shared with him on the south side of Avenue L between 31st and 32nd streets. By 1893—94 Frank and Eva were joined by Clarisse (Clarrie) and the younger son, Thomas, who was employed as an office boy by D. G. Ferrill.[14]

The Galveston *Daily News* of May 8, 1894, carried the announcement of Webb's death. It began, "At 2:45 a.m. May 7, Prof. Frank Johnson Webb, colored, formerly of Philadelphia, Pa., born March 21, 1828, departed this life . . . He had been for years clerk in the Galveston postoffice, followed by thirteen years as principal of the West district public school, for six years licensed lay reader of St. Augustine's Protestant Episcopal church and twenty-four years an esteemed resident of this city." The education community of Galveston activly participated in the funeral ceremonies.

The obituary noted that Webb left "a wife and six children." Thomas, the younger son, evidently remained in Galveston. He worked first as an office boy for Drs. Sampson, then as a delivery clerk for Flatto Brothers. But what was the fate of the other Webbs? Where did they venture next? Frank, Jr., graduated from Howard University Medical School in 1895. Did the others retreat to the island of Jamaica? Did Webb, who seemed so prolific a writer

13. 1880 U.S. Census, Texas. Roll 1297, p. 22.

14. *Morrison & Fourmy's General Directory of the City of Galveston, 1882–1883* (Galveston, Texas: Morrison & Fourmy, 1893); see also for 1884–85; 1886–87; 1888–89; 1890–91; 1891–92; 1893–94; 1895–96.

during his brief Washington stay, also contribute to publications in the Galveston area? All these questions remain to be answered.[15]

For Frank J. Webb the story ended in Galveston. But the themes he set forth in *The Garies and Their Friends* dominated much of twentieth-century African American literature. The novel set precedents in many respects. In his introduction to the 1969 reprint Arthur P. Davis wrote: "It is the first work of fiction to describe the lives and problems of the free northern Negro; the first to treat in depth the 'mixed marriage'; the first to include a lynch mob in its plot; the first to treat ironically . . . the problem of the 'color line' . . . and the first to make 'passing for white' a major theme . . . In short, the novel anticipates much that appears in later Negro American fiction."[16] These are the major themes of the first half of the twentieth century. They are played out in the works of Charles Chesnutt, the writers of the Harlem Renaissance, Richard Wright, James Baldwin, and their successors. These writers echoed the common theme that ran through Webb's writing. Webb urgently desired an equal chance. Like Walters in *The Garies,* he did not ask for any advantage. He just wanted to be free from color discrimination. Given this freedom, he was confident that he would be able to hold his own against any man. If *The Garies and Their Friends* could be judged freely, separate from the antislavery literary tradition, separate from the mystery that surrounded the life of its author, perhaps it would rise from obscurity to its rightful place as the novel that defined the central themes of African American literature for the next one hundred years.

15. *Morrison & Fourmy's,* . . . 1895–1896 through 1901–2. Frederick D. Wilkinson, ed., *Directory of Graduates: Howard University, 1870–1963* (Washington, D.C.: Howard University Press, 1963), pp. 390, 519.

16. Arthur P. Davis, introduction to *The Garies and Their Friends* (New York: Arno Press, 1969), p vi.

*Michel Fabre*

# Paris as a Moment in African American Consciousness

Still in my mind is a long poem on Richard Wright and Paris and me. How crucial to my development as a writer/thinker was my last year in Paris. It wasn't just an "experience" of an American abroad, it was a deep part of my life, and one that I plan to see grow into something lasting and solid.
—MELVIN DIXON, 1973

*P*aris constitutes a privileged "moment" in African American consciousness. By "moment" I do not mean a historical period, however brief, or the experience of an individual residing there; rather, one can conceive of such a moment as a metaphor. It can stand for feelings and concepts reflecting personal discovery or expressing group awareness; one could even speak of a realization comparable to James Joyce's "epiphanies" or to what Charles Baudelaire defined as the "symbol," that is, the experiential (and not merely intellectual) perception of spiritual realities embodied in the spectacle, however ordinary, by which one is confronted. From this perspective the City of Light occupies a privileged place in African American consciousness.

For centuries Paris has been the administrative, political, financial, economic, and cultural capital of France. It thus stands as a metaphor for the whole nation. Even more, as an heir to the architectural splendor of monarchy as well as to the humanistic ideals of the Enlightenment embodied in the 1789 Revolution, it remains an undisputed site of creative excellence and refinement, if not the unchallenged cultural capital of the Old World. As early as 1903 W. E. B. Du Bois, lecturing to a black audience in Louisville, Kentucky, stressed this distinguishing characteristic of "the greatest of the world's cities":

In memory of Melvin Dixon, who died on October 27, 1992.

I say greatest advisedly, for there is not on earth a city comparable in all the things that make a great metropolis to the capital of France . . . In Paris alone have we combined a vast aggregation of human beings under a modern municipal government amid historic surroundings and clothed in an outward magnificence and grandeur unparalleled in history . . . Here is the center of the aesthetic culture of the nineteenth century and from the brilliant cafés of the sweeping Boulevards go forth edicts more despotic than the decrees of Caesar . . . and the man or woman in the civilized world who has not at least a distant acquaintance with the language of the Parisian dare not claim a pretense to liberal culture.[1]

Ever since the times when the French-speaking colored elite of New Orleans repaired there,[2] black Americans have had reasons for living in Paris, in particular the onus of racial oppression at home as well as the desire to advance one's career or to escape the pressure to conform. The choice of France over other places has often been accounted for by the romance of bohemian Paris, the example set by famous black predecessors, the existence of institutions and an atmosphere propitious to artistic creation. Whether this image of Paris corresponds to reality or not, the fact remains that it has been "a city of the mind," conceived as such even by those who never set foot there.

A prime reason for the appeal of Paris to African Americans has been its vaunted racial liberalism. That London ranked first as a cradle of emancipation is indisputable, yet Paris early enjoyed the reputation of a racial haven; the Afro-American press disseminated the notion, mixing myth with eyewitness accounts.[3] This is reflected in *Iola Leroy,* an 1892 novel by Frances Ellen Harper. An educated octoroon whom her white husband cannot impose

1. W.E.B. Du Bois, in *Against Racism: Unpublished Essays, Papers, Addresses, 1887–1961,* ed. Herbert Aptheker (Amherst: University of Massachusetts Press, 1985), p. 57.

2. Among others, Camille Thierry, excluded from Louisiana high society life because of a few drops of black blood, contemplated expatriation in "Le chant de l'exilé": "Who can hold me to these shores / Where I only dwell among regrets? . . . / Take heart! There is another shore/ Where happiness can soar . . . / A foreign land will open its door to me." In *Les Vagabondes, poésies américaines* (Paris: Lemerre, De Laporte, 1874), pp. 41–42.

3. In the 1830s, for instance, *The Colored American* reported lack of racial prejudice in France even though its editors, bent on temperance, regarded theater-going as an evil activity and fiction a source of licentiousness, and branded French novels, especially, leading to "the loss of virtue." At the turn of the century, when culture was no longer considered reprehensible, racial equality in Paris was advertised, even when occasionally challenged, as when E. Azalia Hackley questioned the "liberal treatment accorded the black man by the French" in "How the Color Question Looks to an American in France," *AME Church Review* 23.3 (January, 1907); 210–215.

upon his acquaintances is taken to Paris; only there can their children be brought up "without being subjected to the depressing influence of caste feeling. Perhaps by the time their education is finished, I will be ready to wind up my affairs and take them abroad, where merit and ability will give them entrance into the best circles of art, literature and science." Harper cites the examples of Ira Aldridge and Alexandre Dumas, who "was not forced to conceal his origin to succeed as a novelist."[4] Half a century later young Langston Hughes, eager to become a writer, could cite only the elder Dumas as an example of a commercially successful colored writer in order to convince his father, who remarked: "Yes, but he was in Paris, where they don't care about color."[5]

Being there could be interiorized as a cherished personal project. Countee Cullen testified to the existence of the dream; as a little boy he already wanted to visit Paris. "It was only a thing of the heart . . . In Paris I used to build my castles in the air. Again, when I graduated, we were all filled with dreams and hopes, and each had slightly different ones. But our different hopes were all linked by a hope which bound us together: we all wanted to go to Paris."[6]

Claude McKay has provided a sophisticated analysis of the pro-French attitude of the African American intelligentsia, confirming the prevalence of the myth. The good treatment of individuals by those whom they met in Paris biased their sympathies to the point where they refused to confront French exploitation of Africans. McKay reasoned that African Americans had good reasons to "loosely generalize about the differences in the treatment of Negroes in bourgeois France and in plutocratic America." René Maran's novel *Batouala*, "a denunciation of the activities of the French government in Africa," had brought him the Goncourt Prize and membership in desirable writers' circles in Paris. In contrast, W. E. B. Du Bois, author of a "surprisingly moving work, *The Souls of Black Folk*, written in splendid English," remained "up to the present an outcast in American society."[7]

The sophistication and refinement of Paris have captivated many African Americans. Among them Alain Locke, the "New Negro" aesthete, wrote to Langston Hughes about the exceptional moment when he became infatuated

---

4. Frances Ellen Harper, *Iola Leroy or Shadows Uplifted* (1892; rpt. New York: McGrath, 1969), pp. 84–85.

5. Langston Hughes, *The Big Sea* (New York: Knopf, 1940), p. 62.

6. Countee Cullen, unpublished exercise book, Yale University Library, pp. 109–110.

7. Claude McKay, *The Negro in America* (Port Washington, N.Y.: Kennikat Press, 1979), pp. 50–51.

with the city in 1925: "I needed one such day and one such night . . . in which to see soul-deep and be satisfied—for after all with all my sensuality and sentimentality, I love sublimated things and today nature, the only great cleanser of life, would have distilled anything. God grant us one such day and night before America with her inhibitions closes down on us."[8]

In Paris art and beauty seem to counterbalance sin, even though they do not annul the notion of it. After a night in the Montmartre cabarets the young artist and poet Gwendolyn Bennett never forgot the shock of beauty as she stepped out into the early morning streets and looked up at the "beautiful, pearly Sacré-Cœur, as though its silent loveliness were pointing a white finger at our night's debauchery. I wished then that so worthy an emotion as I felt might have been forever caught in a poem."[9]

Although Paris is often perceived as different from mainstream America, and therefore strange, quaint, and exotic, the cherished experience of "the Parisian moment" sometimes consists in the delighted discovery of a profound consonance between France and the Afro-American soul. There is some ambiguity to this, however. A nineteenth-century visitor, the black Alabamian James T. Rapier, remarked on "French street urchins turning somersaults or walking on their hands to get a centime,"[10] a practice often associated with black "pickaninnies" and, later, with third world children. It must be remembered that France at the time frequently passed for a lazy and underdeveloped country. Booker T. Washington shared the perception of puritanical Americans who held the French in low esteem because of their supposed lack of industry. He saw France as a reprehensibly frivolous nation with the feminine weaknesses sometimes ascribed to the Negro race by white supremacists. Reflecting on the moral inferiority of the Parisians possessed by the "love of pleasure and excitement," he believed that "in the matter of truth and high honor" southern blacks did not suffer from comparison with them.[11]

A more positive temperamental kinship between black Americans and the French has often been noted, opposing Latin-black feeling for life to Anglo-

8. Alain Locke, undated letter to Langston Hughes, August 1925, Yale University Library.

9. Gwendolyn Bennett, unpublished journal, August 6, 1925, p. 27, Schomburg Collection, New York Public Library.

10. James T. Rapier, "Notes of Travel in Europe," unpublished ms., Yale University Library.

11. Booker T. Washington, *Up From Slavery*, in *Three Negro Classics* (New York: Avon, 1965), pp. 181–182.

Saxon uptightness. After he had traveled four thousand miles visiting black American World War I soldiers in France, the Reverend Hugh Proctor concluded: "It was a remarkable thing that a colored person could approach a Frenchman anywhere without an introduction and almost immediately be on terms of *bonhommie*. I believe the Negro and French are affinities. They are both emotional, artistic, musical, fun-loving, and religious. Perhaps that is why they understand each other so quickly."[12] Likewise the journalist Joel A. Rogers claimed: "The French remind me more of colored folks. They are just as noisy, excitable, loveable, and light-hearted. They also take their own time about things."[13]

This natural consonance appears to explain the widespread French acceptance of blacks. The Harlem Renaissance author John F. Matheus thus celebrated the moment of his discovery of Paris together with his pride in French appreciation of black world culture. In "Belle Mamselle of Martinique" he sings of Antillean elegance on French soil:

> You live here? Ah, now, I see
> Why I like gay, old Paree,
> You're the romance that we seek,
> Belle Mamselle of Martinique.

The girl, a "real Parisienne," is asked not to forget her "tropic, foliaged shores / Where the torrid sun restores / Color to the Nordic cheek." And Matheus finally foregrounds the tribute which France, above all nations, pays to black beauty:

> Yes, I know they put a ban
> On crinkly hair and cheek of tan
> Where we live across the sea,
> Knowing not that Gay Paree
>
> Worships just such nymphs as you,
> Colored nymphs, whose eyes are dew,
> Colored faces, copper, bronze,
> Mango, olive, almond, orange.[14]

12. Rev. Hugh Proctor, *Between Black and White* (Boston: Pilgrim Press, 1925), p. 160.

13. "J. A. Rogers Makes Comparison of French and American Customs," *New York Amsterdam News*, October 19, 1925, Schomburg Library files.

14. John F. Matheus, "Belle Mamselle of Martinique," *Carolina Magazine* (1927), clipping.

For Horace Cayton, too, race superseded any other experience in a colored man's existence. After speaking in a Paris café with a young woman from Martinique who identified herself as French, not Negro, he reflected on the difference between the two cultures: "America had me conscious only that I was a Negro yet France had made this girl, though she was perhaps only a prostitute, feel at home, feel that she belonged."[15]

Not only the French lack of racial prejudice but the respect for difference, stemming from a basic belief in the potential equality of persons and peoples, was often noted. Frederick Douglass liked Paris for that reason in the 1890s. The Negro, he remarked, was not an object of ridicule, possibly because he had often been there as an artist or scholar rather than as a slave, also possibly owing to the influence of the Catholic church. Before Douglass, William Wells Brown praised French respect and courtesy.[16] Countee Cullen later endowed Parisians with perpetual politeness, which he ascribed to a "natural inherent streak, something fine and delicate, left over perhaps . . . from the days when France had kings and a court."[17] Admittedly, to Booker T. Washington the recognition granted the painter Henry Ossawa Tanner in Paris was less an indication of lack of prejudice than a reinforcement of his belief that "any man, regardless of color, will be recognized and rewarded just in proportion as he learns to do something well." He acknowledged, however, that in France "the color of the face neither helps nor hinders."[18]

Expressions abound of the African American's delight in experiencing the moment when one ceases to be a member of a group and becomes "just a person." The novelist Jessie Fauset came to appreciate in Paris an unusual freedom on many levels—social, racial, and cultural; it was "lovely just to be oneself and not bothering about color or prejudice."[19] This blessed mo-

15. Horace Cayton, *Long Old Road* (New York: Trident Press, 1965), p. 225.

16. Frederick Douglass, *The Life and Times of Frederick Douglass* (1892; rpt., New York: Macmillan, 1962), p. 562. In Paris in 1849 the fugitive slave Brown asked to be driven to the Elysée Palace. The cabman drove between two lines of soldiers and left him in front of the gates, where a liveried servant opened the cab door and asked if he had an appointment with the president. "Amid the shrugs of their shoulders, the nods of their heads, and the laughter of the soldiers," Brown tried to explain that he was only a tourist. But he later made a point of remarking: "Few nations are more courteous than the French . . . With the exception of the egregious blunder I have mentioned of the cabman driving me to the Elysée, I was not laughed at once while in France." William Wells Brown, *Sketches of Places and People Abroad* (Boston: John P. Jewett, 1855), p. 97.

17. "Countee Cullen on French Courtesy," *Crisis 36* (June 1929): 193.

18. Louis Harlan et al., ed. *The Booker T. Washington Papers* (Urbana: University of Illinois Press, 1976), 5:142.

19. Jessie Fauset to Langston Hughes, January 8, 1925, Yale University Library.

ment was often linked with the monumental architecture and the leisurely pace of the city. It crystallized for Horace Cayton as he wandered up the Champs-Elysées at dusk: "The air was soft and balmy. Crowds of people were sitting at the numerous terrace cafés on either side of the wide street. Paris was wonderful, Paris was beautiful, Paris was free . . . Walking up the broad Champs Elysées, I was just one of a crowd. I felt free and happy as I had never remembered feeling in the United States."[20] This ability to blend in, this allure of free anonymity are quite notable. Richard Wright also repeatedly stated his delight at being in beautiful surroundings, "somewhere where your color is the least important thing about you."[21]

The most perceptive celebration of this newfound freedom of mind probably comes from the pen of James Weldon Johnson:

> From the day I set foot in France [in 1905] I became aware of the working of a miracle within me. I became aware of a quick readjustment to life and environment. I recaptured for the first time since childhood the sense of being just a human being . . . I was suddenly free: free from a sense of impending discomfort, insecurity, danger; free from the conflict within the Man-Negro dualism and the innumerable maneuvers in thought and behavior that it compels; free from the problem of the many obvious or subtle adjustments to a multitude of bans and taboos; free from special scorn, special tolerance, special condescension, special commiseration; free to be merely a man.[22]

Claude McKay, too, would explain: "Why do foreign colonies flourish so easily in France? The secret is France's aloofness; they tolerate strangers and allow them to do as they please as long as they don't meddle in French national affairs or do anything to hurt their pride."[23]

The key point is that France's aloofness and tolerance concretely meant that in Paris people left you alone. Many black Americans desired just this. The individualism of the French prevented them from adopting conformist attitudes, including racism, and when the novelist William Gardner Smith noted "a relative absence of tension in daily life, regardless of what people might be thinking behind polite exteriors," he remarked that the blacks in Europe did not care so much about what people were thinking: "White ac-

20. Cayton, *Long Old Road,* pp. 220–221.

21. Richard Wright to M. Scanton, June 15, 1946, quoted in Michel Fabre, *The World of Richard Wright* (Oxford: University Press of Mississippi, 1985), p. 156.

22. James Weldon Johnson, *Along This Way* (New York: Viking 1933), p. 209.

23. Claude McKay to Arthur Spingarn, July 31, 1933, Yale University Library.

tions were what exasperated us."[24] Likewise, James Baldwin stated glowingly that because the French left him alone, he was free of the "crutches of race." In his novel *Just above My Head,* the narrator makes this momentary and momentous experience more explicit:

> In Paris, one feels free to be an outsider, to watch . . . Here he feels free, more free than he has ever been, anywhere; and, though he has yet to realize it consciously, this freedom is very largely due to the fact that he moves in almost total silence. His vocabulary exists almost entirely in his fingers and in his eyes; he is forced to throw himself on the good nature of the French and he will never, luckily, live here long enough to be forced to put this good nature to any test . . . In the resulting silence he drops his guard.
>
> He could never have done that in New York, where all his senses were always alert for danger, or in London . . .
>
> But nothing is demanded of him in Paris. In Paris, he is practically invisible, practically free.[25]

Baldwin made a point of shunning romantic stereotypes about Paris which others had willingly accepted. The Harlem Renaissance champion Harold Jackman resorted to the familiar image upon discovering the city: "Love here in the springtime must be next to divine for in the summer it is a lovely sight to view two lovers on the boulevard just cooing to each other as it were. I tell you, rather I should ask you, what other place under the sun is like Paris, except somewhere in the tropics under the soft moonlight? I could stay there for ever."[26] As for Baldwin, he defined romantic Paris as "the city where everyone loses his head, and his morals, lives through at least one *histoire d'amour,* ceases, quite, to arrive anywhere on time, and thumbs his nose at the Puritans—the city, in brief, where all become drunken on the fine, old air of freedom." The legend even placed the many inconveniences endured by Americans "in the gentle glow of the picturesque, and the absurd; so that, finally, it is perfectly possible to be enamored of Paris while remaining totally indifferent or even hostile to the French."[27]

Most black Americans have found Paris a city of superlatives. Countee Cullen encountered there more than he had dreamed of. "Somewhat [this

24. Willian Gardner Smith, *Return to Black America* (Englewood Cliffs, N.J. Prentice-Hall, 1971), p. 71.

25. James Baldwin, *Just Above My Head* (New York: Dial Press, 1979), p. 468.

26. Harold Jackman to Langston Hughes, August 13, 1925, Yale University Library.

27. James Baldwin, *Notes of a Native Son* (Boston: Beacon Press, 1955), p. 108.

'somewhat' seems fairly crucial] like New York where I was born, Paris is a peerless city. Liberty, equality, fraternity are not only words. They express the spirit of which Paris is made. I love this café life, this quiet existence mixed with noise and quick motion which is attached to every large city . . . sights, noises in the night, places where one has fun according to one's liking, a sympathetic and tolerant world, in sum, a true civilization."[28]

This blend of beauty, tolerance, leisure, even spirituality to be found in France is already present in Addie Hunton and Kathryn Johnson's book *Two Colored Women with the American Expeditionary Force*. They summed up what Paris as a moment can embody when they wrote that the association of black soldiers with the French in World War I entailed a broader view of life:

> They caught the vision of a freedom that gave them new hope and new inspiration . . . Many hundreds had the opportunity of traveling through the flowering fields of a country long-famed for its wonderful monuments, cathedrals, art galleries, palaces, chateaux, etc., that represent the highest attainment in the world of architecture and art. They looked upon the relics left by a people long gone and saw the picturesqueness of a great and wonderful country . . . they learned that there is a fair-skinned people in the world who believe in the equality of the races, and who practice what they believe.[29]

Even the more down-to-earth visitors often ended up on a high spiritual note. Joel A. Rogers began to praise the Frenchman as a true bohemian, to be seen "in hundreds of thousands sitting at the delightful little tables on the sidewalks of the great boulevards, sipping his café, wine or aperitif and taking his time to get acquainted with life." Rogers's appreciation of café life is quite interesting when compared to the American conception of blacks as "lazy"; here, freedom of leisure is a privilege and the sign of a refined, open mind. Rogers topped it by concluding: "This is perhaps why the French are such an artistic people. Paris is a very beautiful city in spite of the rusty appearance of the buildings . . . I cannot recall having experienced a greater elevation of soul than when I stepped into the magnificent and spacious Place de la Concorde."[30]

Paris can easily be viewed as an embodiment of the spiritual, a Keatsian

28. Cullen, exercise book, pp. 109–110.

29. Addie Hunton and Kathryn Johnson, *Two Colored Women with the American Expeditionary Force* (New York: Brooklyn Eagle Press, n.d.), pp. 253–254.

30. "J. A. Rogers Makes Comparison of French and American Customs."

"thing of beauty." Gwendolyn Bennett remarked after visiting the Luxembourg Museum during her first Sunday there: "There never was a more beautiful city than Paris . . . There couldn't be! On every hand are works of art and beautiful vistas. One has the impression of looking through at fairy-worlds as one sees gorgeous buildings, arches and towers rising from among the mounds of trees from afar. And there are flowers, too, in Paris, oh, just billions of them."[31] As for Richard Wright, as he was driven across the city for the first time in 1946 he became more and more silent, only whispering in awe: "My God, what beauty!" Arriving in front of Notre-Dame he exclaimed, "Can you imagine what this means to me? I never knew a city could be so beautiful. This is something I shall never forget."[32]

At that moment the beauty of Paris struck Wright as a quality brought to environment by age and history, a tangible proof not only of a refined culture but of a successful civilization. He associated it at once with intellectual vitality and the absence of racial pressure. On his second trip in 1947 the same joy prevailed in this ecstatic moment: "Coming again into Paris! The sun was just setting and the pale light shone upon the old buildings and revealed their age. How earthy a people are the French! How squat the buildings sit upon the ground! It was like a dream."[33] Wright analyzed the key reasons for his satisfaction: the French felt so secure culturally that their acceptance of diversity made Paris a truly international scene. Their education provided them with a "universal scheme of reference which imputes to the alien a level of humanity different from his own in outward guise but not in intrinsic substance."[34] The emphasis laid on "universality" in French education allowed Wright to stress criteria for self-definition and social definition other than economic status and race (in Europe poor and rich are not so strictly separated by residence as in America). As a result, tolerance could prevail.[35] Unlike McKay, Wright did not consider the price placed on intellect in France a threat to the dignity of the uneducated. He was attracted to a value system that did not condemn the poor, "even by implication, to

31. Bennett, journal, June 28, 1925, p. 8.

32. Douglas Schneider, letter to Michel Fabre, December 12, 1964.

33. Richard Wright, journal, August 8, 1947, Yale University Library. See Fabre, *The World of Richard Wright*, p. 147.

34. Richard Wright, "I Choose Exile," in Fabre, *The World of Richard Wright*, p. 149.

35. Richard Wright to Ed Aswell, May 15, 1946, in Michel Fabre, *The Unfinished Quest of Richard Wright* (New York: Morrow, 1973), p. 306.

a sub-human status . . . As an American Negro, I felt, amidst such a milieu, safe from my neighbor for the first time in my life."[36]

As a result, racial equality in Paris is not only experienced by black visitors as free sharing of social amenities; it becomes enjoyment of a superior culture on an equal footing, allowing one to function as a member of the world's educated elite. In 1890 Frederick Douglass was gratified to walk the streets of that "splendid city" and spend days in its art galleries; he appreciated it all the more because "to think that I, once a slave on the Eastern shore of Maryland, was experiencing all this was well calculated to intensify my feeling of good fortune by reason of contrast, if nothing more." Yet his conclusion is even more striking: *"Now I was enjoying what the wisest and best of the world have bestowed for the wisest and best to enjoy."*[37]

Although a strong opponent of French colonial domination, W. E. B. Du Bois remained a friend of France during the dark hours of the Nazi occupation. Significantly he began his July 6, 1940, editorial for the *Pittsburgh Courier:* "The greatness of France in her culture and people will not and cannot die." Ralph Ellison also pointed out the exceptionalism of France most tellingly when he confessed, after seeeing the bombed buildings of London: "What are the symbols and monuments of Britain to me that I should feel a sense of loss? But in France, it was different, even the negative symbols contain enough of their lost vitality to make one regret he failed to get there sooner. Certainly, it provided me a new perspective through which to look upon the U.S."[38]

Ellison's evocation of France's "lost vitality" reflected his appreciation of French culture more than of France's overly vaunted racial freedom. His concerns were primarily problems of writing, and he could not believe that a trip overseas would magically solve them. Like McKay before him, he was critical of African Americans "running over for a few weeks and coming back insisting that it's paradise. So many of them talk and act like skulking children and all they can say about France with its great culture is that it's a place where they can walk into a restaurant and be served,"[39] he wrote Richard Wright. Wright, upon discovering expatriate Gertrude Stein's cre-

---

36. Wright, "I Choose Exile," p. 12.
37. Douglass, *Life and Times,* pp. 587–588, emphasis added.
38. Ralph Ellison to Richard Wright, August 18, 1948, Yale University Library.
39. Ibid.

ativity, had been too quick to conclude that one could write like that "only if one lived in Paris or in some out of the way spot where one could claim one's own soul."[40] Ellison thought otherwise. And William Gardner Smith echoed him when he observed that many blacks went "in search of a racial shangri-la, a land of equality, a land of justice where no man would be penalized for the color of his skin."[41] But could they really find it in Paris?

It seems that the role played by Paris as a "moment" in African American group and self-awareness could only result in contradictory (or at best complementary) allegiances. This dialectical relation is best embodied in Josephine Baker's all-time hit:

> J'ai deux amours
> Mon pays et Paris,
> Par eux toujours
> Mon cœur est conquis.
> L'Amérique est belle
> Mais pourquoi le nier,
> Ce qui m'ensorcelle
> C'est Paris, Paris tout entier.

(I have two loves / My country and Paris / By them my heart is always won / America is beautiful / But why deny it / What fascinates me / Is Paris, the whole of Paris.)[42]

Josephine Baker's song encapsulates a definition of Paris as "home" for Afro-Americans. Many have spoken of France as a substitute mother country, compensating for the humiliations of ill-loved children as second-class citizens. Mary Church Terrell put it most clearly when she noted, on revisiting Paris in 1904 as president of the National Association of Colored Women: "The country in which I was born and reared and have lived is my fatherland, of course, and I love it genuinely but my motherland is dear, broad-minded France in which people with dark complexions are not dis-

---

40. Richard Wright, unpublished journal, January 28, 1945, in Fabre, *Unfinished Quest*, p. 145.
41. Smith, *Return to Black America*, p. 63.
42. When he sang these lines at the February 1992 conference on African Americans in Europe, the eighty-odd-year-old Martiniquan academic Louis T. Achille not only wished to convey some of the excitement which presided at his performance at the 1931 Colonial Exhibition in Paris; he wanted to share this spirit with the several hundred African Americans who attended, themselves caught in the exhilaration of a momentous, though momentary, celebration of themselves in the Latin Quarter.

criminated against on account of their color."[43] On a later trip she visited sections devastated by the war, and in the Argonne forest she made a very symbolic gesture: she plucked a piece of ivy which grew near the grave of an American soldier and "although I carried it about with me a long time for many miles from pillar to post, several pieces of it survived, so that in two places I have living things to remind me constantly of France."[44] In Claude McKay's novel *Banjo* a black American character likewise carries some French soil back home in a bottle. Indeed many American soldiers voiced similar feelings in the press and in correspondence. On August 26, 1919, a black private wrote bluntly about his regret that he would "sail for our home in Petersburg, Va. United States of America where true democracy is enjoyed only by the white people. There is an air of liberty, equality and fraternity here which does not blow in the black man's face in liberty-loving, democratic America."[45]

Countee Cullen most movingly epitomized the vision of France as a sub-stitute mother country in his sonnet:

> As he whose eyes are gouged craves light to see,
> And he whose limbs are broken strength to run,
> So have I sought in you that alchemy
> That knits my bones and turns me to the sun
> And found across a continent of foam
> What was denied my hungry heart at home.[46]

Paris, however, is but one pole of this multiple allegiance of African American visitors. Josephine Baker's love for America remains vivid in "the Parisian moment" as the antithetical stage of a dialectical relationship. On the Fourth of July, 1925, loneliness in Paris also filled young Gwendolyn Bennett with renewed patriotism, and she confided to her journal: "There are times I'd give half my remaining years to hear the Star-Spangled Banner." But she quickly added: "And yet when I feel that way, I know it has nothing to do with the same 'home' feeling I have when I see crowds of American white people jostling each other about the American Express."[47]

43. Mary Church Terrell, *A Colored Woman in a White World* (Washington, D.C.: Ransdell Publishers, 1940), p. 209.

44. Ibid., p. 347.

45. William Hewlett to W. E. B. Du Bois, August 26, 1919, in *The Correspondence of W. E. B. Du Bois*, vol. 1, ed. Herbert Aptheker (Amherst: University of Massachusetts Press, 1973), pp. 234–235.

46. Countee Cullen, *On These I Stand* (New York: Harper, 1947), p. 147.

47. Bennett, journal, July 26, 1925, pp. 115–116.

African Americans' elation at feeling free in Paris clearly entails the realization that they are different from Europeans—this is a recurring point in
Baldwin's score of essays about discovering his identity in Europe—and
closer than they originally believed to mainstream American culture, if not
to their white fellow citizens. At the same time comes the painful realization
of everything they have missed because of racial discrimination.

Claude McKay's little-known evocation of Paris in a superb sonnet reflects
a similar ambivalence: far from falling for the City of Light as a "pagan
paradise of courtesans / And cavaliers," he gauged the depths on which the
city's strength rested. To him Paris was a cynical place, mesmerizing in its
fascination for the foreign visitor (whom he cast in terms close to Henry
James's evocation of "innocent" Americans in wicked old Europe), yet less
a (moveable) "feast" than "a school" with lessons for all:

> Paris has never stormed my stubborn heart
> And rushed like champagne sparkling to my head . . .
> Because it is a city more like bread
> Than wine and meat as solid nourishment
> To build the Frenchman and his mind complete
> And fit him for his civilizing part.[48]

McKay disliked the sense of superiority in the French, which he explained
by their conviction that they were called upon to "civilize" the world. He
looked up to the tradition of the French Enlightenment and liked reverence
for the intellect but detested Parisian salons and critics, the intellectual smug-
ness of those who looked down on America as a raw country; reverence for
history he found oppressive. Moreover, for him the lure of Paris as a shining
beacon had already been displaced; he believed that New York held greater
promise for romance in the modern world, with its "mighty business palaces,
vast depots receiving and discharging hordes of humanity, immense cathe-
drals of pleasure, far-flung spans of steel roads and tumultuous traffic."[49]

In a March 1, 1954, essay he submitted to *Ebony,* Chester Himes reacted
much like McKay to the Paris "moment." When he first arrived, he found
the city "hard, sexual," and little conducive to romance. He claimed he liked
America better, despite its many faults, and perhaps because of them: "I am
what America made me and the longer I stay the more I discover how much

---

48. Claude McKay, typescript copy in Jean Wagner's papers, Paris.
49. Claude McKay, *Banjo* (New York: Harper, 1929), p. 68.

of America is in me and how much of me is in America. I have a notion, grown out of the little I have seen, that America offers practically everything but antiquity to be found in the rest of the world. The tragedy for me is I can share only a small part of its great offerings."[50] Himes's discovery of his Americanness as a black citizen, a fact that prevented him from sharing his country's offerings because of discrimination, counterpoints Baldwin's realization of his heritage. It also echoes Horace Cayton's realization, in the aforementioned episode, that he had no choice but to return home to the United States: "In a way I love it. I was more American than most of its population."[51] Yet in spite of his patriotic claims, Himes did settle in Europe.

Of late the alienation following the blissful but possibly naive "Parisian moment" of freedom has even been accompanied by visions of Paris as a "no man's land" where uprooted blacks cannot find a second home. In 1964 the nationalist poet Larry Neal asked in "For Black Writers and Artists in 'Exile'":

> How many of them die their deaths
> looking for sun, finding darkness in the city of light.
> motherless, whirling in a world of empty words,
> snatching at, and shaping the rubbish
> that is our lives
> until form becomes, or life dances to an incoherent finish.[52]

One of Melvin Dixon's poems of the mid-1970s, "Getting Directions," should be seen as an attempt to counterpoint the stereotype of Paris as a "moveable feast" by placing it in a wider global perspective than that of American expatriation. The celebrated phrase by Hemingway is quoted to celebrate not the poetry of bohemianism but the fraternity between blacks and the body of the black man, his "primitive feet danced out":

> Entering Paris
> on a moveable feast of clouds
> thick as an old man's beard,
> I walk the streets kept clean
> by the sweep of black
> and Arab hands.

50. Chester Himes, unpublished article, Chester Himes papers, Amistad Research Center, p. 18.
51. Ibid.
52. Larry Neal, *Hoodoo Hollerin' Bebop Ghosts* (Washington, D.C.: Howard University Press, 1974), p. 68.

The poet's persona encounters an African street sweeper and finds a link between their plights, however separate: ". . . both of us / standing in the flow / leaving Paris."[53] To this momentous discovery of togetherness in race and discrimination, further perspective is added in Dixon's companion piece, "Climbing Montmartre." It is a complex layering of reactions through superimposed visions of Paris—the city of tourists, the city of ordinary people, the city of colored immigrants. The tourists are seen rushing up the steps leading to the Sacré-Cœur, ready to click cameras, buy postcards, and throw francs into the fountains. Among such visitors, many African Americans have been counted:

> Langston in the twenties and old Locke too,
> Cullen from the Hotel Saint Pierre,
> Wright from rue Monsieur le Prince, even
> Martin came to climb Montmartre.[54]

Here the theme is less the moment of an individual African American's reactions to experiencing Paris than the relationship of such an individual moment to the long line of collective memory; it is not essentially a reaction to Paris itself but a reaction (and linking) to previous reactions experienced by African American visitors and the creation of a tradition. What is more, the Sacré-Cœur at Montmartre, geographically the culminating point in Paris, which itself stands for the epitome of Europe, embodies not the religious forgiveness which Gwendolyn Bennett saw in it half a century before, but Western Christianity's lack of pity for the colored underdogs. It seems to coalesce with Notre-Dame in the narrator's accusation: "your green eyes / don't see this body drop on angry gargoyles."[55] It remains that, above all, Paris was for Melvin Dixon the city where countless literary ancestors and predecessors of the black race have found sustenance. His own Parisian "moment" was crucial to his development as a writer and thinker. In that sense he strikingly represents the contemporary African American intuition of Paris and awareness of its present relevance: because it has been haven to a whole sequence of black visitors and expatriates, Paris has become inscribed as a moment and site of memory in the cultural tradition of African Americans.

53. Melvin Dixon, *Change, of Territory* (Lexington: University of Kentucky Press, 1983), p. 18.
54. Ibid., p. 24.
55. Ibid., p. 25.

# Sources of Modern African American Cultural Authority

WENTIETH-CENTURY African American writing is part of a literature of urbanization and modernization which Farah Griffin has
called "the migration narrative." The move from South to North
and from country to city, the rise of modern black music and its
changing international significance, the emergence of a new aesthetically oriented view of Africa that informed the Harlem Renaissance,
the expansion of popular culture in many media, the meaning of
becoming an expatriate, and the growth of popular superstitions
and mysticism are among the many subjects associated with the
modern period which are explored in this part of the book.

Shamoon Zamir, who has completed a study of W. E. B. Du Bois
and American thought, here subjects *The Souls of Black Folk,* a key
text of black American writing, to a novel reading. In " 'The Sorrow
Songs'/'Song of Myself': Du Bois, the Crisis of Leadership, and
Prophetic Imagination," Zamir carefully explores Du Bois's self-
fashioning in his relationship to the sorrow songs, to Alexander
Crummell, and to the American transcendental tradition.

Josef Jařab, who translated Ellison's *Invisible Man* into Czech and
has published widely on African American literature, and among
whose works are *Masky a tváře černé Ameriky* (Masks and Faces of
Black America), here looks at the meaning of black music in central
Europe, focusing on the totalitarian opposition to blues and jazz.
"Black Stars, the Red Star, and the Blues" shows the ironies in communist affinities with Joseph Goebbels's strictures against black mu-

sic and the cultural context in which the music became associated with resistance to political oppression in Europe.

Małgorzata Irek, in her essay "From Berlin to Harlem: Felix von Luschan, Alain Locke, and the New Negro," pursues a remark made by Locke and investigates the work of Luschan, a late nineteenth-century Berlin ethnologist whose early interest in Benin art helped to bring about a reorientation toward African artifacts which proved foundational for the Harlem Renaissance.

Friederike Hajek, the author of *Selbstzeugnisse der Afroamerikaner: Black Liberation Movement und Autobiographie* (Testimonies by Afro-Americans: Black Liberation Movement and Autobiography), develops in "The Change of Literary Authority in the Harlem Renaissance: Jean Toomer's *Cane*" a suggestive approach to the most highly praised and complex African American work of its period as a thematic response and formal expression of a crisis of legitimacy which makes itself manifest in the spirit of secularization and the parodic use of call-and-response patterns.

The critical literature on Zora Neale Hurston has been growing in recent years and has yielded the knowledge that Hurston was born on January 15, 1891, in Notasulga, Alabama (*not*, as had been believed, in Eatonville, Florida), as well as some critical questioning of the way in which her rural identity may have been idealized or used against the harder urban school of Richard Wright. Here Paola Boi—who has previously published on Hurston—takes on, in her "Zora Neale Hurston's *Autobiographie Fictive:* Dark Tracks on the Canon of a Female Writer," a reading of Hurston's little-understood autobiography, *Dust Tracks on a Road.*

Robert Gooding-Williams, who has published the collection *Reading Rodney King/Reading Urban Uprising* and has finished a book on Nietzsche's pursuit of modernism, here offers a novel approach to *Casablanca* which challenges some past views of the film as part of a liberal Hollywood tradition that supposedly represented its black characters with dignity. "Black Cupids, White Desires: Reading the Recoding of Racial Difference in *Casablanca*" calls attention to Sam as an ideologically coded black Cupid figure who brings white lovers together, a motif with broad implications for cultural studies.

M. Lynn Weiss, who has written *Two in France,* a study of Wright and Gertrude Stein as expatriates, here turns her attention to *Pagan Spain,* the late and little-studied nonfiction work by Richard Wright. Her reading shows how the expatriate Wright turned toward writing about Spain and drew parallels between Spanish religious and American racial intolerance in the course of the project; yet his account also makes abundantly clear how closely aligned Wright was with the position of an American observer.

In "Coming of Age: The Modernity of Postwar Black American Writing," Sigmund Ro, the author of *Rage and Celebration,* traces the "catalytic presence" in African American modernism of two seminal metaphors of African American literature—"double consciousness" (W. E. B. Du Bois) and "native son" (Richard Wright). In the face of catastrophic dislocation, which all Western cultures suffered in the wake of the Second World War, the genuine interplay of these two concepts became the basis of what the essay celebrates as "the modernization and coming of age of black literary expression."

Gerald Early's many contributions to African American literary studies constitute a defining moment in their own right. He has, in his edition of Countée Cullen's work, offered the dates of two boxing matches as markers of the beginning and end of the Harlem Renaissance and has, in the collection *Lure and Loathing,* subjected Du Bois's notion of the double consciousness to systematic scrutiny. " 'Black Herman Comes Through Only Once Every Seven Years': Black Magic, White Magic, and American Culture" is the cultural reading of a black magician immortalized by Ishmael Reed. Early takes this magician and his acts as the central focus for an exploration of mysticism in the modern experience.

*Shamoon Zamir*

# "The Sorrow Songs"/"Song of Myself": Du Bois, the Crisis of Leadership, and Prophetic Imagination

*M*uch of the critical discussion of *The Souls of Black Folk* (1903) has focused on the debate between W. E. B. Du Bois and Booker T. Washington regarding the aims and forms of Afro-American education and the nature of Afro-American cultural leadership. Du Bois's well-known humanist critique of Washington's emphasis on the primary importance of technical training is mapped out in "Of Mr. Booker T. Washington and Others," the third chapter of *Souls,* first published in 1901, and in his essay "The Talented Tenth" (1903), published the same year as *Souls.*[1] Most commentators have accepted that *Souls* and "The Talented Tenth" outline a consistent and fundamentally identical program for educational reform and cultural leadership. But such a view can be sustained only if the third chapter of *Souls* is read in isolation from the rest of the book. The fourteen chapters that make up *Souls* constitute more than a collection of disparate essays. They are organized into a complex literary structure that interweaves a series of historical, sociological, political, and cultural commentaries with autobiographical reflections and dramatizations. This structure can best be described as a *Bildungsbiographie.* The interplay of the various elements of this *Bildungsbiographie* does not so much affirm the programmatic optimism of "The Talented Tenth" as open this confidence to critical investigation.

1. The third chapter of W. E. B. Du Bois, *The Souls of Black Folk,* was first published in the *Dial* (1901). "The Talented Tenth" first appeared in *The Negro Problem: A Series of Articles by Representative Negroes of To-Day* (New York: James Pott & Co., 1903); contributors included Booker T. Washington, Du Bois, and others.

The very first chapter of *Souls* acknowledges that "the contradiction of double aims" that is a result of Afro-American "double-consciousness" afflicts not only "the black artisan" and "the Negro minister" but also "the black *savant*" and "black artist"[2] The crisis of the Afro-American intellectual and artist is more fully dramatized in the last five chapters of *Souls*. In this essay I argue that in *Souls* the program of "The Talented Tenth" is confronted with the history of racism and violence that constantly thwarts this program. The confrontation leads to a rupture of the prophetic model of leadership derived from the Afro-American church and represented for Du Bois by Alexander Crummell, the founder of the American Negro Academy. In place of this model there emerges in *Souls* a poetic understanding of the prophetic imagination, represented by Du Bois himself as he attempts to describe and analyze Afro-American culture. This emergence is most clearly dramatized in "Of the Sorrow Songs," the celebrated final chapter of *Souls,* in which Du Bois reflects on the meaning of the great Afro-American spirituals. The structure of the prophetic imagination in *Souls* is, however, quite distinct from the forms that dominate the American transcendentalism of Emerson or Whitman. The structure of *Souls* embodies a very different relationship of consciousness to history and of self to *communitas.*

In his poem "W. E. B. Du Bois at Harvard," Jay Wright understands that "the prosody of those dark voices" that sing the "old songs" is Du Bois's "connection" to his "fledgling history,"[3] but it is a connection that cannot be taken for granted. Du Bois's dramatization of his relationship to the "sorrow songs" is marked by a representational hesitancy. His commentary is not based in an exactly shared history between his post-Emancipation northern self and the roots of the songs in a long history of southern violence and slavery. These differences, determined by factors of geography, class, and education, emerge only very allusively and elliptically in the final chapter of *Souls* because Du Bois appears to be caught between wanting, on the one hand, to disguise them in order to strengthen the political challenge to the white reader and, on the other, to acknowledge them within a nondogmatic art. An immediate and concrete sense of the differences and the strategic hesitancies can be given by comparing Du Bois's accounts of his encounters

2. W. E. B. Du Bois, *The Souls of Black Folk,* in Du Bois, *Writings,* ed. Nathan Huggins (New York: The Library of America, 1986), p. 363; hereafter cited in the text as *SBF.*
    3. Jay Wright, *The Homecoming Singer* (New York: Corinth, 1971), p. 37.

with the sorrow songs in the chapter with his quite different accounts of these same encounters in his later autobiographical writings and also, in one instance, in an earlier part of *Souls.*

"Of the Sorrow Songs" opens with Du Bois's earliest recollection of hearing the spirituals and describes the powerful sense of recognition they evoked:

> Ever since I was a child these songs have stirred me strangely. They came out of the South unknown to me, one by one, and yet at once I knew them as of me and of mine. Then in after years when I came to Nashville I saw the great temple builded of these songs towering over the pale city. To me Jubilee Hall seemed ever made of the songs themselves, and its bricks were red with the blood and dust of toil. Out of them rose for me morning, noon and night, bursts of wonderful melody, full of the voices of my brothers and sisters, full of the voices of the past. (*SBF* 536)

Although there is just glimpse enough of the distance and difference between North and South, as the shadow of strangeness and the "unknown" momentarily passes across the transparent meaning of the songs, the overwhelming sense of the passage is one of an intensely felt cultural identity experienced as an almost familial bond.

When Du Bois returns to the memories of his earliest encounters with the spirituals at the end of his life, there is a much more inflected sense of cultural difference in his account. He remembers in his *Autobiography* (1968) that he "heard the Negro folksong first in Great Barrington, sung by the Hampton Singers. But that was *second-hand, sung by youth who never knew slavery.*"[4] The songs were, then, an importation into the (predominantly white) New England culture of Du Bois's hometown of Great Barrington, Massachusetts—and an importation weakened for Du Bois by divorce from its historic and geographic roots, a divorce that reflects the situation of Du Bois as listener as much as that of the singers. Du Bois goes on to describe how he "heard the Negro songs by those who made them and in the land of their American birth" (*A* 120) when he first went south as an undergraduate and taught school in rural Tennessee. There he attended his first revival meeting. As Du Bois details his curiosity and excitement at the novelty of the situation, his posture is very much that of an ethnographic participant-

---

4. W. E. B. Du Bois, *The Autobiography of W. E. B. Du Bois* (New York: International Publishers, 1968), p. 120 (emphasis added); hereafter cited in the text as *A.*

observer reporting from the field. After the "quiet and subdued" church meetings in the Berkshires, Du Bois finds himself in the midst of "a pythian madness, a demoniac possession" that reveals "a scene of human passion such as I had never conceived before" (*A* 120). This same passage occurs in Chapter 10 of *Souls* (493). The feelings of the young Du Bois reproduce the same exoticism that led the white middle-class reading public at the turn of the century to seek out works that revealed how "the other half" lived.

There is similar variation between Du Bois's recollections in *Souls* of an African song that had been handed down in his own family and his tracing of the genealogy of the song in later autobiographical writing. In the middle part of the final chapter of *Souls* he writes:

> My grandfather's grandmother was seized by an evil Dutch trader two centuries ago; and coming to the valleys of the Hudson and Housatonic, black, little, and lithe, she shivered and shrank in the harsh north winds, looked longingly at the hills, and often crooned a heathen melody to the child between her knees, thus:
>
> > Do bana coba, gene me, gene me!
> > Do bana coba, gene me, gene me!
> > Ben d' nuli, nuli, nuli, nuli, ben d' le.
>
> The child sang it to his children and they to their children's children, and so two hundred years it has travelled down to us and we sing it to our children, *knowing as little as our fathers what its words may mean, but knowing well the meaning of its music.* (*SBF* 538, emphasis added)[5]

Again, the overriding sense here is of a transcendent bond, though at the same time the ambivalent wavering between not knowing the meaning of the words to the song and fundamentally understanding the meaning of the music hints at the fact that although the historical continuity of black culture in America is hardly in doubt, it is nevertheless fractured enough to require a sympathetic leap.

Du Bois's later autobiographical writing presents a less transcendent vision. In *Dusk of Dawn* (1940) Du Bois writes that he is, in fact, not sure if his great-great-grandmother was born in Africa or in America and does not know where she learned the song.[6] This acknowledgment comes at the close

---

5. Du Bois provides musical notation along with the lyrics in *Souls*.
6. W. E. B. Du Bois, *Dusk of Dawn: An Essay toward an Autobiography of a Race Concept*, in Du Bois, *Writings*, pp. 636–637; hereafter cited in the text as *DD*.

of a long section of the autobiography in which Du Bois traces his very mixed and complicated family genealogy back to its French Huguenot, Dutch, African, and even Native American roots (*DD* 630–637). The song sung by his great-great-grandmother then becomes his "only one direct cultural connection" with Africa (*DD* 636). After quoting the passage on the African song from *Souls* at length, Du Bois adds that "living with my mother's people I absorbed their culture patterns and these were not African so much as Dutch and New England" (*DD* 638). His "African racial feeling was then purely a matter of . . . later learning and reaction," of Du Bois's "recoil from the assumptions of the whites" and his "experience in the South at Fisk," though "it was none the less real and a large determinant of [his] life and character" (*DD* 638).

The passages from the final chapter of *Souls* which I have quoted signal certain hesitancies, but these hesitancies are more than securely contained within Du Bois's impassioned acceptance of a common history of oppression. But his dramatization of his own relationship to the songs in *Souls* is more subtle than this. It manages finally to suggests the extent of both separation and identity and so resists the alibi of an essentialized idea of *communitas*. The scene that closes *Souls,* the climax of the final chapter, presents a tableau in which Du Bois's relationship to the songs is represented with greater self-reflexivity and complexity:

> If somewhere in this whirl and chaos of things there dwells Eternal Good, pitiful yet masterful, then anon in His good time America shall rend the Veil and the prisoned shall go free. Free, free as the sunshine trickling down the morning into these high windows of mine, free as yonder fresh young voices welling up from the caverns of brick and mortar below—swelling with song, instinct with life, tremulous treble and darkening bass. My children, my little children, are singing to the sunshine, and thus they sing:
>
> > Let us cheer the weary traveller,
> > Cheer the weary traveller,
> > Let us cheer the weary traveller,
> > Along the heavenly way
>
> And the traveller girds himself, and sets his face toward the Morning, and goes his way. (*SBF* 545–546)[7]

---

7. Du Bois provides musical notation along with the lyrics in *Souls.*

This curious scene is a careful revision of both Du Bois's own description of hearing the spirituals at Nashville's Jubilee Hall, which opens the chapter on the sorrow songs, and of Plato's well-known allegory of the cave in his *Republic,* with Du Bois as Plato's enlightened man caught between the light of the sun and the darkness of the caverns. This double revision embodies a plural intentionality on Du Bois's part. Du Bois tries to dramatize simultaneously the independence and artistic integrity of the collective voice that sings through the songs and his own relationship to this voice as a bourgeois intellectual. Such a representational strategy comes as no surprise within the framework of Herderian organic history which dominates the final chapter of *Souls,*[8] and to some extent Du Bois is inevitably trapped within this historical model's paradox of desired immersion and identity and the distance of interpretive authority. Nevertheless, it would be to misrepresent Du Bois's writing if his own openness to displacement by the songs were ignored.

Du Bois's treatment of the spirituals seems at first to be marked by a pronounced sense of cultural elitism or hierarchization that reinforces pastoral nostalgia. Nashville's Jubilee Hall, "towering over the pale city" at the opening of the chapter on the spirituals, has, by the end, become the academic tower of Atlanta University, where Du Bois taught from 1897 to 1910, and where he sits listening to the songs drifting up from below through the "high windows" of the university building. Whereas the young Du Bois, as an undergraduate in his late teens, had been overwhelmed by his first hearing of the songs and an initial sense of community promised by "the voices of my brothers and sisters," the older professor sits alone in his office, a little more removed and reflective in his attention to the singing of "my children, my little children." This "older" Du Bois was, in fact, only in his mid-thirties at the time he wrote the last chapter of *Souls,*[9] but the kindly (and grating) paternalism of the closing scene belies this fact and offers the reader a self-image that artificially stresses a sense of advanced age and therefore a more pronounced sense of distanced contemplation. There is here, in fact, also a reversal of the genealogy that marks the transmission across the generations

8. For more on Herderian elements of Du Bois's commentary on the spirituals, particularly on the links between Du Bois's work and that of the Harvard communalists, see Bernard Bell, *The Folk Roots of Contemporary Afro-American Poetry* (Detroit: Broadside Press, 1974), pp. 20–24.

9. *Souls* was published in 1903, and the chapter on the sorrow songs was written expressly for the book. This would make the setting of the final scene contemporaneous with the date of publication and would put Du Bois's age at thirty-five.

of the African song handed down in Du Bois's family. That song was sung by the parents of each generation to their children but with its meaning obscure to "the children" and their "fathers" alike; here the children sing to their father, who struggles to read the meaning of their songs.

There is, then, submerged beneath the sociological and aesthetic meditations on black music in the final chapter, an authorial self-fashioning and an autobiographical narrative of Du Bois's development from infancy (when the African song is first heard) to youthful immersion (in Tennessee) and to mature self-consciousness (at Atlanta University). This narrative is told as an ongoing dialectical engagement between Du Bois and the sorrow songs which unfolds primarily across the historically charged landscape of the South, from Nashville to Atlanta. Du Bois's commentary on the songs is itself a product of the older self and represents a discourse of a different, more self-conscious nature than the songs themselves, the organicism of the latter being, within Du Bois's Herderian communalism, by definition unself-reflexive. Du Bois's particular interpretive access to the content at the heart of the songs is therefore guaranteed not simply by his fraternal or paternal bonds with the culture and history of the songs but also by those perspectives available to him as a trained academic, intellectual, and writer (these positions being in no sense identical). The unveiling of the songs appears to be dependent on their mediation by and incorporation into the different order of reflection and art represented by Du Bois's writing. This seems to shift the axis of articulation away from the songs themselves toward Du Bois's written synthesizing.[10]

This self-fashioning on Du Bois's part pushes his dramatization of his relationship to the songs toward what James Clifford has described as the allegorical structure of "salvage, or redemptive, ethnography," where "the recorder and interpreter . . . is custodian of an essence, unimpeachable wit-

---

10. There are similar contradictory tensions in Frederick Douglass's commentary on the slave songs in *Narrative of the Life of Frederick Douglass* (1845; rpt. New York: Penguin, 1982), p. 57. Douglass notes that the words to some of the songs "would to many seem unmeaning jargon"; they were nevertheless "full of meaning" to the slaves themselves. But he then goes on to state that he himself "did not, when a slave, understand the deep meaning of those rude and apparently incoherent songs." The reason for this was that the slave Douglass was himself "within the circle; so that I neither saw nor heard as those without might see and hear." The songs "told a tale of woe which was then altogether beyond my feeble comprehension." This lack of comprehension seems curious, given Douglass's detailed and gruesome description of life as a slave. But Douglass is in fact, like Du Bois, suggesting a difference between orders of understanding, between "meaning" and "*deep meaning*," between immediate response and retrospective reflection and analysis.

ness to an authenticity." As Clifford accurately notes, this structure "is appropriately located within a long Western tradition of pastoral."[11] Within such an allegoric narrative "the self, cut loose from viable collective ties, is an identity in search of wholeness, having internalized loss and embarked on an endless search for authenticity. Wholeness by definition becomes a thing of the past (rural, primitive, childlike) accessible only as a fiction, grasped from a stance of incomplete involvement."[12] Clifford's ethnographic commentary helps describe the radical desire that is the content of both Du Bois's critical nostalgias and his problematic stance of "historical and cultural aestheticism"[13] in the final chapter of *Souls*.

The ambivalences of Du Bois's relationship to black American folk culture, signaled by what I have referred to as the representational hesitancies of "Of the Sorrow Songs" and further highlighted by the comparison of this chapter with later autobiographical writings, are much more fully dramatized in Du Bois's rewriting of Plato's allegory of the cave.[14] Du Bois's revision of the opening scene of this chapter (his encounter with the songs at Nashville) at the chapter's end (with Du Bois hearing the songs at Atlanta) unfolds within this other revision and must be read through it.

Plato's allegory is designed "to illustrate the degrees in which our nature may be enlightened or unenlightened."[15] In a cave there are prisoners, chained and immobile since birth, who know nothing of reality other than the shadows cast on the cave wall by a fire behind them. These simulacra they take to be real. One prisoner becomes free and finds true enlightenment when he leaves the cave and walks out into the sunshine. The allegory is

11. James Clifford, "On Ethnographic Allegory," in *Writing Culture: The Poetics and Politics of Ethnography*, ed. James Clifford and George E. Marcus (Berkeley: University of California Press, 1986), p. 113.

12. Ibid., p. 114.

13. I have taken this phrase from Fredric Jameson's description of "existential historicism," a kind of relativist position, in his "Marxism and Historicism," *New Literary History*, 11, no. 1 (1979): 51. Jameson argues that "existential historicism" replaced geneticist and evolutionary models of explanations with "something like a transhistorical event: the experience . . . by which *historicity* as such is manifested by means of the contact between the historian's mind in the present and a given synchronic cultural complex from the past" (51). This helps highlight the politics of the allegorical structure of relativist ethnography delineated by Clifford.

14. See Plato, *Republic*, 7. 514A–521B.

15. *The Republic of Plato*, trans. Francis MacDonald Cornford (1941; rpt. Oxford: Oxford University Press, 1945), p. 227.

concerned with the dilemma facing this one individual who is fully aware of a higher, transcendent reality but is derided as a fool and rejected by the unenlightened prisoners. Du Bois's location within the academic tower at the end of *Souls* appears at first simply to reproduce this dilemma. He is caught between the vision of freedom promised by the transcendental "Eternal Good" and the "free . . . sunshine trickling down the morning into these high windows" on the one hand and the "prisoned" blacks, the "voices welling up . . . from the caverns of brick and mortar below," on the other. Du Bois's implied self-identification with Alexander Crummell, and the theories of education and progress that undergird that identification, briefly mentioned earlier, suggests the obvious appropriateness of the allusion to the Platonic parable. Plato too is advocating the leadership of a cultured elite as a guarantee of "the welfare of the commonwealth."[16]

In Atlanta, however, not only are the voices from below singing "to the sunshine" and urging on "the weary traveller" in his quest (whereas in Plato the prisoners have no conception of freedom), but also the voices from the caverns are themselves "instinct with life" and as "free" as the sunshine that represents higher enlightenment.[17] Du Bois is not trapped between enlightenment and ignorance but poised between different forms of insight and understanding. "Beneath the conventional theology and unmeaning rhapsody" (*SBF* 541) of the sorrow songs there is a hard and bitter knowledge of historical experience which challenges the transcendental cultural universalism championed in the progressive reformism of "The Talented Tenth." Unlike Plato's prisoners, the slaves who created the sorrow songs and the voices that sing at the end of *Souls* have suffered actual, not metaphorical, enslavement and oppression, and their music give voice to a poetry of experiential truths, not unwitting falsehood. The poised tableau at the end of *Souls*, then, is not so much an allegorical rewriting of Plato as a momentary breaking of the allegorical spell because it acknowledges that the "prisoned" cannot be turned into symbols in support of an idealist political program. In opening himself up in sympathetic understanding to "the souls of black

16. Ibid., p. 234.

17. If the University of Atlanta is supposed to represent the institutional embodiment of the program of educational reform outlined in "The Talented Tenth," then it is also important to note that Du Bois spends some time in "The Sorrow Songs" explaining that Fisk University, where he himself had studied, was founded on $150,000 raised by the Fisk Singers on their national and international tour begun in 1871 (*SBF* 266–267).

folk," Du Bois, like his projected white reader, finds a mirror behind the veil. The image at the close of *Souls* of the "weary traveller" who "girds himself" and "goes his way," cheered on by his "children," is not an image of a false collectivity parasitically recuperated into the promise of messianic leadership but a genuinely tragic and political vision that returns Du Bois for strength to the grounds of solitude.

The Platonic revisions through which Du Bois dramatizes an ambivalence of cultural authority between himself as interpreter and the songs comes as the conclusion to a series of chapters that are meditations on the role of religious leadership among Afro-Americans. After the survey in the first nine chapters of the political, economic, and educational issues that affect black American life, the last five chapters of *Souls* are concerned primarily with religious culture—particularly with the political and social function of the religious leader and with the jeremiad of the preacher-prophet as the dominant model of leadership rhetoric available to Afro-Americans. As in "The Sorrow Songs," Du Bois manages to establish both a historical and a contemporary understanding of Afro-American religious culture by combining anthropological and sociopolitical commentaries. Nonetheless, acute assessments of the centrality of religion in Afro-American culture are juxtaposed with dramatizations of the fracture of faith. It is this fracture that underlies Du Bois's distinction between the political and historical content of the songs and the "conventional theology" of their lyrics. The redemptive biblical typologies of religious prophecy are repeatedly qualified by personal experiences of loss and violence. Du Bois inverts the prophetic models of ascent and uplift. It is within the space cleared by these qualifications that Du Bois's model of his own solitary insight and understanding can be properly described.

The terms in which Du Bois describes himself listening to the sorrow songs at the close of *Souls* refigure the description of Alexander Crummell's growth into enlightenment and leadership earlier in the book. In Chapter 12 Du Bois argues that the education of Crummell at the hands of white abolitionists proved to be a process of mutual transformation. The white schoolboys discovered a realm "of thought and longing beneath one black skin, of which they had not dreamed before. And to the lonely boy came a new dawn of sympathy and inspiration" (*SBF* 514). It is through the sympathy awakened by education that Crummell is able to overcome his hatred for the white world and to see for the first time "the sun-swept road that ran 'twixt heaven and earth" (*SBF* 514), a vision of higher cultural ideals offered by the white world. But it is also because of this newly inspired sympathy that Crummell himself can hear "the bronzed hosts of a nation calling" and "the hateful clank of their chains" from "behind the forests," and can respond with a career of "protest" and "prophecy" as "a priest—a seer to lead the uncalled out of the house of bondage" (*SBF* 514). Educational training and the revelation of higher goals necessarily entail a distancing from the repeated cycles of despair in the dark forest, and though sympathy promises a return to roots, it is a return in which both identity and difference must be acknowledged. Crummell answers the call of his fellow blacks but as the priestly head of "the headless host" (*SBF* 514).

The scene where Du Bois listens to the spirituals "welling up from the caverns of brick and mortar below" as the "free . . . sunshine," the enlightening embodiment of the "Eternal Good," trickles through the "high windows" refigures the dialectic of Crummell's sympathetic imagination moving between "the sun-swept road" and the "forest." Just as Crummell "girded himself to walk down the world" (*SBF* 514), so too Du Bois as "the weary traveller" at the very end of the book "girds himself, and sets his face toward the Morning, and goes his way." Du Bois's placing of this allusive self-fashioning at the end of *Souls* seems at first to suggest that the autobiographical narrative of the book should be read as a teleological ascent. In a way the double ontogenic and phylogenic narrative seems to suggest an optimistic reading as the most appropriate one for the book. The narrative seems, after all, to move from racist alienation to personal enlightenment, from continued social discrimination and exclusion to the fulfillment of educational ideals at the universities of Fisk and Atlanta as "the advanced guard" toils "slowly, heavily, doggedly" up "the mountain path to Canaan" (*SBF* 367). This would align *Souls* with the redemptive biblical typologies and rhetoric of the "American jeremiad" inherited by the slave narratives and the message of uplift in Washington's autobiography *Up From Slavery* (1901), a contemporary version of the slave narrative combined with the Horatio Alger myth.[18] Frederick Douglass's earlier (1845) *Narrative of the Life of*

---

18. On the importance of biblical jeremiad rhetoric in American culture, see Sacvan Bercovitch, *The American Jeremiad* (Madison: University of Wisconsin Press, 1978). For the impact of this typological tradition on American minority writing, see Werner Sollors, *Beyond Ethnicity: Consent and Descent in American Culture* (New York: Oxford University Press, 1986), pp. 40–65.

*Frederick Douglass* had itself produced a version of American individualistic self-genesis.[19] But, as Arnold Rampersad has suggested, *Souls* can also be read as an inverted slave narrative, one that reverses the plot of enlightenment and attained freedom.[20] From this perspective the narrative of *Souls* moves from Emancipation (in "Of the Dawn of Freedom") to the slave songs and their reassertion of continued oppression and violence, from a prelapsarian infancy (in the opening scene of the first chapter) to a repeated return to the condition of the divided self.

There is little in the chapter on Crummell to suggest that Du Bois is in any way critical of or ambivalent about Crummell's political and cultural programs. Crummell was, in fact, the direct inspiration for Du Bois's own proposal for a vanguard of Afro-American leaders. In 1897 Crummell had established the American Negro Academy, whose aim was to promote an interest in literature, science, and art among Afro-Americans as a way of developing a scholarly and refined elite. This program was adopted with almost no modification by Du Bois in "The Talented Tenth."[21] But the unqualified eulogy to Crummell is carefully placed between the threnody for the loss of Du Bois's infant son in "Of the Passing of the First-Born" and the fictionalized dramatization of the negation of his own adult ideals by racist violence and prejudice in "Of the Coming of John." The closing moments of the latter, where the educated John, having returned to work in the South, faces the sea as the lynch mob thunders toward him, refer the reader to the closing moments of the chapter on Crummell, where, on the morning before his death and at the end of a life of solitary struggle and hardship, he sits "gazing towards the sea" (*SBF* 520). If the tragic end of "Of the Coming of John" cuts short the visionary projections of the eulogy for Crummell, these projected trajectories are already threatened by the gothic omen of the death of "the first-born" in the previous chapter.

"Of the Passing of the First-Born" opens with biblical resonance: "Unto you a child is born" (*SBF* 506). Du Bois sees "the strength of [his] own arm

19. See the comparison of Douglass and Emerson and the location of Douglass's text in the American Renaissance of the mid-nineteenth century in the conclusion of Russell Reising, *The Unusable Past: Theory and the Study of American Literature* (New York: Methuen, 1986), pp. 256–272.

20. Arnold Rampersad, "Slavery and the Literary Imagination: Du Bois's *The Souls of Black Folk*," in *Slavery and the Literary Imagination*, ed. Deborah E. McDowell and Arnold Rampersad (Baltimore: The Johns Hopkins University Press, 1989), pp. 106, 121.

21. For further information on Crummell and an assessment of his influence on Du Bois, see Manning Marable, *W. E. B. Du Bois: Black Radical Democrat* (Boston: Twayne, 1986), pp. 32–40.

stretched onward through the ages through the newer strength" of the child's, and hears in "the baby voice" of his son "the voice of the Prophet that was to rise within the Veil." But the "hot winds" that roll into Atlanta from "the fetid Gulf" strangle this redemptive hope almost at birth (*SBF* 508). The sense of loss and personal grief is, however, mixed with a sense of relief:

> All that day and all that night there sat an awful gladness in my heart—nay, blame me not if I see the world thus darkly through the Veil—and my soul whispers ever to me, saying, "Not dead, not dead, but escaped; not bond, but free." No bitter meanness now shall sicken his baby heart till it die a living death, no taunt shall madden his happy boyhood. Fool that I was to think or wish that this little soul should grow choked and deformed within the Veil! (*SBF* 510)

This is perhaps Du Bois's most ironic and bitter condemnation of American racism. As Arnold Rampersad notes, "Of the Passing of the First-Born" is in certain respects "an almost classical elegy, in impassioned yet formal language. But it is one in which the central mourner, as a black, can find no consolation. Thus it is in truth anti-Christian, a bitter parody of the Christian elegy."[22] Du Bois only reinforces the anticonsolatory thrust of his mourning by placing its antireligious reversals after the chapter "On the Faith of the Fathers."

For the most part Du Bois keeps his personal life out of *Souls*. The autobiographical narrative is always woven along the edges of the cultural and political commentaries of the book. It reinforces or counterpoints but is never the primary or sole site of exploration. Those denunciations of racism that draw on autobiographical experience penetrate because their articulation is always so overly restrained. This is precisely why the impassioned grief of the elegy for the dead son is so unexpected and overwhelming. Suddenly a personal loss that has little to do with the history or politics of racism occupies center stage, and stoic reticence gives way to public mourning. Throughout *Souls* Du Bois has struggled to build a refuge of reason against both racism and the irrationality of "the vein of vague superstition" among Afro-Americans themselves. But the death of his son seems to unhouse the faith in rationality and providence alike, even if only for a moment. It is as if the

---

22. Rampersad, "Slavery and the Literary Imagination," p. 120.

seat of arbitrary violence and irrationality were discovered at the very heart of nature itself.

John, the educated black hero who returns to the South to teach in Chapter 13 of *Souls,* is the embodiment of what Du Bois's infant son might have become. But John's death at the hands of a lynch mob also represents the life that the son has escaped through his untimely death. The eulogy on Crummell is placed precariously between the deaths of the son and of John. But prophetic progressivism is threatened by more than white racism or personal tragedy. Crummell's brand of uplift acknowledges the political and economic handicaps that defeat Afro-American struggle, but it also assumes the legitimacy of a dichotomy of civilization and barbarism across the color line. For Crummell, Afro-American folk and proletarian culture must be purged of its rudeness and heathen retentions. At moments Du Bois shares this Victorian moralistic valuation of Afro-American culture. But his commentary on the spirituals also describes a transcendent musical embodiment of the historical consciousness that destabilizes such dichotomizations. The aesthetic relativism that marks the final chapter of *Souls* pushes prophetic cultural self-confidence toward insecurity because it brings this confidence face to face with a collective consciousness of terror and suffering.

At a time when most Afro-Americans were Baptists or Methodists, Crummell was an Episcopalian. The Episcopal church was associated with the black bourgeoisie and the upper classes:

> The church had dignified rituals and was far removed from the plantation culture that [Crummell] identified with barbarism, depravity, and weakness. Episcopalianism, with its principles of "submission to authority, respect for rules, quietness and order," was congenial to Crummell's conservative temperament. The American Episcopal church brought him into contact with Anglicanism and nurtured his sense of participating in the literary and intellectual traditions of England. The Anglican music and architecture appealed to him, as did the Anglican liturgy. His religious sentiments were closely linked to aesthetic preferences that were uncommon among black Americans.[23]

Du Bois's own self-fashioning in his first description in *Souls* of his earliest encounter with plantation culture is very much in the image of Crummell's

---

23. Wilson Jeremiah Moses, *Alexander Crummell: A Study of Civilization and Discontent* (New York: Oxford University Press, 1989), p. 281. For a brief history of the place of the Episcopal church in Afro-American culture and history, see the entry "Episcopalians" in the *Encyclopedia of Black America,* ed. W. Augustus Low and Virgil A. Clift (New York: McGraw-Hill, 1981), pp. 372–377.

Episcopalianism. The young Du Bois, "fresh from the East," is overwhelmed by "a pythian madness, a demonic possession." As he notes with restrained humor, "To be sure, we in Berkshire were not perhaps as stiff and formal as they in Suffolk of olden time; yet we were very quiet and subdued, and I know not what would have happened those clear Sabbath mornings had some one punctuated the sermon with a wild scream, or interrupted the long prayer with a loud Amen!" (*SBF* 493).

Throughout the chapter titled "Of the Faith of the Fathers," Du Bois's Victorian unease persists as he traces the development of Afro-American religion "through its gradual changes from the heathenism of the Gold Coast to the institutional Negro church of Chicago" (*SBF* 495). But at the same time the moralism that denigrates the African origins of Afro-American religion as "Voodooism" (*SBF* 498) is balanced by a political consciousness that sees the transition from "Obi worship" to Christianity as a transformation of the spirit of revolt into "passive submission" (*SBF* 499), though Du Bois also notes that, with the growth of the abolition movement and freedom, religion for the Afro-American "became darker and more intense, and into his ethics crept a note of revenge, into his songs a day of reckoning close at hand" (*SBF* 501).

To summarize the argument so far, Victorian moralism and Herderian romanticism are not the only stances that characterize Du Bois's commentaries on Afro-American religion or religious music. There is also an awareness of social and political function and content. The historical memory that marks the spirituals is the collective resource on which the messianic ardor of a Crummell draws. But at the same time that Du Bois's dramatizations recognize that the tragic sensibility and redemptive longings of the songs must be lifted into the activism of the preacher-prophet's salvationary historicism, they also tether the latter to the historical realism that resonates in the performance and lyrics of the former.

In the end, the literary imagination of *Souls* is not able to propose a model of political leadership that will answer the doubts of the book's deeply negative historical consciousness. The late nineteenth and early twentieth centuries are, for the Afro-American, "a time of intense ethical ferment, of religious heart-searching and intellectual unrest." Such a time of radical doubt "must give rise to double worlds and double ideals, and tempt the mind to pretence or to revolt, to hypocrisy or to radicalism" (*SBF* 502), a division that Du Bois charts along the North-South axis (*SBF* 503). But if the polarization of dangerous "anarchy" (*SBF* 504) and "hypocritical compromise" (*SBF* 505) suggests a defense of the liberal center, Du Bois reveals a middle ground occupied by assimilation or fatalistic acquiescence:

> Between the two extreme types of ethical attitude which I have thus sought to make clear wavers the mass of the millions of Negroes, North and South; and their religious life and activity partake of this social conflict within their ranks. Their churches are differentiating—now into groups of cold, fashionable devotees, in no way distinguishable from similar white groups save in color of skin; now into large social and business institutions catering to the desire for information and amusement of their members, warily avoiding unpleasant questions both within and without the black world, and preaching in effect if not in word: *Dum vivimus, vivamus.* (*SBF* 504–505)

Du Bois adds that "back of this still broods silently the deep religious feeling of the real Negro heart, the stirring, unguided might of powerful human souls who have lost the guiding star of the past and are seeking in the great night a new religious ideal" (*SBF* 505). Crummell is the "guiding star" that promises the incarnation of this ideal, and it is an ideal fully endorsed by Du Bois in "The Talented Tenth." But it is also an ideal whose horizon of possibility perpetually recedes in the face of the political and cultural history charted by *Souls*.

The refusal to give unqualified endorsement to a message of uplift in *Souls* is, of course, no failure at all. It is the very ground on which the book's challenge to American political and cultural idealism is built. By concluding *Souls* with a chapter on the spirituals, Du Bois focuses on an art that embodies a sense of history and memory. The way that "The Sorrow Songs" rounds off the autobiographical narrative trajectory of *Souls* also reveals the poetic conceptualization of the historical consciousness that underlies Du Bois's own literary structure.

In the brief "Afterthought" which concludes *Souls*, Du Bois asks the reader to "vouchsafe that this my book fall not still-born into the world-wilderness," and hopes that from it will "spring . . . vigor of *thought* and *thoughtful deed*" (*SBF* 547, emphasis added). Du Bois as "the weary traveller" is not a reincarnated priest-prophet. He is the companion of Blake's "Mental Traveller."[24] In "The Mental Traveller" "the Babe" liberty is "begot-

---

24. No direct influence is suggested here, only a certain affinity.

ten in woe" and "born in joy." But the child is "given to a Woman Old," society, "who nails him down upon a rock."[25] As Foster Damon explains, Blake's poem "is the formula of the history of the idea of Liberty, showing how it is born, how it triumphs, how in its age its opposite is born, how it is cast out, how it then rejuvenates, until it becomes a babe again, and the cycle recurs."[26] *Souls* also dramatizes the recurring struggles of the consciousness of freedom and of bondage. As in Blake, it is from a knowledge of this struggle that prophetic vision is created in *Souls*.

Prophecy is understood here not in a predictive or futuristic sense but as Northrop Frye describes it (though without his religiosity) in his study of Blake:

> An honest man is not quite the noblest work of God until the faith by which the just live develops into full imaginative vision. The fully imaginative man is therefore a visionary whose imaginative activity is prophecy and whose perception produces art. These two are the same thing, perception being an act . . . It is the superior clarity and accuracy of the prophet's vision that makes him an artist, and that makes the great artist prophetic.[27]

In American transcendentalism, as in European romanticism, poetic prophecy is preoccupied with the dialectics of passivity and activity. On the American side, the primary mode of transcending passivity is through a voluntaristic act of *seeing*. A brief examination of Emerson and Whitman, particularly of the triumph in their work of sight over the other senses and of a self defined by seeing, will provide a context in which the poetics of *Souls*'s structuring can be clearly understood.

In *Nature* (1836), his first major work, Ralph Waldo Emerson seeks to reverse the Pauline relegation of prophetic vision to a future world in which the fall is recovered. For Saint Paul, "now we see in a mirror, darkly," but "when that which is perfect is come," then we shall see "face to face" (1 Cor. 13:12, 10). Emerson, however, argues that "the foregoing generations beheld God and nature face to face; we through their eyes," and asks,

25. "The Mental Traveller," in *The Complete Poetry and Prose of William Blake*, ed. David V. Erdman, rev. ed. (New York: Doubleday, 1988), pp. 483–484.

26. S. Foster Damon, *A Blake Dictionary: The Ideas and Symbols of William Blake*, rev. ed. (Hanover, N.H.: University Press of New England, 1988), p. 288.

27. Northrop Frye, *Fearful Symmetry: A Study of William Blake* (1947; rpt. Princeton: Princeton University Press, 1969), p. 59.

"Why should not we also enjoy an original relation to the universe?"[28] The prophet of the New World restores his vision by becoming "a transparent eyeball" whose Platonic insight transcends society:

> I am nothing; I see all; the currents of the Universal Being circulate through me; I am part or parcel of God. The name of the nearest friend sounds then foreign and accidental: to be brothers, to be acquaintances, master or servant, is then a trifle and a disturbance. I am the lover of uncontained and immortal beauty. In the wilderness, I find something more dear and connate than in the streets or villages. In the tranquil landscape, and especially in the distant line of the horizon, man beholds somewhat as beautiful as his own nature.[29]

By contrast with *Nature, Souls* opens not with a seeing subject but with a moment of being seen. Whereas Emerson seeks solitude in nature, the boy Du Bois is seeking the company of his white and black playmates when he is repulsed by the "glance [of] one girl, a tall newcomer" (*SBF* 364). The black body and not "the tranquil landscape" becomes the field of the "Not Me" in which the white subject unfolds its freedom. The moment when the gaze penetrates is the moment when the biblical veil, Du Bois's favorite conceit for the color line, descends and obscures vision in *Souls*. But if the penetrative gaze sets off a process of objectification and the division of consciousness, it also endows the Afro-American with a "second-sight in this American world" (*SBF* 364). The look of Du Bois's new playmate is like that "certain Slant of light" that is both "an imperial affliction" and a source of tragic understanding in Emily Dickinson:

> Heavenly Hurt, it gives us—
> We can find no scar,
> But internal difference,
> Where the Meanings, are—[30]

Not only does *Souls* open with being seen, but it closes with Du Bois *listening* to the voices singing the spirituals, a more social act than seeing, and sending out into the world his *written* work. This presents a very different ratio of the senses than the one that dominates in Emerson, or even the more "amative"

---

28. *Nature*, in *Selections from Ralph Waldo Emerson,*ed. Stephen E. Whicher (Boston: Houghton Mifflin, 1957), p. 21.

29. Ibid., p. 24.

30. Emily Dickinson, *The Complete Poems*, ed. Thomas H. Johnson (London: Faber and Faber, 1975), no. 258, p. 118.

Whitman, and also a very different conceptualization of visionary action. Emerson's attempts to defend the mind as active in "The American Scholar" (1837) and Walt Whitman's poetic self-fashioning in "Song of Myself" (1855) can help illustrate the differences between Du Bois's formulations and American transcendentalism.

"The American Scholar" is a program for the cultivation of the life of the mind in the new nation. Emerson writes that "the so-called 'practical men' sneer at speculative men, as if, because they speculate or *see*, they could do nothing." Emerson takes this to be a false accusation:

> Action is with the scholar subordinate, but it is essential. Without it he is not yet man. Without it thought can never ripen into truth . . . The preamble of thought, the transition through which it passes from the unconscious to the conscious, is action. Only so much do I know, as I have lived. Instantly we know whose words are loaded with life, and whose not.
>
> The world—this shadow of the soul, or *other* me—lies wide around. Its attractions are the keys which unlock my thoughts and make me acquainted with myself. I run eagerly into this tumult. I grasp the hands of those next me, and take my place in the ring to suffer and to work, taught by an instinct that so shall the dumb abyss be vocal with speech.[31]

Despite this last image of collective toiling, Emerson's formulations of the activity of visionary understanding and cultural leadership describe, for the most part, a solitary and passive process. The sense of self-reliance and mastery in the face of the "Not Me" is, after all, dependent on the passivity of seeing.[32] In the passage from "The American Scholar" the transition from seeing to saying involves no process of hearing. Notwithstanding the image of the ring of grasped hands, the scholar does not work from a social location. What is vocalized is in fact not a social or historical knowledge but the passive emergence of preexisting Platonic forms autonomous of consciousness. In Du Bois's revision of Plato, however, the bright revelation of pure and transcendent forms in the light outside the cave is eschewed in favor of the knowledge embodied in the voices of the prisoned inside the cave. As Denis Donoghue observes:

> The site of [Emerson's] poetry and his sageness is the history of voluntarism. The more we read *Nature,* the more clearly it appears that the whole essay is

31. Ralph Waldo Emerson, "The American Scholar" (1837), in *Selections*, p. 70.

32. See Kenneth Marc Harris, *Carlyle and Emerson: Their Long Debate* (Cambridge, Mass.: Harvard University Press, 1978), p. 69.

predicated upon the capacity of Will. Not knowledge but power is its aim; not truth but command . . . So if we go back to the transparent eyeball passage and read it as a voluntaristic act rather than an instance of the Sublime, we find that the eyeball becomes transparent because a light higher than its own sensory light is made to shine through it . . . We have access to [Emerson's work] only by recourse to the vocabulary of Will and to its social form, a pragmatics of the future.[33]

The interaction of the senses and the social politics in Whitman's "Song of Myself" from *Leaves of Grass* are closer to Du Bois than is Emerson, but they are still marked by a fundamental difference that is useful in describing *Souls*. Whitman, like the author of *Souls,* is "attesting sympathy."[34] The poet of the "Song of Myself" touches and feels in his democratic openness in a way Emerson never does (and with a corporeal candor that is also alien to the Victorian Du Bois): "I believe in the flesh and the appetites, / Seeing, hearing, feeling" (*LG* 53). And the poet's "voice goes after what [his] eyes cannot reach" (*LG* 55). In his social openness Whitman is led to make vocal not just "the threads that connect the stars" but political outrage on behalf of the oppressed and socially excluded:

> Through me many long dumb voices,
> Voices of the interminable generations of prisoners and slaves,
> Voices of the diseas'd and despairing and of thieves and dwarfs,
> . . .
> Through me forbidden voices
> Voices of sexes and lusts, voices veil'd and I remove the veil,
> Voices indecent by me clarified and transfigured. (*LG* 52–53)

It is the poet's transfiguration of the voices that lifts the veil. This is closer to Du Bois, but the transfiguration dramatized in the last chapter of *Souls* is somewhat different.

As Larzer Ziff demonstrates, sight ultimately triumphs over the other senses even in Whitman because the other senses are a threat to prophetic stability and self-confidence. With the appearance of the other senses Whit-

33. Denis Donoghue, "Emerson at First: A Commentary on *Nature*," in *Emerson and His Legacy: Essays in Honor of Quentin Anderson,* ed. Stephen Donadio et. al. (Carbondale: Southern Illinois University Press, 1986), pp. 44–45.

34. Walt Whitman, *Leaves of Grass,* ed. Sculley Bradley and Harold W. Blodgett (New York: W. W. Norton, 1973), p. 50; hereafter cited in the text as *LG*.

man's prophetic power of digesting good and evil, ugliness and beauty, into the incorporative self on equal terms "becomes entangled in self-doubt":

> The doubtings, of course, are plotted. It is through a marvelous series of sights that Whitman arrives at the middle point of *Song of Myself,* where he can stand up and, after naming so much else, name himself: "Walt Whitman, an American, one of the roughs, a kosmos." As he compiles those sights he brushes aside the opposition to his gathering strength that comes from sound and touch: "Trippers and askers surround me." But they are not the "Me myself," and when he affirms, "Apart from the pulling and hauling stands what I am," he does so by showing that he "looks."[35]

Unlike Whitman, Du Bois does not attempt to recuperate a threatened self-confidence or a stable self and its powers of incorporation. In the final moments of "The Sorrow Songs" Du Bois is left listening. He does not master the songs but is sent out into the world by them. Tragedy and evil are not assimilated. It is true that, like Whitman, Du Bois transfigures the voices he hears. But he does not incorporate them into the imperial command of his own voice. Through his "Afterthought" he foregrounds the *writtenness* of his transfiguration and the separation between the spirituals and the "book" that is *Souls.*

In "The Mental Traveller" liberty, crucified by society, is born again, though only to undergo perpetually the cycle of defeat and renewal. Du Bois's fear in his "Afterthought" that his book might fall "still born" into the world metaphorically gathers up the dialogues of fathers and sons, of parents and children, which dominate the last five chapters of *Souls,* from the faith of the fathers and the death of the newborn son, to Crummell as father and John as defeated son, and finally to Du Bois as the father listening to the singing of his children. *Souls,* like Blake's "frowning Babe," is created out of a memory and knowledge of the sacrifice of freedom. The same intertwining of memory and transcendence marks the closing moments of Du Bois's *Autobiography.* There, too, as in *Souls,* there is no surrender of hope; there is only an un-American recognition that democratic idealism must remember the past and that this memory sustains the true human purpose of active knowledge:

---

35. Larzer Ziff, *Literary Democracy: The Declaration of Cultural Independence in America* (New York: Penguin, 1982), pp. 235–236.

This is a wonderful America, which the founding fathers dreamed until their sons drowned it in the blood of slavery and devoured it in greed. Our children must rebuild it. Let then the Dreams of the Dead rebuke the Blind who think that what is will be forever and teach them that what was worth living for must live again and that which merited death must stay dead. Teach us, Forever Dead, there is no Dream but Deed, there is no Deed but Memory. (A 422–243)

The sense of the last sentence is that not only is the dream an activity in its own right but also there can be no meaningful action unless it is also an act of remembering feeding the dream.

*Josef Jařab*

# Black Stars, the Red Star, and the Blues

"But jazz is decadent bourgeois music," I was told, for that is what the
Soviet Press had hammered into Russian heads. "It's my music," I said,
"and I wouldn't give it up for a world revolution."

—LANGSTON HUGHES

t was not only for Czechs that Antonín Dvořák one hundred years
ago discovered the musical America. His symphony *From the New
World,* which drew its inspiration from African American songs,
became one of the most popular pieces in the history of Western music;
those who studied it later may have found out that most of the themes in
the composition belong to the Old World rather than the New, but there
was little doubt that the Czech composer had an ear for the difference in
the musical traditions. And what was more, Dvořák saw with surprising clarity the potential of "the negro melodies or Indian chants," which he called
nothing less than the "inspiration for truly national music."[1]

Did the music that came to be called jazz become a fulfillment of Dvořák's
prophecy? Many people inside and outside America have come to believe
so. As early as in the 1920s Leopold Stokowski and Serge Koussevitzky, two
renowned orchestra conductors, recognized jazz as America's "revivifying"
contribution to modern musical literature. The latter also claimed that "jazz
comes from the soil, where all music has its beginning," thus pointing to
its fundamental and not just superficial significance.[2] In 1928 the avant-garde
Czech theater director E. F. Burian wrote the first book on jazz in Czechoslovakia, in which he took issue with the Australian-American composer Percy
Aldridge Grainger that jazz was not to be considered a deficient development

---

1. Antonín Dvořák, "Music in America" (1895), quoted in Henry E. Krehbiel, *Afro-American
Folksongs: A Study in Road and National Music* (New York: G. Schirme, 1914), p. 153.

2. Quoted in J. A. Rogers, "Jazz at Home," in *The New Negro,* ed. Alain Locke (New York: Atheneum, 1968), p. 221.

in Anglo-Saxon music as "it comprised elements of all races"; in addition, Burian maintained that if America could develop jazz as a national music, it would become an achievement provoking the envy of other nations.[3] His views, combining modern feelings with modernist aesthetics, were shared by Jiří Voskovec and Jan Werich, two versatile artists and intellectuals who founded an experimental cabaret theater in Prague, and by their musical partner Jaroslav Ježek, the first genuine Czech jazz composer. Their "Liberated Theater" (Osvobozené divadlo) became very popular. Not only did these artists introduce Czechs to a lot of what the blues and jazz had to convey, but they also found in the forms and messages an inspiration for their comments on the social and cultural situation of Czechoslovakia in the 1930s. It was only logical that after the Nazi occupation and the onset of the war they fled to America, where they continued their effective artistic reflections on current events in their homeland and in the world at large.[4]

There was a noticeable difference in the reception of Negro culture, or American culture with Negro traits, among people in the performing arts and among academics; for the former, elements of the African American nature were considered characteristic of things American and of the modern age, whereas for the latter such features and qualities were perceived primarily as exotic. For instance, Otakar Vočadlo, a sensitive and erudite literary historian, the first Czech professor to undertake a serious consideration of American literature, was still dealing with American letters, in an essay of 1934 concerning literature in English, as a mere subcategory.[5] In a more comprehensive monographic study on the literature in the United States in the same year, he grouped together all the more "exotic" writers in a chapter tellingly entitled "Bohemia and the Other Races." There, W. E. B. Du Bois was mentioned alongside DuBose Heyward, and Langston Hughes alongside Carl Van Vechten; the very fact that a great number of black writers was included is praiseworthy, though it must also be admitted that the white bohemians interested in black life were obviously given more weight by Vočadlo than the African American artists themselves.[6]

3. E. F. Burian, *Jazz* (Prague: Aventinum, 1928), pp. 40–44.

4. Jiří Voskovec and Jan Werich returned to Czechoslovakia after the war, but after the communist takeover in 1948 the two inseparable friends and colleagues went their separate ways. Voskovec tried his luck as an actor in America, and Werich was in and out of Czech theaters, quite at the mercy of the totalitarian regime.

5. Otakar Vočadlo, "Anglická literatura ve XX. století," in *Dvacáté století: Co dalo lidstvu*, vol. 7, *Z duševní dílny lidstva* (Prague: Vl. Orel, 1934), pp. 280–290.

6. Otakar Vočadlo, *Současná literatura Spojených států* (Prague: Jan Laichter, 1934), pp. 181–186.

A fuller understanding of and a deeper identification with black American artists, musicians, and writers arose among Czech performers rather than historians and critics of culture. E. F. Burian himself composed and sang blues songs in the 1920s and had them recorded, with slow-fox dances, on Ultraphon records. R. A. Dvorský, a composer, bandleader, and singer, incorporated jazz elements with great success into what was basically Viennese popular music. For Jaroslav Ježek, as well as for Bohuslav Martinů, jazz offered a more realistic sensual inspiration for their musical compositions. For Karel Teige, an avant-garde critic of modern culture, jazz was to become the basic formula of a new "antibourgeois" and "proletarian" art.[7] A hypersensitive modernist poet, Ivan Blatný (1919–1990), wrote in the early 1940s a very personal poem in which the blues form and mood were pervasively present, and the name of Langston Hughes was used as a rhyme within the verse.[8] The blues and jazz served as sources of motivation and interesting formal experimentation for quite a few Czech poets and songwriters, as an extraordinarily popular anthology that was later put together by Lubomír Dorůžka and Josef Škvorecký testifies; along with translated jazz-inspired verse by American poets, both black and white, the editors included poems by E. F. Burian, Vítězslav Nezval, Jaroslav Seifert (who later won the Nobel Prize), Josef Kainar, Ivan Diviš, Josef Škvorecký himself, and others.[9] Obviously, jazz had become for Czech artists both a vital source and an admirable expression of creative energy.

As it happened, in Central Europe, totalitarian regimes were imposed on the political, social, and cultural life of the region for more than half a century. It could be said that jazz was a good companion to many Czechs throughout the dark decades. Through its spontaneity it was a reminder of freedom, and was therefore seen as a menace by dictators of whatever political orientation, be they fascist or communist. "When the lives of individuals and communities are controlled by powers that themselves remain uncontrolled . . . then creative energy becomes a protest," Škvorecký observed in an essay, "Red Music," which was printed as a foreword to the writer's own jazz novella, *The Bass Saxophone*.[10] Although the story itself goes back to the

---

7. Antonín Matzner, Ivan Poledňák, Igor Wasserberger, et al., *Encyklopedie jazzu a moderní populární hudby* (Prague: Supraphon, 1983), pp. 191–192.

8. Blatný's poem is titled "Báseň v cizím bytě" (A Poem in Someone Else's Flat). Manuscript privately owned.

9. Lubomír Dorůžka and Josef Škvorecký, eds., *Jazzová inspirace* (Prague: Odeon, 1966).

10. Josef Škvorecký, *The Bass Saxophone* (London: Chatto & Windus, 1978), pp. 9–10.

years of the German occupation of Czechoslovakia, the foreword, written in 1977 when the writer was living in exile in Toronto, enumerates among the evil powers along with "slavers, czars and fuehrers" also "first secretaries" and "marshals,"[11] thus showing clearly why the communists' propaganda could not make fully convincing use of the plight of blacks in America as they would have liked to do, and a few times indeed tried to do, with little success. There is, however, ample material illustrating and supporting the view that the Nazis and the communists shared much in their attitudes toward jazz, for striking similarities issue from biased racial or dogmatic class interpretations of reality.

When, in 1958, Škvorecký presented in one of his short stories Goebbelsian "ten commandments" as to what could and could not be done by performers of jazz, that "Judeonegroid" music, a Czech censor confiscated the text of the story because the anti-jazz exhortations did not appear at all disturbing or funny to him but were taken as quite justifiable arguments. That is, the communist totalitarian official found it objectionable that artists and intellectuals in his country should ridicule "rules" such as these:

> so called jazz compositions may contain at most 10% syncopation; the remainder must consist of a natural legato movement devoid of hysterical rhythmic reserves characteristic of the music of the barbarian races and conducive to dark instincts alien to the German people (the so-called riffs)

or

> all light orchestras and dance bands are advised to restrict the use of saxophones of all keys and to substitute for them the violoncello, the viola or possibly a suitable folk instrument

or even

> strictly prohibited is the use of instruments alien to the German spirit (so-called cow-bells, flexatone, brushes, etc.) as well as all mutes which turn the noble sound of wind and brass instruments into a Jewish-Freemasonic yowl (so-called wa-wa, hat, etc.).[12]

As a cultural phenomenon with obvious political implications, jazz played an interesting role during the cold war period on both sides of the battlefield. "Jazz was often at the front line of the battle," the U.S. ambassador to Po-

11. Ibid., p. 10.
12. Ibid., pp. 14, 15.

land, Thomas Winston Simons, Jr., proclaimed in his speech at the inauguration of the American Studies Center at Warsaw University in 1992. There
were, indeed, times and moments when, for different and yet not entirely
unrelated reasons, jazz was perceived both in America and in the Soviet-
bloc countries as something disturbing which did not quite fit into the idea
of an official culture, something illicit and declassé. And at the same time
there were others who took jazz for a universal music, for a product of what
could be called genuine culture. The cultural classification of jazz, though,
could not entirely escape being seen as an ideological issue. As a latter-day
lover of jazz and an attentive observer of the cold war scene, Ambassador
Simons could conclude that "even before it became universal, its hybrid
character made it the best American rebuttal to the Soviet claim that America
had no high culture, and that its mass culture was soulless materialism. Even
before the word 'soul' had a musical connotation, jazz had both quality and
soul."[13] It is, of course, to the credit of jazz and its vitality that not only did
it survive the rather uninviting if not hostile atmosphere of the totalitarian
world but it helped many people survive the uneasy decades behind the Iron
Curtain. Jazz also managed to bridge the gap between popular and high
culture. It aspired more and more to become America's classical music, as
Antonín Dvořák prophesied a century ago. What is truly impressive is the
scope of jazz, its capacity to absorb and represent. From Wynton Marsalis
it reaches back to Edmond Hall; it ranges from George Gershwin to Duke
Ellington and the early combos, to Louis Armstrong and Bessie Smith. It
was only natural that jazz, and later rock, should frequently acquire within
the totalitarian context a reputation as rebellious or even conspiratorial—
and that it was perceived and treated by the public and the authorities accordingly.

    In 1954 a brochure written by Jaroslav Bouček was published "to help
the working-class readers in their search for cultural and ideological values";
the booklet was called "The Troubadours of Hate," and it rejected as deca-
dents William Faulkner and Ernest Hemingway (spelled "Hemmingway"),
Eugene O'Neill as well as John Steinbeck. Richard Wright was accused of
having willingly become part of an indoctrination campaign of murder, hatred, and crime, a writer who was not only a disgrace to the black proletariat
but who made it his abominable task to depict blacks as beasts.

---

13. Thomas Winston Simons, Jr., "Some Thoughts on the Diplomacy of Culture," inauguration
address, American Studies Center, Warsaw University, March 23, 1992.

It was, of course, difficult for the Czech communist authorities to explain why writers of protest, both racial and social, could nonetheless be published in the United States and taught in American schools while some of the same authors stood little chance of being translated into Czech, to say nothing of our own writers of dissent, who could hardly be mentioned and stood virtually no chance whatever of entering the curriculum of our schools. And it was precisely because open, direct, and explicit protest was hardly possible and rarely effective in modern Czech history, and because Czechs are used to reading and learning and even teaching "between the lines," that our people, even in the reception of American art and letters of any ethnic description have been traditionally more open to identifying with cultural rebels, to identifying in human rather than political or ideological terms. So those who understood the Good Soldier Švejk could feel some kinship with the characters of Sholom Aleichem or with Jesse B. Simple. The notion of "laughing to keep from crying" was always familiar and close to the Czechs, and therefore it became quite obvious that even African American literature would be more appealing when introduced through the frequencies shared by writers and musicians, that is, through the echoes of blues and jazz in the writings. Here begins the history of those Czechs "who liked syncopation more than their government," as Josef Škvorecký put it. Here the history of the Jazz Section has its origin, and its story is one of the most telling examples of cultural protest with very powerful political implications and consequences.[14] Having been a part of the story myself, I joined forces with colleagues and put together a representative anthology of what I deemed the best of African American literature from Frederick Douglass to Ntozake Shange. The collection, called *Masks and Faces of Black America,* was published in 1985 and was intended to destroy the political stereotypes attached to black authors. It succeeded in this goal because it attempted to view African American literature as part of the pluralistic or multicultural scene in the United States and because it relied heavily on the blues and jazz tradition in the selections.[15]

14. Josef Škvorecký, "Hipness at Noon," *New Republic,* December 17, 1984, p. 27. See also Josef Škvorecký, *Franz Kafka, jazz a jiné marginálie* (Toronto: Sixty-Eight Publishers, 1988). Josef Jařab, "The Story of the Jazz Section in Czechoslovakia," in *Cultural Transmissions and Receptions: American Mass Culture in Europe,* eds. D. F. J. Boscher, Rob Kroes, and Robert W. Rydell (Amsterdam: VU Press, 1993), pp. 209–215.

15. Josef Jařab, ed., *Masky a tváře černé Ameriky* (Prague: Odeon, 1985). An English version of the introductory essay to the anthology by Josef Jařab, "Black American Literature and Cultural Pluralism," was published in *In the European Grain: American Studies from Central and Eastern Europe,* ed. Orm Overland (Amsterdam: VU Press, 1990), pp. 88–103.

Now that the red star, which may have looked to some people like a star of promise but did not deliver anything but pain, is eclipsed, the black stars, be they poets, musicians, or narrators, keep shining even from a distance. They are heard, they are seen, they convey a human message that does not come to us as something unfamiliar—the message of the blues and beyond.

# From Berlin to Harlem: Felix von Luschan, Alain Locke, and the New Negro

There are no other savages in Africa than some whites acting crazily.
—FELIX VON LUSCHAN

*D*iscussing the origins of the Harlem Renaissance, Alain Locke observed that Negro cultural awakening would not have been possible had it not been for the European discovery of African art, for, as he put it, "there were no forces in America capable of discovering [it] . . . There was a too much obscured and distorted vision before the eyes of black and white artists alike with the smoke of slavery still on the horizon."[1] Locke mentioned two events that served "to open European eyes to the art values of these African curios which had been almost completely overlooked." The first was the arrival in Europe of the art of Benin in 1897, when,

> acting without official orders, a young curator of the Berlin Museum bought up nearly half of this unsuspected art treasure and founded a reputation and a career. For his auction bargain has turned out to be the most prized and valuable collection of African art in existence: the Benin collection of the Berlin Ethnographic Museum . . . The young scholar, Felix von Luschan, by a four volume folio publication on this art and its historical background, easily became the outstanding authority of his generation on primitive African Art.

The second event, according to Locke, was the discovery of the formal beauty of African fetish carvings by a group of young painters in Paris, among whom Picasso played the major role. These two events came together, and Europe rediscovered Africa, "the new continent of the black man's mind."[2]

Responding to this European interest, Americans began to redefine their images of Africa, which opened the way for the birth of the Harlem Renais-

1. Alain Locke, *Negro Art: Past and Present* (New York: Arno Press, 1969), pp. 34–35.
2. Ibid., p. 35–37.

sance. One can readily agree with Locke's statement about Paris, given the links between "la France Libérale"[3] and progressive America. The assertion about Germany, however, may seem strange and unexpected. How could a country known as a nest of racism, birthplace of the Teutonic-Aryan-Caucasian origins theory which supplied the philosophical foundations for the Ku Klux Klan and the Nazis alike, possibly be a cradle of the racial awakening of the American Negro?

In the literature on the Harlem Renaissance there are not many explicit traces of its European connections, in particular to Germany, not to mention its possible German sources and its links with Luschan, whose name appears only in specific works in anthropology and in bibliographies of West African art. Yet Alain Locke, a graduate of Harvard, a student of Oxford and Berlin universities, was too well educated to blunder where such a basic matter was concerned. Locke's statement may therefore serve as a working hypothesis for the investigation of possible links between Germany, and Luschan in particular, with the Harlem Renaissance. The results surpass one's expectations: it appears not only that the liberal race theories underlying the Harlem Renaissance originated in Germany, but also that we can trace the influence of the Western discovery of Benin art on the birth of the Harlem Renaissance.

The European discovery of Benin art functioned as an important stage between classical and modern taste, an agent precipitating the rise of primitivism in art, and a focus of interest in the heated academic debate over possible external influences on African cultures. The fact that Africans were able to create masterpieces of art employing the complicated *cire perdue* (lost wax) technique was of crucial importance in the creation of liberal race theories, which provided a scientific foundation for the Harlem Renaissance. Moreover, the fathers of the Harlem Renaissance were immediately and personally tied to Germany and Luschan himself.

A detailed description of how the Benin collection reached Europe can be found in the introduction to Luschan's monumental *Die Altertümer von Benin* (1919). Toward the end of 1896 Britain's Niger Coast Protector, a Mr. Phillips, wanted to visit the city of Benin, capital of one of the few independent African kingdoms. The king of Benin refused him permission to enter

---

3. Michel Fabre, *La Rive Noire, de Harlem à la Seine* (Paris: Edition Lieu Commun, 1985). According to Fabre, "The intellectual idyll between liberal France and the blacks of the United States is already an old story" (p. 28).

the city because secret religious rituals were being held at that time. Despite the king's refusal and the warning of friendly neighboring chiefs, Phillips proceeded with his mission. The expedition was surprised by the king's soldiers and almost all its members were killed. The event, known as the Benin massacre, provided the long-awaited pretext for England to penetrate the interior of the country.

Only forty-six days after the incident, nine warships and a transport steamer landed on the coast. The city of Benin was looted and destroyed. One of the British officers, Commander R. H. Bacon, complained about the disappointing results of the expedition: unlike at Ashanti, "silver there was none and gold there was none, and the coral was of little value,"[4] and the ivory was damaged. Having established British rule in the city, the expedition withdrew as quickly as possible, taking with them, as Luschan contemptuously remarked, no plan of the city, no photographs of the surroundings, and no scientific documentation whatsoever.[5] It is indicative of the British attitude toward African cultures that the few photographs of the time were taken by a Herr Erdmann, the chief of a German trading post in Lagos. The members of the expedition had to be satisfied with some "souvenirs of no great value."[6] After several days these "souvenirs" found their way into the hands of traders in Lagos. Whatever remained was shipped to London, where the objects considered most valuable were sold off to private collectors as curiosities. The rest were sold in London auction rooms as "damaged" ivory and bronze.

Having learned from one of his informants that about six hundred *Zentner* (hundredweight) of damaged ivory from Benin was going to be auctioned, Luschan, who was acquainted with Olfert Dapper's description of Benin[7] and with some objects from that region, hurried to London, where he immediately recognized the "damaged ivory" as an art treasure. Acting on his personal responsibility, without official permission from the authorities, he sent a telegram to his Lagos connections, authorizing them to buy anything

---

4. R. H. Bacon, *Benin, the City of Blood* (London: Arnold, 1897), p. 89. Felix von Luschan, *Die Altertümer von Benin* (Berlin: De Gruyter, 1919), p. 3.

5. Luschan, *die Altertümer von Benin*, p. 3.

6. Ibid. Luschan refers to conflict over the origin of the photographs, which was resolved by the fact that Erdmann's wife possessed the negatives.

7. Olfert Dapper, *Umbständliche und eigentliche Beschreibung von Africa Anno 1668* (Stuttgart: Steingruber Verlag, 1964).

they could get hold of, without regard to price. Without waiting for bureau-
cratic procedures, Luschan financed further acquisitions with a loan made
by his family.[8] He bought additional pieces of Beniniana at auctions in Lagos
and London, and, using his extraordinary personal connections, he persuaded some "generous Maecenas" to make donations. He even got a director of the London Museum to sell a series of plaques to him cheaply.[9] In
this way Luschan had acquired 580 Benin pieces by 1904, as well as forty-
four copies of the most beautiful pieces, themselves unobtainable, and ten
pieces of uncertain origin. He was indeed entitled to boast, "The Berlin Museum takes its place above all the museums in the world."[10]

Over the next few years, the prices of Beniniana and Africana in general
rose sharply, and in 1901 Luschan spoke about "hunting" for Benin pieces
at world auctions. When, in his correspondence with the London trader
W. D. Webster, Luschan complained about the "exorbitant" prices, Webster
responded that he wished he could have bought the objects back so that he
might sell them at triple the price.[11] The abrupt increase in values after 1897
is proof of the sudden rise in demand, indicating further that the "fashion"
in Africana had already begun by 1897—not, as was subsequently assumed,
as late as 1907, and thus before the French artists pulled African art out
of the "darkness of the ethnographic museums." (This commonly used
metaphor was appropriate for the Trocadéro, but not for the Berlin
Museum, which, according to German state policy, was a chief means of
propaganda.)

A discussion as to who propagated the idea of the French origins of the
fashion known as "l'art Nègre," and how, is beyond the scope of this essay.
It is, however, relevant to remark that the art of Benin was already well
known to the artistic avant-garde of Paris before Picasso painted his historic
*Demoiselles d'Avignon.* Guillaume Apollinaire, who seems to have been
largely responsible for popularizing the view that the fashion for Africana
had French origins, himself possessed a small beaten copper figure of a bird

8. Kurt Krieger, in *Hundert Jahre Museum für Völkerkunde Berlin* (Baessler Archiv, N.F. XXI, 1973);
see contributions by Kurt Krieger and Sigrid Westfal-Hellbusch, pp. 105–118.

9. Felix von Luschan, "Introduction," in *Die Alterümer von Benin.* Luschan used the terms "opfer-
freudige Mäcen" (the Maecenas who takes pleasure in making a sacrifice).

10. Ibid., p. 9.

11. Angelika Tunis, personal communication. Tunis referred me to the correspondence of Luschan
and Webster, held by the Berlin Museum.

from Dahomey, which he used to call "l'oiseau du Bénin," the name by which he referred to Picasso in "Le Poète assassiné."[12]

It was Luschan, not Picasso, who first insisted on describing ethnographical objects from Africa as works of art ranking with the best European achievements. He also pointed out the formal affinities between Beniniana and the art of neighboring tribes. His line of thinking was later elaborated by the art historian, Carl Einstein (1885–1940), whose *Negerplastik* was the first serious study of primitive art. In Einstein's book, the art of Benin consti- tuted a natural *point d'appui* for the formal study of African art. He has been followed in this by all subsequent writers on the subject.

From Locke's opinion, popularized further by M. J. Butcher, one might assume that Luschan was a naive youngster who, through his more or less accidental discovery, gained "easy fame and reputation." Yet we should do justice to Luschan and throw more light on his personality and his "easy career" as well as on the far-reaching effects of his "auction bargain." Felix von Luschan (1854–1924), born in Hollabrunn, Austria, was a person of broad education: his scholarly titles ranged from M.D., Litt.D., and D.Sc. from Vienna to a Dr.Phil. from Munich. During his lifetime he enjoyed immense authority as an expert in anthropology, archaeology, and ethnogra- phy. In 1882 he wrote his first habilitation in which he formulated the subject matter of his lifelong research—the physical characteristics of the primary human races. When, in 1885, Luschan was called to Berlin as an assistant director of the Museum für Völkerkunde, German ethnology was already enjoying a leading role in Europe, although Germany's colonial possessions were a fairly recent acquisition. This phenomenon can be explained as a product of the fruitful combination of expansionist state policy, German Methodismus, and the established tradition of collecting ethnographic ob- jects.[13]

When Luschan arrived in Berlin, there were already 7,388 objects in his department of the museum; by the time he retired, this number had risen

12. Down Ades, *Dada and Surrealism Reviewed,* exhibition catalog (London: Westernham Press, 1978), p. 31.

13. For biographical data on Luschan, see Staatsbibliothek Preussischer Kulturbesitz, Berlin, De- partment of Manuscripts; Nachlass Fritz Kiffner; *International Dictionary of Anthropologists;* Nachlass Felix von Luschan; Krieger, *Hundert Jahre Museum,* pp. 105–118; Angelika Tunis, "Introduction to the Catalogue of the Benin Antiquities," unpublished manuscript; Hans Virchow, "Gedächtnisrede auf Felix v. Luschan," *Zeitschrift für Ethnologie* (1924): 112–117. Matgorzata Irek, *The European Roots of the Harlem Renaissance* (Berlin: J. F. Kennedy Institut, 1994).

to 48,845, and he could declare, "The Berlin collection is seven times as large as the ethnographic department of the British Museum."[14] Personal contributions by directors such as Leopold Ledebur and Adolf Bastian,[15] as well as Luschan, and the well-developed collecting tradition, added significantly to this "explosion," but it would never have been possible without a systematic method of research which prevented the collection from being a pile of casually heaped up objects illustrating the range of colonial possessions, as was the case with other European museums.

This sudden interest in science and colonial achievements was stimulated by German state policy. As Locke notes, "Germans especially, interested in their new African colonial ventures, were feverishly collecting materials and as might be expected, in a more methodological and scientific way. Not only were the great collections being built up at Berlin, but at Hamburg, Bremen, Leipzig, Frankfurt, Munich, Dresden, and even smaller centers, like Cologne, Lübeck, and Darmstadt."[16]

Significantly, in contrast to the established colonial powers, Germany did not develop anti-savage propaganda in the initial stages of colonialism. The German colonial self-image was one of benevolent German bureaucrats who, unlike other colonizers, maintained rule over the *Naturvölker* with wise understanding and scientific objectivity. Any representations threatening this official image were suppressed and attempts to destroy it punished, as in the case of Gottlob Krause.[17] Toward the end of the nineteenth century, Germany was thus the only colonial power for which the recognition of well-developed cultures in Africa did not contradict state policy. In contrast, "La France Libérale" was at that time greatly interested in justifying its conquest of the kingdom of Dahomey, a modern African state with an elaborate administrative structure, diplomatic ties with European powers, an export-oriented agriculture, and a military armed with machine guns.[18] In an attempt

14. Nachlass Luschan, Berlin.

15. Georg Elwert, "Ethnologie," in *Wissenschaften in Berlin-Disciplinen,* ed. Tilmann Buddensieg and Kurt Düwell (Berlin: Mann, 1987), pp. 134–141.

16. Locke, *Negro Art,* p. 35.

17. Gottlob Krause, an outstanding German Africanist, known in Africa as Malam Musa, claimed publicly that German colonial officials were involved in the slave trade. This lapse of patriotism on his part was punished by the state through a boycott of his work and collections in all German public museums. See Peter Sebald, *Malam Musa G. A. Krause, 1850–1938* (Berlin: Akademie Verlag, 1972), pp. 136–172.

18. Georg Elwert, personal communication.

to cast a shadow over these achievements, the Africans were represented in France as mere savages and their art as an expression of barbarous, homicidal idolatry. Hence, even the finest bronze works and wooden sculptures brought from Dahomey were hidden in the "darkness" of museums and labeled the fetishes of savages.

Similarly, the British conquest of Benin had to be justified in terms of the white man's duty to civilize the bloodthirsty savages. This attitude is shown by contemporary British literature on the Benin expedition, ranging from soldiers' accounts to serious ethnographic studies. Thus, Captain A. M. Bois-ragon's *Benin Massacre* and Bacon's *Benin, The City of Blood*, which appeared simultaneously in London and New York in 1897, threatened the public with images of horror and savagery which fit conventional racist stereotypes only too well, especially in the United States, where these portraits struck a re-sponsive chord in the post-Reconstruction South. From these books a direct line may be traced to suggestive fiction such as T. Dixon's *Leopard's Spots* and to historical research, of which U. B. Phillip's *American Negro Slavery* was the most influential.

R. H. Bacon's book, a soldier's eyewitness account, set the pattern for scholarly research such as Ling Roth's *Great Benin: Its Customs, Art, and Horrors* (1903), and Charles Hercules Read and Ormonde Maddock Dalton's *Antiquities of the City of Benin* (1899), which it was written to show "a selec-tion of the principal objects obtained by the expedition sent to Benin to punish the nations of that city for the treacherous massacre of a peaceful English mission," and praised the Benin collection as a historical document "which has no parallel in the records of savage Africa."[19]

Bacon tells us that his book was written "firstly to have a full account of what happened, and secondly to leave on record certain details of organiza-tion and equipment which may be used in future similar expeditions." As might be expected from such a statement, Bacon was writing from a Euro-centric viewpoint, and as in the case of Dahomey, his description had to serve the ends of anti-savage propaganda to justify war expenses. According to Bacon, civilized, respectful white gentlemen were obliged to "interfere with the native royalty [to stop] savagery of the most debased kind," details of which he described in over a hundred pages, in the manner of the best

19. Charles Hercules Read and Ormonde Maddock Dalton, "Introduction," in *Antiquities of the City of Benin and from Other Parts of West Africa in the British Museum* (London: Longman & Co., 1899), p. 32.

dramatic novels. Among the queen's kind, civilized subjects was the unfortunate Mr. Phillips, whose stupidity caused the massacre of his people. But,
according to Bacon, Phillips was a "gallant, brave man . . . able to treat
natives pacifically," who was murdered by the bloodthirsty savages just as
he pronounced the historic words: "No revolvers, gentlemen, no revolvers."
The subsequent colonial conquest is portrayed by Bacon as a battle between
good and evil, fought not merely in revenge for the massacre but as a moral
duty of civilized people to "destroy the centre of vice" and to restrain the
"blood lust" of savages. Significantly, even the good Africans who cooperated
with the whites in the expedition and who, as Bacon puts it, "already enjoyed
British protection," are described in terms of the "Sambo" convention: they
were "comically dressed, as pleased as children to help the white man, absolutely indifferent to telling a lie or the truth" and "their brains were very
slow."[20]

Although different in kind from Bacon's story, the work of Pitt-Rivers,
Inspector of Ancient Monuments in Great Britain, who was involved in the
Benin event and managed to secure 228 pieces for his private collection of
"curiosities," was written according to the same convention. What he called
"well-formed pieces" of art he attributed to Portuguese influence, compared
with the "rudely formed pieces" characteristic of "barbaric" art.[21] Pitt-Rivers
thus shared the general opinion of the time: "To ascribe these masterpieces
simply to Negroes is pure folly."[22] Indeed, the existing stereotype of African
savagery was so strong that the majority of serious scholars regarded Benin
art as a product of Portuguese, Egyptian, or even German influence.

In this context we may safely say that it was Luschan who rediscovered
Africa for European intellectuals. His opinion of African art and his lifelong
crusade against the "underestimation of the Negro as such"[23] were revolutionary. Already in 1898, in his first publication on Benin art, "Althertümer
von Benin," Luschan insisted that Benin art was absolutely native. "The style
of the works is purely African, absolutely and exclusively only African. To
talk about Phoenician or Assyrian forms here would simply show that one

20. Bacon, *Benin*, pp. 13, 17, 4, 106, and 131.

21. George Henry Lane-Fox Pitt-Rivers, *Antique Works of Art from Benin* (London: Harrison &
Sons, 1900), "Introduction" and pp. 10, 12, 13, 14, 28, and 70.

22. Quoted in Werner Forman and Burchard Brentjes, *Alte afrikanische Plastik* (Leipzig: Koehler
Verlag, 1968), p. 41.

23. Felix von Luschan, "Altertümer von Benin," *Zeitschrift für Ethnologie,* 30 (1898): 153.

knows nothing of either of these, nor of modern African art," he claimed, deliberately using the expression African art without quotation marks, for, as he observed, nothing could have expressed the European underestimation of African societies better than the quotation marks used with words such as *culture* or *art.* Instead, he advocated using quotation marks for ambiguous terms such as "fetish, savage, or primitive."[24] This redefinition of habitual terms and rejection of stereotypical labels represents the first shift in European attitudes toward Africa.

In his numerous publications Luschan repeatedly stressed that the very existence of monumental native Benin art, comparable to contemporary European achievements and technically at the highest possible level—"Cellini himself would not have made these bronzes better, and nobody before or after him to date"—had both cognitive and moral meaning.[25] The latter was of "infinitely greater significance," for it proved beyond any doubt that Negroes were not subhuman. Once Benin art had been discovered, he said, Europeans could no longer think of Negroes as "savages" because "people who have brought bronze techniques to the highest degree of mastery, people to whom one can ascribe, with absolute certainty, the invention of iron-working, people of whom we now know that they have for ages maintained regular trade-exchange relations with the societies which we describe as civilized, can no longer be considered half-apes, the killing of whom is just as pleasant and well-deserved a pastime as, let us say, rooting out pernicious vermin." Reversing the stereotype of good whites versus bad savages, Luschan spoke of "white barbarians" or "white savages." He continually stressed that "there are no other savages in Africa than some whites acting crazily," whom he accused of having destroyed native African social structures with the unprecedented slave hunting that followed the settlement of the Americas. The image of bloodthirsty savages, he noted, was created by so-called colonial circles and by Africans themselves, who, by presenting their culture as uninviting and formidable, hoped to keep out the white barbarians and control the slave trade themselves.[26]

24. Ibid., p. 150.
25. Ibid., p. 153.
26. Felix von Luschan, "Über die alten Handelsbeziehungen von Benin," in *Verhandlungen des VII. internationalen Geographen-Kongresses in Berlin, 1899* (Berlin: Greve, 1900), p. 611, 607; see also Luschan, "Introduction," in *Die Altertümer von Benin.*

Luschan claimed that in a cognitive respect the existence of Benin art questioned the value of dividing societies into superior versus inferior or civilized versus primitive. "The ethnically unfalsified originality of the 'savages,'" he said mockingly, "exists only in the brains of certain ethnologists."[27] In proving that Europeans could no longer consider the culture of "so-called savages" inferior to their own, Luschan was a forerunner of cultural relativism. Not only did he develop the theoretical foundations of nonracial theories[28] and support them with evidence such as Benin art, but he actively propagated these progressive ideas as well.

Luschan spread his progressive theories in his museum activities and through his work with various scholarly societies, as well as through his wide-ranging personal contacts; the fact that he was a Freemason was not without significance. An important forum for his activities was Berlin University, where he was a professor of anthropology. He raised a generation of nonracist scholars, such as the anthropologist Jan Czekanowski and the famous medical doctor Albert Schweitzer. At the university Luschan belonged to the progressive milieu that revolved around the anthropologist, medical scientist, and politician Rudolf Virchow (1821–1902), who also taught W. E. B. Du Bois and Franz Boas. Luschan maintained a lifelong friendship with Boas from the time the latter came to Berlin. Boas, a graduate in physics, learned physical anthropology from Luschan, who was himself a graduate in medicine and anthropology. Given the contribution of Boas's antiracist work to the rise of the Harlem Renaissance, it is important to remember where his antiracism began: it developed in Germany, under the influence of Virchow and Luschan.

After the two world wars the sharp criticism of German nationalism made it impossible to link Germany with the racial revival of American blacks. Yet it is important not to forget that Germany had a strong antiracist tradition dating back to Theodore Waitz. This tradition, along with a high level

27. Luschan, "Introduction," in *Die Altertümer von Benin.*

28. Luschan devoted more than thirty years to the excavations which he carried out in the capital of the ancient Hittite empire, Senschirli (Zincirli). The excavations were to prove his theory of race, disproving the existence of a cranially uniform Jewish type, which, according to Luschan, "exists only in books and not in reality." See "Die anthropologische Stellung der Juden," *Korrespondenszblatt der Deutschen Anthropologischen Gesellschaft* (1892); "The Early Inhabitants of Western Asia," Huxley Memorial Lecture, Royal Anthropological Institute, London, 1911); *Wissenschaftliche Monographie von Ausgrabungen in Sendschirli* (Berlin: Reimer, 1902–1911).

of *Völkerkunde* and, ironically, Germany's colonial policy, created an atmosphere in which the appreciation of African culture was possible. As a consequence, it was one of Germany's antiracist thinkers, Felix von Luschan, who, with his appreciation of the true value of Benin art, started the worldwide reevaluation of Africa in the spheres of art and racial theory, thus significantly contributing to the rise of the Harlem Renaissance.

*Friederike Hajek*

# The Change of Literary Authority in the Harlem Renaissance: Jean Toomer's *Cane*

*T*he dramatic change from a largely oral and rural culture to a predominantly literary and urban one found a very special and also a most complex treatment in Jean Toomer's *Cane.* That small volume published in 1923 with a preface by Waldo Frank was enthusiastically welcomed by a number of prominent critics and authors including W. E. B. Du Bois and Sherwood Anderson; but no more than about five hundred copies of the first and only edition for decades were able to find buyers. Yet there has been a Toomer renaissance since the end of the 1960s. *Cane* is now one of the most widely read black texts of its day and has even been praised as "the most respected." Its author is "ranked among the finest artists in the history of Afro-American literature."[1] Toomer himself called *Cane* a "swan-song" for a dying culture. When he worked as a teacher in Sparta, Georgia, he came to hear the singing of a back-country black family:

> And this was the first time I'd ever heard the folk-songs and spirituals. They were very rich and sad and joyous and beautiful. But I learned that the Negroes of the town objected to them. They called them shouting . . . So, I realized with deep regret, that the spirituals, meeting ridicule, would be certain to die out . . . The folk spirit was walking in to die on the modern desert. That spirit was so beautiful. Its death was so tragic. Just this seemed to sum up life for me. And this was the feeling I put into *Cane* . . . It was a song of an end. And why no one has seen and felt that, why people have expected me to write a

---

1. Darwin T. Turner, "Introduction," in Jean Toomer, *Cane* (New York: Liveright, 1975), p. x; subsequent references will be cited by page in the text.

second and a third and a forth book like *Cane,* is one of the queer misunderstandings of my life. (xxii)

Meanwhile, this swan song has turned into a rich source of inspiration and self-definition for African American authors from Ralph Ellison to Alice Walker. The swan song metaphor has also kept literary scholars busy. Barbara E. Bowen, for example, comes to the conclusion that *Cane* had to remain unique "because the call-and-response form which *Cane* explores and celebrates is exactly the form it shows is no longer possible."[2] Bowen's essay gives a very clear explanation of what had been lost under the impact of modernity; yet the question remains as to what came out in the balance of that change: if the call-and-response form had become an impossibility, what, then, were the new possibilities? What was to take the place of the old formula? This question can perhaps be answered if we try to understand the process in terms of a crisis of cultural authority in the course of which an old authority was replaced by a new one. Not only is *Cane* the product of such a crisis—as, indeed, was the Harlem Renaissance as a whole—but also Toomer's work distinguishes itself equally by the author's effort to make this change the very subject of his discourse, which he structured accordingly. Because of its multitude of forms—poems, songs, stories, sketches, and drama—and also because it does not have a unified plot, the status of *Cane* as a novel has been doubted, though its artistic value has never been questioned by serious critics.

One of its unifying elements, I suggest, is the concept of changing authority as a structuring device. This change occurs in three phases, signified by a division of the text into three parts. The first section introduces us to a rural setting in Georgia. Here the call-and-response form is still intact, or seems so at first sight. So does the old rural authority, which expresses itself in a communal voice. The authority of a preacher such as King Barlo, for instance, depends on the response of the community to which he preaches. It is the community that, by its way of responding, authorizes him to speak as a messenger of God himself. The reason why many critics consider this part of *Cane* the most beautiful has to do with the still strong presence of a unifying spirit of communal authority based on shared (religious and other) beliefs. Verse and lyrical prose sing of the uniqueness of that "purple country," of its terrors and of the beauty of its women. Yet the signs of crisis are

---

2. Barbara E. Bowen, "Untroubled Voices: Call and Response in *Cane,*" in *Black Literature and Literary Theory,* ed. Henry Louis Gates, Jr. (New York and London: Methuen, 1984), p. 202.

already present. King Barlo's authority as a charismatic preacher is corrupted by his having made money from cotton during the war. Karintha is meaningfully endowed with "beauty perfect as the dusk when the sun goes *down*" and with "a soul *ripened too soon*" (2, emphasis added). Signs of a pending crisis of authority are also represented in the more general power structure of the South. The unheard-of rivalry over a black girl between the white master Bob Stone and the black worker Tom Burwell in "Blood-Burning Moon" is seen as a crisis of the authority of racist supremacy in the South. Bob and the lynch mob act according to "southern traditions," thereby apparently reenforcing the latter, but Bob, having been educated in the North, can no longer be sure about the validity of his traditional "rights."

The second part of *Cane* takes us to urban surroundings, and the authority based on call-and-response patterns ceases to function entirely. The voice of the speaker is left without a response. He is isolated, misunderstood, without a community to speak to. There are merely other individuals who are as isolated as the speaker himself. In "Avey" we see an example of how this isolated speaker—now represented in the first-person singular—tries to impose his authority on a young woman, the title character. The man apparently has adapted himself to the new situation, but Avey has not: "I was ambitious," he says. "I was going off to college. The more I thought of it, the more I resented, yes, hell, that's what it was, her downright laziness. Sloppy indolence. There was no excuse for a healthy girl taking life so easy. Hell! she was no better than a cow" (44). Unlike Avey, the speaker has accepted the authority of middle-class urban life. His authority takes on the appearance of being self-defined. In fact, though, it is not his own but the authority of a puritan work ethic which speaks—swearing—through him; he has been appropriated by that outside authority while he himself as an individual is left with no authority of his own at all. Ironically, and very much to the point, Toomer has Avey fall asleep while the young man, who may also be somewhat representative of Toomer himself, is speaking to her—preaching—"about an art that would be born, an art that would open the way for women the likes of her" (46). Withdrawal, then, becomes a way of subverting and refusing this new self-imposed authority which was to replace the old relation by functioning as authoritative *saying* and *passive* listening "to what I had to say." The call-and-response pattern is finally reestablished, but it is literally muted. The speaker figure responds to the silent "call" of the sleeping woman when he decides to guard the sleep of that "Orphan-woman"(47).

The theme of muteness is continued in the third part, which consists of one single piece, "Kabnis." Kabnis has returned to Georgia from the North to work as a teacher. He is not strong enough to resist the many pressures placed on him physically and mentally by southern racism and general backwardness. After a nervous breakdown he begins an apprenticeship as a wagon builder. In truth, though, he wants to become an artist, an "orator." One day his boss, Halsey, gives a feast in the cellar beneath his workshop. A special role is played here by an old man who lives in this cellar, Father John. The crisis of authority is acted out between the old man and Kabnis. The old man sits "in a high-backed chair which stands upon a low platform." He is "like a bust in black walnut. Grey-bearded. Grey-haired. Prophetic. Immobile . . . A mute John the Baptist of a new religion—or a tongue-tied shadow of an old" (104). Insofar, then, as he is to be counted among the living, he is mute; as a representative of an old communal authority he is but a mere shadow: "Dead blind father of a muted folk who feel their way upward to a life that crushes and absorbs them" (105). It should be noted that Toomer speaks of a "muted folk." Robbed of their communal voice as well as of their songs, they are silenced by being absorbed or crushed *by* as much as *into* modern civilization while yet trying to aspire to its standards. In this context it is very important for some of the characters on the scene to reserve some hope for the old folk spirit to speak to them once again. Lewis, Halsey, and Carrie Kate maintain a desire for a communal voice that would speak for all of them and thus enable them to overcome their muteness. But Kabnis, the representative of the new authority, "won't give him [Father John] a chance" (104). He swears at him: "Father of hell" (104). "Just like any done-up preacher he looks to me. Jam some false teeth in his mouth and crank him, an youd have God Almighty spit in torrents all around th floor" (107). Kabnis denounces the old communal authority together with religion and the past in general. He is the one to replace the authority of the dying folk spirit which had been pushed into the underground to rot and die but for the rare occasions when it is celebrated as a monument to a not yet fully obsolete past.

The new authority represented by Kabnis is characterized by self-authorization. Toomer signifies this by his differentiation between "preacher" and "orator." Kabnis claims he "was born and bred in a family of orators." "Preachers," corrects Halsey. And Kabnis replies: "Na. Preachers hell . . . Y misapprehend me . . . All right then, y misapprehend me. I didn't say preachers. I said orators. ORATORS. Born one an I'll die one" (109). As an orator he is, unlike a preacher, no longer dependent on a community that would respond to him and thereby establish his authority. He can do even without their understanding him at all: "All right then, y misapprehend me." He is able to ignore this and go on speaking his text without taking the trouble to explain anything. This kind of estrangement comes out more brutally when he responds to the question whether the old man has spoken: "Huh? Who? Him? No. Don't need to. I talk. An when I really talk, it pays the best of them t listen. Th old man is a good listener. He's deaf; but he's a good listener. An I can talk t him. Tell him anything" (114). Here the distance from orator to dictator seems a very short one. The little scene is highly indicative of the historically dangerous potential of this new authority. The self-authorized "I" has cut himself off from the people of the community and their response. He wants "them" to be only listeners, passive receivers of what he has to say, without any need for further communication. It does not matter even if they are deaf and cannot really hear him. It's enough for the new authority that they *appear* to be listening, that they perform as a silent auditor who does not talk back. The only real listener is the new artist himself, who establishes himself through his performance.

Yet, the old folk spirit has not become totally superfluous. It has enough meaning for Kabnis that he wants to spend the rest of his life "down in this scum-hole . . . th old man an me" (114). The old authority of the folk spirit has become the Other which has to be denied by the new authority but against which, nevertheless, the new authority has to define itself: "Have you ever heard him say th things youve heard me say?" (115). True to the new pattern of "communication," the speaker does not pause for a response from his "audience." The question is merely a rhetorical device to facilitate his speaking. The old man could not have said what he has to say "if he had th Holy Ghost t help him" (115). The change of authority is determined historically and is, therefore, inescapable.

Involved in this process is a redefinition of values. When the old man finally speaks, he speaks of "sin." But Kabnis denies the man's authority on that level, too: "He doesn't know what he is talking about. Couldn't know. It was only a preacher's sin they knew in those old days, an that wasn't sin at all. Mind me, th only sin is whats done against th soul. Th whole world is a conspiracy t sin, especially in America, an against me. I'm th victim of their sin. I'm what sin is" (115). The dissolution of authority of the communal folk spirit is accompanied by the dissolution of the authority of God and, indeed, of rural culture as a whole. At the center of the new urban culture is the individual against whom the whole world is in sinful conspiracy, making him or her a microcosmic representation of "what sin is." The contradiction between artist and the ruling powers of the United States is represented in the individual, thus making the individual representative of society as a whole. Thereby the individual artist's claim to authority becomes valid. The new authority based on recognition of *real* sin against the human soul rather than on *belief* in sin against God (preacher's sin) justifies and realizes itself as artistic activity within the newly developed institution of art as an autonomous sphere of aesthetic production directed against the acquisitive impulses of capitalist society.

Toomer thus has made his own contribution to modernity. In writing *Cane* out of a deep sense of fundamental cultural loss, he fictionalized the historical process of that loss and thereby transcribed the waning oral tradition into a written text, preserving it as a future source of literary tradition and imagination. In this sense Toomer has become one of the fathers of modern African American literature. Langston Hughes, Zora Neale Hurston, Ishmael Reed, Alice Walker, and others took up his gift in their own ways.

The call-and-reponse pattern according to which Toomer structured *Cane* is also the basic pattern of the blues. Over the three parts of the book he sustained the communicative scheme as statement (the first part, in a rural setting), *variation* (crisis in the urban sphere), *response* (the dissolution of the pattern in "Kabnis"). Yet the dissolution of the old authority and communal spirit is at the same time the creation of a new one which is also representative of the more general crisis in the American culture of the 1920s. The black masses had begun to enter the urban centers of civilization at a time when this civilization itself had become highly questionable as to the validity of its own traditional values.

*Cane,* then, was more than a swan song for a dying rural folk culture; it was also a birth chant for a new (black) aesthetic that drew its authority not merely from the denial of an old one but far more from a basic critique of modern civilization in the aftermath of the First World War. By no means does this new authority appear in Toomer's representation as something "higher" or "better" than something that is "inferior." Kabnis is a historically valid representative of this new authority, but he is neither loveable nor heroic nor respectable. We may take this as a sign of the author's critical if not skeptical attitude toward the historical changes represented in *Cane.*

*Paola Boi*

# Zora Neale Hurston's *Autobiographie Fictive:* Dark Tracks on the Canon of a Female Writer

I write in order to lose my name.

—GEORGES BATAILLE

I am one thing, my writings are another. It would contradict my character entirely if I expected ears and hands for my truths today.

—FRIEDRICH NIETZSCHE

Who care anything about no train fare? The train track is there, ain't it? I can ride de blind, can't I?

—ZORA NEALE HURSTON

*T*he association between railroad tracks and writing is a recurrent metaphor in Zora Neale Hurston's *Dust Tracks on a Road*,[1] labeled "autobiography" but undoubtedly much closer to a work of fiction than to a reliable self-portrait. Some of the difficulties in classifying this work lie primarily in the definition of autobiography as such,[2] while others stem specifically from the peculiar way in which Hurston's voice transits heedlessly between the private and the public,[3] thus establishing an ambiguous

---

1. Zora Neale Hurston, *Dust Tracks on a Road: An Autobiography* (1942), ed. with an introduction by Robert Hemenway (Urbana: University of Illinois Press, 1984); subsequent references will be given by page in the text.

2. "And you speak about the autobiographical voice as if there was such a thing, as if the prodigious wealth of recent studies on autobiography, first male, then female, hadn't endlessly questioned its existence as a genre." Nicole Ward Jouve, *White Woman Speaks with Forked Tongue: Criticism as Autobiography* (London: Routledge, 1991) p. 10.

3. Self-reflection and autobiography are both special cases of historical experience and knowledge, according to Hans Georg Gadamer, *Truth and Method*, ed., trans., and rev. J. Weinsheimer and D. G. Marshall (New York: Crossroads 1991). What is of interest here, though, is not the historical validity of an autobiographical text but the way history presents itself to the inner world of the objective consciousness.

link between what she pretends to recall as her "vie vécue" and "l'histoire racontée" tout court.

Before introducing any tentative interpretation, though, I should acknowledge duplicity as the qualifying mark of the autobiographical discourse. What makes an autobiography different from a *narration fictive*[4] is almost imponderable. If autobiography is something out of the text, created by an act of reading,[5] an interrelation between what the autobiographer hands out as her or his reality and the response of the reader who completes the act, we should analyze it, accordingly, more "as process rather than genre."[6] The case of *Dust Tracks on a Road* somehow occupies a significantly oriented position in the *décryptage* of the black text. As a mixture of reality and imagination, it bears a strong resemblance to fiction, being marked as it is by what Paul Ricoeur calls "l'effet de référence."[7] The type of reality it conveys is—always—a rearrangement of "the oral trace of the past" (memory),[8] through the written word. The very act of telling events removes them from mere factuality and transforms them into variable, fictional speech acts. It is not surprising, then, that the classic standards of identity and truth have now become two shifting elements in a scene "of a complex discursive encounter presided over by a self-determined narrator who makes free with text and reader in the name of truth *to* self."[9]

We now seem to be confronting several questions: What is the function of the autobiographical text within the whole production of a writer? How

4. For Northrop Frye all autobiographies "select those events and experiences in the writer's life that go to build up an integrated pattern, and so are inspired by a creative and therefore fictional impulse." Quoted in Thomas Cooley, *Educated Lives: The Rise of Autobiography in America* (Columbus: Ohio State University Press, 1976) p. x. Cooley adds that the art of autobiography is "understood to occupy a middle ground between fiction and history. Often inconsistencies in the record are considered more revealing than consensus" (pp. 10–11).

5. The definition is given by Philippe Lejeune in *Le pacte autobiographique* (Paris: Seuil, 1975) p. 45.

6. The suggestion is made by Valerie Smith in *Self-Discovery and Authority in Afro-American Narrative* (Cambridge, Mass.: Harvard University Press, 1987) p. 5.

7. For Paul Ricoeur the world of the text necessarily clashes with the real world only to remake it; the relationship between art and reality would be incomprehensible if art did not "derange" or "rearrange" our relationship to the real. The real past is hinted at only indirectly through the story-speech; its reconstruction is the work of the imagination. What he describes as *l'effet de référence* is the power that fiction has to redescribe reality. Paul Ricoeur, *Du texte à l'action* (Paris: Seuil, 1982) p. 221.

8. Françoise Lionnet, *Autobiographical Voices: Race, Gender, Self-Portraiture* Ithaca, N.Y.: Cornell University Press, 1987), p. 5.

9. William L. Andrews, *To Tell a Free Story: The First Century of Afro-American Autobiography, 1760–1865* (Urbana: University of Illinois Press, 1986) p. 2.

can we reconcile the internal formal structures of literary language with their external, referential, and public effects? Can we consider autobiography a distinct unit of referential meaning? Is internal meaning an outside reference?

In *Dust Tracks* self-consciousness sometimes produces a sort of "running metadiscourse,"[10] whereas in other cases self-discovery turns into simple self-invention. We should nonetheless remember that there is a special relationship between any woman autobiographer and her final text which "outshines referential considerations, and reduces specific aspects of the individual history to accidents."[11] In dealing with Hurston's *autobiographie fictive* we are mainly concerned, therefore, with the various self-representations and metaphors that the writer projects, the relationship between these images and the reader produced *through* the written text. Virginia Woolf states that in order "to tell the whole story of life the autobiographer must devise some means by which the two levels of existence can be recorded—the rapid passage of events and actions the slow opening up of a single and solemn moment of concentrated emotion."[12] But what is the nature of the dynamic situation represented here?

Although black autobiographers have come to seem more interested in *telling* freedom than in "just tell[ing] *about* freedom,"[13] the female voice still "betrays the confinement from which that freedom is wrested."[14] In the case of Hurston's writing, any attempt to catalogue her discourse or define her person will lead us nowhere. Henry Louis Gates's definition of *signifying* as "the trope of tropes" may help us to clear up the impasse. He illustrates the essence of this rhetorical device in terms of repetition, revision, or reversal.[15] The very ease with which this linguistic substitution can be carried out may

10. Ibid. p. 17.

11. See Elizabeth Fox-Genovese's discussion of Hurston's "troubled" autobiography in "My Statue My Self: Autobiographical Writings of Afro-American Women," in *Reading Black, Reading Feminist, A Critical Anthology*, ed. Henry Louis Gates, Jr. (New York: Meridian, 1990), p. 180.

12. Virginia Woolf, "De Quincey's Autobiography," in *The Second Common Reader* (1932; rpt. New York: Harcourt Brace Jovanovich, 1969) p. 125.

13. William L. Andrews, "A Poetics of Afro-American Autobiography" in *Afro-American Literary Study in the 1990s*, ed. Houston A. Baker, Jr., Patricia Redmond (Chicago: University of Chicago Press, 1989) p. 90.

14. Fox-Genovese, *My Statue*, p. 177.

15. In *Figures in Black*, Gates defines signifying as "a uniquely black rhetorical concept, entirely textual or linguistic by which a second statement or figure repeats, or tropes, or reverses the first". He considers Hurston the "first author of the tradition to represent signifying itself as a vehicle of liberation for an oppressed woman." Henry Louis Gates, Jr., *Figures in Black: Words, Signs, and the Racial Self* (New York: Oxford University Press, 1987), pp. 49, 241.

blur the centrality of its epistemological unreliability. To signify means to exert a certain mischievous power over the truth and falsehood of statements. Writers as different as Nietzsche, Freud, and Harold Bloom assert categorically that to substitute is to falsify, and that the deviant meaning may itself be considered as definite and authoritative as the original. *Dust Tracks* originally derives from a "matrix of literary discontinuities,"[16] in which the author signifies upon communication as a literary discourse, upon herself as a black writer, and upon autobiography as a literary genre.

In a 1988 roundtable on autobiography Jacques Derrida offered a comment appropriate to the aural world that Hurston reinvents in *Dust Tracks* when he said that "it is the ear of the other that signs."[17] In pointing out this double perspective (aural/oral), Derrida displaces the *autos,* the self, as the subject of biography into the *otos,* the structure of the ear of the other, who receives the message and gives it authenticity. In fact, Hurston's "autobiographical" text puts a strong emphasis on the act of communication through an extensive use of the hear/tell semantic reference as the first means for reaching the other. "This is all *hear-say.* Maybe some of the details of my birth as *told* me are a little inaccurate . . . The *saying* goes like this . . . I have never been *told,* but I did *hear* . . . Let me *change a few words* . . . I am of the *word changing* kind" (27; emphasis added). Using this perspective Hurston purposefully stresses the interlocutor's role by constantly summoning the reader to participate. What Derrida says about the shifting identity of the other might suggest that the text does not fully control its interpretation; nor can any single reading preempt the field of other possible readings. The discourse is dispersed into multiple sets of order, thus eliminating the possiblity of achieving an organic whole: differences are not resolved but multiplied. The probability of interpretation is in itself a pluridimensional stance, a shift from self-presentation to discussions on the varieties of interpretation, understanding, submission to facts. In other words, it is a transition from a psychological to a hermeneutical grounding, from an individual experience to the attainment of knowledge.

16. Hortense Spillers, "Cross-Currents, Discontinuities: Black Women's Fiction," in *Conjuring: Black Women, Fiction, and Literary Tradition,* ed. Marjorie Pryse and Hortense Spillers (Bloomington: Indiana University Press, 1985), p. 251.

17. Jacques Derrida, *L'oreille de l'autre,* published in English as *The Ear of the Other: Otobiography, Transference, Translation,* ed. Christie McDonald, trans. Peggy Kamuf and Avital Ronnell (New York: Bison Books, 1988), p. 50. "A keen ear is an ear that perceives *differences*" . . . and is also *double* (49).

Ricoeur states the value of "multiple meaning,"[18] giving resonance to the peculiar way in which Hurston makes history story. If self-reflection and autobiography undoubtedly focus on the distorting mirror of subjectivity, Hurston's private (hi)story—written, one might say, with two hands—can offer a basis for hermeneutical considerations. Her text shows a constant double play, sometimes a double voice, sometimes a fracture, a gap between what she says and what is left unsaid or is purposely distorted. In certain places it is marked by a sort of deletion that makes us read what it rules out, inscribing violently in the text what it tries to command from outside, shifting from *saying* to *hiding,* from the *real* to the *imagined* discourse. In such a space the author outruns any understanding; here the multiplicity of events indicates a series of discursive processes, meanings, and practices that are not synthesized but are rather thrown together through dissension and controversy. Paraphrasing Foucault, one might say that "les choses vécues" are not by any means "les mots dits": meaning is generated out of the restrictions of universality; truth travels half concealed and shows its significance only by being unreadable, thus soliciting and resisting the interpreter. It is in this light that Hurston might be described as "both autobiographically astute and strikingly brilliant."[19] Deceitful as she may be, she seems to emerge from the text "behind a plurality of masks or names,"[20] which leave a silent trace on her writing. There is something outside the text and wholly different from it but complementary to it that is crushed out by the power of discourse. If Hurston's language in *Dust Tracks* is disguised, it is because hiding is a dimension of its disclosure. Her "self-portraying" is not an event, but an appropriation of the event, she destructures the domination of time and opens a way of telling that is not controlled by past events.

The book, this "study in the art of subterfuge," a "less than candid *camouflage,*"[21] did not satisfy her. Her obvious fooling of the reader, herself, or both was only partially masked by her "innocence." The book's relevance, though, evidently lies not in its resemblance to reality but in the extent of its literary value. As an artist in control of her powers, Hurston appears,

---

18. Paul Ricoeur, *Le conflit des interprétations* (Paris: Seuil, 1969) p. 165.

19. See Houston A. Baker Jr., "There Is No More Beautiful Way," in Baker and Redmond, *Afro-American Literary Studies,* p. 140.

20. Jacques Derrida, *The Ear of the Other,* p. 7.

21. The first definition is by Robert Hemenway, "Introduction," in Hurston, *Dust Tracks on a Road,* pp. xi, xiv; the second is by Mary Helen Washington, quoted ibid. p. xxxviii.

at least at a cursory reading, untouched by the alienating effect that self-disclosure seems to bring to the black author's psyche. If her superficial "trace" can be easily erased, the inner track takes a deeper, hidden course. Her hybrid narrative says much more about its author than one might suspect, in spite of the tricks, or because of them. Hurston does not have a monolithic truth to offer the reader on a silver platter to be consummed decorously; her authenticity is attested to by her ambiguity itself.

Before her James Weldon Johnson, a friend and an inspirer of her art, conceived his fictional autobiography as a "way of rendering in fiction the range of sensibility and consciousness of a black character, his ambitions and dreams, his weakness and fears, his aspirations and anxieties."[22] Like him, Hurston introduces "a very complex ego afflicted by self-division, an imperfect character,"[23] with all its unflattering flaws, tortured more by artistic choices than by social pressure. Her artistic gifts lead the receiver/decoder through the subtlest nuances of pathos, lyricism, irony, irresistible relief, uncertainty, doubt. The imprint of her artistic self, *la trace de l'écriture,* runs parallel to her personal trace—elusive, hidden, inscrutable, flashing from the page only in glimpses or guesses, as on a dark track: "I have no intention of putting but so much in the *public ears*" (261).

The historical factuality on which *Dust Tracks* should be built reads from the very beginning like fiction, *histoire fictive.* (Paradoxically, Hurston would be more autobiographical in *Jonah's Gourd Vine* and *Their Eyes Were Watching God* than in *Dust Tracks.*) Her first entrance is a great performance, an act of ironic self-acknowledgment: "I saw no benefits in excusing my looks by claiming to be half Indian. In fact I boast that I am the only Negro in the United States whose grandfather on the mother's side was *not* an Indian chief" (235). Françoise Lionnet defines this self-portrait as "an anamnesis: not self-contemplation but an effort to be *the* voice of that occluded past, to fill the void of collective memory."[24] The mythic origin indispensable to any respectable hero is imbued with ironic aural/oral semantic categories. A doctor (who, we are told, is white) passing by the Hurstons' house, struck by the screams of the half-delivered baby, promptly intervenes and performs

---

22. Henry Louis Gates, Jr., "Introduction," in James Weldon Johnson, *The Autobiography of an Ex-Colored Man* (1927; rept. New York: Vintage 1989) p. xvi.

23. Ibid. p. xix.

24. Françoise Lionnet, "Autoethnography: The An-Archic Style of *Dust Tracks on a Road,*" in *Autobiographical Voices,* p. 118.

his maieutic duty, introducing Zora to this world: "He claimed later that he *heard* me spreading my lungs all over Orange County. He followed the *noise* and then he *saw*."(29; emphasis added). Events are edited through an endless true-false game of *inward-outward:* "*I* have memories *within* that came out of the material that went to make *me. Time and place* have had their *say . . . you* may *interpret* the incidents and directions of *my* life" (3; emphasis added). The stress is on I/you, place/time, memories/interpretation. But in Hurston's discourse the "I" is a mischievous "eye": almost nothing is true, historically speaking, about her place/time memories; self-revelation becomes an act of self-deception, an attempt to think of truth as originating from its opposite. Her place of birth, for instance, given as Eatonville, might just as well be some other town;[25] and records of time, far from being accurate, only confirm her "visions" and deepen the metaphysical dimension of her recollections (59).

The writer's alleged *mensonge* (women-*songe*) is ultimately not to be analyzed through empirical verification so that it might validate our guesses but needs to be looked at from a "logic of probability," as Ricoeur suggests.[26] Hurston's display of certainty combined with an almost as definite uncertainty makes the truth of incidents optional; whatever is related to prior thinking is nothing but interpretation. Her achievement, in fact, derives mainly from her need "to shake off the totalizing traps of historical determinism, in order to subvert the cultural commonplaces" that she abhors.[27]

When the narrator introduces herself as a threefold "I":—" I have been a Negro baby, a Negro girl and a Negro woman" (237)—she wants to insist, against all odds, that being a Negro is *not* that relevant. Contrasts—between inside/outside, hearing/saying, light/darkness, identity/difference—fill the pages: "There was stress and strain *inside* as well as *out*. Being black was not enough. Skins were no measure of what was *inside* people. None of the Race clichés meant anything any more. I began to laugh at both *white* and *black* who claimed special blessings on the basis of race." (235; emphasis added). "A feeling of *difference*" (59; emphasis added) affects her deeply because she

25. In his unpublished memoir "The Story of Zora Neale Hurston, Author," Edwin Osgood Grover tells us that "Zora was born in a small Georgia town, but her family moved to Eatonville, Florida, when she was just a child." Quoted in N. Y. Nathiri, ed., *Zora! Zora Neale Hurston: A Woman and Her Community* (Orlando, Fla.: Sentinel, 1991), p. 30.

26. Quoted in David E. Klemm, *The Hermeneutical Theory of Paul Ricoeur* (Lewisburg, Pa.: Bucknell University Press, 1983), p. 93.

27. Lionnet, *Autobiographical Voices,* p. 107.

is a woman. She foresees her destiny, doomed as she is to be lonely and disgraced. Hurston appears to refuse disclosure, but in fact she is utilizing it as a literary weapon to destructure the dominance of subject terms in the interpretation of human being. Self-revelation does not lead to an illumination of these memories. The author's "lurid data" (186) are woven into a texture of allurement and distraction in which differences are part of ideas and experiences; man is *released* only when his life appears questionable to the other, the reader.

The most tragic moment in the text occurs when Zora, nine years old, faces her dying mother, unable to satisfy her final request: "She looked at me, or so I felt, to *speak* for her. She depended on me for a *voice*" (58; emphasis added). Her track, that impervious personal (and artistic) path, becomes symbolically crucial. She starts to have strange visions: "I would hurry to catch a train and fail to find it when I arrived, then cross many *tracks* to board the train again" (58; emphasis added). The protagonist's estrangement deepens: "Always I stood apart *within*" (60; emphasis added). The train leads her toward an unknown destination. Her feelings of uncertainty underscore an otherwise pervasive feminine attitude: that women carry "a sense of their being somehow 'unfinished' human beings."[28] Hurston's pride would never let such an insinuation burst into the open, though we sense it hovering underneath.

When Barbara Johnson defines Hurston's books as statements about difference, she adds that in *Dust Tracks* "questions of difference and identity are always a function of a specific interlocutionary situation, and the answers, matter of strategy."[29] But in order to define who it is that Hurston wants to differ from, it is important to know whom she is addressing: Who is she talking to? Unlike the first African American autobiographers, she is *not* talking to whites. More probably she is questioning "the better-thinking Negro," the refined and cultivated Negro intellectuals, the "Race Champions, who wanted nothing to do with anything frankly Negroid, . . . who drew color lines within the race" (233). Hurston's text formulates the idea of identity as a process of separation from the group, a matter of self-differentiation which she seems at moments to be denying. The game between the individual and the collective "otherness" is well focused by Françoise Lionnet, who

28. Jouve, *White Woman Speaks with Forked Tongue*, . . . p. 11.

29. Barbara E. Johnson, "Thresholds of Difference," in *A World of Difference* (Baltimore: Johns Hopkins University Press, 1982), pp. 172–183.

defines the latter as a "silverless mirror, capable of absorbing the self into a duplicitous game."[30] Hurston cannot boast any "descendants of royal African blood" (202), but she can look at herself as one (among many) endowed with the community's special gift for inventing, forging, manipulating language: "The bookless may have difficulty in reading a newspaper, but when they get down to 'playing the dozens' they have no equal in America, and in the whole world." (217). "When you find a man chewing up the dictionary and spitting out language, that's My People" (298).

In *Dark Tracks* the biographical cuts through the "body" of writing, *le corps de l'écriture,* as it does through the body of the narrator. The end of Hurston's love story is imprinted with "tracks of blood" (260); her artistic way out passes through "the Hell dark door (308)" following "the urge to write" (168). The text as a body, with all its threatening implications of substitutive tropes, is displaced by the text as a machine, and the illusion of meaning is radically estranged by its performance. We find a fictional discourse on the one hand and an empirical experience on the other: their interaction makes it impossible to decipher either one. Self-portraying, as a special case of historical experience and knowledge, must be understood here as a coherence of meaning that wholly transcends the horizon of the individual's experience: a passage from psychology to hermeneutics. This would perhaps imply that the essence of Hurston's text is self-destructive, displaced by an infinite series of images, metaphors, and rhetorical reversals that keep it suspended between truth and its own negation. What is certain is that the biographical is limited in its development by its inextricable ties to the literary. Hurston's search for knowledge is her driving force, both *inward* and *outward,* toward intellectual action. The description of her (external) homely looks—"Here I was, with my face looking like it had been chopped out of a knot of pine wood with a hatchet on somebody's off day" (150)—is balanced by the mention of her internal drive toward superior, costly knowledge: "He went *down* the well of knowledge to drink and was *told* that the price of a drink from that fountain was an *eye.*" (53; emphasis added).

Signifying, the lying contest, the bright exercise of similes and metaphors—these are Hurston's weapon of feminine and literary power. Sometimes discourse is structured with a balance that tracks the course of musical

---

30. Lionnet, *Autobiographical Voices,* p. 115.

counterpoint: "Black men laughing, singing . . . black men from tree to tree
. . . black men scrambling up ladders" (180–181). Men bustle around Polk
County uttering jokes, songs, invective, whereas the woman performs *a solo:*
"I *heard* somebody, a woman's *voice* 'specifying' " (187; emphasis added).
The voice belongs to Big Sweet,—a real character and another projection
of Hurston's multiple faces—whose excellence positions her higher than any
man in town. Her dexterity stands for the writer's excellence at verbal assault,
the unique privilege of using poetry as a swinging blade.

Hurston's *lieux de mémoir(e)*, the lives that she wanted to write but could
not live, have, however, a configuration of remoteness, of distance, which
can be resolved only through the dimension of telling and hearing: "I put
*in* the words that the *sounds* put *into me* . . . People enjoyed the *telling* just
as much as I did the *hearing*" (197; emphasis added). Her delicate modern
sensibility, and her manifold voices meet but never become one. Zora Neale
Hurston the person stayed out of the text, far from her fictive alter ego,
silently completing her days in a male-dominated unmerciful world. But
feminine irony has a great, undetectable power: Woman—as Derrida says—
can always "burst out laughing at the last moment. She knows, in sorrow
and in death, how to pervert the power that represses her."[31]

Hurston's book may be seen as a powerful gesture of protection and in-
ternment[32] and also as a record of conceptual repression, an open beach
marked by the progressive erasing of a trace.[33] "Le sang blanc de l'écriture"[34]
finally covers her voice, allowing textuality to go beyond the roots of life
and transgress even its own explicit statements.

31. Jacques Derrida, *Glas, Que reste-t-il du savoir absolu?* (Paris: Denoel/Gonthier, 1981), 2:
259–260. See also Jacques Derrida, *Deconstruction and Criticism* (New York: Seabury, 1979), p. 149.

32. Or in Big Sweet's words, "knocking the right hat off the wrong head" (*DT* 189).

33. "L'écriture semble en effet représenter la parole et en meme temps s'effacer devant elle."
Jacques Derrida, *Positions* (Paris: Editions de Minuit, 1972) p. 36.

34. Edmond Jabès, "Lettre à Jacques Derrida," *L'arc,* 54 (1973):62.

*Robert Gooding-Williams*

# Black Cupids, White Desires: Reading the Recoding of Racial Difference in *Casablanca*

W hat can be said about the representation of racial difference in *Casablanca*? Some fifty years after the film's initial release the standard answer to this question seems to be that *Casablanca* marks a defining moment in the history of Hollywood's representation of black characters. Thomas Cripps, for example, writes that "of all the films following the *Gone with the Wind* thaw in racial depictions *Casablanca* (1942) reached the widest audience and probably had the strongest impact within the limits of liberal faith."[1] For Cripps the essence of *Casablanca*'s racial liberalism was its representation of Sam as Rick's friend and equal, and its equally important repudiation of traditional racial stereotypes. More recently Aljean Harmetz has written that the "role of Sam in *Casablanca* was one of a handful in the early 1940s in which an African-American was allowed some dignity."[2] "For a comparison with the roles black actors were usually given," Harmetz claims, "one has only to look at Wilson's previous film, *Night in New Orleans* . . . In that film, Wilson played Shadrack Jones, described by *The New York Times* as the 'inevitable colored servant who makes sounds of appropriate comic alarm when the lights go out or a body suddenly splashes off a fogbound wharf.' "[3] For both Cripps and Harmetz, *Casablanca* belongs to a moment

---

1. Thomas Cripps, *Slow Fade to Black* (New York: Oxford University Press, 1977), p. 370.
2. Aljean Harmetz, *Round Up the Usual Suspects* (New York: Hyperion, 1992), p. 141.
3. Ibid. Harlan Lebo expresses a similar point of view in his *Casablanca: Behind the Scenes* (New York: Simon and Schuster, 1992), pp. 86–88. He writes: "Casting Sam, a black character playing an equal to a white leading player, was an especially delicate matter for [Hal] Wallis. Hollywood's greatest shame for the first fifty years of film production was its treatment of black characters, virtually without exception, as inferior to whites. Black actors were almost never cast in everyday roles, and instead

in the history of Hollywood film in which demeaning depictions of blacks began to give way to representations that, because they did not explicitly mock and insult black characters, can be said to have recognized in blacks a human worth on a par with that of whites.

In this essay I question Cripps's and Harmetz's conception of the representation of race in *Casablanca*. In particular I challenge their suggestion that, in breaking with established norms of racial representation, *Casablanca* affirms black dignity and equality at the expense of received racial stereotypes. The essence of my argument is that *Casablanca,* despite its apparent liberalism, *recodes* racial difference. More exactly, in this film racial difference is not set aside so much as reinterpreted. What Cripps and Harmetz see as a movement *away* from black stereotypes and *toward* a vision of equal black dignity I read as a revaluing of racial difference that reinscribes the assertion of white superiority. In *Casablanca,* Hollywood's "liberal" turn away from racial stereotypes involves a complicated reassertion of racial subordination.

Sam's character in *Casablanca,* though not that of a simpleton or a comic fool, has a functional value the significance of which lends it an innocence according with the view that *Casablanca* is "racially liberal." Cast as the mythical Cupid, Sam is a figure whose primary role is to facilitate the romantic relationship between the film's white male and white female protagonists, Rick and Ilsa. But why, we might ask, should the performance of this function seem to dignify Sam? And what is the difference between the "dignity" Sam acquires in his role as a black Cupid and the "indignity" of economic exploitation that, *Casablanca* hints, he is bound to suffer for the sake of America's fight against Nazism?[4]

## Love Triangles and Outlaw Heroes

My reading of *Casablanca* draws its inspiration from two treatments of the film I have found provocative. The first of these is Umberto Eco's "Casa-

---

were relegated to wide-eyed servants, shuffling shoeshiners, or criminals . . . In spite of the dismal track record for black characters in films produced by all the major Hollywood studios—Warner Bros. included—no one involved in Casablanca ever questioned or attempted to revise the plot point that Sam, while an employee of Rick, was also his closest friend and confidante . . . As a result of the studio's willingness to let Wilson play Sam's character as originally written, the actor portrayed one of the few nondegrading black roles in any film (other than all-black productions) made in Hollywood to that time."

4. Casablanca is just one of many Hollywood films in which "black Cupids" appear. Others include *The Man Who Shot Liberty Valance, Something Wild,* and, more recently, *Ghost.*

blanca: Cult Movies and Intertextual Collage"; the second is Robert Ray's interpretation of *Casablanca* in *A Certain Tendency of the Hollywood Cinema.*[5]

Of particular interest in Eco's essay is his emphasis on the Rick-Ilsa-Victor love triangle. Eco is right, of course, to stress the significance of this "unhappy" trio. Yet he makes no note of the connections between the Rick-Ilsa-Victor triangle and at least three other erotically charged "triangles" that shape the plot of the film. Consider, for example, the threesome consisting of Rick, Renault, and Strasser; here Renault is in the middle, especially in the film's early scenes, in which we see that, though he is drawn to the romantic hero, antifascist, and sentimentalist he senses in Rick, his ultimate allegiance is to the power personified by Major Strasser. Consider as well the trio consisting of Ferrari, Sam, and Rick. In this triangle Sam occupies the middle position of an employee who, because of his heartfelt loyalty to Rick, refuses Ferrari's seductive bid to double his wages. (Despite his claim that he neither buys nor sells human beings, Rick has, by the end of the film, "sold" Sam to Ferrari!) Consider, finally, the triangle consisting of Rick, Ilsa, and Sam. As I have already suggested, Sam in this trio appears primarily in the role of a black Cupid who mediates Rick and Ilsa's romantic love.

Although the primary focus of this essay is the Rick-Sam-Ilsa triangle, a complete reading of *Casablanca* would attend to all of the trios I have mentioned, as well as to the fact that by the end of the film these four trios have been dramatically resolved into three pairs or couples (Victor-Ilsa, Rick-Renault, and Ferrari-Sam).[6] It is inevitable, moreover, that my discussion of the Rick-Sam-Ilsa triangle refers, at least implicitly, to *Casablanca*'s three other threesomes, since each is intelligible only in relation to the others. Still, my decision to emphasize the Rick-Sam-Ilsa triangle is a deliberate one, intended to complicate current discussions of the representation of "love triangles" that foreground gender and sexuality but not race.[7]

My reading of the Rick-Sam-Ilsa triangle takes as its point of departure Robert Ray's claim that *Casablanca* "reincarnated in Rick and Laszlo the

5. Eco's essay appears in his *Travels in Hyperreality* (New York: Harcourt Brace Jovanovich, 1983). The full citation for Ray's book is *A Certain Tendency of the Hollywood Cinema, 1930–1980* (Princeton: Princeton University Press, 1985).

6. Rick kills Strasser and ends up with Renault. He also sends Ilsa off with Victor, and arranges for Sam to work for Ferrari.

7. See, for example, Eve Sedgwick, *Between Men* (New York: Columbia University Press, 1985).

outlaw hero–official hero opposition," an opposition that, he contends, appears repeatedly in the films of Hollywood's classic period. According to Ray, the outlaw hero distrusts civilization, lives "outside" the law, and obeys a private code of justice and morality. The official hero, by contrast, firmly adheres to the law and, unlike the outlaw hero, wholeheartedly embraces the norms of civilization, especially marriage. In *Casablanca* Rick is the quintessential outlaw hero—an unmarried Robin Hood, "operating outside of a corrupt legal system in the name of some higher, private notion of justice . . . Like Robin . . . Rick robbed from the rich to give to the poor, manipulating his own roulette wheel to provide refugees with money for exit visas." Victor, however, is married, and, like the typical official hero, insists on the sanctity of legal rules. "The movie's basic premise," writes Ray, "was the neutrality of the 'frontier' town Casablanca, an abstract principle that Laszlo repeatedly asserted. 'You won't dare to interfere with me here,' he warned Strasser."[8]

Ray's characterization of Rick as an outlaw hero is useful for my purposes because it helps bring into view the specificity of Sam's significance as a Cupid figure who mediates Rick and Ilsa's love. Developing Ray's reading in a direction at which he only hints, in what follows I attempt to elucidate the connection between Sam's role as a Cupid figure and Rick's status as an outlaw. My discussion begins with a consideration of *Casablanca*'s "Paris flashback" sequence.

## Lovers' Desires, Cupid's Song

Drunk in his saloon and awaiting Ilsa's appearance, Rick insists that Sam play "As Time Goes By." "You played it for her and you can play it for me," says Rick. "If she can stand it, I can. Play it!" As Sam begins to play "As Time Goes By," the camera closes in on Rick, and the scene dissolves. The next image we see is Paris in the spring. A shot of the Arc de Triomphe is followed by one of Rick and Ilsa driving along the boulevard.

Sam's singing introduces the Paris flashback. When, during the flashback, we first see Sam with Rick and Ilsa, Sam is playing "As Time Goes By" while Rick displays the same detachment and romantic gallantry we saw him show when he and Ilsa were alone in his Paris apartment (the screenplay tells us

---

8. See Ray, *A Certain Tendency*, pp. 89, 101–102.

that "his manner is wry, but not the bitter wryness we have seen in Casablanca"). Despite the advent of the Nazis, the private sphere of Rick's life seems to him harmonious and secure as he anticipates marrying Ilsa upon arriving in Marseilles or, he jokes, while they are still traveling on the train to Marseilles. But Ilsa has discovered that Victor is alive, that he has escaped from a concentration camp, and so she does not show up at the train station. Left to depart without her, Rick feels betrayed and, we later discover, does not permit Sam to sing "As Time Goes By" anymore. Catching him unawares, the play of political events has drawn Ilsa away from Rick, thus spoiling his happiness.

In Rick's nostalgic vision the world of the Paris flashback is a picture of carefree romantic desire and of the places—the boulevard, his apartment and Ilsa's, the dance hall, an excursion boat on the Seine, a café, and so on—he associates with that desire.[9] Sam appears in this world simply in order to sing and bear witness to Rick and Ilsa's romance; his raison d'être here is to envision their romance as possessing an immutable value tying it to the "fundamental" things (moonlight and love song; hearts filled with passion, jealousy, and hate; woman needing man, man needing his mate) which apply as time goes by. Cheerful and devoted servant that he is, Sam serves Rick and Ilsa by singing a song that represents their love as possessing a self-sufficient and timeless perfection, eternally and everywhere "the same old story." His narrative function in *Casablanca* is, in essence, to reify Rick and Ilsa's love, to make it into an object that each of them can and does invoke to conjure up feelings of romance when one of them is absent.[10] Playing the piano and singing "As Time Goes By," Sam labors on the "raw" material of heterosexual desire, transforming it into a commodity fetish that each of the white lovers appropriates as a sort of erotic surplus value, a value that he creates and they consume.[11]

Sam is a black Cupid, a black producer of erotic value. Cast in a role that

9. For an interesting discussion of the relationship between nostalgia and place, see Edward Casey, "The World of Nostalgia," *Man and World*, 20 (1987): 361–368.

10. Rick has Sam serve this function when, just before the "Paris flashback," he asks him to sing "As Time Goes By." Ilsa does the same, during her first conversation with Sam at Rick's. "Play it once Sam," she says, "for old time's sake."

11. Here, of course, I mean to invoke Marx's famous analysis of commodity fetishism in the first volume of *Das Kapital*. It is worth noting, moreover, that the line "Play it again, Sam," which itself has become something of a fetish in the minds of many *Casablanca* admirers (for example, Woody Allen), never actually occurs in the film.

ties him essentially to heterosexual desire, he is in part the personification of a familiar racial stereotype which equates blackness with sexuality.[12] We must be careful, however, since Sam's tie to sexuality is primarily a tie to a sexuality that belongs to others. Insofar as he sings the song of Rick and Ilsa's love, Sam appears as an asexual and desireless subject, not as a black epitome of sexual potency. Servant Sam, one might say, produces and carries the baggage of Rick and Ilsa's desire yet displays no desire of his own while he does his work. Still, the shadow of the stereotype equating blackness with sexuality haunts Sam's presence, if only because that presence helps mark the difference between Rick's outlaw hero and Victor's official hero. By providing Rick with a black servant who devotedly sings his master's love song, *Casablanca* invests Rick with a romantic allure that the civilized Victor lacks, thus representing him as the inevitable and proper object of Ilsa's desire. Echoing the traditional stereotype, Sam's presence connotes Rick's access to a charismatic sexuality—an implicitly black sexuality—that no official hero could possibly possess.[13]

At only one juncture in the development of *Casablanca*'s plot are we, the film's audience, permitted to imagine that Sam could possibly become the agent of his own desire. The scene I have in mind transpires just a few moments before the Paris flashback sequence. With Sam looking compassionately at Rick, who is getting more and more drunk as he awaits Ilsa's arrival, this exchange occurs:

*Sam:*   Boss, let's get out of here.

*Rick:*   No, sir. I'm waiting for a lady.

*Sam:*   Please, boss, let's go. Ain't nothin' but trouble for you here.

*Rick:*   She's coming back. I know she's coming back.

*Sam:*   We'll take the car and drive all night. We'll get drunk. We'll go fishing and stay away until she's gone.

*Rick:*   Shut up and go home, will you?

*Sam:*   No, sir. I'm staying right here.

12. See, for example, Frantz Fanon's discussion in Chapter 6 of *Black Skin, White Masks*, trans. Charles Markmann (New York: Grove Press, 1967). See also Robert Miles, *Racism* (New York: Routledge, 1989), pp. 27–28.

13. Cameron Bailey addresses related issues in his "Nigger/Lover: The Thin Sheen of Race in 'Something Wild,'" *Screen*, 29 (August 1988):28–40.

Worried that Ilsa is no good for Rick, Sam, for a brief moment, redefines the "love triangle" which he, Rick, and Ilsa compose. He appears suddenly not as the muse singing of Rick and Ilsa's romance but as providing Rick with a promising alternative to confronting his lover. Sam, it seems, would take Rick away from Ilsa and from the pain she has caused him. Together, he suggests, he and his boss should steal away into the night and then lose themselves in the revelry of drunken driving and fishing. Posing more as Dionysus than as Cupid, Sam here appears as Ilsa's rival, a potential carouser who would seduce Rick to exchange the pain and "trouble" that Rick's "lady" is bound to bring him for the nighttime delights of a romp with his servant. The homoerotic connotations of this scenario strike a familiar chord, as they immediately recall the canonical story of Huck and Jim on the lam, running away from women and from civilization, and enjoying on their raft what Leslie Fiedler describes as a "sacred marriage of males."[14] Rick, as we know, resists Sam's seduction, and only a few moments later demands that Sam revert to the role of a black Cupid, insisting, "Play it!" Refusing to become the object of Sam's desire, Rick will nostalgically consume his own desire, which Sam has made into a song.

Rick's nostalgia is for a time of heterosexual bliss on the margins of civilization. Refusing Sam's temptation to lose himself in a night of drunkenness, Rick yet longs for a time when, with Sam at his side, envisioning Rick's love as timelessly perfect, he personified a romantic charisma that made him irresistible to Ilsa. This time, a time gone by, Rick's nostalgia paints as possessing a prelapsarian flawlessness which historical time, the time of human history and politics, can only ruin. Read allegorically—and there is much in *Casablanca* that invites us to read it this way—this Edenic time is the idealized time of America's prewar isolationism, a time when, we are asked to believe, America had excepted itself from the trials and traumas of the European civilization which Victor Laszlo represents. Part of what distinguished prewar America, or so *Casablanca* suggests, was its special and "innocent" way of exploiting blacks; the allure that Rick acquires through his association with Sam is, allegorically, the allure that America acquires through the presence of erotically productive and entertaining black folk. It is essential, of course, that blacks' connection to eros remain subject to white

14. Leslie Fiedler, "Come Back to the Raft Ag'in, Huck Honey," in *An End to Innocence* (Boston: Beacon Press, 1955), p. 148. Ray (*A Certain Tendency*, pp. 107–108) and Harmetz (*Round Up the Usual Suspects*, p. 350) also discuss the connection between *Casablanca* and *Huck Finn*.

control, which is simply another way of saying that in Rick's Eden, though Sam can be a Cupid who labors on the eros of others, he is forbidden to personify a Dionysus who enacts an erotic desire for Rick that perhaps Rick could never master. Here the nostalgia of the outlaw is precise: picturing a happiness on the margins of civilization, Rick will never go so far as to imagine himself lost and helpless in the heart of a Dionysian darkness.[15]

### Ilsa's Plot, Rick's Revenge

It is Ilsa, of course, who bursts the bubble. After she departs, Rick becomes a bitter man. His Eden destroyed, he takes refuge in his isolation, keeping his distance from the political realities about him and insisting adamantly that he won't "stick [his] neck out for nobody." Ilsa gets it right when, having come to Rick's café in order to force him to give her the letters of transit, she tells him, "You want to feel sorry for yourself, don't you? With so much at stake, all you can think of its your own feeling. One woman has hurt you, and you take revenge on the whole world."

The sequence of action following Ilsa's remark is *Casablanca*'s most consequential turning point. When Ilsa left Rick, she caused him pain by acting out of loyalty to Victor. In effect, she initiated a story line that was at odds with Rick's intention that he, she, and Sam run away together. When Ilsa comes to Rick's café looking for the letters of transit, she takes the initiative again, once more attempting to force the story in a direction opposed to Rick's will. After scolding Rick for feeling sorry for himself, she reveals a revolver and says that she will shoot him if he does not hand over the letters. Rick, ready now to resign everything, tells Ilsa, "Go ahead and shoot. You'll be doing me a favor." He then walks toward her until, as he reaches her, she drops her right hand, which is holding the revolver. According to the screenplay Ilsa is "hysterical," and now says to Rick, "Richard, I tried to

---

15. The ambivalence implicit in the white desire to have access to while still controlling "black sexuality" has deep roots in American popular culture. A useful point of departure for thinking about this issue is David Roediger, *The Wages of Whiteness: Race and the Making of the American Working Class* (New York: Verso, 1991). Rick's homophobia, which is perhaps implicit in his resistance to Sam's seduction, appears explicitly when he rebuffs Sasha, the Russian bartender, who kisses Rick after the latter has helped one of Renault's potential victims win at the gambling table. Carl Schaefer, the head of Warner Bros. Research Department, insisted that the representation of Rick's aversion to Sasha's kiss be handled delicately—for the sake of international relations! According to Harlan Lebo, "In the interest of maintaining friendly U.S.-Soviet relations, Schaefer suggested that when Rick is kissed by his Russian bartender Sasha, Bogart's rebuff be done 'in good humor.' " See Lebo, *Casablanca*, p. 115.

stay away. I thought I would never see you again, that you were out of my life. The day you left Paris, if you knew what I went through! If you knew how much I loved you, how much I still love you." Rick at this point takes Ilsa in his arms and kisses her passionately. Just a few moments later, after this most romantic crescendo, Ilsa tells Rick why she kept her marriage a secret and why she went back to Victor without saying anything to Rick. Listening attentively, Rick responds that her story is "still a story without an ending." But now that she has given up her will to enact a storyline that is at odds with Rick's will, Ilsa replies, "You'll have to do the thinking for both of us, for all of us." With Ilsa's head cradled in his arms, Rick confidently replies, "All right, I will."

The pivotal scene which I have described here conflates *Casablanca*'s most compelling representation of expressed heterosexual desire with Ilsa's decision to submit to Rick's will. This decision is in essence a decision to submit to Rick's narrative authority. Relinquishing her effort to plot a course of action that will free Victor from the clutches of the Nazis, Ilsa cedes to Rick the right and the power to complete their story, which is "still . . . without an ending": "You'll have to do the thinking for both of us." As we well know, the plot that Rick invents—which involves sending Ilsa off with Victor—is no less a surprise to Ilsa than it is to anyone seeing *Casablanca* for the first time. Donning the air of self-sacrificial nobility ("I'm no good at being noble, Ilsa"), Rick avenges the pain Ilsa has caused him by insisting that she suffer the pain of renunciation, even after she has told him that she cannot run away from him again. (Rick, I am suggesting, continues to enact the spirit of revenge, what Nietzsche called "the will's ill will against time," and what is here an ill will against historical time, even after he has handed over the letters of transit.) By subjecting Ilsa to the painful consequences of the plot he produces, Rick in effect punishes her, doing to her what she did to him. Where previously Ilsa's assertion of her will caused Rick to suffer, now Rick's assertion of his will causes Ilsa to suffer. Either way, of course, Rick and, allegorically, America suffer the destruction of an isolated paradise. Still, it matters to Rick that it is he, not Ilsa, who charts the way out of Eden. If America is to enter the war and thus embrace the drama of European history and politics, then America must enjoy an autonomy which *Casablanca* represents simultaneously as the patriarchal triumph of a white man's will and the passionate expression of white heterosexual desire.[16]

16. See Doris Sommer, *Foundational Fictions: The National Romances of Latin America* (Berkeley: University of California Press, 1991), pp. 30–51, for a significant theoretical discussion of the ways

## Rick's Plot, Sam's Fate

Rick's plot, the plot that brings *Casablanca* to an end, has consequences for Sam and not solely for Ilsa. Just as, according to Rick, Ilsa will become a part of Victor's work, Sam will become a part of Ferrari's work.[17] In his role as a black producer of erotic value, Sam becomes functionally obsolete just at the point when Rick decides to send Ilsa away with Victor. Sam no longer needs to be available to sing the song that expresses Rick's most passionate heterosexual desire because Rick has deliberately renounced that desire, once and for all (something he has not done before Ilsa appears in Casablanca, even though he has forbidden Sam to play "As Time Goes By").[18]

Working for Ferrari, Sam will be a profit-making economic asset. Viewers of *Casablanca* tend to see Sam's change of employers as a loss for him, in part because the film represents this change as echoing one of America's persistent myths about the impact of the Civil War on the lives of southern blacks. In comparison to the suave and refined Rick, whose relation to his servant seems always genteel—as, according to the myth, the relations between antebellum masters and their slaves were supposed to have been—the disreputable Ferrari, Casablanca's leading black marketeer, reminds us of a carpetbagger. Sam is worse off than before, this post–Civil War construction suggests, because he is now prey to the economic exploitation of a capitalist vulture who will extend to him none of the kindness and consideration shown him by his former master.

But what distinguishes the "indignity" of sheer economic exploitation from the "dignity" that, as Cripps and Harmetz suggest, Sam possesses in his relation to Rick? If the presence of this "dignity" seems self-evident, if it seems to connote some sort of "racial liberalism," it is because Sam's role as a Cupid figure is tied to a vision of a prelapsarian American paradise—before the Second World War? before the Civil War?—that remained somehow untouched by the vicissitudes of human history. But what is Sam's role

---

in which erotic plots and political plots can function as allegories of each other. For a hilarious and heavily sexualized reading/reimagining of the scene I have been discussing, see Robert Coover, *A Night at the Movies* (New York: Linden Press, 1987), pp. 156–187.

17. Rick tells Ilsa that she is a part of Victor's work in the famous airport scene which concludes *Casablanca.* Earlier in the movie Rick makes arrangements to have Sam go to work for Ferrari.

18. Rick's renunciation of heterosexual desire need not be read as a renunciation of desire per se. In fact, much has been made of the homoerotic connotations suggested by the beginning of his "beautiful friendship" with Renault. From the perspective of the reading I have sketched in this essay, it is significant that, after renouncing Ilsa, Rick chooses to run off with Renault and not with Sam.

within that vision? It is in essence to assist the flow of others' desires, to function as the unobstructive medium through which these desires achieve romantic expression. In paradise, then, Sam is exploited, if not as an economic tool then as an erotic one. Even if he lacks dignity in the one capacity, why maintain that he possesses it in the other?

To be sure, Sam never appears as the stereotypical simpleton or fool. Still, he seems to lack a well-defined personality. *Casablanca* thus recodes racial difference not by creating a new kind of personality stereotype but by depriving its only black character of a distinctive personality. Acting essentially as a conduit for the play of white erotic energies, Sam emblematizes not a racially progressive recognition that blacks are complicated and dignified individuals, irreducible to racial stereotypes, but the assimilation of black characters to abstract mythical functions.

*M. Lynn Weiss*

# *Para Usted:* Richard Wright's *Pagan Spain*

The only thing that stood between me and Spain, that beckoned as much as it repelled, was a state of mind.

—RICHARD WRIGHT

In the summer of 1946 Richard Wright went to visit the dying Gertrude Stein. During their conversation she suggested, "Dick you ought to go to Spain . . . You'll see the past there, you'll see what the Western world is made of."[1] Several years later Alva and Gunnar Myrdal made the same proposal, and in August 1954 Wright drove over the French border into the Past. Since its publication in 1957, *Pagan Spain* has provoked confusion. Although contemporary critics commented on the subjective quality of the narrative, most read it as a piece of travel journalism. Even when they did not agree with Wright's Freudian and Marxist analyses, they praised his skill as a writer.[2] But of the many studies of Wright's work since his death in 1960, few have given *Pagan Spain* more than a passing glance; it simply did not fit expectations for a book by Richard Wright.[3]

1. Richard Wright, *Pagan Spain* (New York: Harper's, 1957), p. 1; subsequent references are cited by page in the text.

2. Herbert Matthews, in "How It Seemed to Him," *New York Times Book Review,* February 24, 1957, focused on the subjective qualities of the text. Wright, he said, was a "Negro with a deep sense of race consciousness and a former communist which explains the type of book that he has done in *Pagan Spain*" (7). The black critic Roi Ottley echoed the sentiments of a number of Wright's critics when he reviewed *Pagan Spain*. Ottley did not like the book and urged Wright to return to the States and write about civil rights. See "He Should Stick to Fiction," *Chicago Sun Tribune Magazine of Books,* March 3, 1957, p. 10. In *Books on Trial,* 16 (March 1957):307, Eva Ross criticized Wright's anti-Catholic bias. And in *Current History,* 32 (April 1957):240, the reviewer conceded that *Pagan Spain* was well written but maintained that it was far too subjective to be read as a factual account of contemporary Spain.

3. In *The Ordeal of a Native Son* (Garden City, N. Y.: Doubleday, 1980) Addison Gayle remarks that Wright's reactions to Spain were extremely personal (250). Margaret Walker argues that Wright's Marxist training was responsible for the anti-Catholic bias in *Pagan Spain*. See *Richard Wright Daemonic Genius: A Portrait of the Man and a Critical Look at His Work* (New York: Warner Books, 1988), pp. 249–258.

Wright's journey to Spain in 1956 was an effort to understand the origins of Western culture, particularly in the context of confrontation. In Spain he saw the struggle between modernity and tradition, between the sacred and the secular, and the vestiges of the struggle between the Christian and the Moor (that is, between white and black). For Wright this was a familiar theme. And though many critics missed this point, Wright had made it ex-ɔlicit on the dust jacket of the British edition:

> I'm a self-conscious Negro and I'm the product of Western culture, living with white people far from my racial origins. I began to ask myself how did I get there, who brought me there and why? What kind of people were they who dared the oceans to get slaves and sell them? It was in Spain, where tradition has not changed, that I found my answers . . . But my going to Spain had yet another and deeper meaning, a meaning that I did not know until I got there. I found myself a man freed of traditions, uprooted from my racial heritage, looking at white people who were still caught in their age-old traditions. The white man had unknowingly freed me of my traditional, backward culture, but had clung fiercely to his own. This is the point of *Pagan Spain*.[4]

*Pagan Spain* explores life under a repressive regime. But its larger ambition is to place the history of African Americans (and particularly Wright's own history) in a global context.

Wright's interest in Spain did not begin in 1946. As early as 1937 Wright, then a reporter for the Harlem bureau of the New York *Daily Worker,* had published a series of articles on the Spanish civil war. Wright's task was to describe this war in the terms of the Communist party and praise the efforts of the black American soldiers (of the Abraham Lincoln Brigade) who fought alongside the Loyalists against the Fascists.[5] In one article Wright interviewed a young black soldier from Brooklyn whose career in the Loyalist army sym-bolized the achievement that still eluded blacks in the American armed forces: in less than a year Walter Garland had risen to the rank of lieutenant in charge of an American training base in Spain.[6] Wright's enthusiasm for

---

4. Quoted in *Richard Wright Reader,* ed. Michel Fabre and Ellen Wright, (New York: Harper and Row, 1978), p. 110.

5. New interest in this subject is evident in the publication of James Yates, *From Mississippi to Madrid: Memoir of a Black American in the Abe Lincoln Brigade* (Seattle: Open Hand Publishing, 1989).

6. Richard Wright, "Walter Garland Tells What Spain's Fight against Fascism Means to the Negro People," *Daily Worker,* November 29, 1937, p. 2.

the Loyalists, and his pride in the Afro-Americans who fought for their cause, is everywhere apparent in these articles.[7] It follows that nineteen years later *Pagan Spain* would begin with this confession: "The fate of Spain had hurt me, had haunted me; I had never been able to stifle a hunger to understand what had happened there and why" (2).[8]

Another important factor in Wright's decision to write a book on Spain suggests how expatriation had expanded his perspective on the familiar theme of racial intolerance. By 1954 he had lived in France for eight years, and in addition to a great number of articles, book reviews, and essays, had completed two novels, *The Outsider* (1953) and *Savage Holiday* (1954), and a work of nonfiction, *Black Power* (1954). Although many reviewers approved of *Black Power,* none of these works was awarded the acclaim given *Native Son* or *Black Boy.* The critical consensus held that the expatriate Wright was too out of touch with the reality of contemporary America to make a valid assessment of it. Wright's literary agent, Paul Reynolds, Jr., echoed this sentiment in a letter in May 1954 in which he suggested that Wright work on a novel set during the Civil War or one on the Afro-American community in Paris. But Wright was not interested in returning to fiction just yet. In his reply to Reynolds he admitted: "I'm inclined to feel that I ought not to work right now on a novel. This does not mean that I'm giving up writing fiction, but, really, there are so many more exciting and interesting things happening now in the world that I feel sort of dodging them if I don't say something about them."[9] As this excerpt suggests, Wright was bored by the prospect of writing yet another version of *Native Son* or *Black Boy.* His desire to explore the "exciting and interesting things happening now in the world" was in part a resistance to audience expectations of the "Negro" writer. For this resistance critics both black and white suggested that the expatriate was out of touch with the source of his creativity.[10] Still,

7. The other articles on this subject by Richard Wright in the *New York Daily Worker* are: "Two American Negroes in Key Posts of Spain's Loyalist Forces," September 19, 1937, p. 2; "Harlem Spanish Women Come Out of the Kitchen," September 20, 1937, p. 5; "Bates Tells of Spain's Fight for Strong Republican Army," October 1, 1937, p. 2; "From Spain's Loyalist Trenches Larry Foy Asks about Harlem's Fight against Fascism in U.S.," December 23, 1937, p. 2.

8. In the manuscript the first part of this sentence reads, "The fate of Spain hurt me, haunted me," Beinecke Library, Yale University MS. 374, fol. 1.

9. Quoted in Michel Fabre, *The Unfinished Quest of Richard Wright,* trans. Isabel Barzun (New York: Morrow, 1973), p. 407.

10. See, specifically, Ottley, "He Should Stick to Fiction," 10; and Matthews, "How It Seemed to Him," 7.

Paul Reynolds obtained a verbal agreement from Harper's for Wright's book on Spain. And with the $500 advance from his publisher, Wright set off on the first part of his journey to the Iberian peninsula.[11]

In all Wright made three trips to Spain: from August 15 to September 10, 1954; from November 8 to December 17, 1954; and then from February 20 to early April 1955. He visited every major city, monument, and cathedral. He went to bullfights, attended religious festivals, saw Gypsies and flamenco dancers. He spoke to a barber in Catalonia, an American matador, wealthy aristocrats, and desperately poor prostitutes. He met Catholics, Protestants, and Jews, Republicans and Loyalists, native-born Spaniards and immigrants. For part of the journey he drove or hired a driver; once or twice he took the train. He stayed in pensions and in cheap and average hotels, and once he rented a room with a family. He took photographs and notes and during the entire journey traveled over five thousand miles. The manuscript, completed in March 1957, ran 537 pages and included several photographs.[12] Wright was determined to show that his research was thorough.

As Michel Fabre has observed, Wright began with a hypothesis he then set out to prove.[13] Throughout the study he invoked a number of authorities—Freud, Marx, his own experience of oppression, two critically acclaimed histories of Spain, and personal interviews. Other forms of documentation included a newspaper clipping from the European edition of the *International Herald Tribune* which supported his own observations of prostitution in Spain (189).[14] Wright also interviewed a lawyer who provided

11. Fabre, *The Unfinished Quest,* p. 409.

12. Ibid., pp. 407–413.

13. Ibid., p. 411.

14. Wright had purchased from a group of prostitutes a number of letters, written to them by American sailors. Several of the letters were from black sailors. Wright had included some of these letters in the typescript of *Pagan Spain,* but they were excluded from the Harper edition of the text. In the French translation, *Espagne païenne* (Paris: Buchet-Chastel-Correa, 1958), pp. 36–49, all of the letters appear exactly as in the typescript. The exclusion of the letters from the American edition changes the focus of the section in which they appear. To obtain the letters Wright had asked his guide to tell the women that he wanted to purchase their love letters. Wright's earlier questions had made several of them suspect that he was a police officer. As the women were desperately poor and Wright was unwilling to buy anything but the letters, he soon owned a "thick batch," which he carefully tucked inside the other valuable piece of documentation, *Formación política.* Most significant is the difference between the Wright of the typescript and the Wright of the Harper text. In the typescript he is an aggressive detective; in the American text he is little more than a perceptive observer. See Beinecke Library, Yale University MS. 764, fols. 12–13. Michel Fabre argues that Wright admired and sought to imitate Zola, who copied letters of prostitutes for his novel *Nana.* By purchasing letters from the prostitutes in Barcelona and later in Paris for his book on American GIs in

him with statistics on the cost of living and the level of unemployment (219–221). In addition, Wright visited the UNESCO library in Geneva to obtain an economic profile of Spanish life between his first and second visits.[15] During his first trip to Spain he was given a text issued by the Spanish government, *Formacion política: lecciones para las flechas,* parts of which he included in *Pagan Spain.*[16] He consulted Salvador de Madariaga's *Spain.* Interestingly, Fabre notes that Wright did considerably less research for this journey than he had for his trip to the Gold Coast. After three weeks in Spain and very little reading on the subject, Wright, in a letter to Reynolds, stated briefly that he would show "how a non-western people living in Europe work out their life problems."[17]

The most important historical text Wright refers to in *Pagan Spain* is Americo Castro's *Structure of Spanish History.*[18] Castro was particularly interested in the Jewish and Muslim influences on the formation of the Spanish character. The heterogeneous quality of Spanish culture, with obvious resonances for American culture, fascinated Wright. This was evident from his title, in which the "pagan" refers to the not purely Christian elements of Spanish culture.[19] When he sent Reynolds the manuscript, he included an engraving of Santiago de Compostella overcoming a Moor.[20] This image illustrates the essence of Castro's argument: the Spanish character was developed through an extended and usually violent encounter of the Christian with the "Other." And that the "Other" was black was especially important to Wright.

---

France, Wright obviously had Zola's example in mind. Michel Fabre, "Beyond Naturalism," in *Richard Wright,* ed. Harold Bloom (New York: Chelsea House, 1987), p. 47.

15. Fabre, *The Unfinished Quest,* p. 411. Despite Wright's attention to minute detail, he was wrong on two occasions: he confused the French town of Perthus with the Spanish town of La Junquera, and he put El Greco in the Middle Ages. See Wright, *Pagan Spain,* pp. 2 and 230.

16. One of his critics' chief complaints about *Pagan Spain* was that Wright included more than twenty-five pages of *Formación política.* Although Wright no doubt wanted to illustrate the thoroughness of the government's indoctrination, far fewer than twenty-five pages would have sufficed. Wright's need to document his observations is, in this instance, clearly somewhat obsessive.

17. Fabre, *The Unfinished Quest,* p. 411. Fabre indicates that this letter to Reynolds was dated September 19, 1954, shortly after Wright's first trip.

18. Americo Castro, *The Structure of Spanish History,* trans. Edmund King (Princeton: Princeton University Press, 1954).

19. According to the *Oxford English Dictionary* the Latin *paganus* and the Greek *ethnik* came to have the same meaning—those who were not Christian. Originally, however, these terms did not include Hebrews. See vols. 5 and 11 of the *Oxford English Dictionary* (New York: Oxford University Press, 1989).

20. Fabre, *The Unfinished Quest,* p. 608, n. 5.

The sole footnote in *Pagan Spain* refers to the "pagan" underpinnings of Spanish culture and demonstrates Wright's use of Castro's argument. During lunch with his guide Andre's family, Wright asked if they knew the origin of the word *ole*. They did not. Wright then revealed that it was a Moorish word meaning "for God's sake."[21] Andre and his family were incredulous: "They all stood frozen and stared at me with open mouths. They had been uttering the pagan religious phrases of the Moors and never known it!" (90). Wright saw in this example of acculturation a striking parallel to American English. One need think only of the frequency with which Yiddish or "black English" is incorporated into mainstream American speech. For Wright this was particularly striking because the word *ole* had survived long after the Moor had been defeated and expelled from Spain.

Wright's need to support his own observations with those of other authorities may have been related to his ignorance of Spanish. Throughout the text Wright reminds the reader that his knowledge of the language is rudimentary.[22] Although he had undertaken a review of Spanish before he left Paris, his efforts yielded little result.[23] And yet most of Wright's encounters were with people who spoke little or no English. There were a few interviews in which he had obtained the assistance of an interpreter. In some instances communication took place through gestures and in Wright's simple French or Spanish phrases. Wright's problem with language is apparent from the beginning of his voyage. A vivid and humorous example occurred on his first day in Spain.

En route to Barcelona, Wright stopped at a gas station. There a civil guard armed with a machine gun approached him. The man addressed him in Spanish. Wright's anxiety peaked: "I was in a police state and I thought: *This is it . . .*" (3). He quickly produced his passport, which the guard ignored. Finally, the bilingual gas station attendant informed Wright that the

21. Castro, *Structure of Spanish History*, p. 113. Wright's reference comes from this sentence: "And I believe that in many instances behind the Christian God vibrates the echo of Allah, present in the interjection ole! (*wa-l-lah,* 'for God's sake') with which audiences shout their encouragement to dancers and bullfighters."

22. Nowhere in *Pagan Spain* does Wright admit to having difficulty understanding *Formación política*. Michel Fabre indicates that Wright had included his copy with the manuscript that he sent to Reynolds. He asked to have it returned so that he could answer critics who might accuse him of inaccuracies. But Fabre does not mention who translated the text of *Formación* into English or French (*The Unfinished Quest*, p. 608, n. 2).

23. Fabre, *The Unfinished Quest,* p. 608, n 1. Fabre indicates that Wright got through only the first twenty pages of Spanish grammar before he left. He had, however, spent several months in Argentina, where doubtless he had learned some Spanish.

guard merely wanted a lift. Wright consented, and the officer climbed in, "machine gun and all." The two men, unable to understand each other's language, were "prey to a curious and uneasy compulsion to talk, not to communicate but to try to let each other know that we were civilized and of good will" (3). They spent the next few minutes chattering, each unintelligible to the other, when suddenly the guard touched Wright's arm and began pumping his right foot up and down energetically. Assuming that his passenger wanted him to speed up, Wright stepped on the accelerator. The guard continued pumping his foot so Wright drove even faster. "Finally, he grew desperate and, walling his eyes, he shook his head. I got the point: he had been urging me to step on the brake" (4). Wright then stopped his car and offered to drive the guard back. Not surprisingly, the man refused. After profuse thanks, the guard shook Wright's hand and "lumbered off, his machine gun cradled in his arm" (4). By reporting this incident Wright could support his observation that Spain was a police state: genuine democracies do not require the constant presence of armed guards. But this scene reveals much more about Wright the observer. He finds what he is looking for, but when he finds it he becomes a less perceptive observer. The presence of the machine gun impairs his ability to understand a straightforward gesture.

Throughout the narrative Wright emphasizes his role as protest writer; the many interviews he conducted clearly underscore this purpose. In one of the most striking examples Wright arranged to speak to a Protestant woman who had been arrested for teaching the Bible. Before he relates the particulars of this interview, he asserts his authority on the subject:

> I am an American Negro with a background of psychological suffering stemming from my previous position as a member of a persecuted racial minority. What drew my attention to the emotional plight of the Protestants in Spain was the undeniable and uncanny psychological affinities that they held in common with American Negroes, Jews and other oppressed minorities. It is another proof, if any is needed today, that the main and decisive aspects of human reactions are conditioned and are not inborn. Indeed, the quickest and simplest way to introduce the subject to the reader would be to tell him that I shall describe some of the facets of psychological problems and emotional sufferings of a group of *white Negroes* whom I met in Spain, the assumption being that Negroes are Negroes because they are *treated* as Negroes. (138)

This interview lasted over two hours because it took place through a translator. In the six pages that follow the woman describes a period of many years when she successfully set up and ran Bible classes for impoverished village children. In one village pressure from local authorities forced her to shut down the school. Undaunted, she moved to another village and began a new school. Then one day two police officers arrived, dismissed the children, and arrested the woman and her assistant. Neither she nor the assistant was ever charged with any specific crime, yet they were held in custody for a number of days. The guards and the other prisoners did not know what Protestantism was and therefore did not know what to make of these "criminals." Eventually the women were released, but not before the teacher learned that the police had an extensive file on her activities.

Apart from his introductory comment Wright lets the story speak for itself. The parallel between religious intolerance in Spain and racial intolerance in the United States is underscored in his phrase "the *white Negroes* whom I met in Spain." Despite his deep antipathy for the Protestantism in which he was raised, Wright confesses a "spontaneous and profound sympathy . . . for that exquisite suffering" (138). Once again the situation of Spanish Protestants reminds Wright of his fellow black Americans.

In another encounter communication between Wright and his Spanish hosts took place through an interpreter. But her English was so elementary they were soon forced to employ simple Spanish phrases, gestures, and songs. This strangely moving episode came about when Wright, bored with the sights in Granada, telephoned a woman he had met on a train. During that journey she had observed him taking notes and asked him, in Spanish, what he was writing. They spent much of the long ride engaged in conversation, and although language proved a barrier, the woman's generosity (she gave him a book of flamenco lyrics) and candor had impressed him. When he telephoned, she invited him to dinner. The woman, Lita, and two of her friends met Wright on the sidewalk in front of her apartment building. Upstairs the small apartment suggested its tenant's pride and her poverty. Early on in the long evening Wright learned that Lita's husband had been killed by Franco's forces during the civil war. Wright then asked, "How is life here?" to which Lita replied, "Bad . . . Hard, very hard. We eat, that's all. We eat a little" (170). Wright sensed that his question was ill timed. The tiny living room became profoundly quiet. His courage flagged, and he regretted having come. One of the guests sang a flamenco song about the death of a soldier, which fueled Lita's rage:

> "Franco!" she croaked with fury. "*Comprende?*"
> "*Si, Señora,*" I said.
> "*Hombre malo,*" she said. She lifted her arms and her thin white hands made

a fluttering movement and her mouth imitated the roar of plane engines . . .
'boooooM! boooooooM!'

"*La guerre,*" I said.

"*Si Señor,*" she said. "*Libertad terminada . . . La mitad de la gente española
no come,*" she hissed. (172)

Wright was mute: "They sang and baptized me in their sorrow. I was glad
that we could not talk freely, for words would have profaned what they
communicated to me of their hurt and dejection" (172).

The somber atmosphere was dispelled by songs and pantomimes. At one
point Wright got down on all fours and imitated a charging bull. When he
announced that he had to take an early morning train (he had spent the
entire evening and wee hours of the morning there), Lita and her friends
asked to accompany him. At the station, "I shook hands all around, then
climbed aboard. I opened a window and looked down into their naked plead-
ing eyes and I knew that this love that they were demonstrating was not for
me alone; it was an appeal to that world that they had never seen and whose
reality they had almost begun to doubt. *I represented that world to them . . .*
I took out my fountain pen and waved gently to them.'*Para usted,*' I whispered to them" (175; emphasis added). No passage better illustrates what
Wright felt his role to be. He was a symbol of a freer, more humane world.
The final gesture, waving his fountain pen and whispering "*para usted*" (for
you) was Wright's fittingly symbolic response.

Not all of the interviews yielded the desired response. Wright had arranged
to interview a Spanish Jew. Although the young man had recently immigrated to Spain, his forebears were Spanish, and he spoke the language flu-
ently. Wright does not indicate in what language the interview took place.
But again he provides us with his point of reference: "Jew and Negro, both
from backgrounds of persecution, we sat seemingly securely anchored in a
twentieth century world of sanity and comfort" (222). Wright's direct questions, however, made the man uncomfortable:

"Is there any anti-Semitism in Spain . . .?"

"No . . ."

"Maybe it was all solved back in 1492 when Ferdinand and Isabel drove the
Jews from Spain?"

"Yes . . . You see there are only two thousand five hundred of us here in
Spain . . ."

"And since there are practically no Jews in Spain, there can't be a problem,
can there?"

"That's right . . ."

"Why did you come to Spain?"

"I like Spain . . . You see my people lived here once . . . My ancestors were here . . . I speak Spanish from them." (223)

Wright was clearly irritated with this man's unwillingness to discuss Spanish anti-Semitism openly. After this direct approach failed, Wright took a different tack. He asked the man to describe the laws governing marriage between Spanish Catholics and between Spanish Jews and Catholics. Naturally these laws reflect an intolerance for any faith other than Catholicism. Having made this point, Wright went on to ask about the role of the Jews in Spanish history. This gave the man a chance to try again to explain to Wright why he had immigrated to Spain:

> "You see we Jews either had to leave, or turn Catholic, that is become *conversos.* I've come back to the country from which my ancestors were driven centuries ago. *I feel that I am Spanish.*"
>
> "You *want to be* Spanish . . ."
>
> "I'M SPANISH! . . . Names like Perez, Franco, etc., are Jewish names. Toledo is a Jewish word . . ." (224).

As Wright puts it, "A void hung between us" (224). The interview ended abruptly. The Spanish Jew shook Wright's hand and drove off at a terrific speed. Wright sensed that the man was "seething with shame and burning with fury" (224), but at what and against whom he does not venture a guess. Doubtless he was angry at the presumptuousness of Wright's questions.

Throughout the narrative Wright calls attention to the fact that he is *the* Richard Wright. He reminds the reader that his first encounter with Spain came during his work as a journalist for the Harlem bureau of the *Daily Worker.* The original transcript of the book included an account of the pirated Spanish edition of *Black Boy.*[24] At the train station, Wright, waving his fountain pen, whispered "para usted," the meaning of which is clear. One Spanish woman apologized to him for not having read any of his books (46). The Protestant spoke to him hoping that Wright could write something that would call international attention to the lot of Spanish Protestants. And it is possible that the Spanish Jew refused to speak openly for the same reason. The original title for *Pagan Spain* was *Pagan Spain: A Report of a Journey*

---

24. Ibid., p 414.

*into the Past,* to parallel his autobiography, *Black Boy: A Record of Childhood and Youth.* At this point in his life Wright had begun to evaluate his own career in the context of the American literary tradition.

*Pagan Spain* begins with a description of Wright's last conversation with Gertrude Stein. This reminds the reader of one of Stein's most gifted pupils, who, like Wright, was fascinated with Spain. Wright first encountered Ernest Hemingway in 1937, at the second American Writers' Congress in New York City. Archibald MacLeish, Lillian Hellman, and Ernest Hemingway had co-authored the script of a film titled *The Spanish Earth,* which described the civil war. After scenes from the film were shown, Hemingway addressed the delegates. Although it is not certain that Wright actually introduced himself to Hemingway, it is entirely possible that he did so.[25] There is no doubt that Wright admired the other man's work. With these details in mind, it is clear that *Pagan Spain*'s origins were as literary as they were political. Of course, in all of Wright's work the two were inextricably bound, but during his voyages to Spain, Wright was especially conscious of this literary tradition and of his place in it.

Wright mentions Hemingway in *Pagan Spain,* but he did not have to; simply to describe a bullfight would have been enough to invoke his memory. But he also mentions Washington Irving. In Granada, Wright visited the Alhambra and the Generalife palace. The distance between the perspective of the two writers is vividly illustrated in their descriptions of the palace and the gardens. This is Irving's:

> High above the Alhambra, on the breast of the mountain, amidst embowered gardens and stately terraces, rise the lofty towers and white walls of the Generalife; a fairy palace, full of storied recollections . . . Here were preserved the portraits of many who figured in the romantic drama of the Conquest . . . Ferdinand and Isabella, Ponce de Leon, the gallant marquis of Cadiz, and Garcilaso de la Vega, who slew the Tarfe and Moor, a champion of Herculean Strength.[26]

---

25. Ibid., p. 141. Fabre also notes that this conference was in a small way responsible for Wright's later relationship with Gertrude Stein. Another delegate, Max White, described Wright in a letter to Stein: "There is a young Negro writer we saw a few times before we left New York. His name is Richard Wright and he says he has been immensely influenced by your writings. We haven't seen anything of his but he is at least a very smart person . . . I was wondering whether you know him." Quoted, in Donald Gallup, ed., *Flowers of Friendship* (New York: Knopf, 1953), p. 326.

26. Washington Irving, *The Alhambra* (New York: G. P. Putnam, 1851), p. 200.

And this is Wright's:

> I wandered over the ruins of Alhambra and Generalife . . . and walked through
> the palace, the fortress and the summer gardens, then among the vast brick
> battlements erected centuries earlier by the Moors . . . These relics represented
> the terminal point of influence of the East and Africa in Europe.
>
> Since the vanquishing of the Moors by Ferdinand and Isabella . . . the tide
> of history had reversed itself and Europe, with a long and bloody explosion,
> had hurled itself upon the masses of mankind in Asia and Africa and the then
> unknown Americas. (162)

Unlike Irving, who "had been charmed by this monstrous pile of dead glory
and had woven romantic tales about it" (162), Wright could not accept this
interpretation of history. Instead, Irving's "romantic drama of the Conquest" would become Wright's "long and bloody explosion." In "rewriting"
this passage of *The Alhambra,* Wright accomplished two things. He placed
his own work in the context of a tradition which he obviously shared; and he
illustrated how his vision, born of his own particularly American experience,
contributed to that tradition.

Michel Fabre argues that Wright's account of the bullfight rivals Hemingway's best descriptions.[27] And Wright may have intended this comparison. But when we examine closely the difference between the two writers'
treatments, something interesting emerges. Hemingway's fictional description of the bullfight is perhaps best illustrated in *The Sun Also Rises.* Much
of the drama in the novel is centered on the festival in Pamploma. Hemingway's focus is on the matador and how the act of encountering the bull
reveals the passion of the man and thereby his worth. Similarly, Wright is
impressed by the bravery of the young matador he witnessed in the ring;
but this is not the focal point. Consider this passage from *The Sun Also Rises:*
"Out in the center of the ring Romero profiled in front of the bull, drew
the sword out from the folds of the muleta, rose on his toes, and sighted
along the blade. The bull charged as Romero charged."[28] Wright's description
of this same moment is remarkable for its similarity, but note the difference:

> Chamaco's left hand now grasped the muleta firmly; he turned away from the
> bull, looking at him sideways, letting the red cloth drop below his left knee.
> He now lifted his gleaming sword chin high and sighted along the length of

27. Michel Fabre, *The Unfinished Quest,* p. 415.
28. Ernest Hemingway, *The Sun Also Rises* (New York: Scribner and Sons, 1926), p. 218.

it, pointing its sharp, steel tip at the tormented and bloody mound of wounds on the bull's back. Chamaco's left hand twitched the cloth, citing the bull. The bull saw it and charged. Chamaco charged, meeting the bull. (111–112)

Just as Wright had amended Irving's version of the Generalife, here too his inclusion of "the tormented and bloody mound of wounds on the bull's back" illustrates the important way in which his own account of the bullfight differs from that of his literary predecessor and compatriot. Indeed, Wright's focus in the description of the bullfight is on the sociological and pathological dimensions of the ritual for its participants. Going further than Hemingway, for whom the bullfight embodied the heroic dimension of the matador, Wright argues that it represents a "man made agony to assuage the emotional needs of men" (112). Wright agrees that the matador is the representation of the heroic, but he seeks to understand how and why this quality functioned in the minds of an oppressed people. That Wright could impart this meaning to the bullfight is not surprising to anyone familiar with his work. By addressing this subject, so incontestably Hemingway's, Wright asserted his place in and particular contribution to the American literary tradition.

In one of the most quoted statements from *Pagan Spain,* Wright remarks: "I have no race except that which is forced upon me. I have no country except that to which I'm obliged to belong. I have no traditions. I'm free. I have only the future" (17). This position would seem the logical outcome of his expatriation. Wright felt that he had distanced himself from American traditions, particularly racism; yet expatriation also brought him closer to American thought and literary expression. The last three sentences—"I have no traditions. I'm free. I have only the future"—could have been written by Walt Whitman or Ralph Waldo Emerson.[29] The lack of tradition, the emphasis on the freedom to define oneself, the conviction that one possesses the future are essentially American trademarks.

Throughout *Pagan Spain* the reader is more often encouraged to recall the Wright of Mississippi than the Wright of Chicago, New York, or Paris. David Bakish has noted the connection Wright made between the hooded

29. I am reminded of Walt Whitman's "To a Historian," in *Leaves of Grass* (Boston: Small, Maynard & Co., 1897), p. 11, the pertinent lines of which are "You who celebrate bygones . . . / Who have treated of man as the creature of politics, aggregates, rulers and priests/ I, habitan of the Alleghanies, treating of him as he is in himself in his own rights . . . / I project the history of the future." I am also reminded of Emerson's "Divinity School Address."

participants of a religious festival honoring the Virgin and the hooded Klans-
men of his native Mississippi, who pledged to protect the purity of white
womanhood.[30] This observation is important because it illustrates the "emotional landscape" of Mississippi. But, more significant, it underscores the
difference between Wright's account of Spain and that of any other American writer. Perhaps more significant yet is that Wright wanted to show his
critics that even though he no longer lived in the United States, he could
write skillfully and sensitively about human suffering.

But to write a book on Spain, when he might have gone anywhere in the
world, illustrates a determination to place his work in a literary context that
was specifically American. Wright's journey to Spain may have revealed how
slavery had severed him from the traditions of his ancestral past. But it also
revealed how closely it aligned him with his American origins and his special
role in America's literary history. He might live in Paris and write about
Spain, the Gold Coast, or Indonesia, but his subjects and vision were rooted
in his American imagination.

30. See David Bakish, *Richard Wright* (New York: Frederick Ungar, 1973), pp. 82–83: "In a strong
sense, *Pagan Spain* was really about the emotional landscape of Mississippi. It was to lead Wright
to turn again directly to Mississippi in *The Long Dream* (1958)." In *The Art of Richard Wright* (Carbondale: Southern Illinois University Press, 1969), Edward Margolies argues that Wright's journey
to Spain was a way for him to return to his own past: "By investigating the roots of oppression, he
would be better able to reassess the experiences of his youth . . . He posited his Outsider's sense of
freedom as a point of reference from which he would study the nature of the Spanish people" (43).

*Sigmund Ro*

# Coming of Age: The Modernity of Postwar Black American Writing

*I*n this essay I focus on the process of intellectual modernization which black American letters underwent in the first decade after World War II. In particular, I devote my attention to the catalytic effect of W. E. B. Du Bois's and Richard Wright's two seminal metaphors, those of the black man's "double consciousness" and his native sonship, in the definition of a modern African American literary sensibility. At midcentury black writers and literary intellectuals found themselves catapulted into a new role in a Western culture at once morally depleted and challenged by ethnic and racial pluralism on a global scale. Acutely conscious of the need to express the meaning of the racial experience in terms that would enhance its relevance and utility, they faced a complex task. Reading with the benefit of hindsight the writings of these early postwar years, one cannot but be struck by the pervasive, though frequently submerged, presence of Du Bois and Wright in this process of creative reinterpretation which inaugurated a defining moment and a new maturity in black literary expression.

Thus, there is considerable justification for considering this a period of cultural and artistic coming of age as much as the Harlem Renaissance or the 1960s. Nor should it be forgotten that this was in fact how many culturally articulate black Americans saw themselves in the years following the Second World War. Such is, for example, the self-perception controlling the too often neglected 1950 symposium issue of *Phylon*, together with James Baldwin's two *Partisan Review* essays of 1949 and 1951 the most eloquent public manifestos of the new postwar black literature. Explicit in several of the contributions, this sense is implied in others that speak of the race's cultural and artistic "growth" and newly acquired "maturity." Even the grand old man of black American letters, Alain Locke, shared this postwar vision of a race having reached its long-awaited manhood, placing it in a new relationship both to its own past and to the rest of the world. From the vantage point of 1950, he felt that he could look back on the Harlem Renaissance as the "adolescence" of the race, an inevitable and indispensable stage for the "new spiritual stature" and "added dimension of self-reliance" it contributed, but appearing in all its "gawky and pimply, indiscreet and over-confident, vainglorious and irresponsible" youthfulness, a period of admirable vitality but not to be mistaken for true adulthood in its "pride without poise, vision without true perspective, self-esteem without the necessary tempering of full self-understanding." In contrast to the work of the 1920s, black self-expression had now, Locke felt, taken a decisive step toward becoming objective, a sure sign of a new "cultural maturity."[1]

Racial adulthood also involved a new status and a new role in relation to the majority culture. Black Americans were acutely conscious that the postwar world was a changed world, one that made new demands on black America while it also represented new opportunities. Global vistas were opening up on an unprecedented scale, offering vastly expanded contexts for black self-definition. In a crisis-torn and rapidly shrinking world, the racial experience had suddenly acquired a new significance. The potential inherent in this situation was not lost on the contributors to the *Phylon* symposium. Voicing their concern, Margaret Walker, a leading poet of the period, spoke of the "basis for new conceptions that of necessity lead us in new directions."[2] She, too, saw the "New Negro" of the Harlem Renaissance as having come of age. The test of the new maturity would lie in the ability to express the black heritage in a modern idiom.

This must not be construed to mean that black writers and critics prescribed abandoning racial subject matter and styles. A distinction was made between racialistic literature, of which they felt there had been too much in an adolescent and immature past, and racial art, which for Locke, Walker, Saunders Redding, and Nick Aaron Ford, no less than for Baldwin and Ralph Ellison, was an obvious reference point. Sterling Brown's contribution to the symposium celebrated "Negro folk expression," as did J. Mason Brewer's

1. Alain Locke, "Self-Criticism: The Third Dimension in Culture," *Phylon*, 11 (1950): 391–394.
2. Margaret Walker, "New Poets," *Phylon*, 11 (1950): 345–354. Quotations are from this essay.

research published outside *Phylon*'s pages. Ford urged the continued use of racial themes in his "Blueprint for Negro Authors," and Locke called for a postwar literature "even more racial in the better sense of being more deeply felt and projected." What was needed was a "deep-mining" of the racial heritage and "better artistic smelting of the crude ore" without the chauvinism or "panmining" of the past. Interestingly, Locke's ideal was no longer the Irish renaissance but the literary achievement of nineteenth-century Russia in its fusion of the "cosmopolitan way" and the "nativist way." It is as though in all its youthful exuberance the awakening in Ireland, so much in vogue during the 1920s as an analogy of the "New Negro" movement, appeared to Locke in 1950 as an appropriate equivalent of racial and ethnic puberty, whereas the Russia of Turgenev, Tolstoy, Dostoyevski, Chekhov, Gogol, and Gorky offered a more fitting image of true cultural and artistic maturity. The ultimate desideratum in a literature come of age lay in a quality of "universalized particularity" with the emphasis as much on the second as on the first component.[3]

Positive spurs to moving in new directions were inherent in the postwar situation. Already before the first peacetime euphoria had waned there was a sense that this postwar period was different from previous postwar periods, a sense of—in the words of Eric Goldman—a "terrifying newness"[4] which undermined faith in the possibility of a return to normalcy. The war had opened up vistas of nuclear destruction, and it had dramatically speeded up the process of integration of continents, races, and cultures on a global scale.

It was this climate of disaster and impending adjustments to new cultural realities which interacted with a characteristic American search for regenerative energies to produce a situation of tremendous potential for black literature. In times of moral and cultural exhaustion there has been a traditional impulse in American letters to go in search of redemptive countercultures among minority groups, whether professional, regional, or ethnic. A generation earlier this had been done by Van Wyck Brooks, who, seeing America in bondage to the combined forces of puritanism and the commercialism of the Gilded Age, had looked for a saving "remnant" first to a class of civil servants placed above the vagaries of national politics, later to a class of "engineers" and technocrats capable of rescuing society from rivaling ideolo-

---

3. Locke, "Self-Criticism," pp. 391–394.
4. Eric Goldman, *The Crucial Decade—and After* (New York: Random House, 1960), p. 5.

gies. As Arnold Goldman points out, however, the search had traditionally been for "specific sub-groups *within* an Anglo-Saxon hegemony."[5] After the Second World War conditions had changed enough to offer ethnic and racial subcultures outside this hegemony their chance.

This situation thrust on black America the challenge of a new messianic role. In its heritage of folk wisdom born of suffering and alienation was felt to lie the potential for a unique gnosis, conferring on the race a special authority in a crisis-torn Euro-America, and it was felt that in an age of global cultural convergence the black American's unique three-hundred-year experience of intimate racial coexistence might represent a resource of great value. Such perspectives frequently permeated black cultural comment in the postwar years, and their relevance to the race's literary expression was often noted. In 1949, in his annual review of literature on the Negro, Alain Locke saw Du Bois's prophecy as having come true. No longer a domestic American problem, the "color-line" had become "the number one problem of the world." Of "global significance and proportions," it reached beyond economics and politics into those "more fundamental psychological and cultural dilemmas of human group relations" on which the survival of Western civilization depended. "Many of us," he concluded, "are deeply concerned to discover whether we are a death-watch or a dawn patrol."[6] Ultimately, Locke chose to be optimistic, and to urge black writers to put the racial experience to new and broader uses.

Similar calls came from critics and artists alike. "The possibilities of a literature dealing with the life and ways of Negro peoples in the Western world seem beyond comprehension,"[7] wrote Ira de A. Reid, echoing the voices of many others in emphasizing the privileged position of the black writer. In contrast to the white artist who is envious to the point of "longing almost for major indignities because he knows that such make the pen run wild," blacks, wrote Gwendolyn Brooks, find themselves in the unexpected situation of having come into sudden possession of "a moving, authoritative and humane subject" as well as "great drive and high emotion" to fuel its

---

5. Arnold Goldman, "A Remnant to Escape: The American Writer and the Minority Group," in *American Literature since 1900*, ed. Marcus Cunliffe (London: Sphere Books, 1975), pp. 312–344.

6. Alain Locke, "Dawn Patrol: A Review of the Literature of the Negro for 1948," *Phylon*, 10 (1949):5.

7. Ira de A. Reid, "The Literature of the Negro: A Social Scientist's Appraisal," *Phylon*, 11 (1950): 390.

artistic expression.[8] In a scene in John A. Williams's novel *The Man Who Cried I Am,* a white European character articulates the postwar response to Harry Ames (Richard Wright): "He was very much in demand . . . We needed the confidence of someone who had taken more of a beating than we, generations and generations of beatings, and who could still see *le chemin de la liberte*."[9] This scene captures accurately the postwar moral vacuum and the broad relevance which the black heritage had suddenly acquired. What the white Western speaker voices is the need of her civilization for a redemptive ethos purged in the crucible of history. Such a potential regenerative force was what her generation saw in the American Negro.

With the newly acquired authority of someone whose neglected history has finally become recognized as a resource, the black writer could now proceed to fashion out of the racial experience a new sensibility capable of coping with disaster without losing sight of the road to freedom. According to a *Paris Review* interview, this was precisely Ellison's concern in a vision of black writing which is simultaneously backward-looking and forward-looking. Ellison saw his own art as a contribution "not only to the growth of literature, but to the shaping of the culture as I should like it to be,"[10] and his dream was to help remake the American novel into what it had been in the days of Melville and Twain: the conscience of the nation. But his conception extended further to include the creation, out of racial folk materials, of a new vision suited to the pluralism of the postwar age. Worked out in fictional terms, this was the educational process through which the author put his symbolically nameless hero in *Invisible Man.* Out of the legacy left by his black southern grandfather and the music of Louis Armstrong he molded a heightened modern sensibility. The pivotal process of the novel is the metamorphosis of the black experience into a paradigm of tribulation and overcoming in a crisis-ridden and shrunken world.

In the achievement of this aim, conventional protest was felt to be as unsuitable as direct transcription of folk forms. The racial heritage had to be expressed in a mode of thought that wedded it to modern existential insights. The submerged catalyst shaping that synthesis was the updating

8. Gwendolyn Brooks, "Poets Who Are Negroes," *Phylon,* 11 (1950): 312.

9. John A. Williams, *The Man Who Cried I Am* (New York: The New American Library, 1968), p. 126.

10. Ralph Ellison, "The Way It Is," in *Shadow and Act* (New York: New American Library), p. 183.

and joining together of the two classic metaphors of black literary self-reflection: the African American's "double consciousness" and his native sonship.

The first of these had made its initial self-conscious appearance in the pages of *The Souls of Black Folk* in the early years of the century. Du Bois had suggested that the entire psychohistory of black America could be written in terms of two kinds of *Lebensgefühl*, two separate aggregates of consciousness coexisting within the black mind, and the struggle to "merge this double self." Ultimately he chose to see this divided sensibility as an asset rather than as fate, as endowing the African American with a "second sight," a special truth-seeing power and a sense of the "seventh son." His "double consciousness" put the black man in possession of a subtle psychological peculiarity, amounting almost to a unique spirituality, of great value. This condition conferred on him a messianic "mission" and "responsibility" to "the darker races of men whose future depends so largely on this American experiment, but especially a responsibility to this nation." Du Bois's concern was to invest the experience of black America with a transracial significance on the same level of importance as the contributions to civilization made by other races in his historical roll call. Its impact is envisioned in terms of a black "oasis" in the white American "dusty desert of dollars and smartness" and as an advance guard to nonwhite peoples around the world.[11]

The second self-reflective metaphor—that of the native son—had first been made explicit in Jean Toomer's *Cane*, in the separately published and award-winning "Song of the Son." It remained for Richard Wright, however, to sharpen and expand the idea for further literary use. But before he could turn it into a creative resource for a postwar generation exploring new artistic paths, its dependence on the character of Bigger Thomas and the naturalistic-sociological idiom of the author's Chicago and New York years had to be overcome. In his postwar exile Wright redefined his vision of sonship in a way that brought it closer to the mode of thought pioneered by Du Bois. Psychologizing the idea, he now saw at the core of the black condition "an abiding schism," a split between his "Westernness," which resided in his intellectual skepticism, and that other, more elusive quality, his blackness. Wright's vision was a divided one: "I stand, therefore, mentally and emo-

11. W. E. B. Du Bois, *The Souls of Black Folk*, in *Three Negro Classics* (New York: Avon, 1965), pp. 215, 214, 215, 218, 249, 220.

tionally, looking in both directions." From this split condition there followed a unique and self-conscious detachment, a sense of "psychological distance." Being neither a Westerner nor a non-Westerner, or rather being both, he saw "both worlds from another and third point of view."[12] This mental and cultural trauma also enabled Wright to place the black American experience in a larger context, thus endowing it with a vastly generalized and enriched meaning. Telescoping post-Renaissance history in terms of unprecedented social change, he located black America within this process as the group that most intensely symbolizes its meaning. No other group is more intimately familiar with disruption and chaos, suffering, confusion of identity, and re-adjustment. The black man's history is "the history of Western man writ small," especially in the United States: "The Negro is America's metaphor."[13] In the Western black man is found in distilled and condensed form both the drama of modern man trying to cope with change and a model of how to turn this experience into opportunities for liberation. Wright found the clue to the Negro's sonship in the modernity of the divided sensibility born of his group experience.

By thus hitching the concept of the black man's American and Western sonship to that of his peculiarly dual cast of mind, African American creative writing fashioned a myth to which could be assigned a regenerative role while conferring on the artist a priestly office. In the postwar years the stage was being set for a defining moment based on the reinterpretation of the black experience in terms of a divided sensibility which, while closely attuned to the contemporary sense of catastrophic dislocations, possessed a will and a strength to survive, tested in the crucible of the race's history. In this direction could be found vast opportunities for the modernization and coming of age of black literary expression.

It is this perspective that permeates and informs the work of James Baldwin and Ralph Ellison in the first decade after the war. Baldwin's image of the black man as a "bastard of the West" and a "stranger in the village" and Ellison's of his "invisibility" share a similarity of outlook in the midst of diversity which draws its sustenance to a considerable extent from the combined insights of Du Bois and Wright. In their work all these figures

12. Richard Wright, "Tradition and Industrialization: The Historic Meaning of the Plight of the Tragic Elite in Asia and Africa," in *White Man, Listen* (Garden City, N.Y.: Doubleday, 1964).

13. Richard Wright, "The Literature of the Negro in the United States," in *White Man, Listen*, p. 72.

come together: the man of dual consciousness, the native son and "Western man of color," the invisible man, and the self-conscious stranger in the Euro-American village. The composite image extractable from this cluster of self-reflective metaphors is at the very center of the postwar generation's effort to wrest racial iconography from the captivity of the white-controlled literary marketplace and fashion a sensibility relevant to a new age of moral uncertainty and global racial-ethnic integration. By making the African American's double consciousness the locus of his native sonship, black literary expression and cultural self-understanding can be said to have come of age in this period in a deeper and truer sense than in the 1920s. The situation is summed up in capsule form and with great emblematic power in Baldwin's artistic self-myth in "Stranger in the Village." Behind his veil with only his typewriter and a stack of Bessie Smith records, the young black novelist blows his blues and shouts his testimony from the Swiss mountaintop, near the cradle of Western Protestant culture, peered at by the as yet uncomprehending villagers awaiting the catalytic agent that will help them overcome their moral confusion, their ethnocentrism, and their dangerous supremacist notions in a world no longer white.

*Gerald Early*

# "Black Herman Comes Through Only Once Every Seven Years": Black Magic, White Magic, and American Culture

> Just so the conjurer never reveals in advance the full nature of a trick, that the spectator may not know where to center his attention.
>
> —MAX DESSOIR AND H. J. BURLINGAME, "The Psychology of Conjuring"
> (in Burlingame's *Herrmann the Magician, His Life; His Secrets*)

*A*lthough the books possess the same covers and deal with the same subject matter, there are a number of differences—both major and minor—between the 1934 Martin Publishing Company edition of *Black Herman's Easy Pocket Tricks Which You Can Do* and the 1938 Dorene Publishing Company edition of the same work. The Dorene edition is about twenty-eight pages shorter than the earlier one. Moreover, the earlier edition makes no claim to be "four volumes in one," as the later one does, although there were apparently four distinct sections in every edition of the book. These "volumes," or chapters really, are titled "The Life of the Great Black Herman," "The Study of Legerdemain," "The Signification of Dreams," and "The Story of Oriental Magic I Found in the Orient, An Ancient Practice." The 1934 edition is divided into sections called "The Life of the Great Black Herman," "The Study of Magic," "Horoscope," and "The Signification of Dreams." The two books share most of their material except in three significant instances: the earlier edition is much more profusely illustrated than the later one, which is hardly illustrated at all; there is no section in the earlier book corresponding to "The Story of Oriental Magic I Found in the Orient"; and, finally, in the later book Herman works out an elaborately complex number system for his interpretation of dreams which is absent from the earlier volume, where the dream section reads like any standard dream book for people who play the numbers.

What is curious here is not simply the nature of the revisions but the fact that the revisions even exist. Black Herman died in April 1934 in Louisville, Kentucky, at the age of forty-two from, as the *Chicago Defender* put it in its banner headline, "Acute Indigestion." The immediate suggestion to some minds was that he had been poisoned. This was precisely the kind of death that would have had many of his followers thinking that poor Herman had been hoodooed or had met a conjurer more mighty than he. (In truth, Black Herman's death resembles in its unexpectedness and its strangeness the deaths of Harry Houdini, who died in October 1926 of a ruptured appendix, and Alexander Herrmann the Great, who died in December 1896, apparently of a heart attack, two of the most famous performers in the history of stage magic. Perhaps they were hoodooed too. Or perhaps famous magicians often die in ways that seem to have been caused by supernatural agents; perhaps even in death, ambiguity and theatrics cast a certain surreal verisimilitude.) Still, one wonders who was responsible for the changes in the 1938 edition of Herman's book. Perhaps it is simply a reprint of an earlier edition. Nonetheless, there is no indication in the 1938 edition that it is a posthumous work or that Black Herman had died. Herman's funeral was held at the Mother A. M. E. Zion Church, and he was buried in Woodlawn Cemetery in New York, the same place where Herrmann the Great was interred.

At the time of his death Black Herman was the most famous black magician in American history, as is evidenced by the prominence the report of his death received in black newspapers, where it was invariably a page-one story. Even today, among people who know about black history and the history of performance magic, he is still considered one of the most colorful and charismatic of American magicians. Over six feet tall, with a magnificent physique and a showman's flair for grabbing attention through the most flamboyant, if tawdry, kind of publicity, Herman was certainly a figure to be reckoned with. For many, however, Herman was the fraud of frauds, a magician whose technique left much to be desired. The article about his death that appeared in the April 28, 1934, issue of the New York *Amsterdam News* was at times more morosely arch than laudatory: the headline read "BLACK HERMAN REGULARLY RAISED THE 'DEAD' BUT THEY BURIED HIM LIKE ANY MORTAL MAN." Herman was immortalized by Ishmael Reed in *Mumbo Jumbo*, his 1971 novel about the "New Negro" or Harlem Renaissance, as one of the book's two heroes. (I assume that Reed was also influenced in the creation of both the fictitious Black Herman and PaPa LaBas not only by Chester

Himes's Jones and Johnson but also by the Harlem detective of the 1920s, Herbert Boulin, who frequently appeared in stories in the black New York press. Boulin's initials are, of course, Black Herman's in reverse, just the sort of arcane symbolism that would appeal to Reed.)

Finally, Herman, as an entrepreneur and great magician of color, must have had in mind the model of Richard Potter, the first great American-born conjurer, who also happened to be a mulatto. Potter, who was born near Boston, in 1783, was the son of a British tax collector and one of his black slaves. The slight young man began a career as a performing conjurer in his mid-twenties, after having served as an apprentice to John Rannie, a noted Scottish magician. Potter was extraordinarily successful on his extended tours, where he was often mistaken for a Hindu or an American Indian. He eventually invested more than $10,000 in about two hundred acres of New Hampshire farmland and became a prosperous landowner. In a novel based on the life of Potter titled *Conjuror's Journal* by Frances L. Shine (1978), the central character is shown to be just as enterprising but haunted by his love for a white woman and by his rejection at the hands of his white father (neither of these is biographically accurate). In short, the character in the novel is, in effect, paradoxically bedeviled by the lack of acknowledgment of his blackness by his white father and by his need to assimilate as a result of the egoistic inadequacy of his blackness. However Potter's real life may have differed from the author's version, the novel nonetheless suggests a set of psychological problems associated with blackness (or the taint of it) that, in truth, may be of little concern for the pioneering black male who, in the end, learns to negotiate white fathers (real or surrogate) and white women as a sort of minor aside to the real business of taking a distinct disadvantage and transforming it, if not into a virtue, then certainly into a neutralized necessity. Herman's opportunistic use of racial pride and nationalism were simply ways for a black male with some sense of bourgeois ambition in a largely difficult and at times quite daunting social setting to go about the business of making an independent career in a legal activity. If Herman knew about Richard Potter, what the life of the early black magician may have suggested was that there are ways to work as a black itinerant adept and, even, to make money at it.

Black Herman's most famous illusion was burying a woman alive—the trick was always performed with a woman as the fictive corpse—for a certain period of time and then resurrecting her unharmed. The time that the woman would remain buried varied—sometimes just a few hours, sometimes as long as six days. This trick had become so famous, such a signature, that Black Herman's performance of it was something of a news event. For instance, in the July 4, 1923, issue of the *Amsterdam News* there appears this story:

BLACK HERMAN TO BURY WOMAN 6 HOURS

At the Independence Day Jubilee and Aviation Carnival and Athletic Meet at Hasbrouck Heights aviator field Hasbrouck Heights, New Jersey, Professor Black Herman, the magician, will hypnotize and bury a woman under six feet of earth at 11 o'clock and raise her at 4:45 p.m. Lieut. Herbert Julian will drop 4,000 feet in a parachute and alight exactly over the grave of the sleeping woman. In addition, there will be track races, boxing, baseball, tennis, cricket, a potato race, a three-legged race, etc. This promises to be an afternoon of thrills.

It is much to Black Herman's credit and a signal indication of how successfully he advertised himself as merely a harmless entertainer that he was able to perform a conjuring act at a black picnic. Normally, especially among good Christian black folk, this sort of activity would have been considered the rankest form of the devil's work. Remember the lines from an old Negro spiritual: "De devil is a liar an' a conjurer too / If you don't look out he'll conjure you." The conjurer, the magician, was someone not to be trusted, yet many poor black folk found him irresistibly attractive. Herman asserted in his book that he performed in churches such as Saint Paul's A.M.E. and Metropolitan A.M.E. Zion Church, both in St. Louis, and that he was "a devoted Christian . . . [who] recognizes no man as his superior save God and Christ." This last clause about recognizing no superior in any man resonates with the kind of implicit nationalistic claim one could expect from a man whose very name suggests a deep race consciousness and who was proud to have played at Liberty Hall, Marcus Garvey's headquarters, when he first came to New York in March 1923—interestingly, around the time of the start of the Harlem Renaissance. In fact, Herman gave a number of performances in connection with Garvey, and Herman's own entourage of fancy cars could be found among Garvey's Black Legion and other units in the U.N.I.A.'s grand parades. Herman always seemed quite interested in politicizing performance magic in ways that were subtle yet, ironically, cheaply blatant and sensational: to awaken a black woman—the life bearer—from a simulated death was to symbolize Garvey's cry, "Up, you mighty race." With this trick Herman was uplifting the race from its spiritual death and confinement.

Whenever Herman performed in schools, he never failed to mention his friendship with Booker T. Washington, which was initiated when he played Tuskegee before the great race leader died. Although several sources claim that Washington wrote an introduction for one of Herman's books, I have been unable to locate an extant copy. No doubt such a book did once exist, for Herman often mentioned it. Whatever the merit of Herman's claim of intimacy with Washington, it clearly suggests two things: first, that Herman was a noteworthy performer before 1915—the year of Washington's death— and that he was known in important black circles long before he came to New York (this is exactly what Herman claims in the brief autobiography in his book); and second, that he possessed a political consciousness that invariably influenced his art even if it was not apparent in any of the tricks he performed. This political consciousness was partly an idealized racial na- tionalism and partly a practical understanding of how to get along and get ahead in the world. He melded, in a particularly fascinating way, the twin pillars of the black bourgeois dream-wish—race pride and self-sufficiency. Herman revealed Marcus Garvey's influence by stating in the autobiographi- cal section of his book that he was "born five miles from a small town in the dark jungles of Africa" and suggesting that somehow his powers as a performer were tied to his origins. He revealed Washington's influence by becoming—through the sale of his books and extensive herb collection— one of the most successful black businessmen of his age. He was Afrocentric mysticism incarnate and a hardheaded money-maker; he was *Homo faber* (the man who makes things, including himself) and *Homo economicus* (the man who exploits his circumstances for control and gain) with few peers. We know that from the most ancient times the juggler, the conjurer, has been not just a performer but a salesman as well. For instance, the magic historian Edward Claflin writes about the alchemists of the Middle Ages who sold books and pamphlets containing their "secrets" and strange medicines which were wonder cures. Black Herman was purely and simply within the traditions of both the absolute conceit of the charlatan and the pure hustle of the Yankee peddler. He was truly The Magician.

Herman's success as a stage magician in black churches and at black family gatherings suggests that in a way he was able to detheologize his act, which means that he made magic an obvious or self-evident trick; that is, its fakery was explicit and intelligible by the very context of acceptability in which the acts were performed, in schools, at churches, at picnics—in short, at respectable bourgeois social gatherings and institutions. The tricks ceased to have any significance as rites or spiritual rituals as they became mere demonstrations of technique, of a kind of secularized charisma, without the signification of spirit control or spirit summons. Like the relentlessly mechanical father of modern magic, the clockmaker Robert-Houdin, or his neurotically rationalist and antispiritualist namesake, the escapist and lock specialist Houdini, Black Herman would have been considered a scientist, an inventor, an engineer, a tinkerer (in the spirit of the hero of Ralph Ellison's *Invisible Man* and Benjamin Franklin), and finally, just as he called himself in one of the sections of his autobiography, a detective. (It should be noted here that magicians were the first to introduce clockwork mechanisms for operating dolls or animal figures, including full-scale human mannequins that could do such things as change their clothes, write, and tell fortunes, according to Edward Claflin's 1977 book *Street Magic*. It was thus the magician who gave the world the fulfillment of the automaton, the prototype for the scientific robot. In keeping with this tradition, several magicians today have an act that involves putting together mechanical parts to create a living human, or an act in which a disembodied part becomes mechanized.)

Ishmael Reed did not reinvent or reimagine Black Herman when he made him a detective; he simply made him, as the magic historian Milbourne Christopher has noted, exactly what the magician in the modern world has become. Interestingly, in the mythology constructed by the Nation of Islam (the Black Muslims), the evil Yacub who invents white people is called a scientist and not a magician; yet, as W. B. Yeats makes clear in the first part of his 1901 essay "Magic," the archetype on which the Frankenstein and Faust stories are based is in fact the tragic magician whose insistent uncovering or discovering is the cause of his tragedy. The magician's tragedy, in truth, is the hubris of hardheaded knowledge and engineering dexterity, not of mysticism. The modern world has fused the scientific urge to explain with the magician's urge to dominate and command, so that explanation as the modernist version of the magician's prophecy has indeed become a form of domination, and formularized discourse as the modernist version of the magician's recipe or spell has become a form of control. Herman's book is not simply a book of formulas. It is a book of "explanations," all obviously fake, from the pictures that show Herman with a collection of ventriloquist's dummies which are plainly real children or with a supposedly dead man in a coffin who is really alive, to the "explanation" of dreams that explain nothing, and to explications of simple tricks which are often either incomplete or unclear. Here is a cunning magician's book which offers explanations and formulas while thwarting the very possibility of explanation and formula, but which was accepted by its readers as self-evidently containing explanations and formulas of incredible power. Herman's autobiography itself, a blatant narrative of lies, of fantastic escapades reminiscent of the memoirs of other famous magicians but even more closely linked to heavyweight champion Jack Johnson's 1927 autobiography, *In the Ring—and Out,* operates as a set of fictive recollections that thwart and question the very act of narrative memory, but which, again, his readership would accept as self-evidently the only life story Herman could have had. His acts of explanation become little more than virtuosic displays of the manipulation of obscurity.

Black Herman's magic was an outdoor vaudeville of entertainment, not a grandiose gesture of pure mysticism. As he writes at the very beginning of his book: "In offering to you my solution of the troubles and difficulties that beset your pathway, I wish to state so that there will no misunderstanding at any time, that I do not claim to be the possessor of any supernatural or unnatural power whatsoever, nor do I claim to be able to accomplish anything that is impossible to the average mind, were it to be devoted to specializing along these lines entirely." Here is the preachment of practice and discipline, of learning skills, which characterized both Garvey and Washington. At his stage shows Herman frequently denounced fortune-tellers and spiritualists. "If they can read your fortune," he would say with venom, "why don't they read their own and know when the cops are after them?" The trick for Herman is not mysticism but the irony of the detective presenting the audience with a mystery that can be solved only through rational and deductive logic and an understanding of simple ingenuity but that seems to defy both logic and ingenuity as the magic mystery offers itself as an expression of the utterly inexplicable.

Burying someone alive and then resurrecting the person is quite an old illusion; some even say that Christ performed a variation of it at his entombment. It apparently originated with Indian fakirs; at least they are the best-known performers of living burial as a signification of bodily discipline and the power of the mind to display its force through a simulation of the very negation of that force. Yet I am inclined to think that Black Herman performed this trick in part because it was both an answer and a complement to the famous trick performed by Alexander and Carl Herrmann, German Jews who became very famous magicians and from whom Black Herman may well have taken his name (Herman never acknowledged in his books that his real name was either Herman Rucker or Benjamin Rucker, as the newspapers variously asserted). The white Herrmanns' trick was known as "The Cremation." As reported by Francis Joseph Martinka, an old intimate of the Herrmanns and other magicians in a 1916 issue of the *Brooklyn Eagle,* the trick worked thus: "In this feat a [hypnotized] woman was folded in a coffin and set afire. The audience plainly beheld the feminine form shrivel into a skeleton. After a long moment of suspense, the woman would again appear from behind a curtain at the other end of the stage. The machinery of this trick involved days of ingenious plotting and combined illusions, and brought in nearly $100,000 to Herrmann at the end of his tour." Black Herman wanted an act that was at least as grand as the Herrmann brothers' trick of giving women—the life bearers—the gift of life out of an elaborately induced death that could occur only through a pantomime of submission imitating the gestures of hypnotism, a well-known tool for the psychoanalytic treatment of hysterical women. Aside from this obvious feminist interpretation of symbolic sexual politics given a masculine metaphysical and theatrical veneer, the contrived display of which may have appealed to Herman and his black audience, Black Herman was also very competitive, constantly comparing himself to the best magicians. He had to feel that his illusions were on a par with theirs. If the white Herrmanns had a cremation, he would have a burial.

Among blacks the fakery of the resurrection trick was made even more explicit and more comic when the 1950s rhythm and blues singer Screaming Jay Hawkins of "I Put a Spell On You" fame decided to open his act by rising from a coffin holding a skull. Hawkins conflated the images of the magician, the conjurer, the hoodoo doctor, the spiritualist, the medium, and the vampire—the entire cast of necromantic wonder-workers that lurks in the Western, and particularly the black Western subconscious mind—into a pop culture parody of the arcane and the occult which was meant to make explicit the roots of black American showmanship while mystifying the implicit sexuality and authorial premises of male rhythm and blues singing.

The fact that Black Herman, who was a herbalist and an astrologer in addition to being a magician, was often written about in black newspapers was not very unusual, for during Herman's heyday in the 1920s the doings of black magicians and conjurers seem to have blanketed such newspapers, just as, one supposes, they themselves blanketed black neighborhoods. These "professors" (only black ragtime piano players were so commonly referred to by the same learned appellation—and of course ragtime and magic occupied the same twilight world of black vaudeville and nightclubs, the devil's world, yet one perceived as a world of learning and skill) straddled the realm of the mystic and that of the scientist, and yet they were in truth both the negation and paradoxically the essence of both. (In James Baldwin's 1953 novel *Go Tell It on the Mountain,* Elizabeth, the protagonist's mother, arrives in Harlem from the South in 1920—the era of Black Herman and the Renaissance—to live with Madame Williams, a spiritualist and seer. The narrator condemns her for not noticing or caring about Elizabeth's final tragedy. Thus, although Baldwin may have been, at best, ambivalent in the novel about Christianity, he had nothing but outright scorn for spiritualists as being both the parody and negation of Christianity. This is made explicit in his 1948 essay "The Harlem Ghetto.")

Ads for fortune-tellers and spiritualists—Professor Edet Effrong, Native of Africa; Professor N. Phoenix, Spiritualist, Magician, Healer; Professor Ejo A. Mohammedan, Scientist; Professor J. Du JaJa, A Mohammedan Scientist; Professor S. Indoo; Professor Alpha Roktabija, Arabian Mystic Seer; Professor S. M. Haffaney; and Professor Akpan Aga, Wonderful Magician by Alchemy and Fire—were common in major black newspapers, whose readers were attracted not only by the fortune-telling or spiritualism of these magicians but also by the claims that they were physicians, healers who were often more accessible, more sympathetic, and seemingly more powerful than many medical doctors. (It must be remembered, as Norton Smith notes in *Jesus the Magician,* that Christ's charismatic authority stemmed largely from the fact that his miracles or tricks were mostly feats of healings among the poor.) Professor Joseph Domingo, "World's Wonder, African Spiritualist and Occulist [sic], and Mohammedan from Kano, West Coast, Africa," who frequently advertised in black newspapers of the day, was twice arrested for fraudulent medical practice, both of which instances were front-page stories in the *Amsterdam News.* These black newspapers often ran stories about voodoo doctors, cult murderers, jailed boy healers, quack fortune-tellers, dishonest mediums, and the like, obviously because their readers were interested in them. Although most of these grotesque yet comic stories were written with a certain derisive dismissiveness, there was much coverage of the black vaudeville circuit, where many magicians, wonder-workers, and spiritualists performed. For instance, Coy Herndon, who was featured at minstrel shows and circuses as one of the most extraordinary hoop rollers in the world and one of the great wonder-workers of his time, wrote a regular gossip column for the *Chicago Defender*, "Coy Cogitates," mostly about black vaudeville, but with the suggestion of being about something mystical.

Black Herman did not lack competitors, yet he seems to have risen above them in some way—not because he was, in the end, any less a charlatan or a quack or a confidence man but because he was something else, possibly something more than merely a predator on the ignorant and unlucky poor. His nationalistic pretensions and his business acumen implied a distinct nobility. He was one of the few magicians who advertised himself not merely as a wonder-worker but as a sort of race hero. Of course, the others, with their Islamic trappings and African or Arabic pretensions, made a similar gesture toward being considered race heroes as well. But Herman's own claims were never really atavistic but rather synthetic. He may have claimed an African birthplace, but he was also a professed Christian of a very American, albeit black, nature. Nor, in the end, despite his claims to an African origin, did he try to mystify the concept of race. Herman, like, say, the black nationalist Hubert H. Harrison (a contemporary), really tried to mystify the *power*, while paradoxically demystifying the *act*, of acquiring knowledge. When Herman spoke of knowledge as a discipline open to anyone of "average mind," he was undermining one of the assumptions on which fake spiritualists make their claims to priestcraft. Herman was undoubtedly a hustler but possibly less a fraud than a shrewd fox.

There is one final distinction between the 1934 and 1938 editions of Black Herman's *Easy Pocket Tricks Which You Can Do*. His slogan is slightly altered. In the earlier work it reads "Black Herman Comes Through Only Once Every Seven Years," and in the later edition "Black Herman Comes Through Once Every Seven Years." This minor revision does not really change the sense of the statement. His detractors said that Herman could come to a town only once every seven years because the uproar he caused and the dissatisfied people he left behind virtually ensured no return engagement in the near future. Perhaps this was true. But he was surely no worse than local magicians and wonder-workers in any given community, and probably a bit better than the many religious vultures who picked bones clean with their revival meetings. Who knows why the slogan was altered? Someone, perhaps Herman's ghost, realized that "only" was, after all, a redundancy.

*Defining*
*Moments*
*since*
*the*
*1960s*

"HE IS a friend of my mind," Sixo, one of the slave protagonists in Toni Morrison's novel *Beloved* (1987), says of his lover, the Thirty-Mile Woman. "She gather me, man. The pieces I am, she gather them and give them back to me in all the right order. It's good, you know, when you got a woman who is a friend of your mind."[1] This passage from Morrison's novel formulates the challenge faced by the various attempts to invent and constitute African Americanness since the 1960s: the empowering optimism of the civil rights movement was based on the conviction "that history's lies can be corrected and its omissions restored."[2] There was no doubt about the need to free the African American experience from its entrapment in white definitions, from what Deborah McDowell calls "the betrayal of blacks by the written word."[3] Yet how can African Americanness define and position itself within this confusingly fragmented, heterogeneous, and contradictory scenario of representation, misrepresentation, and self-representation, of race, ethnicity, class, and gender? The contributions in this section characterize African American struggles for definitions in the past thirty years as a vast genealogical revisionist poem that, in the words of Kimberly

1. Toni Morrison, *Beloved* (New York: Knopf, 1987), pp. 273–274.
2. Deborah McDowell, "Negotiating between Tenses: Witnessing Slavery after Freedom—*Dessa Rose*," in *Slavery and Literary Imagination*, ed. Deborah McDowell and Arnold Rampersad (Baltimore: Johns Hopkins University Press, 1989), p. 145.
3. Ibid.

W. Benston, "attempts to restore continuity and meaning to the ruptures or discontinuities imposed by the history of black presence in America."[4]

Using the Organization of Black American Culture (OBAC) writers' workshop in Chicago as his example, David Lionel Smith's "Chicago Poets, OBAC, and the Black Arts Movement" focuses on art and culture as a complex process of generation and formation. Starting with a historical definition of the workshop, its organization, and its activities, Smith—author of the study *Racial Writing, Black and White*—presents its basic ideas and discusses critical works by OBAC members in order to encourage new, multifaceted inquiries into the Black Arts movement.

Phillip Brian Harper, in "Around 1969: Televisual Representation and the Complication of the Black Subject," scrutinizes the cultural moment when black characters entered television programming in a new and intense way. Harper, the author of *Framing the Margins: The Social Logic of Postmodern Culture,* shows that the demand for "relevancy" set off conflicting expectations for both the rise of black TV stars and a critique of the newly emerging figures as being too "middle class" and hence not truly "representative" of African Americans. The contradictions that are amusingly exposed here are suggestive for other areas of the culture industry as well—including, perhaps, present-day academic life.

Ugo Rubeo, whose book *Uomo visibile* (Visible Man) is a critical study of contemporary African American poetry, discusses in "Voice as Lifesaver: Defining the Function of Orality in Etheridge Knight's Poetry" Knight's use of what Rubeo calls "the inner dynamics of the modes of oral communication" in order to ensure the poet's multifaceted dialogue with his own creativity, his audience, and his tradition. It becomes clear that orality both renders this dialogue possible and guarantees its effectiveness as it controls its continuity and represents its inner dynamics "in a telling, suggestive flow of metaphoric images."

Fritz Gysin's "Predicaments of Skin: Boundaries in Recent African American Fiction" is a subtle, insightful reading of "moments" of boundary construction and transgression in the novels of Charles Johnson and John Edgar Wideman. Gysin, best known for his classic study *The Grotesque in American Negro Fiction,* argues here that the experience delineated in these texts tran-

---

4. Kimberly W. Benston, "I Yam What I Am: The Topos of (Un)naming in Afro-American Literature," in *Black Literature and Literary Theory,* ed. Henry Louis Gates, Jr. (New York: Routledge, 1990), p. 152.

scends the exclusive emphasis on the sinister aspects of boundaries which dominates the contemporary discourse of ethnicity and multiculturalism. Instead, the African (American) countervision which energizes these novels is based on the awareness "that the cultural blends within an ethnic group are utilized to formulate the dividing issues within the same group as well as those between this group and the mainstream or the majority at large."

A small cluster of essays by Jeffrey Melnick, ("'What You Lookin' At?' Ishmael Reed's *Reckless Eyeballing*") Katrin Schwenk, ("Lynching and Rape: Border Cases in African American History and Fiction"), and Sämi Ludwig ("Dialogic Possession in Ishmael Reed's *Mumbo Jumbo*") is dedicated, in the manner of a representative case study, to Ishmael Reed's work—which has also been the subject of a special issue of *Callaloo* edited by Shamoon Zamir. The three contributors have read one another's essays as well as other materials. Melnick's and Schwenk's essays both take as their point of departure Reed's novel *Reckless Eyeballing* in the contexts of Black-Jewish relations and the contradictory discourses of racism and sexism. Melnick develops his argument in a close reading of Reed's text against the background of the Leo Frank case, the history of the Emmett Till lynching, and Reed's debates with feminists, whereas Schwenk focuses on the "rape-lynching" complex as developed by Trudier Harris and concludes with a comparison between Reed and Alice Walker. Both essays, most especially in their attention to the conflicting interpretations of the Till case generated by Susan Brownmiller's book on rape, *Against Our Will*, point to virulent problems that are still very much alive at this moment; this became obvious in the process of editing this volume. The publisher's anonymous reader expressed concern that both these essays were too hard on Susan Brownmiller and too easy on Reed, taking him at face value in his attack on white feminists. When the essays were subsequently sent, together with the reader's report, to Reed and Brownmiller, they elicited rather contradictory responses. Reed thought that they were, if anything, "very gentle with Susan Brownmiller," but commended the authors for "their intellectual courage for challenging Ms. Brownmiller, a feminist Ikon, at a time when feminist political correctness has created an atmosphere . . . of fear and intimidation on American campuses." Worried that the report by the anonymous reader, "obviously a member of the feminist thought cops," might lead to the suppression of these essays, Reed warned one of the editors that it "would be unfortunate for [his] project to yield to this kind of pressure." In her response, Susan

Brownmiller confessed that reading the essays had caused her some grief. She questioned whether the critics had actually read her book and its source notes, and restated her position of 1977. In response to Melnick she called attention to sources she had used in addition to Eldridge Cleaver; commenting on Schwenk, she reviews her position on the Emmett Till case: "Yes, I did think Till whistled. Nowhere do I say (or imply) that he should have been lynched for it." Interestingly, Brownmiller complained—as did Reed—about political correctness, finding it "exceedingly troubling that in 1993 people are still terrified of offending the PC canon in regard to the Till case." Yet Reed's and Brownmiller's understandings of political correctness seem, as Schwenk points out in a note, diametrically opposed to each other.

Whereas Melnick and Schwenk highlight the uneasy relationship of African American and feminist concerns, Ludwig offers a new reading of Ishmael Reed, focusing on some analogies between Bakhtinian dialogism, concepts of voodoo, and Reed's notion of the multiculture. Ludwig's interest in Bakhtin makes him part of other new approaches to African American culture, represented in the present volume by Pedersen and Piccinato. In his comments on *Mumbo Jumbo*, Ludwig calls attention to Reed's car imagery as part of a broader concern for "vehicles," and touches on the figure of Black Herman—the subject of Gerald Early's contribution to the present collection.

A twentieth-century female *griot* who insists that "anything I have ever learned of any consequence, I have learned from Black people," the Nobel Prizewinner Toni Morrison takes an approach to African American history that is based on her intention to demystify the "wonderful lies" of some past historiography as well as to defy the self-protective taboos of African American discourse in order to reconstruct the authentic black experience.[5] Sylvia Mayer's " 'You like huckleberries?' Toni Morrison's *Beloved* and Mark Twain's *Adventures of Huckleberry Finn*" documents that Morrison achieves this end not only by relying on the authority of the nineteenth-century slave narrative's black narrative voice but also by reconceptualizing, from a black woman's perspective, the white male discourse on slavery as it was expressed in canonized novels such as Mark Twain's *Huck Finn*.

Hélène Christol's "Reconstructing American History: Land and Geneal-

5. Bettye J. Parker, "Complexity: Toni Morrison's Women—An Interview Essay," in *Sturdy Black Bridges: Visions of Black Women in Literature,* ed. Roseann P. Bell, Beverly Guy-Shaftall, and Bettye J. Parker (Garden City, N.Y.: Anchor Books, 1979), p. 251.

ogy in Gloria Naylor's *Mama Day* (1988)" is more than a sophisticated close reading of Naylor's fiction. By deciphering the intricate relationship between the topographical and the genealogical elements of the text on the one hand and its narrative voices on the other, it illuminates the broad historical concept on which Naylor's writing is based. *Mama Day* becomes, to quote Mae Gwendolyn Henderson, "an expressive site for a dialectics/dialogics of identity and difference."[6]

In "Charting a New Course: African American Literary Politics since 1976," Abby Arthur Johnson and Ronald Johnson, the co-authors of the classic study of Afro-American periodicals from 1900 to 1976, *Propaganda and Aesthetics,* pay tribute to the contributions various journals have made in shaping and documenting the turn toward an exploration of and experimentation with a plurality of theoretical approaches that characterized African American literature and scholarship in the post–Black Aesthetics era. Determined to decipher what E. Ethelbert Miller called the "unchartered waters" of African American cultures, these periodicals have substantially supported and advanced the greater acceptance of varied aesthetic approaches and the acknowledgment of dissent as a constructive, dynamic element of scholarship in African American studies.

6. Mae Gwendolyn Henderson, "Speaking in Tongues: Dialogics and the Black Woman Writer's Literary Tradition," in *Changing Our Own Words,* ed. Cheryl A. Wall (London: Routledge, 1990), p. 37.

*David Lionel Smith*

# Chicago Poets, OBAC, and the Black Arts Movement

*T*he Black Arts movement had several points of origin, and its genesis cannot properly be traced to any one of them. It must be understood, rather, as emanating from various local responses to a general development within American culture of the 1960s. The politics of that decade provided one central element in the origins of this movement: the civil rights movement and its radical heir, Black Power; the collapse of the McCarthyite suppression of the American left and the emergence of a New Left critique of American society and its institutions; and the reaction against imperialism, provoked especially by American, Soviet, and French incursions in Cuba, the Caribbean, Africa, and Southeast Asia. These and other such forces politicized the consciousness of young Americans in the 1960s. Similarly, the rebellion by young people against the rigid, racist, and puritanical culture of the 1950s resulted in a general cultural movement in the 1960s that was, at its extremes, fluid, transgressive, and libertine. The Black Arts movement reflected the America of its era, but it was not merely a darker mirror image. The movement was refracted through the complex dynamics of racial, class, and regional consciousness, as well as through the conflicted imperatives of political and personal agendas.

Although certain individual writers, such as Amiri Baraka, Sonia Sanchez, and Nikki Giovanni, transcended their regions, gaining fame and influence as national figures, we should not lose sight of the regional tendencies that the movement comprised. New York City produced several factions within the movement: writers such as Amiri Baraka and Ted Joans began their careers among the Beats and bohemians of Greenwich Village; the Umbra

Workshop writers were arguably the earliest major collective associated with the movement; and there were also independent figures such as Audre Lorde and June Jordan. On the West Coast the Watts Writers' Workshop was the best known Black Arts organization, though several writers previously associated with Umbra settled in San Francisco. Whether writers such as Ishmael Reed and Al Young are best understood as Black Arts movement writers is a very interesting question, though one that I cannot pursue here. In St. Louis the Black Artists Group (BAG) was best known for its musicians and visual artists. Chicago, however, was the city that produced the greatest variety and the most enduring of Black Arts organizations. This essay concentrates on Chicago's Organization of Black American Culture (OBAC) writers' workshop (OBAC) and the efforts of those writers to develop a black poetics.[1]

The purpose of this essay is to provide three basic elements of the inquiry into a black poetics. First, it offers a historical definition of OBAC, describing its founding, organization, activities, and procedures. Second, it discusses some of the basic ideas associated with OBAC. Third, it considers briefly some critical work by OBAC poets who attempted to articulate the principles of a black poetics. Obviously the inquiry into black poetics cannot be complete without a careful study of actual poetic works to ascertain the relationship between theory and execution. This kind of discussion, unfortunately, cannot be included within the space limitations of the present essay. Nonetheless, the purpose of this discussion of OBAC and black poetics is to provide the groundwork for subsequent examinations of work by OBAC poets.

On its surface the concept of black poetics appears more precise than "the black aesthetic," a phrase commonly associated with the movement but deeply compromised by its troublesome combination of ideological heat and substantive vagueness. "Black poetics" at least suggests a literary genre and a set of technical issues. Unfortunately, in actual use the term was often no

---

1. Eugene B. Redmond, "Festivals and Funerals: Black Poetry of the 1960s and 1970s" in *Drumvoices: The Mission of Afro-American Poetry* (Garden City, N.Y.: Doubleday Anchor, 1976), pp. 294–417, on the Black Arts poets remains the most comprehensive account available. Although he does not provide detailed discussions, he does include a great deal of valuable information. For example, he discusses the major writers' workshops and lists the names of many writers associated with each of them. Hence, this book is an indispensable source. On the Umbra Workshop, see Lorenzo Thomas, "The Shadow World: New York's Umbra Workshop and Origins of the Black Arts Movement" *Callaloo*, 1 (1978): 53–72; and Tom Dent, "Umbra Days," *Black American Literature Forum*, 14.3 (Fall 1980): 105–108.

more focused than "the black aesthetic." For example, Don L. Lee (Haki R. Madhubuti) published an essay in 1968 titled "Black Poetics/For the Many to Come." He begins it by offering his definition of black poetry:

> Blackpoetry is written for/to/about & around the lives/spiritactions/human-ism & total existence of blackpeople. Black poetry in form/sound/word/usage/intonation/rhythm/repetition/definition/direction & beauty is opposed to that which is now (& yesterday) considered poetry, i.e., white poetry . . . Whereas, blackpoets deal in the concrete rather than the abstract (concrete: art for peo-ple's sake; black language or Afro-american language in contrast to standard english, &tc.). Blackpoetry moves to define and legitimize blackpeople's reality (*that* which is real to us).[2]

While this definition conveys the political and ideological yearnings of the movement, it fails to articulate anything specific about poetry. It could easily refer to fiction, journalism, or any other expressive form. This problem of vagueness was ubiquitous in the movement.[3] Consequently, a major chal-lenge for historians of this period is to derive definitions from a study of the actual poetic practices of these writers, recognizing that their published statements about writing are often framed with nonliterary concerns in mind.

OBAC provides an especially interesting case for study because it is the only one of the workshops from the 1960s that still remained active in the 1990s. Thus, one can examine its development over nearly three decades. Founded in 1967, OBAC was conceived as a broadly based organization, with its initial leadership provided by Hoyt Fuller, Gerald McWorter (Abdul Alkalimat), and Conrad Kent Rivers (who died just a few months later). Its acronym, pronounced "o-bah-see," is designed to echo the Yoruba word *oba*, denoting royalty and leadership.[4] To facilitate its vision of cultural revo-lution, OBAC was created as an umbrella group comprising three work-shops: the writers' workshop, the visual artists' workshop, and the commu-nity workshop. This choice of workshops reflects an acknowledgment of other organizations already established in Chicago and a commitment not to overlap their efforts. For example, the Association for the Advancement

2. Don L. Lee, "Black Poetics/For the Many to Come," in *Nommo: A Literary Legacy of Black Chicago (1967–1987)*, ed. Carole A. Parks (Chicago: OBAhouse, 1987), p. 13.

3. Daivd Lionel Smith, "The Black Arts Movement and Its Critics," *American Literary History*, 3.1 (Spring 1991): 93–110.

4. Gerald McWorter, "How OBAC Was Born: Personal Notes," unpublished manuscript.

of Creative Musicians (AACM) had been founded in 1965 (and continues to be active). Thus, OBAC had no musical component. Similarly, there were already black theater organizations in Chicago; and furthermore, Val Gray Ward, who was originally on the OBAC leadership council, soon left to found Kuumba Workshop, a theater group that shared the basic principles of OBAC. Therefore, the OBAC writers' workshop concentrated on poetry and fiction. McWorter was the first chair of OBAC, with Fuller leading the writers' workshop, Jeff Donaldson leading the visual arts workshop, and Joe Simpson leading the community work.[5]

OBAC's original statement of purpose articulated an eight-point program that aspired to define a "Black Aesthetic," to produce work reflecting "the Black Experience," to develop black critics and appropriate standards by which black writing might be judged, to develop an atmosphere of constructive collegial criticism within the workshop, to provide a forum for local and visiting writers, and to maintain publications disseminating the work of OBAC writers.[6] These basic principles informed the operations of the workshop and were reiterated and elaborated in numerous essays by OBAC members over the years. An excellent sampling of them has been collected in *Nommo: A Literary Legacy of Black Chicago (1967–1987)*, an anthology edited by Carole A. Parks to commemorate the twentieth anniversary of the workshop. Of these essays Hoyt Fuller's "Towards a Black Aesthetic" is the most broadly known. It was the lead essay in Addison Gayle's book *The Black Aesthetic*. In it Fuller uses OBAC principles as a basis for discussing the goals of the Black Arts movement in general. What all of these OBAC position papers have in common is their commitment to expressive modes developed out of ordinary black experience and to a direct communication between black artists and a black audience.

As we have already seen with Madhubuti's discussion of "black poetics," a clear and resolute political position does not necessarily translate into definitive literary claims. Similarly, the attempt to define blackness often leads to troubling inconsistencies, such as one finds in one of the earliest documents, McWorter's "OBAC Position Paper: Some Ideological Considerations." McWorter begins with the premise that "a primary fact about the

---

5. Many details of this history are derived from Gerald McWorter's unpublished essay. I have also relied on comments made during panel discussions at the OBAC twentieth-anniversary celebration in Chicago in November 1987, which I have collected on audio tape.

6. Parks, *Nommo*, p. 10.

life-style of Black People is the intensity of the 'now.' We must incorporate this into OBAC and avoid being static in the current context of Black life."[7] Yet most of the essay is concerned with the organization's goals, bespeaking a future consciousness, and it concludes with an assertion that the denial of black history is "among the most denigrating aspects of" the African American experience.[8] Thus, McWorter's clear recognition of the need for total historical consciousness, encompassing past, present, and future, apparently contradicts his premise, identifying black consciousness with the immediacy of present experience.

Actually, this apparent contradiction is primarily a matter of overstatement. McWorter's point really seems to be to emphasize flexibility and the capacity of artists to adapt themselves to their social environment. Still, the problem here is far more than mere exaggeration. It derives directly from the impulse to claim singularity for black consciousness, distinguishing it in some fundamental way from white consciousness. This results in claiming for black consciousness a character that is in fact much more limited than what is attributed to white consciousness: that is, black consciousness is immediate and truncated while white consciousness is historical and inclusive. Worse, this argument endorses precisely the stereotype of black people that the essay ends by condemning. Such entailments are inherent to the essentialist notion of race that this essay takes as its premise.

The point of emphasizing this flaw in McWorter's essay is neither to single him out for special criticism nor to imply that this essay is uniquely deficient. On the contrary, his essay is quite representative of both OBAC and the Black Arts movement in general in its espousal of a racial essentialism. Again and again the inherent contradictions of racial essentialism undermined efforts to articulate a coherent black aesthetic theory. I do not mean to suggest that the quest for a black aesthetic was entirely misguided. Rather, it seems to me that the theorists of the Black Arts movement erred in their preoccupation with defining a single correct ideology of blackness. What was needed instead of uniformity was a far more pluralist, accurate, and historically detailed understanding of racial identity in America than our culture had previously offered. Thus, the error of the movement's theorists was not that they were too radical but rather that they were too conventional. By remaining within essentialist conceptions of race, they bound themselves to a system

7. Ibid., p. 11.
8. Ibid., p. 12.

that was designed explicitly to preclude the revolution they sought. A satis-factory black aesthetic would have liberated them to embrace the multifari-ous particularity of African American experience. Instead, they subscribed to an ideology of blackness that left them trapped in the fun house of racial essentialism.[9]

Naturally this theoretical dilemma reflects a social dilemma. Many of these writers used the ideology of essential blackness to mask their own complex background. OBAC's chair, McWorter, for example, was a University of Chi-cago doctoral candidate, and Hoyt Fuller was as erudite and cosmopolitan as any American journalist of his generation. To note that they failed to articulate a theory of blackness that could account for how much they them-selves owed to white and European culture is not to impugn either their honesty or their theoretical sophistication. It is more useful, it seems to me, to understand this general failing of the movement's writers as an object lesson illustrating how closely theory is constrained by social factors. These men wrote the theory that their circumstances allowed them to write. From our own historical perspective we ought to be able to retheorize their move-ment, and furthermore to do the close literary analysis that the movement's writing has, with a very few exceptions, still not received.

What, exactly, was the OBAC writers' workshop, and what did it do? First and foremost it was a community-based organization. From the outset OBAC members decided that the organization would remain autonomous, eschewing formal affiliations with any other institution. Thus, it has never been connected with any college, university, museum, or cultural center. It has, however, rented meeting space in a variety of locations, including the DuSable Museum, the Southside Community Arts Center, and various store-fronts. It was a group in which members and visitors met every Wednesday (except the fourth Wednesday of the month, which was reserved for business meetings, or for rent parties in the early years) to read their works and offer critical (or appreciative) commentary. Usually writers join OBAC after a pe-riod of attending meetings as visitors. Official membership is gained by invi-tation. Ordinarily only members are permitted to participate in OBAC's pub-lic readings or to publish in its journal, *Nommo,* and its newsletter, *Cumbaya.*

In the early years of OBAC, established black writers who visited Chicago often attended meetings of the workshop and read from their recent work

9. I have pursued this argument in some detail in other essays. See, for example, Smith, "The Black Arts Movement and Its Critics," esp. pp. 98–101.

or work in progress. For example, Alex Haley read from the manuscript of *Roots* at an OBAC meeting in 1968. Generally, visitors received the special consideration of being allowed to read even if they were not celebrities. Members, however, did not necessarily read at each meeting. By the early 1970s OBAC had developed a system of rotating the chairmanship from month to month. The chair had the responsibility to record who was in attendance and what each one had brought to read. When there was not enough time for everyone to read, the chair was also responsible for deciding who would read and how much, taking into account individuals' contributions at previous meetings. After each reading, the floor was open for commentary.[10]

The nature of the commentary could vary. Much of it was typical writing workshop discussion about matters of technique: diction, characterization, imagery, rhythm, and the like. Issues of racial politics and gender relations were frequently debated. (Contrary to some characterizations of the Black Arts movement, women always had a strong and vocal presence in OBAC, beginning with Carolyn Rodgers, Ronda Davis, and Jewel Lattimore [Johari Amini] in the early years. By the late 1970s OBAC was predominantly female.) Certain issues, however, were constants in OBAC—in particular, a concern with the relationship of writers to their audience, the accessibility of the work, and the saturation of the work with black culture. This last point especially focused on the issue of how to use vernacular language in poems and the limitations of the vernacular. For example, Carolyn Rodgers's use of the word "muthafucka" provoked sharp argument, both inside and outside the workshop. She comments on this in her poem "The Last M.F." For the public the issue was propriety. OBAC members addressed this question but were also concerned with aesthetic value: the distinction between sensationalism and creativity. In their public declarations and published writings OBAC members often seemed concerned only with the ideological aspects of writing, but within the workshop, away from public view, they could turn more freely to the subtle details of literary craft.

Most obviously the workshop offered to writers immediate and informed conversation about their writing; but like the other workshops of the time, OBAC provided many other benefits as well. In addition to discussions about specific pieces of writing and about the general values and concerns of the movement, it also provided young writers a sort of literary education. This

10. For some of these details I am indebted to conversations with Angela Jackson. I have also drawn on my own experiences as a member of the workshop in the late 1970s.

was especially valuable in terms of sharing knowledge about works by black writers. After all, black literature courses were generally not taught in schools and were only beginning to enter college curricula at that time. Knowledge of black writers beyond Langston Hughes and Richard Wright had to be derived from independent reading. Thus, the discussions in OBAC provided crucial information regarding past and present black literature. By no means, however, were these discussions limited to black writing. In discussions of fictional technique, for instance, James Joyce's *Dubliners* was frequently mentioned, as well as the works of Hemingway, Steinbeck, and many others. The public polemics of these writers notwithstanding, their attitude toward white writers was not so much a blind rejection of all things white as it was an insistence on choosing their own literary models, on their own terms. Finally, in addition to providing literary education, OBAC also facilitated the development of literary friendships. For young writers this is no small matter.

Workshops such as OBAC represented an attempt by these writers to seize control of the literary means of production. Workshops allowed the writers to shape collectively the nature of their own literary work and to define their relations to the public through their publications and other public activities. In the case of OBAC these other activities included poetry readings not only in places such as schools, museums, and churches but even in bars and other sites where ordinary black folk, not normally considered an audience for poetry, gathered.[11] Furthermore, this pursuit of creative self-determination led people associated with OBAC to develop related organizations. I have already mentioned the founding of the Kuumba Workshop, a theater institution, by Val Gray Ward. Haki Madhubuti and Johari Amini founded Third World Press; it published books of poetry by OBAC members and others, including Amiri Baraka, as well as books on black history and politics. These outlets were immediately available to people associated with the workshop.

The most important publishing connection, however, derived from Hoyt Fuller's involvement with the workshop. Fuller was editor of *Negro Digest/ Black World*, the most widely read and distributed black intellectual journal of its time. Fuller published OBAC writers along with black writers from all over the United States, Africa, and the Caribbean. The importance of Hoyt

---

11. Readings in such unconventional locations were fundamental to OBAC's sense of identity and were not mere digressions or indulgences. For example, one of the programs during the twentieth-anniversary celebration was a "poetry and blues jam" on Saturday night at Gerri's Palm Tavern on Forty-seventh Street. It featured blues by Billy Branch and the SOBs and readings by numerous past and present OBAC poets.

Fuller to OBAC was nonetheless more closely related to his personal charisma than to his editorial status. Erudite, urbane, and incisively articulate, Fuller was a commanding figure. His presence attracted people to the workshop and inspired them to behave themselves once they were there.

One of OBAC's declared objectives was to develop critics; accordingly, some of the workshop members published notable works of criticism. Carolyn Rodgers's essay "Black Poetry—Where It's At" has often been cited,[12] and Don L. Lee's *Dynamite Voices* remains the only book-length study of the Black Arts poets.[13] The two works differ in important ways, but they both endeavor to introduce readers to a variety of poets and poems while at the same time providing critical terms and categories for understanding the new black poetry. Rodgers lists her categories in outline form:

1. *signifying*
   a. open
   b. sly
   c. with or about

2. *teachin/rappin*

3. *coversoff*
   a. rundown
   b. hipto
   c. digup
   d. coatpull

4. *spaced* (spiritual)
   a. mindblower (fantasy)
   b. coolout

5. *bein* (self/reflective)
   a. upinself
   b. uptight
   c. dealin/swingin

6. *love*
   a. skin
   b. space (spiritual)
   c. cosmic (ancestral)

12. Carolyn Rodgers, "Black Poetry—Where It's At," in Parks, *Nommo*, pp. 28–37.
13. Don L. Lee, *Dynamite Voices: Black Poets of the 1960s* (Detroit: Broadside Press, 1971).

   7. *shoutin* (angry/cathartic)
     a. badmouth
     b. facetoface (warning/confrontation)
     c. two faced (irony)

   8. *jazz*
     a. riffin
     b. cosmic ('Trane)
     c. grounded (Lewis)

   9. *du-wah*
     a. dittybop
     b. bebop

   10. *pyramid* (getting us together/building/nationhood)

Rodgers intends these categories to describe a wide range of black poetry, and a close analysis of them reveals a great deal about her conception of poetic form. In contrast to conventional formalist poetics, which describes the elements of the poems by treating the poems as self-contained objects, nearly all of Rodgers's categories are rhetorical stances, reflecting the poet's manner of addressing the audience. Even her choice of vocabulary, using slang terms rather than conventional literary terminology, indicates her commitment to present herself as a writer of the people and for the people. This image of the black poet speaking to black people is perhaps the most characteristic and definitive trait of OBAC writers, and it is fascinating to note that it informs Rodgers's criticism as well as her poetry.[14]

It is also interesting to note that Rodgers lists "signifying" as the first of her categories. Indeed, she devotes more space to "signifying" than to any other of the categories—about a third of the essay. Her examples range from Richard Wright to Amiri Baraka, Don L. Lee, and Nikki Giovanni, and she discusses many forms of signifying. Her emphasis on this category is noteworthy especially because the concept of signifying, as enumerated by Michael Cooke and Henry Louis Gates, Jr., became central to the academic criticism of African American literature in the 1980s. Even before Stephen

---

14. I have discussed the similarities and differences between Gates and Black Arts critics in Smith, "The Black Arts Movement." For a more detailed discussion of Gates and his theory of "signifyin(g)," see Smith, "Black Figures, Signs, Voices," *Review,* 11 (1989): 1–36.

Henderson,[15] Rodgers had already identified and begun to analyze signifying as a definitive element of the black literary tradition.

Don L. Lee's *Dynamite Voices* (1971) is essentially a survey of the new poetry. The most eminent poet of the movement, Amiri Baraka, is conspicuously missing from the survey, but Lee offers an excellent mix of writers, ranging from celebrities such as Nikki Giovanni and Sonia Sanchez to emerging poets such as Everett Hoagland and Ebon. Like Rodgers, Lee offers a set of critical categories; but he is much more concerned than Rodgers with evaluative judgments and questions of aesthetic value. His categories for describing the new poetry are much more conventionally formal than Rodgers's, though his comments on particular poets clearly reveal that he shares her fundamental concern with the stance of the poet relative to his or her audience. Indeed, he quotes Ron Welburn's assertion that black poets are the most "priestly"[16] poets in America.

According to Lee, "the common characteristics of the Black poetry of the Sixties" are:

polyrhythm—uneven, short and explosive lines
intensity—deep, yet simple; spiritual, yet physical
irony—humor, signifying/the dozens
sarcasm—the new comedy
direction—positive movement, teaching, nation-building
concrete subject matter—reflection of a collective and personal life style
musicality—the unique use of vowels and consonants with the developed rap, demanding that the poetry be read out loud[17]

Some of these categories overlap with those provided by Rodgers, but Lee clearly has a greater concern with specific issues of poetic craft. His comments on particular poets, sometimes appreciative and sometimes critical, reflect such concerns. In the book's conclusion Lee makes a rather surprising criticism of his fellow black poets:

We see in some of the poets' current work that they are not reading their own contemporaries and therefore are duplicating, repeating without noticeable advancement. It is clear that the poet must devote to his craft the same time and practice that "good" musicians devote to learning their art form . . . The Black

15. Stephen E. Henderson, *Understanding the New Black Poetry: Black Speech and Black Music as Poetic References* (New York: Morrow, 1973).

16. Lee, *Dynamite Voices*, p. 35.

17. Ibid., p. 35.

poet should understand that there is a tradition of Black writing—conditioned, yes, but still Black. Like the musician, the Black writer/poet must be hip to the present and past in Black letters—in this country, Africa and the West Indies.[18]

He then proceeds to mention a long list of writers, including Robert Hayden, a poet much maligned by many younger poets of the 1960s. This emphasis on the very conventional literary values of disciplined study and respect for tradition are not what one might expect from a Black Arts poet. Nevertheless, Lee/Madhubuti was and remains one of the most broadly read poets of the movement, a man whose reading passions range beyond literature into anthropology, history, sociology, politics, and health and nutrition. His arguments bear his personal stamp, yet they are also clearly rooted in the principles and practices of OBAC.

The relationship between the literary criticism of these writers and their own poetic work is an issue that remains to be explored. Unfortunately, that cannot be pursued within the scope of this essay. The broader point, however, is that these works of criticism are elements of the larger discourse regarding literature, culture, and politics that emanated from the OBAC writers' workshop. The collective activity within the workshop did not necessarily make writers of people who would not otherwise have become writers, but it surely influenced the kinds of writers they became. In order to understand the writers of the Black Arts movement, we need to take into account the role of writers' workshops and other collectives in shaping them. The general attitudes about politics, aesthetic value, the definition of an ideal audience, and the relationship of writer to audience translate themselves into very specific forms of literary praxis. By "literary praxis" I mean both literary gestures, such as the choice of vocabulary and diction, subject matter, and rhetorical stance, and social forms of literary activity, such as selecting publishers, choosing other modes of literary dissemination (for example, broadsides and readings), and managing one's role as a public figure. We must study the literary technique of these writers, but we must also recognize that technique is predicated on ideas about the nature and purposes of literary expression. Thus, we need a multifaceted inquiry that examines the movement, the tendencies or collectives within the movement, and the individual forms of expression associated with it.

18. Ibid., p. 77.

*Phillip Brian Harper*

# Around 1969: Televisual Representation and the Complication of the Black Subject

f we sought to identify one term that served as a signal buzzword in commentary about U.S. mass media culture during the late 1960s and early 1970s, we would be hard-pressed to come up with a better choice than *relevancy*. The term was widely invoked in demands that contemporary culture faithfully "reflect" the myriad social and political issues that so urgently commanded public attention during that volatile period. Insofar as the insistence of those demands corresponded to the relative audience impact enjoyed by any given medium, it is not surprising that broadcast television became a prime target for them. Moreover, insofar as racial politics—and, specifically, black-white race relations—was among the period's most pressing issues, it is understandable that it should have constituted a rallying point for relevancy demands.

A 1970 article by the African American author John Oliver Killens fairly exemplifies the sort of critique to which television was subjected during the period in question. In this piece Killens notes that, through the mid-1960s, a black person could "stare at television and go to an occasional movie and go through the routine from day to day, month to month, and year to year and hardly (if ever) see himself reflected in the cultural media. It was as if he had no real existence, as if he were a figment of his own imagination, or, at best, if he had an existence it wasn't worth reflecting or reflection." Killens goes on to admit that, at the point at which he is writing, "progress *has* been made, in that there are more actors employed in the medium."[1]

---

1. John Oliver Killens, "Our Struggle Is Not to Be White Men in Black Skin," *TV Guide,* 25 (July 1970): 6; subsequently cited by page in the text.

This development, however, is not sufficient in Killens's view, which places a premium not on the mere *quantity* of African Americans appearing on TV, but rather on the medium's reflection of authentic African American social experience, evidenced in the specific *quality* of the images presented on the screen.

This is not to say that increased employment of black actors is an insignificant matter. On the contrary, by the time of Killens's writing network television had already aired a number of successful programs with African American performers in prominent roles, and the publicity surrounding these shows manifested some very interesting features. In 1965, for instance, a substantial amount of press attention was accorded Bill Cosby when he became the first African American to star in a dramatic series on network television—NBC's *I Spy*, also featuring Robert Culp. What was most interesting about Cosby's statements in press profiles, however, was not his claim that his television work might further the agenda of the civil rights movement, but rather the indications he gave as to his prime motivation in taking on such work. A *Saturday Evening Post* article provides a summary of the stand-up comedy experience that preceded Cosby's being hired for *I Spy*, and notes his plans for the future:

> If he clicks in the show [which, at the time of the article's publication, was just beginning its first season], Cosby hopes to phase permanently out of nightclub humor into TV heroics, for one simple reason—money. And he plans to retire from all strenuous activity within 10 years, when he expects to have saved a cool million dollars. "That doesn't mean I don't care about the show," he says. "I'd be upset if I looked like a dodo on that TV screen. But I've got no great artistic ambitions. What show business mainly means to me is cash."[2]

This sentiment was repeated in a *TV Guide* interview from the same period, in which Cosby bluntly asserts, "Money is of the utmost importance to me"; and he muses further, "If this series goes five years, I will be only 33 and rich."[3]

Similar references to material gain characterize feature stories on Diahann Carroll, whose infamous NBC series *Julia*—about a young black war widow raising her son in a racially integrated environment—debuted three years after *I Spy*. A December 1968 *Time* magazine article observes:

2. Stanley Karnow, "Bill Cosby: Variety Is the Life of Spies," *Saturday Evening Post*, 25 (September 1965): 88.

3. Robert de Roos, "The Spy Who Came in for the Gold," *TV Guide*, 23 (October 1965): 15.

Diahann has made a life for herself that is considerably better than the main-stream. She rents a handsome three-bedroom furnished house in Beverly Hills; it came complete with gardens, swimming pool and a grey Bentley. That is in keeping with Diahann's tastes . . .

Diahann's clothes are by Donald Brooks and Scaasi. In restaurants she asks the wine steward for Lafite-Rothschild '55.

The text is accompanied by a photograph of Carroll posed in front of her Bentley on the lot of the 20th Century–Fox studios.[4]

Thus it is clear that black actors' increased employment in television had potentially profound consequences for the performers themselves, whose material wealth was readily registered in media accounts of their success. That success and wealth, however, became deeply problematic for commentators such as John Killens as soon as they began to characterize not the off-screen lives of black performers but the experiences of the characters those actors portrayed on screen.

By the time Killens's article appeared, network television programs featuring African American performers included not only *Julia* but also *The Bill Cosby Show,* in which Cosby, in a transition from the now defunct *I Spy,* portrayed a high school basektball coach; *The Leslie Uggams Show,* an hour-long variety program; and *Room 222,* a classroom "comedy-drama" to which I will give sustained attention shortly. The problem with all of these programs, according to popular critiques, was that they weren't really "black shows." As one black man interviewed by John Killens puts it, "They're just shows with Black people acting like they White," or, to cite another of Killens's interviewees, "White folks masquerading in Black skin" (7, 8). In his own summation, Killens charges that "the television establishment is attempting to give to the world the image of an integrated society in all facets of American life . . . which is all well and good except that it is a colossal lie, because America is not an integrated society. It is a segregated society" (8). And while in this formulation Killens associates television's failure to mirror faithfully the conditions in which black people live their daily lives with its presentation of an integrated society that has no basis in "fact," later on in his piece he offers a slightly different account of what, really, is wrong with the televisual picture. Commenting specifically on *Room 222,* Killens asserts that "the black folk here are full of understanding and wisdom, sym-

4. "Wonderful World of Color," *Time,* 13 (December 1968): 70.

pathetic all the way. No basic problems between the races. All men are brothers, right? An undramatic, middle-classish situation that hardly has anything
to do with the Black experience" (9). In this rendering the inauthenticity
of the televisual representation of black life is expressly identified with the
presentation of a specifically "middle-class" situation in which "the black
experience" apparently cannot, by definition, inhere. This fact indicates an
interesting feature of Killens's critical position regarding television's treatment of blacks, whereby, on the one hand, concern for the financial success
and professional advancement of black performers such as Cosby and Carroll—we might call it their social mobility—is simultaneously registered and
bracketed (through Killens's fleeting recognition that "progress has been
made . . . there are more actors employed in the medium"), while, on the
other hand, the call for authenticity is manifested precisely in the demand
that the black characters portrayed in the medium demonstrate no such
socioeconomic advantage.

Paradoxically, therefore, the insistence that television faithfully represent
a set of social conditions conceived by Killens and others as composing a
singular and unitary phenomenon known as "*the* black experience" runs
smack up against a simultaneous implicit demand that it both recognize and
help constitute the diversity of African American society. The tension inherent in this situation was vividly expressed in the debut of *The Leslie Uggams
Show,* in which Uggams exhorted her presumedly white audience to recognize that "not all black people look alike. I'm not Diahann Carroll. I'm not
Julia." At that moment Marc Copage, the young boy who played Corey,
Julia's son in the Diahann Carroll series, ran onto the stage toward Uggams,
arms outstretched, calling, "Mama, mama!"[5] The shock of this gag consists,
I think, in its simultaneous chastisement regarding the conceptualization of
black people as a monolithic stereotype and its exposure of profound anxieties about the political ramifications of actually instantiating difference
among African American subjects. Thus, if *Room 222* upset John Killens, I
would suggest that, the ostensible import of his protest notwithstanding, this
was precisely because it worked to negotiate an intraracial social difference
that was seen as potentially disruptive to the political solidarity of the African
American community.

*Room 222* ran on ABC from September 17, 1969, through January 11,

---

5. John Garabedian, "Unseasonable," *Newsweek,* 6 (October 1969): 113–114.

1974. Generally a critical success, it won the Emmy award for outstanding new series of the 1969–70 season. In that same season Karen Valentine and Michael Constantine won Emmys for their supporting performances in the series.[6] But neither of these white actors was the primary focus of *Room 222*. As *The Complete Encyclopedia of Television Programs* indicates, the series was conceived as a "comedy-drama" presenting "life in an integrated urban high school as seen through the eyes of Pete Dixon, a black American history instructor, whose classes are held in Room 222."[7] Pete was played by Lloyd Haynes, and his "love interest," to use the industry terminology, was black guidance counselor Liz McIntyre, played by Denise Nicholas. It was these two characters, and especially Pete, who provided *Room 222* with its unique focus and allowed it to serve its particular function in the construction of an African American social collectivity.

In his criticism of the show, cited earlier, John Killens implies that it did not satisfactorily present or otherwise address race-based dissension among the characters who populated the halls of fictional Walt Whitman High School, where the action took place. While it is true that few of the story lines from *Room 222*'s five-year run treat race relations directly or explicitly,[8] the show was characterized from the beginning by drily oblique statements about racial politics, the ambiguity of which I think actually evidences the show's canny awareness of the impossibility of its otherwise speaking to the issue except through platitudes and well-meaning clichés. This ambiguity on racial issues became clear in the first episode, in which Karen Valentine's character, student teacher Alice Johnson, apologetically introduces herself to Pete Dixon, saying, "I know I have a lot of the middle-class hangups. I went to a segregated school." Pete replies evenly, "It's OK—so did I."[9]

A similar exchange takes place in the episode I want to examine now. First broadcast November 2, 1973, during *Room 222*'s final season on the air, this episode depicts the trials of another young white student teacher, this time a man named Arthur, whose eagerness to be a friend to the students actually hinders his effectiveness as an instructor. The opening exchange

6. Craig T. and Peter G. Norback and the editors of *TV Guide* magazine, *TV Guide Almanac* (New York: Ballantine, 1980), pp. 303–304.

7. Vincent Terrace, *The Complete Encyclopedia of Television Programs 1947–1979*, 2d ed., rev. (New York: A. S. Barnes & Co., 1979), 2:847.

8. These story lines are summarized in David Krinsky and Joel Eisner, *Television Comedy Series: An Episode Guide to 153 TV Sitcoms in Syndication* (Jefferson, N.C.: McFarland and Company, 1984).

9. Quoted in Cleveland Amory, review of *Room 222*, *TV Guide*, 25 (October 1969): 52.

between Arthur and Pete again manifests a refined ambiguity on issues of race relations. It is the beginning of the school day, and the scene opens in Pete's classroom, where Arthur is busily distributing papers to the students, who are already gathered for class. Pete, equipped with a very professional looking briefcase, enters the room and greets Arthur:

*Pete:*   Good morning, Arthur.

*Arthur:*   Hi, Pete. I already passed out the test papers so you wouldn't have to take up class time.

*Pete:*   Well, that's no way to get the students to love you.

*Arthur* [*with a slight chuckle of hopeful anticipation*]:   If I get along with all my classes the way I do with this one . . . [*The bell rings, signaling the beginning of the class period.*]

*Pete:*   Well, we'd better get started. I wouldn't want to waste that time you saved me.

*Arthur:*   I'll go sit in the back of the bus. [*Starts to walk to the rear of the classroom, then realizes what he's said. Pete eyes him with mock wariness. He turns back to address Pete again.*] Hey, uh . . . I didn't mean, uh . . .

*Pete* [*flatly*]:   Arthur, you've been student-teaching with me long enough to know better.

*Arthur* [*hesitantly, as he bemusedly ponders this remark*]:   Thanks, Pete. [*He ambles awkwardly away from Pete's desk as Pete looks on in smirking amusement.*][10]

Now, I have claimed that such scenes are evidence of the show's canniness about the dubious project of making definitive statements about racial politics on prime-time television. I can certainly see, however, that the noncommittal quips by Pete Dixon might be interpreted as ineffectual efforts to gloss over the profound difficulty of race relations—and especially of racial integration—during the contemporary era. Even if we read the statements in this way, however, we would have to recognize that such "glossing over" can really only constitute the show's repression of racial concerns into a sort of "political unconscious" that will necessarily inform the working-through of the surface-level plot for any given episode. In other words, the cool shrugging off of racial-political concerns that the show regularly enacts actually signals its profound engagement with racially inflected social difference at a

10. Martin Donovan, "Pete's Protege," episode of *Room 222*, Gene Reynolds and William D'Angelo producers, broadcast on ABC, November 2, 1973. The dialogue presented here represents the author's transcription.

subtextual level, but also its containment of such concerns within conceptual parameters subjectively constituted by Pete Dixon indicates that their import will become manifest specifically with respect to intra- rather than interracial considerations. Thus, contrary to what it might superficially suggest, *Room 222* is not primarily about racial integration at all; rather it always represents an allegorical narrative about social differentiation among black subjects and, in particular, thematizes the articulation of different black subjects into various socioeconomic class positions.[11]

Let me approach the matter from a different direction for a moment in order to buttress my claim that *Room 222* is not first and foremost about integration. It will be helpful to consider first a bit of advance ad copy for another ABC series that premiered in the same season. The premise of *The Brady Bunch* involved a man and a woman, each widowed and raising three children—he boys, she girls—who marry and thus consolidate their fragmented households into one big happy family, weekly overcoming the obstacles to that consolidation inherent in their children's gender difference. Thus, as the network put it in its preseason publicity campaign, *The Brady Bunch* dealt with "the most difficult integration of them all, that of the sexes."[12]

If we conceive of integration in this unique way, identifying it as the consolidation—however difficult and problematic—of disparate elements into a single, undifferentiated social entity, which on U.S. network television has always been represented as the nuclear family, then we must recognize *Room 222*'s singular disengagement from the networks' integrative mission. That singularity is emphasized if we refer to the programming schedules from the time of *Room 222*'s run, which evidence a contrast between its function and that of the other ABC shows broadcast in prime time. Throughout its history on the air *Room 222* was juxtaposed in ABC's schedule with programs that depicted variations on the consolidated nuclear family within a specifically

11. Indeed, Pete Dixon's joking response to racially charged situations makes it all the more possible to conceive racial group politics in *Room 222* as undergoing a type of *repression,* and to consider the series itself as an instance of *allegory.* After all, jokes are a primary affective indicator of the repressive process, acccording to Freud's foundational theorization; and, as Craig Owens has suggested, repression itself constitutes allegory as the governing structure of both the psyche and psychoanalysis. See Sigmund Freud, "Repression" (1915), in *General Psychological Theory,* ed. and intro. Philip Rieff (New York: Collier/Macmillan, 1963), pp. 104–115, esp. pp. 108 and 110–111; and Craig Owens, "The Allegorical Impulse: Toward a Theory of Postmodernism," pts. 1 and 2 (1980), in *Beyond Recognition: Representation, Power, and Culture* (Berkeley: University of California Press, 1992), pp. 52–69 and 70–87, esp. p. 53.

12. "Premières: Old Wrinkles," *Time,* 3 (October 1969); 84.

domestic context. The show was always preceded in the schedule by one or more such programs—*The Courtship of Eddie's Father* with Bill Bixby; *Make Room for Granddaddy* with Danny Thomas; *The Partridge Family* with Shirley Jones, David Cassidy, and Susan Dey; *The Odd Couple* with Tony Randall and Jack Klugman; and the aforementioned *Brady Bunch* with Florence Henderson and Robert Reed. The classroom series was followed in the schedule, most notably, by *The Odd Couple* and *Adam's Rib,* an adaptation of the Katherine Hepburn–Spencer Tracy movie which again depicted the difficult reconciliation of the genders within the domestic context, with Ken Howard and Blythe Danner in the starring roles.[13]

Unlike all of these shows, *Room 222* was emphatically not set in the context of the traditional nuclear family (indeed, to my knowledge, it never depicted a single functional nuclear family in all of its five-year run); nor did it set up relations among its characters that could be construed as metaphorically figuring familial ties. Thus, however harmoniously unified the Walt Whitman High School community might have appeared, *Room 222*'s disengagement from the familial vocabulary that is the predominant televisual mode for indicating stable social synthesis suggests that this was not its major concern. By contrast, the classroom setting offered an ideal configuration through which to enact a social *division* that always implicated black subjects specifically, owing precisely to the show's focus on Pete Dixon rather than on the various white characters.

While Pete—like Liz McIntyre—is a solidly middle-class professional figure, there is, as Cleveland Amory put it in an early review, a "menace in *Room 222*" as well: "Student Jason Allen (Heshimu) for example, could have stepped out of 'The Blackboard Jungle.' "[14] Indeed, particularly in the early seasons, Jason presented a strong antidote to Pete's and Liz's upright middle-classness. A product of the Los Angeles slums, Jason was portrayed as an angry outsider, deeply suspicious and given to thievery. Over the years his character mellowed quite a bit, but he still provided the perfect foil to Pete's professionalism by clearly representing socioeconomic disadvantage. The means of this representation was partially explained by John Wasserman, in his 1969 profile of Denise Nicholas titled "The Girl in 'Room 222' ": Black people, like whites, have different vocabularies and speaking styles for different situations. There are accents, phrasing and sounds for one's peers and

---

13. Larry James Gianakos, *Television Drama Series Programming: A Comprehensive Chronicle, 1959–1975* (Methuen, N.J.: The Scarecrow Press, 1978).

14. Among, review, p. 52.

friends. There are other noises for outsiders . . . It is a subtle point, and one which is generally ignored in integrated theater."[15] Wasserman implicitly praises *Room 222* specifically for *not* ignoring this point, but he might have gone even further since, even *within* a given racial group, there exist different modes of speech corresponding to, among other things, differences in socio-economic class, and these also are represented in the series. Thus, even as Jason Allen became a respectable member of the Walt Whitman High School community, his dialectal speech (which, like that of the other students, was also marked by the youth slang of the period) set him apart from the profes-sional class represented by Mr. Dixon and Miss McIntyre. In the episode I am considering here, this is evidenced in Jason's brief commentary (the dialectal cadences of which I can only imperfectly suggest in print) regarding the erection of a statue of Walt Whitman in front of the school: "Man, it must be a real groove to have you a statue put up in front of a big buildin'."

Thus, Jason implicitly represents one of the various social classes into which the black community can be differentiated, in contrast to that repre-sented by the black faculty at the school. With the difference between profes-sionals like Pete and less advantaged students like Jason always operative as a subtext to the main action of *Room 222,* the explicit differentiation of the black community into various subcategories can be played out as the division between teacher and student that is regularly the ostensible subject of series episodes. In the one I am considering here, titled "Pete's Protege," Pete has to correct student teacher Arthur Billings's too close bonding with his stu-dents, thus reinforcing the necessary division on which the community is founded. Having to take over Pete's class when Pete is out sick, Arthur finds himself confronted by a roomful of unruly students whose respect he cannot gain precisely because he has identified with them too closely as a "friend" rather than establishing himself as an authority figure. In response he harshly criticizes the work of a slow student whom Pete has been tutoring privately, undermining what little self-confidence the boy has begun to achieve. On learning of this development after returning to school, Pete confronts Arthur with his error:

Pete [*angry and exasperated*]:   A teacher can make mistakes. He can have his good days and he can have his bad days. But the one thing that he's *got* to do is stimulate his students! The one thing he *cannot* do is discourage them.

Arthur [*dejectedly*]:   I know that.

15. John L. Wasserman, "The Girl in 'Room 222,' " *TV Guide*, 20 (September 1969): 26.

*Pete:*   Then why did you tell Leo what you did? Now he wants to quit his tutoring; he doesn't think it makes any difference anymore.

*Arthur:*   I didn't think it was a good report.

*Pete:*   It wasn't the best report I've seen, but it's the best report that Leo's done. You know, I think that you took it out on him because of what the kids did to you, and you knew he would take it from you.

*Arthur* [*defensively*]:   You weren't here Friday.

*Pete:*   Yeah, but I can guess what happened.

*Arthur:*   I've been nothing but a friend to those kids, all of them—a real friend! I've played ball with them, I've eaten with them . . .

*Pete:*   That's fine! don't stop doing that; but you're not a student anymore!

*Arthur* [*subdued*]:   I know that.

*Pete:*   You can't be one of the class and in charge of it at the same time, it's too confusing.

Pete's invocation of "confusion" is apt, of course, but it serves just as well in relation to an undifferentiated black collectivity as it does with respect to an undisciplined high school classroom, suggesting the show's engagement in the process of distinguishing Pete's subject position from that of his black students, on more levels than one. As far as the show's critics are concerned, what is *most* confusing and ill-defined is the show's exact stance on the politics of interracial relations. But that confusion, as I have demonstrated, is evidence not necessarily of any fundamental weakness in the program itself, but rather of its problematic situation at the intersection of demands for televisual fidelity to a unitary "black experience" and the increasingly evident illusoriness of such a social phenomenon. To attempt to represent the latter in 1969 was to engage an extremely complex set of exigencies within African-American cultural politics; hence the controversy caused by *Room 222* among many black critics. What that controversy most strongly suggests, however, is that the means of the show's engagement with those exigencies are prime objects for study and analysis—just as the mere fact of that engagement is something to be remarked—amidst the difficult demands of the contemporary context, as what is too easily summed up as the "black experience" becomes increasingly conflicted and dis-integrated.

*Ugo Rubeo*

# Voice as Lifesaver: Defining the Function of Orality in Etheridge Knight's Poetry

*T*hroughout the 1970s and 1980s critical studies on the particular relevance of orality within the African American cultural context have grown increasingly numerous and specific. Although the origins of this critical approach can be traced back to the beginning of this century, in more recent years the branching out of this area of research in several different directions has enormously enhanced its scientific consistency as well as its overall impact on academic circles both in Europe and in the United States. The centrality that the analysis of oral patterns of communication has acquired among critics researching the various facets of African American literature, arts, and folklore is by now well known and commonly accepted—all the more so for anyone who happens to dedicate his attention to the poetic side of that tradition.

Starting from this assumption, the soundness and viability of which are largely self-evident, I propose to define—in the hope of providing some new critical details—the primary role that orality plays in Etheridge Knight's poetry, a body of work that, to this date, does not seem to have earned the attention it deserves. This is all the more surprising as the author's deep perception of and extensive adhesion to oral techniques not only are apparent but also provide an original basis for much of his poetic production. I center my discussion on the inner dynamics of the modes of oral communication that Knight commonly uses in his poetry as a conscious means of establishing a close and deep relationship both with tradition and with the audience—a goal that he deems essential to the poetic experience. Envisioned as a continuous dialogical interaction, that idea soon acquires the status of a fundamental prerequisite for Knight's theoretical framework—an asset that helps give his verse ideological consistency, at the same time ensuring a considerable degree of integration between its thematic and formal textures. While this characteristic intimately links Knight's poetic production to the core of the African American expressive tradition, that same trait seems to connect him to a more general line of linguistic research that goes back to the early years of modernism and to its subsequent developments. Unfortunately, for lack of space, this kind of connection is destined here to remain for the most part implicit, though it must be admitted that Knight's use of intertextuality—primarily but not exclusively addressing the works of African American authors—certainly suggests his consciousness of that continuity. Though somewhat scanty, Knight's critical comments and theories concerning poetry help us ascertain his awareness of the complexity of the problems related to oral forms of communication, as well as the essential coherence with which he always relates to them. This is what makes Knight's own statements a particularly valuable source for verifying my critical propositions, and this is also the reason why I use them as a direct commentary on his poetic choices.

"Poetry is primarily oral utterance, and the end of a poem belongs in somebody's ears rather than their eyes," Etheridge Knight writes in the opening paragraph of one of his rare articles in print.[1] While stated in an extremely colloquial, almost offhand manner, Knight's contention provides a valuable starting point for an evaluation of the role that the dialogical pattern of oral communication plays in his poetry. That concise statement serves the double purpose of acknowledging the preeminence of orality as a basis for the poetic experience while at the same time implicitly placing his own work in a direct line of descent within the rich tradition of African American folk poetry. Knight thus tends to emphasize that the exchange the voice of the poet establishes with the "body" of his audience is of a tangible, concrete nature. He characteristically describes that interaction in strictly physical terms: "If it's true that as I'm talking to you bones are moving in your inner ears, I'm physically touching you with my voice."[2] This commitment to oral forms of communication as the most effective means of activating a deep, dynamic dialogue with the public contains what in itself amounts to a first

---

1. Etheridge Knight, "On the Oral Nature of Poetry," *Black Scholar,* 19 (Fall 1988): 92.
2. Ibid.

ideological statement of some importance, since it helps identify Knight's poetry as openly projected toward a concrete social context. What, in his thinking, substantially differentiates the voice from writing—indeed, it could easily be objected that this latter form guarantees a more durable, objective type of exchange than the former—is the innate capacity of oral language to establish a close, immediate connection with the subsequent stages of the evolution of collective experience. The voice, in other words, not only registers but incorporates and can immediately render the "progress" the language makes in its dutiful definition and interpretation of whatever aspect of the daily experience it gets in touch with. It is this continuous process of checks and balances between the two that, according to Knight, makes the oral medium a more comprehensive and effective—let alone more flexible—vehicle for meaningful communication.

All of this, of course, is particularly true for artistic communication, or whenever language is intentionally used, as in poetry, to provoke an emotional reaction—the value of the expression, in that case, depending on what it "tells," just as much as on the way it is "told." In Knight's own words:

> Too great an emphasis on the written word leads to a distance between poet and audience. Then the poet begins to speak in a language that's not relevant to the audience. If you stay too long on the mountain-top, you will miss the development of the language, you will be speaking in dead metaphors, and the people down here will have gone on to something else. You know, by the time language gets into the dictionary, we done moved on to something else.[3]

Intimately connected to this idea of the spoken language as a fluid "body" is Knight's vision of the relationship that links him, as a poet, to tradition. By activating a dialogical flow with his audience, his voice actually provides a connection between the present and the poetic tradition with which he identifies, one that not only inevitably forms an integral part of his linguistic experience, but that he also may purposefully decide to use as a significant part of his material. Again, the difference between the oral and the written rendering of that intertextual process seems to be made exclusively by the "response" of the audience, which completes and enriches the poet's statement while at the same time making of that tradition a living thing of the present.

Similarly, in bridging that time gap Knight sees himself as engaged in a

3. Ibid, pp. 94–95.

personal struggle to extend his own physical existence beyond its material boundaries—for as long as his words are being spoken (that is to say, physically used in the historical present), he can reasonably hope to avoid falling into oblivion. Hence his insistence on life's being intimately connected to the spoken word: "What I want to emphasize is life, living. Live metaphor. Living poets. I think it's a valid ambition to want the words you strung together to live on the lips of ordinary people."[4] Knight's identification of a referent for his poetic "call" helps make his aesthetic program concrete, avoiding the danger of an abstract construction that would altogether defeat the main purpose of his artistic endeavor—that is to say, communication. His siding with an audience made of "ordinary people," moreover, is in itself a way of reinforcing his connection with the African American folk tradition, as this decision immediately calls to mind similar choices made in the past by a number of major figures who were instrumental in determining the course that future generations of poets would eventually follow.[5] As I suggested earlier, however, the importance of that continuity to Knight is neither absolute nor abstract; it is the audience's response, as a vital component of the entire process, which makes the poem function, which even legitimates it as a form of art: "The Poet, The Poem and The People: When the three come together, the communion, the communication, the Art happens."[6] Knight's poetry constantly tends to register that double dialogue with past and present in which the African American artist is simultaneously involved, representing it through an increasingly tight compound of formal and thematic options that give his verse epistemological consistency as well as an uncommon linguistic thrust.

This mutual, dialogical pattern of oral communication—already apparent in much of his earlier verse—is clearly reproduced in his "To Dinah Washington," a poem in which the soothing voice of the deceased "Queen of the Blues" performs precisely that same unifying function between the "call" of the dead and the "response" of the living which Knight judges to be the essential aim of the artist's work:

4. Ibid, p. 95.
5. I refer, in particular, to Langston Hughes and Sterling Brown, who, in the 1920s and 1930s, helped establish and consolidate folk poetry as a literary genre. On various occasions both Hughes and Brown made clear in critical statements their interest in the "low-down folks" as a subject for their poetry, as well as their commitment to a language that could stir an audience made of "common people."
6. Etheridge Knight, *Born of a Woman: New and Selected Poems* (Boston: Houghton Mifflin, 1980), p. vii.

I have heard your voice, royal and real,
Across the dusky neighborhoods,
And the eyes of old men grow bright, remembering;
Children stop their play to listen,
Remembering—though they have never heard you before,
You are familiar to them:
Queen of the Blues, singing an eternal song.[7]

What the singer's voice sets in motion is a process of group identification that starts with an act of recognition of the song's inner relevance to the experience of various components of the black urban community, that gradually leads to the reinforcement of the bonds of solidarity within that same context, and that implicitly ensures the survival both of its members and of its culturally significant forms. That voice, of course, is recorded, and the reaction of the common people is essentially mute—though it is precisely their intense reaction to the blues singer's call and not the recording per se which ultimately gives its meaning to, and effects the survival of, the dead artist's performance.[8] It is that new performance which, completing that fluid, circular type of exchange, is able to annul any discontinuity between time past and time present—as evidenced by the voice's power to bridge existing generation gaps—finally reestablishing a close relationship between the time of the community and that of the tradition, as exemplified by the "eternity" of the song.

In the early 1980s Etheridge Knight's concern for his craft deepened, and his speculations on the nature of language grew more intense as well as slightly more numerous. Circularity did indeed become the keystone concept of his poetics as well as one of the recurring patterns of his later verse. This concept—always closely connected to the idea of dialogical communication—gradually achieved greater weight and expanded its influence outside the proper limits of single poems, eventually becoming the organizing principle that gives direction and meaning to the entire body of his work. Perhaps nowhere does this appear more evident than in his collection of published and unpublished poems, *Born of a Woman*, a comprehensive edition pub-

---

7. Etheridge Knight, "To Dinah Washington," in *Poems from Prison* (Detroit: Broadside Press, 1968), p. 29.

8. This interpretation of Knight's poem is based on his insistent use of the present tense ("grow bright," "stop their play," "you are familiar," in the first stanza; and "suck in their bellies" and "raise their chins" in the second stanza), which emphasizes the differences in age and behavior of the people who listen, but who are nevertheless all directly touched by the same song.

lished in 1980, which, lamentably, has attracted only limited attention.[9] As Shirley Lumpkin writes, the poems contained in this volume are arranged "in clusters or groupings under titles which are musical variations on the book's essential theme—life inside and outside of prison."[10] Surprisingly little attention, however, was paid to the fact that the headings of the three sections—"Inside-Out," "Outside-In," and "All About and Back Again"— also describe the consecutive stages of a circular course—an ideal guide to the entire complex of his work supplied by the author to his reading public, and one he obviously wishes to be given due consideration. A fuller interpretation of this authorial choice may thus help shed more light on a variety of issues that would otherwise risk going partially unnoticed, but whose impact is significant for what appears to be the highly coherent development of Knight's poetic vision.

The first, almost obvious consideration deals with the author's deliberate use of circularity as a self-reflexive signifier. Images related to that semantic point are used to connote the uninterrupted thread that, uniting one stage of his linguistic progress to the next, makes the evolution of language, its continuous refinement, and the consequential improvement of its communicating potential possible. Essentially, this evolutionary process is envisioned and represented by Knight as moving along a circular path—a pattern he sees as opposed to a linear type of development, based on what he judges to be a restricted, too rigid interpretation of the concept of authority.[11] He writes:

> Another thing I believe is that there are two sides to a word. What I call the masculine, lineal side: the authority for that side of the words comes out of Webster's or the Oxford dictionary. In the connotative side, the authority comes from common agreement. That's the side of the language where nuance and inflection come in . . . The nuance is something that the speaker and the listener must agree on. That's more circular and its authority rests on now . . . That's the side the poet deals with.[12]

9. Knight's book, which went out of print shortly after publication, offered a large selection of his poetry; it obtained only sporadic and, for the most part, minor reviews.

10. Shirley Lumpkin, "Etheridge Knight," in *Afro-American Poets since 1955*, Vol. 41 of *Dictionary of Literary Biography* (Detroit: Gale Research, 1985), p. 209.

11. In "On the Oral Nature of Poetry" Knight develops a theory based on the opposition between linearity and circularity; the first term connotes a language whose authority is based on a rigid objectivity (which he describes as "masculine"); the second ("feminine") type of language gets its authority from the consensus of a group or audience.

12. Knight, "On the Oral Nature of Poetry," p. 95.

According to Knight, then, poetic language reaches its highest degree of "openness" only when the dialogical circle between the artist and the audience is "closed"—that is to say, when the interaction based on the call-and-response pattern of the performance has validated the poem as the product of a collective voice. This of course implies that its authority is strictly temporary and relative, and that it must be sought anew each time the poem is performed. Indeed, the entire experience of the folk poet, then, is a matter of moving along a circular path, going "all about" just to come "back again" to the point of origin, tracking the steps of the course followed by his own voice.

As I suggested earlier, to avoid the dangers of sheer abstraction Knight consciously talks (and writes) of oral communication as of a bodily type of interaction. Indeed, he goes so far as occasionally to describe that process borrowing his terminology from the language of human anatomy.[13] Consequently, all the symbolic images and metaphoric implications traditionally associated with the geometry of the circle (for example, unity, fertility, perfection, harmony, dynamic balance, and the like) tend increasingly to be represented in his poetry through a series of concrete, tangible, often physical terms. In his "Genesis 11"—a powerful lay paraphrasis of John's Gospel—all the various denotations of circularity so far discussed seem to be brought together and effectively intertwined with one another so that the ethereal, impalpable substance of which the Word is made is turned in the end into a womanly image of timeless human fertility. Thus, owing to a suspended finale that completes the circle, leading back to the title itself, the "Word," turned into "Verb," succeeds in defeating time:

> The WORD, Was, Is, Will, BE;
> The Beginning and the End, BE;
> And the Word /is/ Round
> And Warm and Rolling;
> And the Word /be/ a Verb,
> And the Verb /be/ a Woman . . .[14]

13. In the first part of "On the Oral Nature of Poetry" Knight explains in some detail his theory of the physicality of language: "Another thing I believe is that language is not only physical, it's a living thing, a living organism. It's informed by the physical environment, by how we breathe and our speech patterns" (p. 93). Although in this case he does not acknowledge any debt for his theory, it is clear that his research shows several points in common with Whitman's thinking and with poetic experiments made by early modernists such as Gertrude Stein, Amy Lowell, H.D., and Ezra Pound.

14. Etheridge Knight, "Genesis 11," in *The Essential Etheridge Knight* (Pittsburgh: University of Pittsburgh Press, 1986), p. 102. Knight's insistence on this biblical motif is demonstrated by the opening poem of his earlier collection, *Belly Song and Other Poems* (Detroit: Broadside Press, 1973), reprinted in this same volume.

Although it does not seem that Knight ever made any explicit comments to this end, it is hard to resist the temptation to read this poem as his "Ars Poetica," so numerous and sound are the possibilities of a metalinguistic interpetation of those few packed lines, so consequential to his general aesthetic program—and to his views on orality in particular—does the poem's general meaning appear to be. Even more clearly than in the earlier example, in this poetic parable the basic component of orality becomes the multinatured agent of a quasi-religious process of collective survival, the mythical and historical implications of which are undoubtedly enhanced by the effective "variation" the author performs on the linguistic texture of the Scriptures. What lends Knight's poem an uncommon degree of unity and objective "authority" seems to be primarily his skillful handling of incremental repetition and parataxis—two fundamental structures of what Walter J. Ong defines as the "additive oral style" of the Bible.[15] It is as a result of both those devices that each verse of the poem—indeed, each word—adds new possible meanings to the rest, while at the same time reproducing, in a extremely compact structural sequence, the stratifying progress on which orality builds. The highly self-reflexive quality of this piece, moreover, is perfectly integrated with both the account of the Creation—the subject of its biblical model—and the nonreligious denotations of the term *genesis,* (that is, "beginning," "birth," and by extension "artistic creativity").

Etheridge Knight's allegiance to the main stylistic forms of the African American oral tradition is proved by his suggestive reperformance on the linguistic canvas of the Bible, which provides both a powerful rhetorical frame for a considerable part of his work and an essential ground for extratextual communication. But also the vitality of the dialogue he entertains with that tradition is apparent in his frequent use of other forms that branch out of that same base, even though, as in the case of his "toasts," its structure, imagery, and linguistic texture are strikingly different from those so far discussed. The performer's skills in linguistic improvisation—a common prerequisite for all forms of orality—become of paramount importance in this folk style, which, like "the dozens," owes much of its effectiveness to the velocity and spontaneity with which the "general badness" of both the hero and the speaker is rendered. Far from being a simple accessory, or an embellishment of doubtful taste, the language of the "toast," replete as it is with

15. Walter J. Ong, *Orality and Literature* (London: Methuen, 1982), p. 37.

profanities, sexual allusions, heavy innuendoes, and the like, works essentially as an instrument of defense against potential dangers, or as a practical weapon to be used in critical situations. As Knight himself puts it, dexterity in funk is a literally vital quality for the teller: "In Black culture, if you talk about another guy's mother or sister and make it rhyme, it's a heavy weapon. You can keep guys off that way. I learned a lot of poems that we call 'toasts' . . . and I wrote them down. 'Stagger Lee,' 'The Signifying Monkey,' 'The Sinking of the Titanic.' All those classical ones."[16] Even more clearly than on other occasions, Knight's words show his perfect awareness of the innate potential of language as a vehicle for ensuring one's survival—a feature that he must have come to appreciate fully in the seven years he spent as a prison inmate, and that his practice of the toast certainly helped refine. As Geneva Smitherman recalls in her *Talkin and Testifyin,* it is mostly inside correctional institutions nowadays that this folk style is being kept alive "among black prisoners who sit around for hours passing the time away reciting various toasts learned in their adolescence."[17] "Dark Prophecy: I Sing of Shine"—Knight's well-known poetic reinterpretation of the traditional toast on the sinking of the *Titanic*—is a particularly apt example for evaluating how he manages to turn that awareness into the thematic core of his poem. An exceptionally good toaster, Shine, the black stoker of the sinking ship— who happens to be also an excellent swimmer—survives the disaster thanks to his ability to outplay his first two "contendants"—a white millionaire banker who offers him money, and his daughter who blandishes Shine with sex—who engage him in a verbal challenge that could cost him his life. Finally, when he is confronted by a preacher whose aggressive rhetorical prowess ("in the name of the Lord") may seriously prove more effective than his own, "Shine pulled his shank and cut the preacher's throat," silencing him forever, thus escaping what could have turned out to be his fatal embrace.[18]

16. Knight, "On the Oral Nature of Poetry," p. 94.

17. Geneva Smitherman, *Talkin and Testifyin: The Language of Black America* (Boston: Houghton Mifflin, 1977), p. 158.

18. Etheridge Knight, "Dark Prophesy: I Sing of Shine," in *Belly Song and Other Poems,* p. 25. The section of the poem in which Shine is confronted by the preacher reads: "How Shine swam past a preacher afloat on a board / crying save me nigger Shine in the name of the Lord— / how the preacher grabbed Shine's arm and broke his stroke— /how Shine pulled his shank and cut the preacher's throat—." When reprinted in *The Essential Etheridge Knight,* "Prophesy" was turned into "Prophecy," and some other changes were made in the text.

The exemplary conclusion of this narrative poem—Shine's merry celebration upon his safe return home, "up in Harlem"[19]—leads to one last aspect of this discussion, namely, Knight's insistent use of oral modes—and the blues in particular—as an aesthetically accomplished solution to the problematic core of his poetics: his overriding concern to avoid the danger of rootlessness. This danger, which Knight sees as both a personal and a general problem for African American artists and intellectuals,[20] consists in a concrete risk of losing touch with one's own familiar history, cultural background and geographic context, but most of all in being unable to continue the dialogue with own's audience—hence the necessity to "*keep* the language alive" through "the word—the spoken word" that "is the main tool of the poet."[21] Knight's own artistic predicament becomes, then, the underlying concern of a consistent part of his poetry, while the thematic, stylistic, and ideological possibilities that the oral tradition offers him—themselves an explicit evidence of his adhesion to his cultural roots—often turn into instruments that directly reflect and enhance the aliveness of that same "tool." In "Con/Tin/U/Way/Shun Blues," a poem in which Knight takes an unequivocal stand in the debate waged by a number of black aesthetic intellectuals on the supposed political inefficacy of the blues, that argument is directly incorporated into the text, thus helping reverberate, as in a miniature medallion, the impact of the blues structure in which it is inserted:

> "blues are more than cries of oppression"—Mary Helen Washington
> They say the blues is just a slave song
> But I say that's just a lie . . .[22]

Undoubtedly, it is precisely because of his dexterous use of the blues form that, as in this case, Etheridge Knight's poetry seldom slips into that boister-

19. In the *Essential* version of this poem, the concluding lines originally read: "And when the news hit shore that the titanic had sunk / Shine was up in Harlem damn near drunk— / and dancing in the streets. / Yeah, damn near drunk and dancing in the streets." From this was taken away the repetiton "and dancing in the streets." It is also interesting to note that, in reaching Harlem, Shine is faster than the telegraph's voice.

20. In a 1985 interview published in Sanford Pinsker, *Conversations with Contemporary American Writers* (Amsterdam: Rodopi, 1985), pp. 107–116, Knight talks at length of this problem, comparing Richard Wright's and William Faulkner's relations to Mississippi: "Richard Wright was constantly rootless . . . He was always the outsider. He didn't *stay*. I've always had a thing about artists who expatriate. I can see *moving*. Artists are gonna move and go, but to expatriate . . . you get away from what you know, from your primary audience. Being from Mississippi, I can feel that Faulkner is addressing me, at least on a secondary level. He's still in touch with me" (p. 112).

21. Ibid., p. 110.

22. Etheridge Knight, "Con/Tin/U/Way/Shun Blues," in *The Essential Etheridge Knight*, p. 93.

ous, redundant tone that, between the late 1960s and early 1980s, became an all but infrequent trait among a variety of African American poets. The ideological substance that runs through his verse, smoothly integrated in the familiar, apparently subdued structure of the blues, often ends up hitting its target much more effectively than a straight political poem, thus proving the intrinsic validity of the thesis he supports.

At other times the self-reflexive quality of Knight's poetic language is used to convey the sense and difficulties of his personal striving as an artist, the intricate dialogue with past and present in which he is actually involved. "One Day We Shall All Go Back" is a good example in which to see this intent at work, as the poem's thematic impact—based on the "down home" motif—is strongly reinforced by the poem's structure as a direct answer to Langston Hughes's "One-Way Ticket,"[23] a feature that obviously helps expand the poem's implications into the realm of the author's literary ascent. Knight's recurrent use of the "longing for home" blues motif in his poetry acquires the value of an artistic "signature"; it is a consistent, complex, and aesthetically accomplished method for avoiding the dangers of isolation, fulfilling the multifaceted dialogue (with his audience, his tradition, his own creativity) that he sees as his artistic goal. Orality not only makes that dialogue possible but also ensures its effectiveness; it registers and checks its continuity; and finally it represents its inner dynamics in a telling, suggestive flow of metaphorical images.

23. Knight's most obvious reference to Hughes's poem is in the substitution of a long catalogue of southern cities for that of northern centers included in Hughes's text. More intertextual connections related to this same subject can be found between Knight's "A Poem for Myself," in *Belly Song,* p. 50. and Hughes's "Our Land," published in *The Weary Blues* (New York: Knopf, 1926).

*Fritz Gysin*

# Predicaments of Skin: Boundaries in Recent African American Fiction

*I*n the current discussions of ethnicity and multiculturalism in the United States we often find a tendency to ignore or dismiss the concept of boundaries,[1] to accentuate only their sinister aspects, to attack their "reification," or to treat them as manifestations of bad faith. Scholars and critics alike either tacitly assume the superiority of only one form of assimilation or embrace a gratuitous and rather formless kind of cultural syncretism, reminiscent of the hotchpotch that often graces American folk festivals with their combinations of "ethnic food," "ethnic rock music," and "ethnic dancing." Especially in the field of African American culture, proponents of accommodation, assimilation, or unification, such as the advocates of an American melting pot and the adherents of the Afrocentric idea, tend to exclude one another without paying sufficient attention to the boundary they are creating in the process.[2] At the same time, the move from the margin

---

1. I am using this term because it contains the meanings of "division" and "periphery," a combination that is important to the minority experience of marginality.

2. See, for example, Molefi Kete Asante [Arthur L. Smith, Jr.], *The Afrocentric Idea* (Philadelphia: Temple University Press, 1987); Werner Sollors, "Theory of American Ethnicity, or: '? S ethnic?/Ti and AMERICAN/TI, DE OR UNITED (W) STATES S SI AND THEOR?,' " *American Quarterly*, 33.3 (1981): 257–282; Werner Sollors, "A Critique of Pure Pluralism," in *Reconstructing American Literary History*, ed. Sacvan Bercovitch (Cambridge, Mass.: Harvard University Press, 1986), pp. 250–279; Werner Sollors, *Beyond Ethnicity: Consent and Descent in American Culture* (New York: Oxford University Press, 1986); see especially, in Steven Thernstrom, Ann Orlov, and Oscar Handlin, eds., *Harvard Encyclopedia of American Ethnic Groups* (Cambridge, Mass.: Harvard University Press, 1980), Harold J. Abramson, "Assimilation and Pluralism"; Philip Gleason, "American Identity and Americanization"; Michael Novak, "Pluralism: A Humanistic Perspective"; William Petersen, "Concepts of Ethnicity"; Werner Sollors, "Literature and Ethnicity"; and Michael Walzer, "Pluralism: A Political Perspective."

to the center, which is a result of actual dislocation or of a change of focus, is frequently celebrated by the minority involved as an act of crossing or overcoming age-old boundaries, disregarding the fact that what is centralized is often the condition of marginality and "boundaricity."

It seems to me that, in contrast to a number of fashionable cultural theories, some recent works of African American fiction do pay attention to this phenomenon of boundaries, highlighting it in fresh and unusual ways. In these works we witness a new concern with inner and outer boundaries, or rather a concern with new inner and outer boundaries. To cope with this we need a more complex model of boundary formation, one that takes into consideration that the cultural blends within an ethnic group are utilized to formulate the dividing issues within the same group as well as those between this group and the mainstream or the majority at large. I have written about this elsewhere.[3] Here I briefly discuss two imaginative approaches to the articulation of "the spaces of contradiction," to borrow a phrase from Hortense Spillers,[4] both of which offer novel and significant approaches to one of the most essential types of boundary, that of skin.

In an exemplary way the human skin is, to quote from Roberta Rubenstein's definition of boundary, an area "of both separation and connection between contiguous entities."[5] Moreover, the skin possesses the double status that the anthropologist Anya Peterson Royce attributes to the boundary as a social and cultural phenomenon: it is "maintained from within" and "imposed from outside."[6] The skin contains and protects the body of the individual human being and displays and signals its surface and its shape, but it also enfolds an individual's identity, mind, or soul, as is evident in the expression "to jump out of one's skin." And yet in the larger category of human groups and societies skin functions as boundary largely because of its variety and shades of color. This, to be sure, is its timeworn aspect in African American literature, which thus often reflects and reacts to a simpli-

3. Fritz Gysin, "Centralizing the Marginal: Boundaries in Recent African American Fiction," in *Modernism, Modernity, and Ethnicity*, ed. Josef Jarab (forthcoming).

4. Hortense Spillers, "Response [to Deborah E. McDowell]," in *Afro-American Literary Study in the 1990s*, ed. Houston A. Baker, Jr., and Patricia Redmond (Chicago: University of Chicago Press, 1989), p. 72.

5. Roberta Rubenstein, *Boundaries of the Self: Gender, Culture, Fiction* (Urbana: University of Illinois Press, 1987), p. 238.

6. Anya Peterson Royce, *Ethnic Identity: Strategies of Diversity* (Bloomington: Indiana University Press, 1982), p. 29.

fying social and linguistic practice of racial, often racist, differentiation. In some of the more imaginative works of recent African American fiction, however, prevalent social and cultural concerns are questioned, subverted, challenged, or even inverted by means of an uncommon foregrounding of the physical implications of skin. There are many ways in which this process takes shape. Raymond Andrews's first novel, *Appalachee Red,* for example, traces the success story of a mulatto who skillfully uses his white skin to seize power over the black section of a doubly segregated town and then becomes the catalyst of the community's violent racial conversion.[7] The black ghost in Toni Morrison's *Beloved* in quite a different fashion comes across as an empty shell; her skin is bare of creases and wrinkles; significantly the whites in *Beloved's* famous "rememory" of the Middle Passage, or the land of the dead, are called "men without skin."[8] In the present essay I discuss briefly two cases of this preoccupation with skin in which the relationship between skin and boundary highlights the significance of skin *as* boundary in rather unusual ways: Charles Johnson's use of tattoos and John Edgar Wideman's treatment of albinism.

Charles Johnson's *Oxherding Tale* (1982) is a combination of a slave narrative and a novel of passing and a parody of both.[9] Its form and content recall the postmodern satires of Ishmael Reed, Neo-HooDoo aesthetics being replaced by traditional philosophy, especially phenomenology, and an interest in Eastern thought. According to an early reviewer, the novel "translates the Zen enigma of in-betweenness to the ante-bellum South."[10] It traces the comic adventures of Andrew Hawkins, a light-skinned mulatto, the offspring of a playful drunken exchange of partners between a master and his slave. Andrew receives an education in anarchism from a crazy white transcendentalist, is trained by a white vamp to become a male concubine, and escapes to illusory freedom with a black coffin maker by passing for white, only to fear detection of his black heritage in his new white surroundings.

Andrew's perception of slavery is dominated by the confining properties of skin: "The wretchedness of being colonized was not that slavery created

7. Raymond Andrews, *Appalachee Red* (New York: Dial, 1978); see esp. pp. 65–66, 117, 135, 215, 255–256.

8. Toni Morrison, *Beloved* (New York: Knopf, 1987), p. 55, 50, 214. The term "men without skin" is also applied by Sethe when she imagines Schoolteacher coming back to get her baby (p. 262).

9. Charles Johnson, *Oxherding Tale* (Bloomington: Indiana University Press, 1982); all subsequent references are cited by page in the text.

10. Steven Weisenburger, "In-Between," *Callaloo,* 7.1 (Winter 1984): 153.

feelings of guilt and indebtedness . . . nor that it created a long, lurid dream of multiplicity and separateness . . . but the fact that men had epidermalized Being" (52). At the end of the novel his physical and spiritual antagonist, a slave hunter named Horace Bannon, becomes a manifestation of this epidermalizing process. Even more than Andrew, Bannon is "a racial mongrel": his "deltoid nose of a Wazimba" and "snotcup" (67) vie for prominence with the thin line of his lips; his coarse, curly hair contrasts with his blue and green eyes (68). His black voice and "deep-fried Mississippi Delta twang" do not prevent him from frequenting the best white circles, although he is, in Andrew's words, "a slave who, for reasons too fantastic to guess, hunted slaves" (68).

This frightening "slack-shouldered monster" (67) is a compulsive serial killer, a black version of Flannery O'Connor's Misfit,[11] who is, however, hired by the system to maintain its racial barriers. In this capacity Bannon is, paradoxically, allowed to function as a professional crosser and straddler of boundaries, yet he crosses and straddles not only horizontal ones such as the borders of plantations but also what we might call vertical ones, such as that between life and death. His metaphysical dimension is indicated by his nickname, "Soulcatcher"; he is a spiritual technician of execution, who hunts and haunts escaped slaves and exhausts their mental power of resistance until his victims beg him for the coup de grace. Toward the end of the novel he appears as a personification of Death and the Devil, only to retire into harmless vulgarity and happy marriage to a whore after his first failure to catch a runaway.

Andrew, needless to say, profits from this failure and gains his freedom, but not before he has gone through the harrowing experience of taking what he thinks is to be his last journey on the Soulcatcher's wagon. And this is where he has his epiphany of skin, arguably the most imaginative moment of the entire book. Questioned about the way Andrew's father died, Bannon (who has murdered him) suggests that Andrew ask his father directly, opening his shirt and pointing to his own chest and arms,

> where the intricately woven brown tattoos presented . . . an impossible flesh tapestry of a thousand individualities no longer static, mere drawings, but if you looked at them long enough, bodies moving like Lilliputians over the surface of

---

11. Flannery O'Connor, *"A Good Man Is Hard to Find" and Other Stories* (New York: Harcourt, Brace, 1955).

his skin. Not tattoos at all, I saw, but forms sardined in his contour, creatures Bannon had killed since childhood: spineless insects, flies he'd dewinged; yet even the tiniest of these thrashing within the body mosaic was, clearly, a society as complex as the higher forms, a concrescence of molecules cells atoms in concert, for nothing in the necropolis he'd filled stood alone, . . . and the commonwealth of the dead shape-shifted on his chest, his full belly, his fat shoulders, traded hand for claw, feet for hooves, legs for wings, their metamorphosis having no purpose beyond the delight the universe took in diversity for its own sake, the proliferation of beauty, and yet all were conserved in this process of doubling, . . . where the profound mystery of the One and the Many gave me back my father again and again, his love, in every being from grubworms to giant sumacs, for these too were my father and, in the final face I saw in the Soulcatcher, which shook tears from me—my own face, for he had duplicated portions of me during the early days of the hunt—I was my father's father, and he my child. (175–176)

In this revelation the trophies of Bannon's murders, of infinite crossings of boundaries, are shown to inhabit the ultimate boundary, the mongrel creature's skin, an epidermal cemetery, in which the dead are (re)animated only to succumb to infinitesimal transformations into one another. Thus, Andrew obtains his liberty only at the cost of an awareness that he is forever bound to an ancestry of suffering victims. And yet, through the Soulcatcher, a liminal figure, the issue of slavery, by being "epidermalized" in a Melvillean projection of depth to surface, is extended to metaphysical proportions. Bannon's animated skin provides insights into the law of correspondences, "the profound mystery of the One and the Many" (176), the enigma of duplication. No longer merely protective or stigmatizing, skin in this passage becomes a mirror into another world, a stage, or rather a screen, on which the eternal cycle of life and death is played out in shape-shifting swarms of ambiguous creatures, paradoxically promising access to the amorphous sources of creation.

The protean nature of this "theater of tattooes" (176) fascinated Johnson so much that he took it up again in *Middle Passage* (the novel that earned him the National Book Award in 1990) and made it the major characteristic of the Allmuseri god that the dwarfish white slave trader is trying to carry back from Africa in the hold of his ship.[12] This is a dangerous god who absorbs people, appears to them in the shape of their ancestors, and confronts them with their mirror images. But the process of absorption goes in

12. Charles Johnson, *Middle Passage* (New York: Atheneum, 1990); all subsequent references are cited by page in the text.

both directions: "This blistering vision licked itself clean, as cats do, and had other beings, whole cultures of them, living *parasitically* on his body" (168; emphasis added).

The coal-black god's appearance represents as much of a descent and return to the protagonist's ancient African roots as the latter will ever experience; it "confused my lineage as a marginalized American colored man," he says (169). Yet the shift of the image is significant. The mulatto slave hunter of *Oxherding Tale* is in this novel replaced by another outsider: the captain of the slave ship is a white dwarf. The emblem of Soulcatcher's "boundary condition," his grotesque tattoo, however, is transferred to the Allmuseri ("all misery") god. By absorbing into his epidermis the people who are sent to feed him, this god becomes a god of the boundary, of the in-between, literally of the Middle Passage.

If *Roots* (or the books from which Alex Haley allegedly borrowed) introduced a formerly remote Africa into black American fiction and thus extended fictional Afro-American history backward, far beyond slavery, Johnson's novel introduces the crossing of the boundary between the two continents, between the two cultures, and centralizes the experience of this boundary by treating it as a liminal experience. His imaginative treatment of tattooing as microcosm combines the functions of skin as dividing line, as zone of exchange, and as edge to the unknown. This has a profound effect on the narrator-protagonist, for it means that the principles of division and multiplicity have always already been an essential issue of his ethnic condition. The adventurous return to his roots, therefore, paradoxically leads to a heightened awareness of his marginality. Hence, it is no wonder that the message he receives from this weird deity is that "identity [is] imagined," that "the (black) self is the greatest of all fictions" (171). This, perhaps, is the reason why in Johnson's novels the concern with boundaries has replaced the concern with roots, but also the reason why his boundaries no longer merely separate, divide, or protect but instead function as signifiers of the biological, physical, cultural exchanges going on across them as well as of the blending of disparate and contradictory elements out of which they have been constructed.

My second text, taken from John Edgar Wideman's *Homewood Trilogy*,[13]

---

13. John Edgar Wideman, *The Homewood Trilogy: Damballah, Hiding Place, Sent for You Yesterday* (New York: Avon, 1985); all subsequent references are cited by page in the text. Reprinted as *The Homewood Books* (Pittsburgh: University of Pittsburgh Press, 1992).

is the prizewinning novel *Sent for You Yesterday*.[14] On the surface it is a nonlinear account of the lives of three generations of members and friends of the narrator's family. On a deeper level it is the record of a writer's search for the mythical forces of survival in the dilapidated black section of Pittsburgh and of his digging for the roots of his art in the collective memory of the black community. Through continual shifting of time levels and focalizers the author blends memory and prophecy and makes the characters echo and reflect one another. In this way, and by means of highly figurative language, Wideman creates an imaginative texture that extends far beyond his dense and tightly structured novel.

The emotional center of the collective memory is a black blues pianist named Albert Wilkes, who had been kept on the run for seven years for murdering a white policeman and was finally shot while playing the piano in the parlor of his former foster mother. With his big black hat and his long gray coat, Wilkes has become a mythical figure for the later generations of Homewood residents: visitors to his favorite bar think they see his shadow on the walls; his piano playing pursues people in the street; and another foster child, who had to clean up the mess after the shooting, even claims to possess a relic in the form of a piece of his skull. Not only is Wilkes the ideal erotic black hero who defies all taboos, especially those of segregation, but also he embodies the soul of black music, its creative freedom, its ability to structure chaos and to tiptoe across the void. And just as his brains were scattered when he was killed, his musical legacy has been disseminated, passed on to fertilize the imagination of later generations. According to the critic Matthew Wilson, this is a version of *sparagmos*,[15] the dismemberment of fertility gods, and thus an orphic analogue to the dissemination of tales, which is one of the narrator's major concerns.[16]

The spiritual successor to Albert Wilkes, his antitype as it were, the mediator between the legendary musician and the storytelling narrator, and thus the protagonist of the novel, is a nameless albino, ironically called Brother Tate or simply Brother, an appellation that is used by African Americans to indicate membership in a community based on religious affiliation or more

14. John Edgar Wideman, *Sent for You Yesterday* (New York: Avon, 1983).

15. Matthew Wilson, "The Circles of History in John Edgar Wideman's *The Homewood Trilogy*," *CLA Journal*, 33.3 (March 1990): 243, 251.

16. On the development from letters to songs and on listening, see Ashraf H. A. Rushdy, "Fraternal Blues: John Edgar Wideman's *Homewood Trilogy*," *Contemporary Literature*, 32.3 (1991): 312–345.

generally racial identity (a white "soul brother," therefore, is a contradiction in terms). The central function of Brother's albinism is apparent from the way he is introduced in the first chapter:

> If you looked closely Brother had no color. He was lighter than anybody else, so white was a word some people used to picture him, but he wasn't white, not white like snow or paper, not even white like the people who called us black. Depending on the time of day, on how much light was in a room, on how you were feeling when you ran into Brother Tate, his color changed. I was always a little afraid of him, afraid I'd see through him, under his skin, because there was no color to stop my eyes, no color which said there's a black man or a white man in front of you. I was afraid I'd see through that transparent envelope of skin to the bones and blood and guts of whatever he was. To see Brother I'd have to look away from where he was standing, focus on something safe and solid near him so that Brother would hover like the height of a mountain at the skittish edges of my vision. (357)

Readers familiar with Ralph Ellison's *Invisible Man* will find here a striking reference to the epilogue of that novel, where the anonymous narrator, living in a cellar on the edge of Harlem, links his invisibility with guilt, signifying on Armstrong and Kierkegaard by troping on the sin of skin:

> It came upon me slowly, like that strange disease that affects those black men whom you see turning slowly from black to albino, their pigment disappearing as under the radiation of some cruel, invisible ray. You go along for years knowing something is wrong, then suddenly you discover that you're as transparent as air. At first you tell yourself that it's all a dirty joke, or that it's due to the "political situation." But deep down you come to suspect that you're yourself to blame, and you stand naked and shivering before the millions of eyes who look through you unseeingly.[17]

For Ellison's antihero, however, invisibility has a mirroring function, whereas Wideman's young narrator fears exactly those aspects which Ellison's observers in the prologue cannot or do not want to see: Brother Tate's bones, blood, and guts.[18] Moreover, whereas for Ellison albinism represents an aspect of invisibility, invisibility, or at least transparency, for Wideman appears only as an aspect of albinism, as one of the many shades of white mentioned in the quoted passage.

Brother Tate's fate is a direct result of his albinism, and the reaction of

17. Ralph Ellison, *Invisible Man* (New York: Random House, 1952), p. 434.
18. Ibid., p. 3.

the others to his skin reflects his inner development and vice versa. His three-year love affair with a black nationalist woman, the birth of an albino son (in a caul, a "bag of skin," by the way), and the child's rejection by his black brothers and sisters are followed by a sudden miraculous display of musical talent in Brother, which makes him appear to be a reincarnation of the dead blues pianist. The half-accidental burning to death of his six-year-old albino boy, which is experienced by the child's mother as an act of lynching, strikes him dumb; he survives a few more years as a scat-singing fool and finally dies a mysterious death playing a children's scare game, crossing the boundary of the railroad tracks in front of an engine. The mother goes insane.

Through a combination of physical defects and supernatural powers this albino becomes a representative of a different black generation in Homewood, a generation of outsiders and marginal people; at the same time, however, he takes over from Albert Wilkes as disseminator of the ancient knowledge of blackness and becomes an absurd carrier of the old myths. In the description of the haunting scene in which Brother Tate holds a wake for his dead son, we read:

> That's when I sang to Junebug. Sang to him to save his life. Because he was just a baby. Because he didn't know a thing about leaving or coming back again. So I had to tell him what I knew. Where I had been . . .
> . . . But then I told him the secret. That there was more. More fire and pain and singing. That I had been through it before. That nothing stopped. That I had crossed the ocean in a minute. That I had drowned in rivers and dangled like rotten fruit from trees. That my unmourned bones were ground to dust and the dust salted and plowed. That I had been chained and branded like an animal. That I had watched my children's brains dashed against a rock. That I had seen my mother whipped and my woman raped and my daddy stretched on a cross. *That I had even lost my color* and lost my tongue but all of that too was only a minute. (496–497; emphasis added)

In this song "white" Brother Tate relates himself to generations of black martyrs, reaching back to slavery, to the Middle Passage, to capture in Africa. Above all, it is striking how in his metaphoric foreshortening of African American history he experiences his albinism as a final phase of this black suffering and connects it with his loss of speech.

In a study of 1936, one of the rare books on the subject, the ethnologist Fritz Sarasin lists a whole range of reactions to albinism around the globe, ranging from disgust and rejection to veneration as a token of wisdom and holiness; several so-called savage populations treat albinos as the wild people (generated by sexual involvement of humans with orangutans), displaying an interesting tendency to demonize whiteness.[19] Melville's famous chapter titled "The Whiteness of the Whale"—in a book fascinated by skin and skin color—adds, among other things, a philosophical dimension to the demonization of the albino.[20] African American fiction has followed suit. George Schuyler provides a satirical version of this fascination in his utopian novel of 1931, *Black No More*,[21] and Richard Wright's "white blurs," "white bags," and "white spider" in his fiction from *Native Son* to *Eight Men* emphasize the frightening aspects of whiteness.[22] Wideman's albino draws on many sources, black as well as white; the work thus exemplifies one of the features I have pointed out as typical of the boundary in African American fiction: the separating barrier is created by a blending of elements from different cultures.

Moreover, from its marginal position as an element in a simile of Ellison's epilogue, albinism has in this novel been transformed into a central symbol of Brother's position on the boundary between black and white. With the promotion of this albino to a central position, however, the theme of the tragic mulatto in African American fiction is given an additional twist: whereas the mulatto is a double victim because he is rejected equally by black and by white society, this albino attains his status as a double victim by becoming a substitute for the white man in the black ritual of reverse racism against his son and by experiencing his lack of pigmentation as the last stage of black exploitation and abuse. In other words, the complex existential situation that Brother Tate represents and endures through his albinism remains predominantly within the domain of the African American community. Thus we might say that with Wideman, black invisibility has become visible, but as an off-white counterimage, as it were, comparable to the white negative picture on a photographic plate.

19. Fritz Sarasin, *Die Anschauungen der Völker über den Albinismus* (Basel: Helbing & Lichtenhahn, 1936).

20. Herman Melville, *Moby-Dick. An Authoritative Text,* ed. Harrison Hayford and Hershel Parker (New York: Norton, 1967), pp. 163–170.

21. George S. Schuyler, *Black No More* (1939; rpt. Boston: Northeastern University Press, 1989).

22. Richard Wright, *Native Son* (New York: Random House, 1940); *Black Boy: A Record of Childhood and Youth* (New York: Harper & Row, 1945); *The Outsider* (New York: Harper, 1953); *Eight Men* (Cleveland: World Publishing Co., 1961); *The Works of Richard Wright* (New York: Library of America, 1991).

Critics have found linear development and circular repetition in *The Homewood Trilogy,* and much has been made of the transmission of family history and what Matthew Wilson calls "subversive counter-knowledge"[23] in the form of stories told and songs sung across generations. Doot (John Lawson), the general narrator, is considered the recipient of the *griot*'s gift, because at the end of the novel he replaces Brother Tate in the trio with Lucy and his uncle Carl, and because he has learnt to listen to the blues.[24] What such interpretations tend to ignore is the indirect nature of this transmission. Doot, after all, is only the second choice. The first recipient of ancestral lore is Junebug, Brother Tate's dead albino son. As in the first story of the trilogy, ancient wisdom is transmitted only across the threshold of death—and so Albert Wilkes has to die to pass on his musical knowledge to Brother Tate.[25] But whereas in "Damballah" it is the teller of the tale who has to die in order to pass the message on to the boy, in the quoted passage the message is passed on to a dead boy. Brother Tate, in a radical withdrawal from society typical of the bebop musician, reduces communication to scatting and refuses to talk to the living. Here, as nowhere else in the trilogy, the tradition is at risk because it is told to a dead recipient.[26] Thus, Doot can become Junebug's substitute only by means of an act of creative imagina-

23. Wilson, "The Circles of History": 242, 249.

24. In his attempt to show that *The Homewood Trilogy* moves from letter to story to song, Rushdy finds it necessary to consider John Lawson, alias "Doot," the protagonist of the novel. The narrator, by learning to listen, becomes able to reenact the tale that contains the essential wisdom of the community. Rushdy, "Fraternal Blues": 340–342; see also Wilson, "The Circles of History": 242. The problem is only that Doot plays a comparatively minor role as an actual participant. The major events in the fictional present center around Brother Tate. This is confirmed by the author: "The working title is *Brother Hall,* but I think I am going to have to change the name because there was a 'Brother Hall,' and his sister is still alive . . . I'll probably change the title. But I would like the title to have something to do with this character, Brother, who is an albino. He appeared before in *A Glance Away.*" Quoted in Wilfried D. Samuels, "Going Home: A Conversation with John Edgar Wideman," *Callaloo,* 6.1 (1983): 46.

25. In one of his nightmares Brother Tate even imagines that it is he who betrayed Albert Wilkes to the police, and again the imagery of skin is essential: "Albert Wilkes's life was hanging on him like a skin to be shed, a skin he couldn't shake off, so it was squeezing, choking all his other lives. It would kill him forever if he didn't shrug it off, so he ran from the living room and up Tioga to Homewood and Frankstown and said to a white policeman he'd never seen before that Albert Wilkes was back. That he had killed a white policeman seven years ago and now he's back in Homewood at the Tates' on Tioga." Wideman, *Homewood Trilogy,* p. 488.

26. Wilson finds a similar condition in *Hiding Place,* claiming that "In Tommy, a continuity has been broken" ("The Circles of History": 249); the difference being that in *Sent For You Yesterday* Brother Tate does possess the knowledge and refuses to pass it on, except to his dead son, whereas Tommy refuses to receive the knowledge.

tion, by collecting the scattered pieces and by (re)imagining the past—in other words, by becoming a writer, by reliving and re-creating the dream-narrative of Junebug's death through an incredibly intricate chain of focal-izers (Carl—Lucy—Samantha).[27]

Doot survives by writing. His imaginary dancing at the end of the novel is a celebration of the community spirit he has successfully been able to capture in his work. But the center of that work is occupied by Brother Tate, the marginal figure, the other brother,[28] or the Other as brother, an adopted uncle, a prince of boundaries, whose existential dilemma is a function of his extremely unusual skin, and whose absurd endurance beyond his death[29] testifies to the strength of the African countervision, without which the work would not exist.

Thus, in both works discussed here the predicaments of skin as boundary impede a direct linear tracing of one's roots; or, to turn things around, the African countervision, which energizes the text, is shown to have its origins in the experience of the boundary.

27. See Rushdy, "Fraternal Blues": 335.
28. John Lawson's real brother is, of course, Tommy, one of the protagonists of *Hiding Place.*
29. The prologue of *Sent for You Yesterday* finds him in heaven, telling his worst nightmare.

*Jeffrey Melnick*

# "What You Lookin' At?" Ishmael Reed's *Reckless Eyeballing*

shmael Reed—like Norman Mailer, another writer fond of boxing metaphors—seems to go out of his way to court controversy.[1] It is tempting to summarize Reed's career by presenting a kind of photographic negative image; one could learn much about Ishmael Reed by studying a random collection of quotations about him from his numerous enemies, rivals, and critics.[2]

Reed is an inveterate writer of letters to the editor, a peerless conspiracy theorist, and an individualist who consistently defies attempts to categorize him, although he has often been pushed unwillingly (if understandably) into a conservative pigeonhole.[3] Amiri Baraka has described Reed as a "rightwing

1. This essay is a part of my Harvard University Ph.D. dissertation, "Ancestors and Relatives: The Uncanny Relationship of African Americans and Jews" (1994), a study of episodes in the construction of African American–Jewish relatedness. All references to Ishmael Reed's *Reckless Eyeballing* (1986; rpt. New York: Atheneum, 1988) are cited by page in the text. On Reed's penchant for fight imagery, see especially his collection of essays, *Writin' Is Fightin': Thirty-Seven Years of Boxing on Paper* (1988; rpt. New York: Atheneum, 1990). See the contributions by Katrin Schwenk and Sämi Ludwig in this volume for more on, respectively, Reed's interests in lynching and Neo-HooDoo. While I agree with Schwenk's general claim that Reed is particularly interested in historiography, I find her contention that Reed privileges racial over gender politics somewhat misleading; in Reed, as I note in the text, it is impossible to discuss race and gender separately.

2. Robert Murray Davis suggests that Reed has been received with "relative neglect" because of his iconoclasm. Davis writes that Reed has "gone out of his way to reject . . . the New York literary establishment; Jewish critics of Black literature; other Black writers and critics of differing political, esthetic, and even physical hue." See Robert Murray Davis, "Scatting the Myths: Ishmael Reed," *Arizona Quarterly* 39.2 (Summer 1983): 406. Of course Davis does not even mention Reed's most frequent and vociferous antagonists, feminists and womanists.

3. In "The World Needs More Guys Like Pee Wee," in *Shrovetide in Old New Orleans* (1978; rpt. New York: Atheneum, 1989), Reed writes that his critics are "always calling me 'conservative' and 'right wing' but all I know is when you lose your spine, you can't walk" (p. 242).

art major," a "capitulationist" who is representative of "House Negroes" and is "part of the 'bribed element' " to whom "we say, Fuck You!"[4] Baraka has gone so far as to suggest that comments Reed has made about Malcolm X could, in certain circumstances, "easily get [him] iced."[5] But Reed has gone to great pains to form alliances with a wide range of other marginalized artists. It is important to Reed, as we shall see in his 1986 novel *Reckless Eyeballing,* that ethnic writers not let themselves be conquered by division.[6]

Another important ingredient of Reed's broad approach to art is an embrace of all cultural forms. In one catalogue of constitutive American items, Reed lists "comic books, movies, World War II, Milton Berle, Redd Foxx, Yiddish theater, John F. Kennedy, Muhammed Ali, Toscanini, John Coltrane, Black Power, KKK, Ice Cream, Mickey Mouse, etc."[7] The second page of his *Reckless Eyeballing* contains its own catalogue, this time of the objects found in lead character Ian Ball's hotel room: Kentucky Fried Chicken, *Life* magazine's World War II issue, a Hagler versus Hearns fight poster, a typewriter, and perhaps most tellingly of all, the Kronos Quartet's interpretation of Thelonious Monk—in other words, the long-dreamt-of meeting of Western "classical" and jazz music (2).[8]

4. The first phrase is quoted in Robert Elliot Fox, *Conscientious Sorcerers: The Black Postmodernist Fiction of LeRoi Jones/Amiri Baraka, Ishmael Reed, and Samuel R. Delany* (New York: Greenwood Press, 1987), p. 82. The rest of the epithets are from Amiri Baraka, "Afro-American Literature and Class Struggle," *Black American Literature Forum*, 14.1 (Spring 1980): 10.

5. Baraka, "Afro-American Literature and Class Struggle," p. 12.

6. In one essay Reed cautions other African American writers not to become hypnotized by manipulation, and to examine themselves for feelings of competition with other struggling writers. "We will have to admit," he writes, "that some of us are flattered when the Colonialists . . . tell us that we have better 'craft' than the Chicanos, or that we have more balls than Asians." Ishmael Reed, "The 'Liberal' in Us All," in *Shrovetide*, p. 42.

7. For this catalogue, see Ishmael Reed, "American Poetry: Is There a Center?" in *God Made Alaska for the Indians: Selected Essays* (New York: Garland Publishing, 1982), p. 112. Indeed, cross-cultural exchange has always been central to Reed's work. For instance, unlike most African American intellectuals Reed does not dismiss Norman Mailer's imagined White Negro out of hand: he admits to some sympathy for Mailer's frustration at being white (although his sympathy, of course, is laced with irony) and imagines that maybe someday there will be an "identity delicatessen where one can obtain identity as easily as buying a new flavored yogurt." On Mailer and the identity delicatessen, see Ishmael Reed, "The Fourth Ali," in *God Made Alaska for the Indians*, p. 48.

8. The issue of *Life* magazine mentioned here (December 22, 1941) included a post–Pearl Harbor guide for distinguishing between Japanese and Chinese citizens, titled "How to Tell Japs from Chinese" (p. 81). For a recent gloss on this special issue, see Maxine Hong Kingston, *Tripmaster Monkey: His Fake Book* (New York: Knopf, 1989), p. 76. The hotel sounds like the famed Chelsea, long a bastion of New York bohemian life, where Bob Dylan lived for a while, and where ex–Sex Pistol Sid Vicious stabbed Nancy Spungen. On the Chelsea, see Florence Turner's memoir *At the Chelsea* (San Diego: Harcourt Brace Jovanovich, 1987); and Claudio Edinger's photoessay *Chelsea Hotel* (New

One way to understand Reed is to pay attention to what he says about his own art. He has delineated an artistic vision which he calls the "Neo-HooDoo aesthetic."[9] Neo-HooDoo is necessarily undefined: it places a premium on improvisation and individual expression, and opposes attempts to codify art or separate it from its roots in folk expression. Neo-HooDoo is an attempt to move away from false oppositions such as East and West, artist and audience, history and myth. In his battle against monoculturalism, parochialism, and racism, Reed's major weapon has always been humor. He consciously invokes and parodies the most sacred texts and genres of American culture in order to demystify and subvert them. At times this leads Reed (by his own admission) to deal in "types" rather than in deep characterization as he searches for rhetorical clarity.[10]

*Reckless Eyeballing* takes great joy in the playful delineation of types who just barely qualify as characters. Reed claims to have written this book primarily as an exploration and revision of overly optimistic views of African American–Jewish relations, but the appearance of a number of straw-womanists makes it clear that he has at least one other major ax to grind as well.[11] Reed has described *Reckless Eyeballing* as a "part whodunit in which the first clue is contained in the book's title," and presumably he means that

---

York: Abbeville, 1983). The Chelsea has been home to William Burroughs, Thomas Wolfe, Edgar Lee Masters, O. Henry, Brendan Behan, and James Farrell. Recall the hilarious reference to Farrell during Lieutenant O'Reedy's death scene (Reed, *Reckless Eyeballing*, p. 124).

9. For Reed's initial HooDoo pronouncements, see "Black Power Poem," "Neo-HooDoo Manifesto," "The NeoHooDoo Aesthetic," and "Catechism of d Neoamerican Hoodoo Church" (originally in his collection *Conjure: Selected Poems, 1963–1970* [Amherst: University of Massachusetts Press, 1972]), in Ishmael Reed, *New and Collected Poems* (New York: Atheneum, 1989), pp. 19–27, 36. Various critics have striven mightily, if quixotically, to formalize Reed's intentionally slippery HooDoo conceptualizations. See, for instance, Reginald Martin, "Hoodoo as Literary Method: Ishmael Reed's 'True Afro-American Aesthetic,' " in his *Ishmael Reed and the New Black Aesthetic Critics* (London: Macmillan, 1988), pp. 63–108; James R. Lindroth, "From Krazy Kat to HooDoo: Aesthetic Discourse in the Fiction of Ishmael Reed," *Review of Contemporary Fiction*, 4.2 (1984): 227–233; James R. Lindroth, "Generating the Vocabulary of Hoodoo: Zora Neale Hurston and Ishmael Reed," *Zora Neale Hurston Forum*, 2.1 (Fall 1987): 27–34; and Sämi Ludwig's essay in this volume.

10. See Ishmael Reed, "The Great Tenure Battle of 1977," in *Shrovetide*, p. 232.

11. In Mel Watkins, "An Interview with Ishmael Reed," *Southern Review*, 21.3 (July 1985): 609–611. There has, so far, been little scholarly reaction to *Reckless Eyeballing*; Daniel Punday argues, among other things, that Reed's attacks on feminists here are best read as an ironic cooptation of the charge of sexism so frequently levied against him. Daniel Punday's, "Ishmael Reed's Rhetorical Turn: Uses of 'Signifying' in *Reckless Eyeballing*," *College English*, 54.4 (April 1992): 446–461. See also Janice Doane and Devon Hodges, *Nostalgia and Sexual Difference: The Resistance to Contemporary Feminism* (New York: Methuen, 1987), pp. 39–42.

as soon as we learn of the crimes of the Flower Phantom, we should know that Ian Ball (I. Ball) is responsible.[12] But Reed has also suggested that the title refers to his own daring in writing about Jewish issues. He argues that there is a long tradition of appropriation of African American experience by Jews (he cites Jewish television producer Norman Lear in particular) but that attempts by African Americans "to write about other major cultures is considered a case of 'Reckless Eyeballing.' What you lookin' at?"[13] I will return to this issue, but first I want to sketch out the implications of one other central hint which the title of the book gives us.

The concept of reckless eyeballing most significantly refers to the charge historically made against African American men who are caught (or imagined to be) staring at white women. In Reed's novel this accusation is made within Ian Ball's play about Ham Hill. In this play, which Ball has written to appease the feminists who have "sex-listed" him as a result of his misogynistic first play, Ham Hill is a young African American who is lynched for "eyeballing" a white woman. Here one of Reed's major targets becomes obvious. The Ham Hill story is a retelling of the 1955 Emmett Till case, in which an African American teenager, visiting Mississippi from his home in Chicago, wolf whistled at Carolyn Bryant, a white woman. Till was killed for it by Bryant's husband and his half-brother.[14]

It is not the case itself that Reed is responding to but the interpretation of it presented by Susan Brownmiller (one model for Reed's Becky French) in

12. Ishmael Reed, "The Tradition of Serious Comedy in Afro-American Literature," in *Writin' Is Fightin'*, p. 137. There are other clues in the title, too. First, it is an ironic rewriting of Ralph Waldo Emerson's famous image of the "transparent eyeball" from his 1836 work *Nature*, where he writes of "standing on the bare ground—my head bathed by the blithe air and uplifted into infinite space— all mean egotism vanishes. I become a transparent eyeball; I am nothing; I see all; the currents of the Universal Being circulate through me . . . I am the lover of uncontained and immortal beauty." Of course for Ian Ball it is the beauty of women's bodies—not "the Universal Being"—which circulates through him when he becomes a transparent eyeball. See Ralph Waldo Emerson, "Nature," in *Selected Writings of Emerson*, ed. Donald McQuade (New York: Modern Library, 1981), p. 6. For a brief account of the surrealist obsession with eyeballs, see Vicki Goldberg, "A Spooky Fascination with Disembodied Eyes," *New York Times*, January 24, 1993, section 2, p. 29.

13. On Lear, see Reed, "The 'Liberal' in Us All," p. 39. In "300 Years of 1984," in *Writin' Is Fightin'*, pp. 60–61, Reed contends that attempts by African American writers "to write about other major cultures is considered a case of 'Reckless Eyeballing.' What you lookin' at? This is none of your business." Similarly, in Mel Watkins's *Southern Review* interview Reed argues that African American writers "can write about those other groups with more class and knowledge than they can write about us." See Watkins, "An Interview with Ishmael Reed," p. 612.

14. For the most complete account of this case, see Stephen J. Whitfield, *A Death in the Delta: The Story of Emmett Till* (New York: Free Press, 1988).

her influential 1975 book *Against Our Will: Men, Women, and Rape*. Calling Emmett Till's whistle "more than a kid's brash prank," Brownmiller concludes that he "had in mind to possess" Carolyn Bryant.[15] Brownmiller's hyperbolic and insensitive interpretation of the Till case was derived in large part from her reading of Black Panther leader Eldridge Cleaver's *Soul on Ice* (1968), in which Cleaver recounts seeing a picture of Carolyn Bryant: Cleaver comes to the painful realization that he is attracted to Bryant and suffers a nervous breakdown. When he "recovers," he decides to become a rapist; Cleaver concludes, in a notorious formulation, that rape is an "insurrectionary act."[16] That Brownmiller relied on this report for her understanding of the Till case is scandalous; notwithstanding later denials, she plainly and egregiously derives her argument from this single—and singular—piece of rhetoric. But Reed's location of Brownmiller as the basis for his attacks on all feminists replicates her offense. By 1986 numerous African American feminists (about whom Reed has said few kind words) had already roundly criticized Brownmiller's unfortunate use of the Emmett Till case; Reed's invocation of this controversy seems intellectually dishonest for what it neglects to mention.[17]

Ishmael Reed has had "female troubles," as the title of a Michele Wallace essay once put it, for a long time.[18] Since at least the mid-1970s it has ap-

15. Susan Brownmiller, *Against Our Will: Men, Women, and Rape* (1975; rpt. New York: Bantam, 1976), pp. 272–273. We should be careful about trying too hard to denote the "real" identities lurking behind Reed's characters. *Reckless Eyeballing* flirts with being a roman à clef but never quite commits. Ian Ball displays similarities to Ishmael Reed, but so too does Lieutenant O'Reedy. (Reed has often written and spoken of his own Irish heritage.) Jake Brashford seems, in some ways, a parody of Ralph Ellison, but, again, it is an incomplete representation.

16. See Eldridge Cleaver, *Soul on Ice* (New York: Dell, 1968), pp. 10–14.

17. See especially Angela Davis's response to Brownmiller in "Rape, Racism, and the Myth of the Black Rapist," in *Women, Race, and Class* (1981; rpt. New York: Vintage, 1983), pp. 176–201, esp. pp. 178–180. Additionally, and quite unfortunately, Reed goes far beyond a mere rebuttal of Brownmiller's appallingly divisive rhetoric. There are, throughout *Reckless Eyeballing*, brazen instances of men staring at women with at least implied violence in their gaze. The representative of white male authority, Detective Lawrence O'Reedy, can hardly concentrate on the Flower Phantom case because he is too busy staring at Tremonisha Smarts's "serendipitous buttocks moving beneath her silk pants" (p. 11). The most egregious example of reckless eyeballing comes on page 61. While Ian is speaking with Becky French, we hear this interior monologue: "She put her hand down her back for a moment and scratched. As she did this her ass shifted on the sofa's pillow. He didn't know anybody who had fucked her, but he could look at her and know that she was a gasper. One of those kind who took short breaths when you gave it to her hot."

18. Michele Wallace, "Ishmael Reed's Female Troubles," in *Invisibility Blues: From Pop to Theory* (New York: Verso, 1990), pp. 146–154. This essay appeared originally in the *Village Voice Literary Supplement*, no. 51 (December 1986): 9–11.

peared to Reed that an alliance between white and African American feminists (as well as between white men and African American women) has been forged—primarily through assaults on the African American man. In light of Reed's very public rhetorical battles with Alice Walker and others, it is not hard to see why he would create Tremonisha Smarts as his vehicle of retribution. The name Tremonisha comes from Scott Joplin's 1911 opera (Joplin spelled it "Treemonisha"), in which, according to Reginald Martin, Tremonisha "represents the powers of assimilation into American culture in opposition to" HooDoo power.[19] In *Reckless Eyeballing* Tremonisha is first presented as similar to "those women who collaborated with the Nazis" (4). She is accused of fostering a "blood libel" against black men, and it is with this reference that Reed opens his investigations into the connections between African American and Jewish history and the present-day interactions of these two groups.[20]

Reed's examinations of gender and racial politics are inseparable and represent an extended demonstration that, as James Weldon Johnson claimed over fifty years earlier, "in the core of the heart of the American race problem the sex factor is rooted."[21] The link is nowhere more clear than in Reed's daring reenactment of the Leo Frank case—a re-presentation of a sacred text of American Jewish history—which Reed playfully includes as an example of his own reckless eyeballing. Reed's reference to the Frank case is glancing and oblique but still significant. Ian Ball's friend Jim Minsk is invited to Mary Phegan [*sic*] College, where he is forced to watch an anti-Semitic performance which culminates with a dramatization of Frank's alleged murder of Mary Phagan. This performance reaches it climax as Jim Conley, the African American janitor at the factory managed by Frank, discovers Frank carrying Phagan's lifeless body; in an echo of Joseph Conrad's *Heart of Darkness*

19. Martin, *Ishmael Reed*, p. 106. Joplin's *Treemonisha* was published in 1911 and performed only once during the composer's lifetime.

20. The "blood libel," of course, is the age-old charge that Jews use the blood of Christians in certain religious rites. The most famous blood libel incident is the Mendel Beiliss (also spelled Beilis) case which took place in Russia from 1911 to 1913. It came to a close in the same year in which the Leo Frank case, discussed later in this essay, began. Bernard Malamud used the Beiliss case as a rough model in his book *The Fixer* (New York: Farrar, Straus and Giroux, 1966). On Beiliss, see Maurice Samuel, *Blood Accusation: The Strange History of the Beiliss Case* (Philadelphia: Jewish Publication Society of America, 1966), and Albert S. Lindemann, *The Jew Accused: Three Anti-Semitic Affairs (Dreyfus, Beilis, Frank), 1894–1915* (New York: Cambridge University Press, 1991), pp. 129–193.

21. James Weldon Johnson, *Along This Way* (1933; rpt. New York: Penguin, 1990), p. 170.

("Mistah Kurtz—he dead") Conley asks, "She dead, Mr. Frank? She dead?" (45). Following this ritualized interpretation of the Frank affair, Minsk himself is lynched. This episode seems to have little direct connection with the rest of *Reckless Eyeballing*, but a brief overview of the Frank affair might help us to understand Reed's revisionist take on African American-Jewish relations.

Leo Frank was an American Jew who was tried and convicted in Atlanta in 1913 for the murder of Mary Phagan, a young white woman who worked in the pencil factory he managed. Although Frank was not formally charged with raping Mary Phagan, much of the testimony at the trial centered on his alleged sexual perversions: various charges made included that he was a homosexual, that he was unable to perform like a "normal" man, that he was addicted to oral sex, and that he used his nose sexually.[22] The composite picture that developed showed Frank as totally alien, a deviant who had defiled a young flower of the South.

Perhaps most interesting for Reed's purposes, Frank was also accused of being a reckless eyeballer: he was charged with peeking into the dressing room of the factory while women workers changed into and out of their work clothes. Of all the many commentators on this case, only Leslie Fiedler, in his 1966 essay "Some Jewish Pop Art Heroes," pushes this accusation to a rhetorical conclusion outrageous enough to attract Ishmael Reed: even if Frank were not sexually exploiting young women in the factory he managed, he did walk "in on their privacy with utter contempt for their dignity. Like most factory managers of his time, he was—metaphorically at least—screwing little girls like Mary Phagan."[23]

The case also revived the popular question (as Eugene Levy pointed out in 1974) of whether Jews "counted" as white—or if they should be considered equivalent to African Americans, or something else altogether.[24] The key tes-

22. For the basic historical outlines of the Frank case and its implications, see Leonard Dinnerstein, *The Leo Frank Case* (New York: Columbia University Press, 1968); Harry Golden, *A Little Girl Is Dead* (New York: World Publishing, 1965); Nancy MacLean, "The Leo Frank Case Reconsidered: Gender and Sexual Politics in the Making of Reactionary Populism," *Journal of American History*, 78.3 (December 1991): 917–948; Eugene Levy, " 'Is the Jew a White Man?': Press Reaction to the Leo Frank Case, 1913–1915," *Phylon*, 35.2 (June 1974): 212–222; and my dissertation, "Ancestors and Relatives." For specific information on Frank's perversions, see Dinnerstein, *The Leo Frank Case*, pp. 17–19, 41, 51; MacLean, "The Leo Frank Case Reconsidered," p. 932; Jeffrey Melnick, "Leo Frank's Perversion," paper delivered at the 1993 American Studies Association Conference in Boston.

23. Leslie Fiedler, "Some Jewish Pop Art Heroes," in *The Collected Essays of Leslie Fiedler* (New York: Stein and Day, 1971), 2:135.

24. On this point, see Levy, "Is the Jew a White Man?," in particular.

timony leading to Frank's conviction came from the janitor, Jim Conley. Never before had an African American's testimony been accepted in a capital case against a "white" man in the postbellum South. In addition, much of the evidence suggested that if Frank did not kill Mary Phagan, then Jim Conley must have. (Of course, a rarely uttered but real possibility is that both the Jew and the African American shared some responsibility for the crime.)

Frank was sentenced to death, but after two years of legal appeals the governor of Georgia finally commuted his sentence during the summer of 1915. Soon after this Frank was abducted from the prison farm where he was incarcerated and was hanged outside Marietta, the birthplace of Mary Phagan. The case led to the founding of the Anti-Defamation League and contributed to the revitalization of the new Ku Klux Klan. When, in *Reckless Eyeballing*, Jim Minsk sees the campus of Mary Phegan College looming on a mountain in the distance, we are reminded that the legend of the new Klan has it that their first ritual was held on top of Stone Mountain in Georgia (36).[25]

The "lynching" of Ian Ball's friend Jim Minsk is more or less tangential to the major plot line of *Reckless Eyeballing*, so it is worth asking why Reed summons the memory of the Frank case. Given the "truly tasteless" joke that serves as epigraph to *Reckless Eyeballing*—"What's the American dream? A million blacks swimming back to Africa with a Jew under each arm"— one possibility is that Reed believes Jews and African Americans are in the same boat as marginalized groups in American society.[26] Indeed, David Levering Lewis's influential 1984 study of African American–Jewish relations locates the Frank case as the moment when Jews realized that they too were vulnerable in America, and decided to throw in their lot with their African American brothers in suffering.[27] (My use of gendered language to

25. Leonard Dinnerstein suggests that the Knights of Mary Phagan, organized to avenge her death, formed the nucleus of the new Klan. See Dinnerstein, *The Leo Frank Case*, pp. 149–150.

26. As such, it might be more accurate to say that African Americans and Jews are in the same ocean—without even a boat to keep them afloat.

27. See David Levering Lewis, "Parallels and Divergences: Assimilationist Strategies of Afro-American and Jewish Elites from 1910 to the Early 1930s," *Journal of American History*, 71.3 (December 1984): 543–564. This important essay has been reprinted in *Bridges and Boundaries: African Americans and American Jews*, ed. Jack Salzman, with Adina Back and Gretchen Sullivan Sorin (New York: George Braziller in association with the Jewish Museum, 1992), pp. 17–35. My own archival research into the discourses in and around this case suggest a much more ambiguous conclusion. The Frank case, rather than serving as a first entry in a utopian version of the relationship of Jews and African Americans, is better understood as a site of much struggle, specifically over whether

describe the putative alliance is intentional; the rhetoric around African American–Jewish relations is almost completely masculinized.)

I think Reed would demur from this dominant interpretation. Reed's adaptation of the Frank case, especially in the context of Jake Brashford's strong anti-Jewish sentiments in *Reckless Eyeballing*, suggests that the case provides a matchless example of how the veneer of similarity in the tribulations of Jews and African Americans has often covered up important differences. These differences have festered in a culture of avoidance and ultimately have given the lie to the simple dreams of alliance which depend on analogy.[28]

Most broadly, I think Reed is intent on reminding Jews of their provisional whiteness. Ian Ball tells Jim Minsk: "Brashford says that you're not a white male, you're Jewish, that white men and Jewish men have been fighting for centuries and for you to call yourself a white man is strange" (14). Randy Shank, in his own incoherent way, also promotes this viewpoint, arguing that "there's really no such thing as a white Jew. Real white people call Jews and the Arabs sand niggers behind their backs. Back in the 1900s and 1910s in this town they called the Russian ones Asiatics and Orientals" (67). Much of *Reckless Eyeballing* serves as a reminder of a time when the social and racial status of Jews in the United States was ambiguous and contested.

There are many voices in this book saying many contradictory things. It would do violence to the complexity of Reed's vision of African American–Jewish relations to simplify his message to the old line that these two oppressed groups were natural allies. Instead, through Ian Ball, Randy Shank, Jake Brashford, and Paul Shoboater, Reed includes a fairly representative sampling of modern African American opinion on relations with Jews. Reed himself harbors no romantic illusions about a golden age of African American–Jewish relations in anybody's recent memory. In an interview published in *Southern Review* in 1985, Reed claims with characteristic overstatement that "the last time Jews cooperated with blacks was in the Middle

---

Frank or Conley should have been punished for this crime, and more broadly over which group was "safer" and more Americanized.

28. In the Frank trial even the images of perversion which surrounded the defendant marked him off as particularly alien and totally unlike the mythical phallic rapist of the southern imagination. Jim Conley claimed to have seen Frank with a woman who was "sitting down in a chair and she had her clothes up to here, and he was down on his knees" (Dinnerstein, *The Leo Frank Case,* p. 41): I think it is instructive that the focal point of this Jewish man's sexual perversion is not organized around a powerful vision of genitality, as it would have likely have been for an African American man at the time. See Melnick, "Leo Frank's Perversion."

Ages when the Jews showed Africans how to get into Spain—how to take over the country. They provided the Moors with an invasion route because the Jews were catching hell in Spain. There were Spanish Christian fundamentalists who were trying to force the Jews into conversion; together the Jews and the blacks created a renaissance. It happened about 900 A.D."[29] With this, Reed reveals his project in *Reckless Eyeballing* to be a subversion of older, more quiescent views of African American–Jewish relations.

This is not to suggest that Reed rejects all comparisons of the two groups. It is safe to say that he takes the extermination of Jews in Europe during the Second World War as an extreme cautionary tale. But where Malcolm X and Amiri Baraka, for instance, focused on the negative lessons of attempted assimilation by besieged minority groups, Reed is more interested in the specific ways that the group in power demonizes threatening outsiders—in other words, how in-groups make out-groups killable.[30] Reed has stated in a flagrant and purposeful misreading of Susan Brownmiller that he has

> found some interesting parallels between the period leading up to the [German] denunciation of Jews . . . and some things that are going on in America today. That's what makes Susan Brownmiller and people like that frightening to me . . . She wrote that the black man encouraged rape and supported rape,

29. Watkins, "Interview with Ishmael Reed," p. 609. *Bridges and Boundaries* is a good place to begin an investigation of the liberal optimism surrounding this subject. See also Lenora E. Berson, *The Negroes and the Jews* (New York: Random House, 1971); Hasia R. Diner, *In the Almost Promised Land: American Jews and Blacks, 1915–1935* (Westport, Conn.: Greenwood Press, 1977); *Black Anti-Semitism and Jewish Racism,* intro. and ed. Nat Hentoff (New York: R. W. Baron, 1969); *Negro and Jew: An Encounter in America,* ed. Shlomo Katz (New York: Macmillan, 1967); Jonathan Kaufman, *Broken Alliance: The Turbulent Times between Blacks and Jews in America* (New York: Scribner, 1988); Robert Weisbord and Arthur Stein, *Bittersweet Encounter: The Afro-American and the American Jew* (Westport, Conn.: Greenwood Press, 1970). For more from Reed, see "Is There a Black-Jewish Feud?" *Airing Dirty Laundry* (New York: Addison-Wesley, 1993), pp. 33–42.

30. Malcolm X wrote that "history's most tragic result of a mixed, therefore diluted and weakened, ethnic identity has been experienced by a white ethnic group—the Jew in Germany." See Malcolm X with the assistance of Alex Haley, *The Autobiography of Malcolm X* (1965; rpt. New York: Grove Press, 1966), pp. 277–278. For Baraka on Jewish assimilation, see his poem "Black Dada Nihilismus" ("the / ugly silent deaths of jews under / the surgeon's knife") and his "Letter to Jules Feiffer," where he wonders rhetorically, "Why so much fuss about Negroes wanting to call themselves Afro-Americans? . . . If you want to call yourself a Judeo (Judaeo?) American, it's perfectly all right with me. In fact, I think that if perhaps there were more Judeo-Americans and a few less bland, cultureless, middle-headed AMERICANS, this country might still be a great one." In Amiri Baraka, *Home: Social Essays* (New York: William Morrow, 1966), p. 67. For "Black Dada," see *The LeRoi Jones/Amiri Baraka Reader,* ed. William J. Harris (New York: Thunder's Mouth Press, 1991), pp. 71–73. This poem originally appeared in *The Dead Lecturer* (New York: Grove Press, 1964). I am grateful to Werner Sollors for these references.

which suggests that one person stands for the whole group and implicates all black men. This is the kind of generalization that you used to hear about Jewish males in Germany.[31]

So when Reed mentions a Nazi film replete with images of dark Jews compulsively raping pure German girls, the subtext is clear: the kind of cultural work this stereotyping does can open the door to genocide.[32] Understanding how much emphasis Reed puts on the power of popular culture, we might also come to understand his committed attempt to brand any "negative images" of African American men as representing a concrete danger.

Even as Reed derives from the Jewish experience of the Holocaust crucial lessons for African Americans, he has little patience for what has been the most dominant version of African American–Jewish relations. This general line of thought argues two main points: (1) African Americans and Jews are similarly oppressed and ought to team up to fight their enemies together; and (2) since the Jews have had such success assimilating into American culture, African Americans should look to them as a role model and Jews should aid their progress.[33] For much of this American century it has been assumed by many African American and Jewish leaders that friction between the two groups was atypical and unnatural. (Of course, the contest of potential villains in the Leo Frank case gives us one poignant example of how African American and Jewish interests could clash.)

We can see how little stock Reed puts in this view by taking a look at the character who reproduces this argument, Paul Shoboater. Shoboater (perhaps modeled on Stanley Crouch) writes for the *Downtown Mandarin*, a

31. Watkins, "Interview with Ishmael Reed," p. 611.

32. Reed has noted that one of the white men accused in the Howard Beach incident was reputed to have seen the movie of *The Color Purple* with his African American girlfriend and to have been "real emotional" about it. (The Howard Beach incident took place late in 1986, when a gang of young white men chased and beat a group of African American men in this now infamous section of Queens, New York. One of the victims, Michael Griffith, tried to cross a highway to escape his attackers and was struck and killed by a car. The man Reed is describing is Jon Lester.) Reed's inference is that the depredations of African American men encouraged by the movie and its ilk were no longer abstract. See Reed's essay "Steven Spielberg Plays Howard Beach," in *Writin' Is Fightin'*, pp. 145–157.

33. As early as 1899 Booker T. Washington described Jews as "a very bright and striking example" for Negroes, a people who have "unity, pride, and love of race . . . Unless the Negro learns more and more to imitate the Jew . . . to have faith in himself, he cannot expect to have any high degree of success." Booker T. Washington, *The Future of the American Negro*, reprinted in *The Booker T. Washington Papers*, vol. 5, 1899–1900, ed. Louis R. Harlan and Raymond W. Smock (Chicago: University of Illinois Press, 1976), pp. 369–370.

thinly veiled version of the *Village Voice,* a weekly for which Reed harbors no little enmity.[34] His name is meant to remind us of *Show Boat*—the novel (1926) and Broadway play (1927)—a prime example of the adaptation of African American materials by Jewish artists.[35] Shoboater is presented as a sellout, a tour guide for white people "who wanted to become acquainted with the trends and styles of Afro-American culture" (79). Shoboater is himself a "showboat," an inane, affected, and superficial man who covers the waterfront of standard assimilationist opinion on African American–Jewish relations. He tells Ian Ball that the Jews were responsible for the success of many African American writers, but "instead of expressing gratitude, the fellas keep coming down hard on the Jews." He then goes on to advise Ball that "instead of fight the Jews, you ought to be more like them" (82). In addition to presenting the old "Jews as model" construct, Shoboater also suggests that "if it wasn't for Jewish morality . . . people would be burning niggers left and right" (84). In an exceedingly slippery novel where authorial intent is almost always in doubt, Reed makes it clear that Shoboater's position deserves scorn, not support.

A good question to ask at this point is: what does Ishmael Reed want anyway? He doesn't want the old "natural allies" argument (although there is the hint that if African American and white women can team up across race lines, then so should African American and Jewish men—which would recapture one important aspect of New Left politics). Reed doesn't really seem to believe that Jews are black or Hitler was a Jew or Hitler was a Moor passing for Nordic, or that Jews are not really Jews, or any of the other mumbo jumbo he plays around with either.

Two messages come clear, finally, out of the mass of satire and misdirection in *Reckless Eyeballing.* First, rigid segregation of the subjects of art into sets of ethnic ownership is unfair, limiting, and potentially dangerous; and second, there must be a freer, louder conversation among African Ameri-

---

34. Recall that Michele Wallace's attack on Reed was first published in the *Village Voice Literary Supplement.*

35. Edna Ferber, *Show Boat* (1926; rpt. New York: Grosset and Dunlap, n.d.). The musical was frequently lauded for its modern integration of music and story and its dignified presentation of African Americans. On the one hand, this Jewish-produced fantasy seems just the type of "tour" into African American culture that Shoboater is accused of leading; on the other, it does have a fairly progressive miscegenation plot. On the meaning of *Show Boat* as play and film for Paul Robeson's career, see Richard Dyer, *Heavenly Bodies: Film Stars and Society* (London: Macmillan, British Film Institute Series, 1986), pp. 105–109, 126–128.

cans, Jews, and other ethnic Americans in order to stave off the divide-and-conquer tactics of the white power elite.

On the first point, Jake Brashford's complaints about Jews' stealing all the good material have to be taken seriously, especially since they reflect Reed's own beliefs as he has displayed them in essays and interviews. Brashford tells Ball: "Every time you turn on the TV or go to the movies or read a new play or novel, there's some Jewish writer, director, or producer who thinks that he knows more about niggers than they know about themselves, and who's cashing in on the need of Americans to consume the black style without having anything to do with niggers" (30). Then, in a self-reflexive moment which echoes Reed's own contentions about how he is recklessly eye-balling by telling a Jewish story, Brashford tells Ian Ball that he's going to write about Armenians (30–32). For all of the intended humor in this, Reed does seem to be making a serious protest against artistic apartheid. If various ethnic artists are going to mine African American culture, then African Americans must be considered authorized interpreters of other cultures as well.[36]

On the second point, Reed believes that certain white ethnic groups, Jews in particular, have been used in American culture to keep African Americans in check. Randy Shank suggests that powerful white people "let" the Jews be white now "because they serve the white man by keeping an eye on us, monitoring us, providing him with statistics about us, and interpreting us to the white man" (67). Jews, then, become "deputy" whites, who maintain their status as long as they do their jobs as social scientists, artists, and television producers. Ball recounts that Brashford completes the argument with this proposition: "Jews are not being innocently manipulated, but are consciously using blacks to keep the goyim off their case. All this stuff about pathology—welfare, crime and dope, single parent households . . . conservative Jews keep those issues on the front burner so's the goyim will be so angry with blacks that they will ignore the Jews and leave them alone" (86).[37] Reed has argued elsewhere that "white" ethnic groups which "stave off the

---

36. For relevant reflections, see Reed's essay "Chester Himes: Writer," in *Shrovetide*, pp. 77–99.

37. The reference here is to the proliferation of social science literature about rampant dysfunctions in the African American community, a stance that was actually given its most influential articulation by Daniel Patrick Moynihan. "The Moynihan Report," as it is commonly called, was originally titled *The Negro Family: The Case for National Action* and was published in March 1965 by the Office of Policy Planning and Research of the U.S. Department of Labor.

'nonwhite' hordes" are rewarded in American culture with "Angloness."[38] Reed's own cultural work—including his outrageous caricatures of ethnic conflict in *Reckless Eyeballing*—has often been focused on trying to avoid this kind of atomization.

But Reed doesn't get overly pious about all of this, as Tremonisha's "conversion" letter to Ian makes clear. Tremonisha, having escaped from the control of white feminists, is presumably the voice of informed reason here. She suggests that African Americans and Jews need to be more open to criticism and hard dialogue if they are going to make progress together. But listen to how treacly her language is: "Same thing with the Jews and the blacks. If they are afraid to tell the truth for fear of furnishing ammunition to their enemies or if they're trying to deflect legitimate criticism by dismissing it as anti-Semitic, or racist, then the Nazis will have won and the Klan will have won, and all of the other bigots under the sheets, and setting fires to synagogues will have won" (132). This scarcely sounds like the toughminded feminist playwright Tremonisha is supposed to have been. It is hard to imagine this is the payoff Reed has been working toward. This kind of piety is certainly not part of Reed's cherished Neo-HooDoo aesthetic. The obvious flatness of Tremonisha's rhetoric suggests that Reed believes that reverence is not the only proper attitude to bring to discussions of cross-ethnic encounter; humor, too, may have a place. (Of course, Tremonisha's language might also be evidence of a wicked act of ventriloquism on Reed's part; here, finally, he can put the "proper" words in the mouth of a recovered feminist.)

But the serious point should not be lost: the manipulation of ethnic boundaries can cause real divisions, and usually serves ruling-class interests. It is the responsibility of the committed multicultural artist to reveal and combat discourses that marginalize "ethnic" expression. Jake Brashford's wife remarks at one point that Brashford has been "trying to write a play of universal values, but everywhere he turns, he runs into ethnicity" (117). So, too, does Ishmael Reed continue to run into ethnicity, but in his hands Mrs. Brashford's disconsolate binary opposition becomes (ap)positive.

38. Ishmael Reed, "Hymietown Revisited," in *Writin' Is Fightin'*, p. 81.

*Katrin Schwenk*

# Lynching and Rape: Border Cases in African American History and Fiction

/t has been said that our country's national crime is lynching." These words open James Cutler's study of the history of lynching in America, published almost a century ago.[1] Lynching has in fact constituted a defining and traumatic moment for the lives of black people. It was more than a punishment for offenses in the absence of a court; it was an instrument of the systematic terrorizing and social and economic subordination of the black population. What made lynching so effective was the accompanying cultural narrative that justified and encouraged it—the myth of the black rapist. Although roughly one third of the persons lynched were white men (and a small percentage black or white women), and although fewer than a third of the black men lynched were charged with rape in the first place (and many of these charges were unfounded), lynching has come to be inevitably associated with the myth of the black rapist.[2] Because of this cultural narrative, the specter of real and imagined lynchings has continued to haunt the black community today.

Cutler's meticulous study has proven valuable for many academic writers after him; he became "the leading authority on nineteenth century lynch law."[3] Cutler, a white scientist teaching at Wellesley and Yale, indicted

1. James Elbert Cutler, *Lynching: An Investigation into the History of Lynching in the United States* (1905; rpt. New York: Negro Universities Press, 1969), p. 1; subsequent references are cited by page in the text.

2. NAACP, *Thirty Years of Lynching in the United States, 1889–1918* (1919; rpt. New York: Negro Universities Press, 1969), p. 10.

3. David M. Tucker, "Miss Ida B. Wells and the Memphis Lynching," *Phylon*, 32.2 (Summer 1971): 121.

lynching as a "national disgrace" (277) and called for "a strong and uncompromising public sentiment against it" (279). His intentions were clearly laudable, and his arguments may not have gone unheeded in the early debates on lynching. A closer look, however, reveals his stance as highly questionable. Cutler criticizes the lawlessness and brutality of lynchings but concedes that "they may be the administration of deserved and well-merited punishments" (279), that is, an unlawful but understandable retaliation for the sexual crimes committed by the "thoroughly lewd and vicious" part of the black population (274). The special American character of lynchings, Cutler explains, lies in the democratic self-confidence of American citizens: "They make the laws; therefore they can unmake them" (269). In other words, lynching is nothing more than an undesired by-product of the democratic process. In this context any national, centralized response to lynching would be undemocratic. Thus, although Cutler speaks decidedly against lynching, it "is a question with which the South alone can properly deal" (278).

The ironies of Cutler's arguments indicate that the historiography of lynching is full of contradictions which point to the difficulties involved in trying to take a clear-cut, unequivocal stance on an issue marked by complexity and controversy. Writing about the problem of interracial rape, Valerie Smith has borrowed from Mary Poovey the term "border cases"—cases in which binary oppositions are doomed to collapse.[4] In this essay I elaborate the complexities of lynching and rape and try to see how they are encoded in the general critical discourse and, more specifically, in and by African American literature. Taking examples from Ishmael Reed and Alice Walker, I show that their novels, despite glaring differences, are closely connected in complex ways.

In her book *Exorcising Blackness* Trudier Harris analyzes how black writers have dealt with the phenomenon of lynching.[5] Blacks, and especially black writers, Harris states, must know their history in order to understand themselves and their literature (ix). Lynching, a particularly violent part of that history, has been a recurring theme in African American literature. The liter-

---

4. Valerie Smith, "Split Affinities: The Case of Interracial Rape," in *Conflicts in Feminism*, ed. Marianne Hirsch and Evelyn Fox Keller, (New York: Routledge, 1990), p. 272.

5. Trudier Harris, *Exorcising Blackness: Historical and Literary Lynching and Burning Rituals* (Bloomington: Indiana University Press, 1984); all subsequent references are cited by page in the text.

ary description of the grisly ritual has itself become a ritual; the lynchers' efforts to exorcise blackness is echoed by the black authors' attempts to "exorcise fear from racial memory" (195). Harris's book is highly informative and in some respects very convincing, and yet it is not without ironies and omissions, as we shall see.

Ishmael Reed's novel *Reckless Eyeballing*, which appeared in 1986 and shows much concern with history, seems to fit Harris's thesis.[6] The fear of lynching is indeed central to the novel; Reed calls it "a justifiable paranoia" that inflicts all black men.[7] *Reckless Eyeballing* suggests that black men are as jeopardized today as ever before by the myth of the black rapist. The novel's several subplots demonstrate the persistence of the myth of the black rapist and its immediate and real dangers. Ian Ball, a playwright, has great hopes for his new script, "Reckless Eyeballing." In it he stages the judicial revision of a lynching case, having adopted a militant feminist perspective to mollify the white feminists who control the theater market and who have "sex-listed" Ball for writing misogynistic plays. When Ball's Jewish friend and director suddenly dies (he is killed by an anti-Semitic lynch mob), Ball finds himself at the mercy of two women—his new black director and his white, man-hating producer. Both rewrite Ball's script until it fits their taste; in the end, it becomes a Broadway success.

The case Ball has set out to rewrite concerns the death of a young boy, Ham Hill, who was accused of "recklessly eyeballing" a white woman, Cora Mae, and was subsequently lynched by her husband and his friends. A historical parallel to this fictional lynching is close at hand: in 1955 fourteen-year-old Emmett Till of Chicago, who was visiting relatives in Mississippi, was lynched for allegedly whistling at a white woman, Carolyn Bryant. The lynchers, Bryant's husband and his half-brother, were acquitted. The event traumatized the black population and turned out to be one of the motivating moments for the civil rights movement.[8]

Ball's play recalls this event, but with a twist. Cora Mae reappears twenty years after the lynching and demands that Hill's corpse be exhumed and tried in court. She wants to prove that she was an innocent victim of Hill's

6. Ishmael Reed, *Reckless Eyeballing* (New York: Atheneum, 1988).

7. Ishmael Reed, "Stephen Spielberg Plays Howard Beach," in *Writin' Is Fightin': Thirty-Seven Years of Boxing on Paper* (New York: Atheneum, 1988), p. 157.

8. Harvard Sitkoff, *The Struggle for Black Equality, 1954–1980* (New York: Hill and Wang, 1981), p. 49.

stare. "Reckless Eyeballing" thus enacts the conflicting charges of racism and sexism. Ian Ball plans to have Hill acquitted after Cora Mae realizes that he and she were both victims of a racist-sexist ideology directed at keeping both blacks and women under control (106). His script, however, is rewritten several times by his director and his producer. In the final version Ham Hill is found guilty by the jury after Cora Mae's lawyer remarks in closing: "This man knew what his eyes were doing. He was raping her, in a manner of speaking . . . He eye-raped her, ladies and gentlemen" (104).

There is a factual parallel to this twist as well. Twenty years after Emmett Till's death, Susan Brownmiller published *Against Our Will: Men, Women, and Rape.*[9] The merit of the book is that it brought into the open a problem that had long been denied and ignored. Brownmiller wrested the myth of the black rapist from the control of white men and rewrote it from the perspective of a white feminist. Nonetheless, one particular passage of that book turned out to be offensive to many black critics. In her interpretation of the Emmett Till case, Brownmiller deplores the death of Emmett but insists on reinterpreting the whistle as an expression of a male chauvinistic abuse of power: "Emmett Till was going to show his black buddies that he . . . could get a white woman . . . In concrete terms, the accessibility of all white women was on review" (247). The next passage particularly enraged the black critics and is the basis for Reed's characterization of Cora Mae and her lawyer: "We are rightly aghast that a whistle could be cause for murder but we must also accept that Emmett Till . . . understood that the whistle was no small tweet of hubba-bubba or melodious approval for a well-turned ankle . . . It was a deliberate insult just short of physical assault, a last reminder to Carolyn Bryant that this black boy, Till, had in mind to possess her" (247).[10]

It is important to acknowledge that Brownmiller's book displays a remarkable sensitivity toward the problems of racism and sexism which come to-

9. Susan Brownmiller, *Against Our Will: Men, Women, and Rape* (1975; rpt. New York: Penguin, 1977); subsequent references are cited by page in the text.

10. This well-known quote has been cited by many black critics. See Paula Giddings, *When and Where I Enter: The Impact of Black Women on Race and Sex in America* (1984; rpt. New York: Bantam, 1988), p. 310; Barbara H. Andolsen, "Daughters of Jefferson, Daughters of Bootblacks," in *Racism and American Feminism* (Macon, Ga.: Mercer University Press, 1986), pp. 84–87; Angela Davis, *Women, Race, and Class* (New York: Random House, 1981), pp. 178–199; bell hooks, *Ain't I a Woman: Black Women and Feminism* (Boston: South End Press, 1981), p. 51.

gether in the issue of lynching, and that before discussing the Emmett Till case she spends thirty-five pages describing "the national obsession" with interracial rape and lynching and its racist, and deadly, implications.[11] Why, then, did Brownmiller choose to phrase this passage in a fashion that seemed to equate whistling with lynching as crimes of equal weight and that could almost be interpreted as suggesting that Emmett Till was guilty? White feminists before the 1980s had indeed not always been able to escape racism or racist implications. But then again, why did Brownmiller's critics focus exclusively on this and a few other passages without acknowledging her fundamental awareness of the unnerving complexities of rape and lynching? Despite apprehension on both sides, the discourses of antiracism and antisexism seem to be disconnected, as if irreconcilable.[12]

According to Trudier Harris, the literary exorcism of lynching has been a particularly male tradition. To be sure, black women artists have also concerned themselves with lynchings, real and symbolic. Nonetheless, Harris notes: "Black women writers have been more willing to let some portions of their history be, and the lynching of black males for sexual crimes against white women is one of these portions" (195). Her thesis, however, ignores the complexity of the context in which lynching must be seen. A look at a novel by Alice Walker may be of help here. *The Color Purple* (1982) contains a lynching scene (which Harris fails to mention).[13] After having lived all of her life with the oppressive memory of having been raped and impregnated by her father in her early youth, the protagonist, Celie, finally learns that the man she thought was her father was only her stepfather. Her real father had been a farmer and shopkeeper whose success brought losses to his angry white competitors. A lynch mob destroyed the shop and killed him.

Alice Walker, like Reed, is preoccupied with history. In fact, the story of Celie's father resembles a historical case of 1892. The People's Grocery Store was a successful black-owned enterprise in Memphis.[14] Several violent incidents were instigated by a white competitor, and after a fatal misunder-

---

11. Brownmiller, *Against Our Will*, chap. 7.

12. Any effort to take a position between these two discourses inevitably invites charges from both sides. Having read an earlier version of this essay, both Brownmiller and Reed warned me in personal communications of succumbing to the pressure of political correctness. Their respective notions of PC, however, seem diametrically opposed.

13. Alice Walker, *The Color Purple* (New York: Washington Square Press, 1982), p. 160.

14. The enterprise Celie later founds in Memphis is called Folkspants (ibid., p. 192).

standing a lynch mob seized the president of the store and two of his friends from jail and killed them.[15]

Walker's novel, which interprets the lynching in a very personal way, seems to confirm Harris's thesis that black women are less interested in lynching scenes per se than in the psychological development of their characters. The lynching case reveals to Celie that her supposed father was in fact her stepfather. This means that she was not raped by her own father; her children were not begotten in incest. The death of the father paradoxically reinstates order in the family. This interpretation, however, depoliticizes the importance of the lynching scene; the belated news of the death of Celie's father is the prelude to the classic fairy-tale happy ending.[16] But, lynching takes on a new function in the novel: it does not refer to the politics of racism but helps lessen the pain of Celie's personal history, of her rape.[17] The novel establishes a connection between lynching and rape which has so far been neglected. A preliminary response to Harris's thesis could be that Alice Walker, far from "letting this portion of black history be," is in fact actively dealing with it by pointing out rape as its underside.

In any case, Walker's interpretation of lynching sets the novel in sharp contrast to *Reckless Eyeballing*. Reed is commonly (and not without reason) assumed to have written his novel in answer to *The Color Purple;* he was indeed alarmed by the fact that the leader of the lynch mob at Howard Beach had seen, and may have been motivated by, the movie *The Color Purple*.[18] Reed sees black men jeopardized by the feminist outrage against rape and black machismo, which fits all too well the myth of the black rapist. This is in fact the general tenor of the debate around *The Color Purple* which was sparked after the movie was released in 1985. Many blacks (mostly, but not

15. See Tucker, "Miss Ida B. Wells," pp. 115–116. This lynching, incidentally, motivated the activist Ida B. Wells to start her lifelong antilynching crusade.

16. See Lauren Berlant, "Race, Gender, and Nation in *The Color Purple*," *Critical Inquiry*, 14 (Summer 1988): 831–859.

17. Nonetheless, Berlant argues, this focus plays down the weight of both the lynching and the rapes (ibid).

18. Reed, "Howard Beach," p. 155. In 1986 in New York City a group of young blacks was attacked by a mob of white teenagers in the Queens neighborhood of Howard Beach; one of them was chased to a nearby highway, where he was hit by a car and killed. I am aware that most of the attacks against *The Color Purple* have been leveled not against the novel but against the Hollywood movie, whose plot and characters are mostly sentimentalized and overdrawn. Reed, however, does not adhere to this distinction.

only, male) felt threatened by the movie's depiction of black men. They charged Walker with presenting one-sided images dominated by violence and sexism. Walker, in their eyes, was airing dirty linen in public and therefore catering to the interests of white feminists. Reed can thus be seen as taking part in another cultural narrative that counters the myth of the black rapist from a black male perspective.[19] From this point of view the alliance of black women with white feminists should prove devastating to the situation of black males, as the myth of the black rapist is resurrected and exploited for the feminist cause.[20] This debate is as old as black feminism itself; one of the incidents that revived it was the production in the 1970s of Ntozake Shange's feminist play *For Colored Girls Who Have Considered Suicide/ When the Rainbow Is Enuf.*[21]

The feeling of immediate jeopardy is central to this black male counternarrative and is a recurrent theme in Reed's novel. Reed describes the hysteria of a neofascist crowd ready to revenge rape; in the end Ball's Jewish producer, Jim Minsk, is lynched in a reenactment of the 1913 Leo Frank case: "He looked about the crowd, and they were all looking at him . . . From the look in [their] eyes, Minsk knew there would be trouble ahead . . . Some members of the audience hiss . . . People in the audience begin to sob . . . The audience was now screaming, 'Death to the Jews' " (41–44). There is a striking similarity to an audience later in the novel, which is watching a feminist play about Eva Braun (who is presented as an oppressed heroine who eventually kills Hitler and manages to escape): "There's a chorus of boos from the women in the audience . . . The audience goes wild . . . The audience is on its feet applauding, hooting, cheering, and the two women sharing a table with Ball stare at Ball, menacingly. Come to think of it, he's the only man in attendance" (98–100).

Both scenes echo a 1979 review of Shange's *For Colored Girls* by the black

19. It is important to note that what I call a black male perspective can be shared by men and women alike.

20. The history of white feminism is in fact full of examples of blatant or subtle racism. White feminism of the 1960s and 1970s was marked less by racism itself than by the tendency to ignore the importance of race and racism; since the 1980s the number of contributions combining the discourses of race, gender, and class has been steadily increasing.

21. Ntozake Shange, *For Colored Girls Who Have Considered Suicide/When the Rainbow is Enuf* (New York: Bantam, 1980). The debate is understandable only in the context of the role of responsibility that has traditionally been assigned to black writers.

critic Robert Staples. The similarity suggests that a ritualization of the argument has taken place: "[The] sell-out audiences throughout the United States [are] composed mostly of black women and whites . . . Watching a performance one sees a collective appetite for black male blood." Staples half-jokingly adds: "Reports that a black male is offered as a sacrificial lamb at the end of her play are greatly exaggerated."[22]

The black male counternarrative justly warns of the dangers inherent in a feminist discourse structured by only one element, namely, gender: a one-sided feminist narrative stressing the terror of rape will render the terror of lynching invisible. If rape is seen as a male-female problem only, one will be blind to the discourse of race that cuts across it and differentiates between black and white rapists in terms of power and persecution.

The reverse is true as well, however. The narrative of the threatened black male has relied heavily and one-sidedly on the discourse of race without taking into account the complexities of gender. A look at Harris's *Exorcising Blackness* shows that Harris, writing from this "black male perspective," ignores the complex relation of rape and lynching; in her eyes lynching has to do with black men, rape with white women. Harris talks little about the rape of black women: to be exact, the index lists no more than four references under the heading "black women"; only one concerns black women and rape. "Black women," she writes, "though equally powerless [in comparison to black men], and equally dehumanized by rape, did not have a part of their anatomy comparable to a penis physically taken away from them . . . More often than not, when black women were raped, they were psychologically warped, but the violation led to a tainted addition, not to a subtraction from their persons" (188). To be sure, there is a difference between castration (Harris's metonym for lynching) and rape, and the former kind of violent act was usually fatal for the victim whereas the latter was not. Nonetheless, the way Harris bluntly hierarchizes lynching over rape is cynical as well as unacceptable, and it serves to justify her dismissal of the importance of rape in her analysis of lynching.

In fact, Harris plays down rape as a crime throughout her book. She is correct in stating that the threat of lynching denied black men "any privileges

---

22. Robert Staples, "The Myth of Black Macho: A Response to Angry Black Feminists," *Black Scholar*, 10 (March–April 1979): 25.

of manhood, whether sexual, economic, or political" (x). But to define economic or political autonomy as privileges of *manhood* is questionable in the first place; yet, claiming *sexual* privileges of manhood for black men effectively ignores the situation of women of either color. This claim may be understandable in a context of prefeminist history and literature, but it is problematic for Harris, writing in the mid-1980s. Harris's terms describing the rape of black women by white men are revealing: "White men . . . had coupled with black women in a leisurely way during slavery" (16). She in fact describes rape in terms of "sexual preferences" (20). In this Harris not only ignores the question of rape by turning it into a problem of fatherhood, but also is blind to the economic implications of the rape of female slaves. "No matter how perverse we consider such actions today, a black woman in slavery who had several children from her master could feel a degree of pride in her 'accomplishments.' No matter the father of her children, she still was able to fulfill—in spite of the conditions under which the fulfillment was carried out—her traditional role as woman within society, that of bearer of children" (188–189). It is true that traditional family and gender roles offered some degree of satisfaction and stability for the slaves.[23] But what Harris does not mention is that black slaves continually feared losing their children; and if the female slave carried out the traditional role of bearing children, she was also fulfilling the economic role of increasing the master's property.[24]

Another problem is that Harris defines her topic as "the lynching of black males for sexual crimes against white women" (195). This focus implies that these crimes had in fact always been committed. But Harris contradicts herself; after all, in her introduction she acknowledges that lynching often took place for offenses other than rape and that the rape charge was often unfounded (x). She does not see that the contradiction is resolved if the myth of the black rapist is incorporated into the context of a complex cultural narrative, structured by gender, race, and class considerations and involving all gender and race groups alike, not just the relation between black men and white women.

---

23. This is the argument of Jacqueline Jones, *Labor of Love, Labor of Sorrow: Black Women, Work, and the Family from Slavery to the Present* (New York: Vintage Books, 1986), pp. 29–43.

24. Another revealing passage is Harris's question, "How could [the black man] assume the role of man when he could not protect his own bed?" (*Exorcising Blackness*, p. 189). "His own bed" is, of course, his wife; the question indicates the pivotal role of property in the lynching-rape complex.

This cultural narrative, which becomes visible only if one acknowledges the perspective of black women, includes the black rapist and the fragile white woman as well as the promiscuous black woman and the white protector. The myth of the black rapist held black men in check and justified violence against them. The myth of the virtuous woman not only legitimated the lynchings but also served to solidify the relations between white men and white women: protection was traded for white women's acquiescence to their status as property. But of course the myth of virtuous womanhood did not extend to black women. Their status as promiscuous women justified their rape by white men, increasing white men's property during slavery and further humiliating not only black women but also black men. Lynching and rape, then, were central to a cultural narrative that ensured the perpetuation of gender, race, and class hierarchies and still continues to affect race and gender relations today.[25]

Efforts to protect the dignity of black men or women of either color were problematic as the arguments frequently threatened to backfire or to harm the status of the respective other. James Cutler's questionable efforts to condemn lynching and the case of Susan Brownmiller are two examples. A third is Ida B. Wells's argument in 1892 that "nobody . . . believes the old thread bare lie that Negro men rape white women."[26] Wells used this claim to protect black men from lynching, but in doing so she "den[ied] the veracity of any white woman's testimony against a black man."[27]

As many black feminist critics have pointed out, the situation of black women has always been particularly problematic as they are caught between two discourses that stress the importance of either race or gender and seem to be blind to the connection of the two. Valerie Smith writes: "As members of a community under siege, [black women] may well sympathize with the black male who stands accused. At the same time, as women they share the victim's sense of violation." In short, "black women represent the most

25. See Smith, "Split Affinities"; Davis, *Women, Race, and Class;* Bettina Aptheker, *Lynching and Rape: An Exchange of Views* (New York: American Institute for Marxist Studies, 1977); Hazel Carby, *Reconstructing Womanhood: The Emergence of the Afro-American Woman Novelist* (New York: Oxford University Press, 1987). The class hierarchies that cut across race ensure that not every white man profits from that narrative.

26. Ida B. Wells-Barnett, "Southern Horrors," in *On Lynchings* (1892; rpt. New York: Arno Press and the *New York Times,* 1969), p. 6.

27. Smith, "Split Affinities," p. 273. Walter White, assistant secretary of the NAACP, makes a similar argument by hinting at the instability and unreliability of white women raising rape charges, in *Rope and Faggot: A Biography of Judge Lynch* (1929; rpt. New York: Arno Press, 1969), p. 261.

vulnerable and least visible victims of rape."[28] Black women were defined as promiscuous, and the rape of a promiscuous woman was seen as a contradiction in terms and was thus downgraded. According to public sentiment, the crime when committed against a black woman seemed less of an outrage; her body was valued less than that of a white victim.[29]

With this complex narrative in mind, we again turn to Reed's and Walker's novels. Both stress only one of the elements, race or gender, lynching or rape. As we have seen, neither rape nor lynching can be named separately without invoking the other. The novels thus represent an opposition that is an impossible one.

Nonetheless, in some instances both authors display an awareness of the complexity of the problem. Walker's subsequent novel, *The Temple of My Familiar,* shows an explicit acknowledgment of Reed's position: "White men were steadily accusing [blacks] of raping white women, looking at white women—they called this 'reckless eyeballing,' and many a black man found himself in jail on this charge!—or even speaking to a white woman who was speaking to them."[30] Ishmael Reed's hints are more subtle: Ian Ball, the living parody of a habitual sexist who sees women in fragments and respects them only when he is at their mercy, has a one-night stand with an actress and later wonders about her comments, which he could not understand because they were in German. Only to the German-speaking reader will they reveal that she did not enjoy their sexual encounter, and they may even suggest that he (date)raped her (109, 113). The book thus shows an awareness of the possibility of date rape.[31]

If both authors nonetheless decline to incorporate effectively the view of the respective other into their novels, it may be concluded that they are

28. Smith, "Split Affinities," p. 275.

29. Ibid., p. 275. Deb Friedman has demonstrated that between 1930 and 1979, 455 men were executed for rape; 405 of them were black. This statistic already gives food for thought; matters appear even more sinister when one realizes that although some black men were executed for raping black women, the overwhelming majority of the victims were white, and no white man was executed for raping a black woman. Deb Friedman, "Rape, Racism, and Reality," *Quest,* 5.1 (Summer 1979: 40–52.) I mention this only to support Smith's thesis that the bodies of black women do not seem to count as much as those of white women. In pointing out the difference among victims, though, I do not wish to suggest the appropriateness of the death penalty.

30. Alice Walker, *The Temple of My Familiar* (New York: Harcourt Brace Jovanovich, 1989), p. 168.

31. It is disturbing, however, that the clue to this scene is written in German. Reed thus simultaneously reveals and veils the information. In addition, he invites a tongue-in-cheek complicity between himself and the educated reader which serves to play down the possibility of rape.

trying to make a specific point in doing so. It then becomes easy to see the target of both novels. Their goal is not primarily to come to terms with *history*. Harris's thesis simply does not fit here. Rather, their concern is *historiography*, and their aim is to establish a counterposition to what each writer perceives to be the dominant story. Reed and Walker may thus be said to be working on the same project of revising (African) American history, and, using the examples of lynching and rape, stressing different but complementary elements of it.

The connection is a bit more complex, though. The history that Alice Walker reconstructs is a counterhistory, an alternative to the male-oriented perspective. She seems to oppose not historiography fundamentally but only its specific content. She wants to make room for black women in history, and she demonstrates that the newly accepted black history, with its stories of and by black men, has not offered black women any feeling of identity. Celie's comment on the death of her mother, who had never dared face the reality of Celie's rape or challenge the explanations Celie's stepfather gave of the incident, is revealing: "I felt sorry for mama. Trying to believe his story kilt her."[32] History, in the context of *The Color Purple*, has been turned into "his story" and needs to be replaced by "her"—Celie's—story. The form of the novel also supports this need: Walker's use of the vernacular as well as of the genres of the historical and the epistolary novel are intended to suggest Celie's authenticity.[33]

In contrast, *Reckless Eyeballing* does not make the effort to find a new and "truer" history; its subject is historiography in general, no matter who has written it. Reed has claimed to be engaged in "artistic guerrilla warfare against the Historical Establishment."[34] The establishment has traditionally been white and male-dominated, although Reed's special target is a newcomer to the establishment: feminism and feminist revision. "These feminists," he writes, "like zealots and ideologues everywhere, desire to rearrange history so that it includes only the parts supporting their feminist arguments, and leave out the parts that don't."[35] But Reed, despite holding onto the one-

32. Walker, *The Color Purple*, p. 15.

33. Walker's use of these two traditionally white genres is of course tongue-in-cheek. But her aim is authenticity: "Celie speaks in the voice and uses the language of my step-grandmother . . . And I say, yes, she did exist, and I can prove it to you." Alice Walker, "Coming In from the Cold," in *Living by the Word: Selected Writings, 1973–1987* (San Diego: Harcourt, 1988), p. 64.

34. In John O'Brien, ed., *Interviews with Black Writers* (New York: Liveright, 1973), p. 179.

35. Reed, "Howard Beach," p. 10.

sided black counternarrative, points to the arbitrariness of *every* incidence of storywriting, including that by black men, as soon as it comes into power, and to the danger of all-too-determined revisions. His novel is a parody; its goal is not to *replace* but to *unmask* historiography.[36]

At the risk of oversimplifying the matter, one could describe Walker's novel as demonstrating the uses of revising history, while Reed's parody would point to the abuses of history writing. Both moves are familiar to those who take part in the larger project of revising American history. Revisionists of all disciplines have set out to prove the danger and arbitrariness of one-sided traditional historical narratives in order to replace them with what they perceive to be more appropriate versions. But the new versions may be exclusionary and arbitrary as well. I would therefore argue that both moments—that of reconstruction and that of deconstruction—are essential to the revisionist project, which needs a high degree of self-reflexivity in order to live with its contradictions. Without necessarily suggesting too much harmony between *Reckless Eyeballing* and *The Color Purple,* one can see that the two novels are united in their contradictory messages. The tension they present is to be found at the heart of any sincere project of revising American history undertaken by African American (or) feminist criticism.

36. Obviously the parody makes fun of readers' trying to pinpoint Reed's viewpoints. But Reed in fact echoes Walker's insistence on authenticity: he quotes data and facts that support some of his novel's arguments and claims that his "remark was based upon research" ("Howard Beach," p. 147).

*Sämi Ludwig*

# Dialogic Possession in Ishmael Reed's *Mumbo Jumbo:* Bakhtin, Voodoo, and the Materiality of Multicultural Discourse

Languages quarreled with each other, but this quarrel—like any quarrel among great and significant cultural and historical forces—could not pass on to a further phase by means of abstract and rational dialogue, not by a purely dramatic dialogue, but only by means of complexly dialogized hybrids.

It is necessary to come to terms with discourse as a reified, "typical" but at the same time intentional phenomenon.

—M. M. BAKHTIN

I'm convinced there's a connection between early New Orleans music, what people call Dixieland, you know, and religious rites. Because in the Voodoo rites a lot of loas [voodoo spirits] show up at the same time, and they start quarreling, everybody talking at the same time. You get that in Dixieland. The instruments take over from the usual drums as a vessel for the loas. So you hear the talking trombone, the wah-wah trumpet and all that, Erzuli's showin' up, you know. . . . Which makes Louis Armstrong the most important jazz musician of the century. He maintained the tradition.

—ISHMAEL REED

The novel form itself was invented by Cervantes, a Moor.

—ISHMAEL REED

My aim in this essay is to relate "voodoo rites" to Bakhtin, to sketch out some surprising analogies between the imagery and processes in Bakhtin's critical idiom on the one hand and manifestations of Ishmael Reed's polytheistic "Neo-HooDoo aesthetic," especially the concepts of possession and the houngan (voodoo priest) as we find them in voodoo religion and in Reed's *Mumbo Jumbo*[1] on the other. In doing so we

1. Ishmael Reed, *Mumbo Jumbo* (Garden City, N.Y.: Doubleday, 1972); all subsequent references are cited by page in the text.

find a certain figural overlap of constituents as well as systems. If, following cognitive linguists such as George Lakoff and Mark Johnson, we assume that the metaphors we use determine the structure of our thinking, they become an ideal focus of comparison: "Our ordinary conceptual system, in terms of which we both think and act," they write, "is fundamentally metaphorical in nature."[2] Even literary theorists claim that metaphor is the "founding stone of conceptualization and abstraction" and "the prime instrument for the discovery of meanings."[3] Thus, in this view metaphors also define what theorists call *terminology*. If, furthermore, we now follow Roland Barthes and define myth as a kind of discourse,[4] we may look at Bakhtin's theory of language beyond an abstract terminology (such as "complexly dialogized hybrids") to the dialogic animist way in which the "invisibles" concretely *exert influence on* and at the same time *are used by* humans in a voodoo ceremony. I hope to convince readers unfamiliar with Haitian rituals that there are interesting dynamic structural properties to such a system of representation, which, like Bakhtin's discourse in the novel, can integrate and express the views of multiple (sub)cultures and may to a certain extent serve as a concrete model for multiculturalism. Let me first present Bakhtin, then voodoo and Reed, and end with a comparison.

For Bakhtin all languages are voices of ideology, and in the novel they become stylized into active "ideologemes."[5] His most often quoted definition, from *The Dialogic Imagination,* expresses the tension between being controlled by a language and utilizing it as a tool to get one's own intentions across: "The word in language is half someone else's. It becomes one's own only when the speaker populates it with his own intention" (293). Novelistic

2. George Lakoff and Mark Johnson, *Metaphors We Live By* (Chicago: University of Chicago Press, 1980), p. 3. Focusing on the "experiential" nature of metaphors, Lakoff and Johnson link cognitive categories to physical experiences and maintain that even abstract notions are ultimately expressed concretely: "*No metaphor can ever be comprehended or even adequately represented independently of its experiential basis*" (p. 19).

3. Liliane Papin, "This Is Not a Universe: Metaphor, Language, and Representation," *PMLA*, 107.5 (1992): 1259. Papin contrasts the "limitation" of metaphor to its "potential." She defines "metaphorical leaps" as theoretical insights which can come about only if a model is defined by new metaphors (her example is the issue of light as either particles or waves in physics; ibid., 1260).

4. See Roland Barthes, "Myth Today," in *Mythologies,* trans. Annette Lavers (1957; rpt. New York: Hill and Wang, 1972), pp. 109–159.

5. M. M. Bakhtin, *The Dialogic Imagination: Four Essays,* ed. and trans. Michael Holquist (Austin: University of Texas Press, 1981), p. 333; all subsequent references are cited by page in the text.

"heteroglossia" tackles this "difficult and complicated process" of self-expression by choosing among many different languages: "Consciousness finds itself inevitably facing the necessity of *having to choose a language*. With each literary-verbal performance, consciousness must actively orient itself amidst heteroglossia, it must move in and occupy a position for itself within it, it chooses, in other words, a 'language'" (295). This very ability to use language rather than be used by it is what makes Bakhtin's realm of discourse a "treasure-house" (278) of ideologemes rather than a "prisonhouse" of ideology. It is an obvious consequence that only the person who consciously has access to many "languages" is ultimately "free" to negotiate his or her "intentions" in a position of choice.

This dynamic and multilayered process of motivated semiosis cannot be described with a static "Ptolemaic" model (65), that is, in terms of a logo-centric universe of discourse. Moreover, abstract Platonist notions cannot explain motivated language "behavior." Thus, in the novel, Bakhtin's exemplary medium, intersecting languages are often made concrete[6] and personified: "Heteroglossia . . . enters the novel in person (so to speak) and assumes material form within it in the images of speaking persons" (332). Characters represent certain types.[7] "Language" in the novel is often "styl-ized," that is, it "highlight[s] certain elements while leaving others in the shade" (75). Time and again Bakhtin relates the novel's dialogic nature to a cognitive kind of competition, "an intense struggle within us for hegemony among various available verbal and ideological points of view, approaches, directions, and values" (346). The novel offers a "zone of contact" (39), in which multiple languages, familiarized into a reality of human form, can interact. Its "double-voiced discourse," moreover, can integrate the novel-ist's meta-intentions: "The author utilizes now one language, now another, in order to avoid giving himself up wholly to either of them; he makes use of this verbal give-and-take, this dialogue of languages at every point in his

6. Bakhtin, like Lakoff and Johnson, insists on "the brute materiality, the typicality, that is the essential attribute not only of actions, gestures and separate words and expressions, but the basic ingredient as well in point of view, in how the world is seen and felt, ways that are organically part and parcel with the language that expresses them" (ibid., p. 367).

7. Bakhtin observes that "certain kinds of internally persuasive discourse can be fundamentally and organically fused with the image of a speaking person: ethical (discourse fused with the image of, let us say, a preacher), philosophical (discourse fused with the image of a wise man), sociopolitical (discourse fused with an image of a Leader)" (ibid., p. 347).

work, in order that he himself might remain as it were neutral with regard to language, a third party in a quarrel between two people (although he might be a biased third party)" (314). He is a kind of referee who has himself *expressed by* these "languages" and yet keeps his *distance from* them. For Bakhtin "parodic-travestying forms" can liberate thinking from "the thick walls that had imprisoned consciousness" (60); a new dialogism appropriates and relativizes the functions of old monoglossia.

Many of these processes and metaphors can also be found in voodoo and in Reed's fiction. In voodoo Bakhtin's "ideologemes" are personified by the spirits. Maya Deren writes that these loas, or voodoo spirits, are "supernatural in the same sense that a principle is super-natural or abstract."[8] Milo Rigaud even relates them to the French word *loi,* "more frequently spelled *loa* when used as a Voodoo term. The *lois,* (the 'laws of creation') create the *loas* (animistic spirits) in visible manifestations such as plants, animals, and men, but chiefly as ancestors, because Voodoo is essentially a cult of ancestor worship."[9] Like Bakhtin's "languages," the loas are fundamentally rooted in history; they represent the "socio-ideological" points of view of ancestral tradition. Being "super-natural" entities of memory, they "can be perceived only when manifest in matter, the serviteur addresses himself to material objects and phenomena, particularly in ritual."[10] As "intentions" manifest themselves in concrete words, the loas "live" in personifications, that is, by possessing voodooists.

Whereas the notion of ancestor worship may predominantly indicate a movement from human society to myth (the gods' historical origins), the term *possession* traditionally stands for exactly the opposite. It indicates a top-to-bottom movement, namely, the dependence of humans on their gods, the control the gods have over them:

> Guedé [a loa] is never visible. He manifests himself by "mounting" a subject as a rider mounts a horse, then he speaks and acts through his mount. The person mounted does nothing of his own accord. He is the horse of a loa until

8. Maya Deren, *Divine Horsemen: The Living Gods of Haiti* (New York: McPherson, 1953), p. 88. In my short presentation of voodoo phenomena I consciously limit myself to books that have been used by Ishmael Reed (see the bibliography appended to *Mumbo Jumbo*). As voodoo is not an orthodox matter, I concentrate on sources that are philologically relevant to "Neo-HooDoo."

9. Milo Rigaud, *Secrets of Voodoo,* trans. Robert B. Cross (San Franscisco: City Lights Books, 1985), p. 11. Although voodooists may believe that the *loas* are transcendent forces, the context of ancestor worship makes it clear that they are historically developed entities.

10. Deren, *Divine Horsemen,* p. 10. This seems to correspond to the "living impulse . . . toward the object" of Bakhtin's "language" (*Dialogic Imagination,* p. 291).

the spirit departs. Under the whip and guidance of the spirit-rider, the "horse" does and says many things that he or she would never have uttered un-ridden.

*Parlay Cheval Ou* (Tell My Horse), the loa begins to dictate through the lips of his mount and goes on and on.[11]

It is very important to note that possession has nothing to do with self-expression at all: "The actions and utterances of the possessed person are not the expression of the individual, but are readily identifiable manifestations of the particular loa or archetypal principle."[12] The role acted by a possessed voodooist can be recognized by cognizant houngans, or voodoo priests, who know a loa's typical voice and behavior.[13]

The first loa to be addressed in a ceremony is Legba, "the doorkeeper of the loas. [He will] 'open the gates' and allow the loas to enter the temple. His title is Maître Carrefour."[14] Legba mediates between *serviteur* and loa; thus his symbol is the cross.[15] As an inspirational communication facilitator he complements the houngan's efforts from the other side. Legba appears in *Mumbo Jumbo* personified as PaPa LaBas, the main protagonist and "metaphysical detective."

In Reed's fiction we find the definitions of "loa" and "possession" applied to forces beyond the Haitian tradition. Robert Gover writes on the loas in Reed: "The university, the corporation, the government. These are our loas, a few of them, the entities that have power over our life and are fed by us. Each exists in our mind as a complex of forces, thoughts, spirits, moods, the composite of which is a loa."[16] He shows how voodoo can be applied

11. Zora Neale Hurston, *Tell My Horse* (Berkeley: Turtle Island, 1981), p. 234. Obviously Reed's cowboys in *Yellow Back Radio Broke-Down* (Garden City, N.Y.: Doubleday, 1969) are loas which "possess" other characters. Reed also relates possession to the ventriloquism of Black Peter and his dummy in *The Terrible Twos* (New York: St.Martin's / Marek, 1982), pp. 22–28. Actually this imagery coincides with Bakhtin's words: "Thus a prose writer . . . speaks, as it were, *through* language, a language that has somehow more or less materialized, become objectivized, that he merely ventriloquates" (*Dialogic Imagination*, p. 299).

12. Deren, *Divine Horsemen*, p. 16.

13. The narrator in *Mumbo Jumbo* describes how "the loa is known by its signs and is fed, celebrated, drummed to until it deserts the horse and *govi* of its host and goes about its business" (p. 50). Also compare this to Bakhtin: "The action and individual act of a character in a novel are essential in order to expose—as well as to test—his ideological position, his discourse" (*Dialogic Imagination*, p. 334).

14. Sheldon Williams, *Voodoo and the Art of Haiti* (Nottingham: Oxley Press, n.d.), p. 5.

15. See the Watson cross, worn by many of Ishmael Reed's HooDoo heroes, for example, all the Workers in *The Last Days of Louisiana Red* (New York: Random House, 1974).

16. Robert Gover, "An Interview with Ishmael Reed," *Black American Literature Forum,* 12.1 (1978): 19.

to the American scene: "In Voodoo, the eternal loas are always there, history is always present. Down the street in your neighbor, the loa of Benjamin Franklin lives—if only very faintly—and the other basic archetypes live in your other neighbors, of whatever creed or color."[17] What Reed means by "loa" is the ideas that prestructure our experiences as well as our interpretations, the principles that govern our minds and our souls *and* the forces and institutions representing them. This includes different means of expression, of education, ideology, and art. Such a conception of "loa" may be more graspable for a western mind if one removes its exotic veil and defines it as any concrete, de-Platonized idea. Loa "is" conceptual practice, an ideologeme that represents ideologies as alive and kicking (that is, motivated) and is therefore best imagined as a person interacting with other persons,[18] very much like Bakhtin's "languages" which "struggle" for hegemony in the novelistic discourse.

In the landscape of Reed's novels we find possession as a general metaphor of control. The most striking example occurs in *Yellow Back Radio Broke-Down*, when the Loop Garoo Kid steals Drag Gibson's green mustang and, like a loa, rides away on "MY SYMBOL," as Drag hollers.[19] It is their hunger for power that reveals the type-protagonists who are the main possessors in Reed's fiction. Most political figureheads are dominated by ambitious figures in the background.[20] In *Mumbo Jumbo* President Harding is a mere peon manipulated and ultimately sacrificed by the Atonist Ohio Gang. This logocentric and monocultural force and its proponents are opposed by a multicultural group of metaphysical detectives and "art nappers" associated with Jes Grew, the revival of ancient loas which Reed relates to jazz, in a context of prohibition, gang warfare, and competing "secret societies." In this way multiple possessions, the symbolic "quarrels" of the "invisibles," of "languages" or "loas," and the values they contain are made concrete in Reed's plots. In a cognitive laboratory of fiction their typical behavior is exposed.[21]

17. Ibid., p. 15.

18. Voodoo semiotics thus may also explain why Roland Barthes's myth can appropriate language.

19. Reed, *Yellow Back*, p. 81.

20. Thus, in *The Free-Lance Pallbearers* (Garden City, N.Y.: Doubleday, 1967) Harry Sam dominates Nixon; in *Yellow Back Radio Broke-Down* Drag Gibson dominates the Banker, the Marshall, and the Doctor of the town; in *Flight to Canada* (New York: Random House, 1976) Swille dominates Lincoln; and in *The Terrible Twos* the Colorado Gang dominate President Dean Clift (Reed here creates an analogy between the Harding and the Reagan administrations).

21. Compare this situation to Bakhtin's wording: "Stylized language" is projected into "new scenarios, testing it in situations that would have been impossible for it on its own" (*Dialogic Imagina-*

The multiple incidents of loa possession roughly cover the aspect of "double-voicedness" which in Bakhtin is defined as the "intention of others" in language—forces that come from above. Interestingly, in *Mumbo Jumbo* we also find a motif that suggests the other side of Janus-faced language, in which "the speaker populates it with his own intention," that is, in which the "ideologeme" serves the user.[22] Let me illustrate this countermovement with a short analysis of the concept of vehicles in Reed's text. Almost every character can be recognized by his own particular means of transportation— an emphasis on individualism which seems to coincide with functional pragmatics of variety in voodoo and which can, as I will show, also be related to possession.

Reed's preoccupation with cars is almost fetishistic. He describes the 1920s as a "drag race," a competition of fast vehicles for victory (20). Schlitz, "the Sarge of Yorktown," and his gang roll up in Harlem in "3 Packards" on collection day (19).[23] The Sarge's classy black rival Buddy Jackson presides over a fleet of Studebakers, which suggest a combination of tradition and progress: "You can still see the influence of the carriage upon this automobile's design, this Studebaker which was characterized by its vendors as 'Knight Motored' " (107). The Haitians pick up a group of distinguished black poets at a Harlem "intersection" in "3 black Buicks" (149). The "Rev. Jefferson . . . pastor from Ré-mōte Mississippi" and his "3 deacons" (142) take the prodigal son Woodrow Wilson back home in "3 T Model Fords which at the time had such a reliable engine you could plow with it" (143). The different groups drive a great variety of trinities.

Yet individuals have extravagant cars as well. The mayor of New Orleans sports a Stutz Bearcat (3). PaPa LaBas relies on his sturdy "Locomobile, the name of which amused many of his critics" (24). Later this vehicle is specified as "his 1915, 2-passenger Town Coupe Locomobile. It is a car designed to accommodate the philosophy 'small numbers make for distinction, quantity destroys' and its production is limited to 4 per day" (48). Black Herman, who helps LaBas with his detective work, owns an outlandish car called

*tion*, p. 363). "In a word, the novelistic plot serves to represent speaking persons and their ideological worlds" (ibid., p. 365).

22. Bakhtin, *Dialogic Imagination*, p. 293. This aspect is already implied (though unwittingly) in the arbitrary selectiveness of voodoo ancestor worship. Only useful spirits will be "fed" and thus can survive.

23. The specification of the vehicles is important because they are the clue to who murdered two Wall Street bankers at a Harlem intersection. Reed, *Mumbo Jumbo*, p. 23.

"President Straight 8" (130, 197). All of these examples emphasize individualism as far as vehicles are concerned, a predilection that is also confirmed by a negative statement we find in *The Last Days of Louisiana Red:* "Sherwood Anderson, the prophet, had warned of the consequences of standardization and left Herbert Hoover's presence when he found out that Hoover was a leveler: I don't care if my car looks like the other fellow's, as long as it gets me to where I'm going was how Hoover saw it."[24] Obviously the make of the car seems to matter to Reed's narrators, who advocate a special and singular relationship between each user and his vehicle.

Actually the preoccupation with "vehicles" in *Mumbo Jumbo* goes beyond cars in the literal sense and metaphorically branches out into semiotic notions described in terms of "vehicle" and "tenor." Jes Grew, the jazz phenomenon of loa possession who shakes up the 1920s, has appropriated the radio as an (oral) medium to spread out and reach people.[25] Though the Atonists control other (print) media such as the powerful *New York Sun,* their attitude toward "vehicles" is problematic. The radio reports that Biff Musclewhite, the curator of the Center of Art Detention (CAD), a kind of prison for ritual objects of ethnic culture, is sailing "FOR HOME ON THE INVINCIBLE SHIP THE TITANIC" (205). This ardent disciple of "Western Civilization" limits himself to a single gigantic vessel[26]—which is a risky anachronism, as we know from history. Even worse is the situation of LaBas's old rival, the Guianese art critic Hank Rollings. LaBas meets the low-down "ideological tramp" (217) again in the 1960s. The old Locomobile, which "by this time has developed a mind of its own," simply runs him over: "He doesn't appear to be hurt because he lifts himself from the pavement and begins a ponderous trot in pursuit of the car. He stops and clutches his chest as if in pain" (218). Rollings obviously has no vehicle at all. In the context of Reed's attitudes we may assume that his "devotion to empirical method" (215) has left Rollings without cognitive tools. His "ponderous trot" exemplifies the culmination of Western religion and philosophy in a kind of absolute skepti-

24. Reed, *Louisiana Red,* p. 7.

25. The "inventor of the 3-element vacuum tube which helped make big time radio possible," Dr. Lee De Forest, is blamed at a press conference because "his invention [is] now in the grips of Jes Grew." Reed, *Mumbo Jumbo,* p. 94.

26. Reed also uses the term "vessel" in the context of possession by loas in jazz. Gover, "Interview," p. 15.

cism, in atheism and existentialism.[27] Without belief and without language it is hard to progress in the landscape of ideas.

The most important metaphor concerning the question of metaphysical "transportation" in *Mumbo Jumbo,* however, is the emblem of the Knights Templar. It is depicted on the upper right-hand corner of the hardback book jacket and is described as "2 Knights riding upon 1 horse" (131), "a symbol of the Templars' poverty vow" (191). LaBas later lectures to his assistants that all Atonists in general "comfortably share a single horse like two knights. They will try to depress Jes Grew but it will only spring back and prosper" (204). Their sharing one single ideology is symbolized in the single horse, the one and only "vehicle" they all have vowed to use. Again we find on the Atonist side no expressive choice, no variety, no individualism.[28]

Riding a horse in the context of voodoo necessarily refers to possession by a loa.[29] Surprisingly we thus encounter in Reed's vehicle fetishism an inversion of possession, the metaphorical term so elaborately worked out earlier. Yet what happens to hierarchy if we depict not the ideologemes as riders and the human beings as horses but, suddenly, the humans themselves as riders of "vehicles" which they use for their own purpose—if, in short, the loa is, from a different perspective, treated as a vehicle? What kind of discourse defines itself in these metaphors? Is the "riding" directed down *and* up at the same time? It looks as if the notion of possession, though useful for the description of a single incident of monitoring control—that is, for defining one momentary situation—cannot be generalized into an overarching strategy forever fixing the path of ideological causality. The specific use of vehicle imagery in *Mumbo Jumbo* indicates that possession goes both ways: not only does the superstructure, the multiple divine wills, "own" its share in the consciousness and ultimately the behavior of humans as its playground, but also the humans themselves, if they have enough *connaissance,* can "own" the realm of loas or Bakhtin's "languages" and "drive"[30] it by their own control and for their own use. As Milo Rigaud ob-

27. Ishmael Reed defines existentialism as "A Way of Saying Nothing," in *Shrovetide in Old New Orleans* (Garden City, N.Y.: Doubleday, 1978), p. 93.

28. Yet the speckled ("piebald"; Reed, *Mumbo Jumbo,* p. 71) nature of the horse indicates that variety resurges *within* the single symbolic vehicle. This is, however, possible only through linguistic ambiguity and thus loss of precision.

29. Thus the "poverty" vowed by the Templars seems to be a spiritual one, see also Matthew 5:3.

30. "Driving" seems a natural modernizing of the "riding" metaphor.

serves: "Functionally, [the loas] are all under the houn'gan's control who, in point of hierarchy, is their chief."[31] The houngan "works" or does "business" with loas, just as Bakhtin's novelist negotiates intentions with "languages."

Reed the houngan/writer thus operates with the stereotypes of American ideology in terms of conjuring.[32] He appropriates a heathen model to deal with what Bakhtin calls the "difficult and complicated process" of expropriating "languages" (294). Like Bakhtin's novelist, Reed is a "biased" mediator in a special type of "verbal give-and-take" situation. His own role model seems to be the Legba-figure.[33] "My reading," he says, "leads me to believe that HooDoo or as they say in Haiti and other places 'VooDoo' or 'Vodoun' was always open to the possibility of the real world and the psychic world intersecting. They have a principle for it: Legba (in the U.S., 'LaBas')."[34] The "metaphysical detective" PaPa LaBas simply traces "supernatural" forces and exposes mythological crimes. He does not personify any authoritative myth or closed knowledge (we might call this *monoglossia*), but he has an inspirational function. In that sense the Neo-HooDoo aesthetic offers a mode of communication rather than a statement: there is no written Bible, no authoritative "Book of Thot" left at the end of *Mumbo Jumbo,* only a possessive dynamic process called Jes Grew.

Let me conclude with a tentative chart suggesting certain parallels between Bakhtin's "dialogic imagination," voodoo structures, and Reed's Neo-Hoo-Doo aesthetic:

| *Bakhtin* | *voodoo* | *Reed* | *Principle*[35] |
| --- | --- | --- | --- |
| languages | loas | protagonists | ideologies |
| stylization | attributes | typification | highlighting |
| image of language | personified principle | type character | familiarization |

31. Rigaud, *Secrets of Voodoo,* p. 69.

32. See also Ishmael Reed's two jazz albums with the band Conjure and his collection of poetry containing the "Neo-HooDoo Manifesto," in *Conjure: Selected Poems, 1963–1970* (Amherst: University of Massachusetts Press, 1972), pp. 20–25.

33. Ishmael Reed sometimes wears the Watson cross himself. Reed, *Shrovetide,* p. 271.

34. Ibid., p. 132.

35. Of course the notion of principle is problematic in a context of concrete theory. The fourth column is thus not paradigmatically consistent (or systematic), but merely provides additional explanatory points of reference.

| *Bakhtin* | *voodoo* | *Reed* | *Principle*[35] |
|---|---|---|---|
| "brute materiality" | manifestations | concrete metaphors | plasticity |
| novel | Guedé ceremony | fiction | manifestation |
| zone of contact | Legba | PaPa LaBas | communication/interaction |
| voices | "speak through" | jazz | orality |
| intention | possession | "riding," "driving" | symbolic control |
| language intention | loa | stereotype | given meaning |
| struggle | quarrel | gang wars | hegemonic urge |
| user intention | conjuring | using "vehicles" | expressive choice |
| heteroglossia | polytheism | Neo-HooDoo | variety (multiculturalism) |
| monoglossia | — | Atonism | logocentrism |
| novelist | houngan | author | monitoring (negotiation) |
| language ≠ intention | loa ≠ human | stereotype ≠ self | map ≠ territory, difference |
| reified discourse | symbolism | surrealism | distanced discourse, respect |

I am aware that some of the analogies presented here go beyond the scope of this article, yet I hope that future work can further systematize the metaphors expressing heteroglot and possessive phenomena. Similarities between Bakhtin and Reed may become somewhat less surprising if we consider that both writers base their respective approaches to discourse on paganism and multiculturalism, which they see as causally connected. Reed claims that "Voodoo is the perfect metaphor for the multiculture,"[36] the figure of a system that can integrate multicultural communication.[37] Bakhtin similarly traces heteroglossia back to polyglossia, which could only come into being in the Roman and Hellenistic age of "hybrid culture and hybrid literary forms" (63).

Is there anything we can learn from observing these analogies? In "putting da hoodoo" on Bakhtin I intend to show that a heathen "aesthetic" can to a certain extent do the work of a theory, not because it creates a mental world of abstract ideals, but because it offers useful concrete concepts, metaphors which are tied to experiential reality. Reed's Neo-HooDoo approach to

36. Reed, *Shrovetide*, p. 232.
37. On Reed's multiculturalism, see also the essay by Jeffrey Melnik in this volume.

language may offer insights into the life of discourse which merely "abstract" theories, because of their metaphorical poverty, foreclose. Thus, not only can Bakhtin's "double-voiced" terminology "explain" Reed's use of "loas" and "vehicles" but, conversely, the voodoo aesthetic can integrate some of the discursive phenomena merely suggested in Bakhtin's concrete metaphors into an old oral tradition, which in addressing itself to "material objects and phenomena" shuns abstractons.[38] This approach does not decry the "predicament" of the metaphor as imprisoning, but searches in a "treasure-house" of many metaphors for the one that best defines, explains, or represents a situation. Voodoo terminology uncompromisingly insists on familiarization and personification, on the interaction between myth and physical reality in ritual, and on the priority of function. Moreover, it can integrate a Lakoffian view of experiential concepts. If Bakhtin moves halfway out of abstract terminology and into concrete metaphors, voodoo does so radically, something, furthermore, it *can* do because it differentiates between principle and manifestation and in the metaphor of "possession" also explains their interaction. Thus, voodoo needs no vague discursive formations which combine representation and reality; it can disentangle the often confusing issue of meta-language.[39] In the manner of differential calculus, such an aesthetic tackles the "ocean of heteroglossia"[40] by way of multiple defining moments of possession. All of these issues may offer a fresh outlook on the nature of a decentered hermeneutic circularity and, more important, may in the future also help us better understand multicultural discourse.

38. Deren, *Divine Horsemen,* p. 88. Deren also relates material metaphors for voodoo processes of the mind to contemporary Western education: "In effect, this use of ritual constitutes the primitive version of the new theory underlying audio-visual aids and the contemporary appreciation of the efficacy of movies and television as means of concretely conveying the operation of scientific principles and theories" (ibid., p. 89).

39. This primitive tradition takes for granted Magritte's insight that the picture of a pipe "is not a pipe." Papin, "This Is Not a Universe," p. 1259.

40. Bakhtin, *Dialogic Imagination,* p. 368.

*Sylvia Mayer*

# "You Like Huckleberries?" Toni Morrison's *Beloved* and Mark Twain's *Adventures of Huckleberry Finn*

Commenting on the essential goal she intended to achieve in her novel *Beloved*,[1] Toni Morrison stressed its focus on the experience of the individual, on the "interior life"[2] of the slaves, on perceptions of slavery and its aftermath which have been predominantly absent from any kind of historical narrative. Her novel consists of many voices. It is cast into a maze of personal recollections—often called "rememories," recollections that surface forcefully in the consciousness of a character after a long time of suppression. The interplay of these voices reflects the cultural background from which Morrison writes, the rich resource of African American oral and literary traditions. The novel's nonlinear, episodic plot structure points toward the communal process of storytelling—both within the text, with respect to the characters' and the omniscient narrator's voices, and between text and reader.[3] Concentrating on her black characters' interior lives, Morrison accomplishes a revision of the dominant historiographic narrative which has obliterated the black perspective altogether, and she critically revises African American slave narratives by adding or expanding dimensions of experience which the authors of these texts omitted.

1. Toni Morrison, *Beloved* (New York: Knopf, 1987), subsequent references are cited by page in the text.
2. Toni Morrison, "The Site of Memory," in *Inventing the Truth: The Art and Craft of Memoir*, ed. William Zinser (Boston: Houghton Mifflin, 1987), p. 111.
3. For a more comprehensive analysis of Morrison's employment of African American cultural resources with respect to narrative technique, see Trudier Harris, *Fiction and Folklore: The Novels of Toni Morrison* (Knoxville: University of Tennessee Press, 1991), esp. pp. 164–172, and Maggie Sale, "Call and Response as Critical Method: African-American Oral Traditions and Beloved," *African American Review*, 26.1 (1992): 41–50.

In addition to these, Morrison performs a third kind of revisionary writing which signals her concern with the depiction of the slave experience in earlier texts by European-American authors—another group of texts characterized by crucial omissions.[4] One of these texts which explores the moral and ethical implications of slavery is a "classical" of nineteenth-century American literature: Mark Twain's *Adventures of Huckleberry Finn* (1885).[5] Focusing on her choice of narrative point of view and on her delineation of character, I demonstrate in this essay how Morrison in two episodes of *Beloved* engages in a profound revision of central themes posed by Twain's novel. It should become apparent how her intertextual engagement—her simultaneous actualization and revision of *Huck Finn*—both sharpens the reader's awareness of crucial absences in it and creates the necessary space for the introduction of the most conspicuous one: the absence of the black female perspective.[6]

It is the story of Denver's birth, the story of the encounter between Sethe and the "whitegirl" Amy, on which Morrison grounds her revisionary project. With this encounter she recreates the central character constellation in *Huck Finn:* two fugitives—one a slave, the other a white social outcast—meet at a river. Moreover, an attentive look at the details of the story reveals several further parallels between *Huck Finn* and *Beloved*. In both texts the reader is confronted with a pre–Civil War situation: Twain's novel is set in the 1830s and 1840s; Sethe's flight takes place in 1855, five years after the U.S. Congress passed the Fugitive Slave Act, a law which, in essence, allowed slave owners to pursue escaped slaves into free territory and reclaim them as their property, and which, in the novel, has such fatal effects on Sethe and her children. In both novels a river—the Mississippi in *Huck Finn,* the Ohio in *Beloved*—provides the setting for the crucial event: respectively, Huck and Jim's raft journey and the birth of Denver. There are also signifi-

---

4. For a discussion of Morrison's critical rewriting of Harriet Beecher-Stowe's *Uncle Tom's Cabin,* see, for example, Maria Diedrich, "Black Antiphrasis: *Uncle Tom's Cabin* and the Sweet Home Episodes in Toni Morrison's *Beloved,*" in *Profils américains: Toni Morrison,* 2 (1992): pp. 37–45, and Lori Askeland, "Remodeling the Model Home in Uncle Tom's Cabin and Beloved," *American Literature,* 64.4 (1992): 785–805.

5. Samuel Langhorne Clemens, *Adventures of Huckleberry Finn,* ed. Sculley Bradley (New York: Norton, 1977); subsequent references are cited by page in the text.

6. Wilfred D. Samuels and Clenora Hudson-Weems have hinted at intertextual correspondences between the novels in *Toni Morrison* (Boston: Twayne, 1990), p 116. They do not, however, engage in detailed textual analysis.

cant similarities between Huck and Amy. They are roughly the same age, about fourteen years old, and both are trying to escape from a cruel father or father figure. Just like Huck, Amy is strongly affected by the perverted moral codes of the slaveholding society in which she has grown up, a feature that becomes strikingly apparent in her use of language. At the same time, however, she is able to transcend this influence and act on pure moral impulse. In her solitariness and in her musings about death she resembles Huck as well. Acknowledging these parallels, we may thus clearly identify Morrison's use of the word "huckleberries" as an overt allusion to Twain's protagonist. Amy come into the pine woods where Sethe is hiding because she is looking for something to eat. She tells Sethe: "Thought there'd be huckleberries. Look like it. That's why I come up in here. Didn't expect to find no nigger woman . . . You like huckleberries?" (32).

While Morrison establishes these obvious parallels in character, setting, and theme, she at the same time introduces several significant alterations. The most crucial one is her shift in narrative point of view from the white male to the black female perspective. In contrast to Jim and Huck in *Huck Finn*, the two fugitives in *Beloved* are female, and it is Sethe, the slave woman, whose perceptions provide all information about the encounter. Yet Morrison goes even further. The shift in point of view gains even more complexity as she ultimately has not Sethe but her daughter Denver relate this part of the flight. In two versions Denver renders the story of her own birth: the first one (29–35) shows her remembering the story that her mother has told her; the second one (76–85) presents her as storyteller, urged by Beloved to recreate the story for, and with, her. Morrison thus confronts the reader with not only one but two black female perspectives, Sethe's and Denver's. With this complex reversal of perspective she achieves several goals. First of all, she depicts in detail the viewpoint, the interior life, of the fugitive slave. Second, in contrast to Twain, who focuses on his protagonist's growth of consciousness, she limits her use of the Huck Finn character Amy to explore only two thematic issues. One is crucial to Twain's novel, too: the conflict between "freedom" and "civilization" in a society deeply affected by slavery. The other is absent from it: the relationship between black and white women who have grown up in such a society. Finally, Morrison's use of Denver as dominant narrative voice links her, the young black woman, to Twain's first-person narrator Huck Finn—a link that allows her an even more sustained, and in its revisionary implications highly significant, treatment of the conflict between "freedom" and "civilization."

Jim, the black fugitive slave in *Huck Finn,* emerges from behind the stereotypical mask of the minstrel figure for only a short time. During the raft journey his human dignity becomes discernible in his friendship with Huck. The boy gets to know him as a reliable and circumspect individual, and he witnesses Jim's suffering over the separation from his wife and children. In fact, Jim's reason for running away from his owner closely resembles Sethe and her husband, Halle's, motivation for running away from Sweet Home: the risk of permanent separation of the family. On the raft Jim tells Huck that "he would go to saving up money . . . and when he got enough he would buy his wife . . . and then they would both work to buy the two children" (73–74). Yet, not only does it become impossible to carry out these plans after Jim and Huck pass Cairo in the fog, but also, in the third part of *Huck Finn,* Jim vanishes again as a complexly drawn human being. The depiction of his thoughts and feelings abruptly ceases in the narrative when, at the Phelps farm, Tom Sawyer is allowed to carry out his plan of "freeing" the already manumitted ex-slave. Jim is again reduced to the minstrel figure.

As the information about the encounter between Sethe and Amy is based on Sethe's accounts, no similar reduction of the fugitive slave's perceptions can occur in *Beloved.* Instead, Sethe's response to her situation, and to Amy, is described in its full complexity. Denver's first version of the story begins with her recollections of this scene: there is nineteen-year-old Sethe, pregnant and severely wounded after the whipping at Sweet Home, physically and emotionally exhausted. Concerned about her three small children, whom she has sent ahead with the Underground Railroad agent, haunted by the memory of physical abuse by Schoolteacher's young nephews, she is afraid of dying in the pine woods, close to the Ohio River, with a six-month baby moving inside her. Despite her exhaustion, however, Sethe's reaction on hearing a young white voice is to summon all her remaining energy in a fierce determination to fight the white boy she assumes she will encounter. By beginning the first version of the story with this extended description of Sethe's fear, despair, and anger, Morrison stresses the desperate situation of the fugitive slave. Perceptions of such intensity are lacking in Chapter 8 of *Huck Finn,* in which Huck meets the fugitive Jim on Jackson Island.

After this introductory scene Morrison proceeds to focus on Sethe's perceptions. She stresses that the ensuing relationship between the two young women rests firmly on Sethe's ability to keep Amy from leaving. When Sethe finds that the voice belongs not to a white boy—another "nephew"—but to a girl, her anger subsides. Intuitively, out of a growing awareness that without help she would have only a small chance to survive, she tells the girl that she is "running" (32), and when she realizes that Amy intends to leave, she successfully makes her stay by beginning a conversation. Amy's answer to her first question, "Where you on your way to, miss?" (33), provides Sethe with the topic that keeps Amy talking: her "utopia" of Boston and velvet. The answer to her second question, "Your ma'am know you on the lookout for velvet?" (34), is essential in that it establishes a firm bond between the two. When Amy tells Sethe that her mother died when she was still a small girl, Sethe is reminded of her own mother. In fact, as Sethe crawled through the thicket shortly before Amy's arrival, her "dying thought[s]" (30) had focused on memories of the plantation where she was born and where she had had to witness the cruel death of her mother. The sorrow Sethe perceives in Amy's words and in her voice when she sings the lullaby she remembers her mother singing (80–81) corresponds closely to her own feelings and recollections, and the realization of this similarity of experience makes her trust Amy. Apparently it affects Amy in the same way. She stays with Sethe, takes her to a shed nearby, and starts to use the healing power of her hands on Sethe's feet and back.

Even though Sethe is anxious to keep Amy with her, she never drops her guard completely. She remains aware of the danger of the situation, of the general unpredictability of the behavior of any white person, and so, for example, does not tell Amy her true name. The depiction of such caution adds to Morrison's complex drawing of the fugitive slave woman's response, stressing her determination to reject any kind of simplistic characterization.

In a passage closer to the end of *Beloved*, Morrison even engages in an explicit rejection of Jim's reduction to stereotype. Working with name allusions, she evokes the setting and events of the final part of *Huck Finn* and has Sethe refuse the treatment Jim suffers at the hands of Tom Sawyer. The restaurant in which Sethe finds work after her release from prison is owned by a man whose name is Sawyer. In him Morrison presents one version of a Tom Sawyer grown up. Sethe reflects on him in this way: "He used to be a sweet man. Patient, tender in his dealings with his help. But each year, following the death of his son in the War, he grew more and more crotchety.

As if [her] dark face was to blame." (191). Sawyer is a Tom Sawyer in whom reality has finally taken hold; the Civil War and the loss of his son have confronted him in an existentially painful way with the inhumanity of a social order based on the institution of slavery. He struggles within himself against a facile assignment of guilt, against his impulse to blame the black population for the events that have occurred.[7] Sethe does not allow him to treat her in a humiliating way. She talks back when he "shout[s] at her" (188) for being late one morning, and, later that same day, expresses her rejection a second time when, on her way home, she passes a store significantly called Phelps', and recalls her anger at the owner's discriminatory practices when serving black customers and her own subsequent refusal to buy there: "She just didn't want the embarrassment of waiting out back of Phelps store with the others till every white in Ohio was served before the keeper turned to the clusters of Negro faces looking through a hole in his back door" (189). In the context of these allusions to Tom Sawyer and his relatives the Phelpses, Sethe's reaction, her pride and her resistance, must be read as Morrison's refutation of the stereotypical depiction of Jim in the final part of *Huck Finn*.

In her delineation of the character Amy, Morrison is not—as Twain is with respect to his narrator Huck—interested in a detailed description of her consciousness and conscience, in thematizing the white predicament concerning slavery. Amy's thoughts, her feelings, and her moral attitude, must and can be inferred from Sethe's and Denver's recollections of her talk and behavior, and there can be no doubt that her moral integrity closely resembles that of Huck. Morrison, instead, focuses on the crucial issue of the conflict between "freedom" and "civilization," a theme that she regards as inscribed in the character of Huck: the "resistance to the loss of Eden and the difficulty of becoming a social individual."[8] In addition, she introduces a theme necessarily absent from the male-centered world of *Huck Finn:* the relationship between black and white women.

7. A second example of a Tom Sawyer grown up can be seen in Mr. Garner, the first owner of the Sweet Home farm in Kentucky. In contrast to Sawyer, he never realizes the inhumanity of the society he lives in and the way his pseudo-liberal practices perpetuate this situation. It is Baby Suggs who most poignantly unmasks his character in a remark that directly evokes the character of the boy Tom Sawyer: "Mr. Garner acted like the world was a toy he was supposed to have fun with." Morrison, *Beloved*, p. 139.

8. Toni Morrison, *Playing in the Dark: Whiteness and the Literary Imagination* (Cambridge, Mass.: Harvard University Press, 1992), p. 55.

The first theme is expressed in one trait Amy shares with Huck: the desire to escape from the morally corrupt and cruel society in which she has had to live. This desire becomes apparent in her favorite topics of conversation, Boston and velvet. Huck's announcement at the end of *Huck Finn,* "I reckon I got to light out for the Territory" (229), parallels Amy's repeated assertions that she is going to Boston to get herself "some velvet." For Amy, "velvet is like the world was just born" (32); its quality signals a place which is as untouched by "civilization" as "the Territory" is for Huck. In neither case does the text provide information about the characters' eventual success or failure: Twain ends his novel with Huck's announcement, and Morrison has Amy disappear right after Denver's birth. In both cases, however, the texts do cast severe doubt on the outcome of their respective goals. Twain stresses the ultimate impossibility of escaping to a place of freedom and innocence when he has Jim and Huck pass Cairo in the fog. He thereby points out that slavery is not a regional but an ethical and moral problem which transcends the border between slaveholding and "free" states. Morrison, for her part, reinforces this argument by employing once more an overt allusion to another of Twain's novels. Amy knows "exactly" where the finest kind of velvet can be obtained in Boston, "in a store [. . .] called Wilson" (32). In the context of Morrison's intertextual engagement with *Huck Finn,* the name of the store must be read as an allusion to *Pudd'nhead Wilson* (1894), a novel in which Twain again addresses the theme of slavery. Its plot bears a striking resemblance to that of *Beloved* in that it unfolds around the pivotal action of the (fair-skinned) slave mother, Roxana, who, out of despair over the fate of her child, first thinks about killing him and herself and then decides to interchange her son with her owner's. In *Pudd'nhead Wilson* Twain vehemently attacks southern racism (Leslie Fiedler reads this novel as a complement to *Huck Finn* in which Twain drops all lyricism, and has the reader fall "into a world of prose," showing him or her "the failures of our humanity").[9] Locating David Wilson's "store" in Boston, Morrison insinuates that Amy will not find this city a world "just born," that her desire for an uncorrupted society will not be that easily fulfilled in the North.

In her study of various nineteenth- and twentieth-century texts, both fictional and autobiographical, Minrose Gwin has analyzed what she calls "the

9. Leslie Fiedler, "As Free as Any Cretur . . .," in *Samuel Langhorne Clemens: "Pudd'nhead Wilson" and "Those Extraordinary Twins,"* ed. Sidney E. Berger (London: Norton, 1980), p. 222.

peculiar sisterhood in American literature," the relationship between black and white women. The tensions "of connection and rejection, of request and refusal"[10] that characterize this relationship also surface in *Beloved*. Although Morrison's white characters are marginal, it is in small gestures and in short verbal responses that her white female characters such as Mrs. Garner, the slave owner, and Miss Bodwin, the abolitionist, betray a racist attitude marked by ignorance and an unwillingness to perceive and acknowledge the humanity of the black woman. With respect to Amy, however, Morrison suggests an alternative. By focusing on the work the two young women perform together at Denver's birth, by stressing the healing power of Amy's hands, she allows the impact of human commitment to dominate this relationship. Other than Clytie Sutpen's touch upon Rosa Coldfield's arm in William Faulkner's *Absalom, Absalom!*—for Gwin an "epiphanic gesture"[11] marking an opportunity for mutual recognition which is, however, at once wasted in the white woman's violent cry of horror and rejection—Amy's life-preserving and life-giving "good hands" (81) testify to a behavior and an attitude free from discriminatory features.

In this context it is important to note that Morrison uses Denver as storyteller. As Denver focuses her narration on the women's successfully performed work, she reveals her growing awareness of the essential quality contained in it: the ability to act responsibly. Learning to practice this ability as well will become the crucial lesson in her own further development. As Morrison depicts this process of maturation, as she picks up again the theme of the difficulty of becoming a social individual, she endows Denver with traits that directly link her, the young black woman, to Twain's protagonist, Huck Finn.

Denver and Huck are, first of all, linked in their respective positions as dominant narrative voice. In the same way that Huck's narrative displays his gradual growth of consciousness, Denver's becoming a storyteller shows her increasing awareness of the complexity that characterizes the circumstances of her birth. Moreover, while shaping the story Denver develops a sense of the responsibility that these circumstances call for; she senses that "a bill was owing somewhere and she, Denver, had to pay it" (77). But it

10. Minrose C. Gwin, *Black and White Women of the Old South: The Peculiar Sisterhood in American Literature* (Knoxville: University of Tennessee Press, 1985), p. 120.

11. Ibid., p. 4; for Gwin's discussion of the passage in the context of Faulkner's novel, see her third chapter, " 'Twin Sistered to the Fell Darkness': Clytie, Rosa, and the Mystery of Racism", pp. 111–129.

is only after a crisis of conscience—the second trait she shares with Huck—that she realizes where, to whom, and how to pay that "bill." Both Huck and Denver suffer a crisis of conscience which demands that they cross painful borders. In *Huck Finn*, after the King and the Duke have sold Jim into slavery again, Huck must decide whether to obey or to violate socially sanctioned moral and religious laws. Memories of their time on the raft lead to his decision to "steal Jim out of slavery again" (170), even though this implies the risk of having to "go to hell" (169). Denver's crisis of conscience occurs after she has realized that her mother needs to be freed from the destructive presence of Beloved, and that it is Sethe to whom she owes the "bill." Distressed by an immense fear of leaving her house, 124, and entering the world outside in order to find help—a world that means "hell" to her—Denver stand hesitantly on the porch. And in her case it is her memory of Baby Suggs that helps her to overcome her fear, to risk crossing the threshold and by so doing initiate the community women's help for Sethe. A short "dialogue" occurs which presents Baby Suggs once more as the spiritual center of the novel. Denver asks her: "But you said there was no defense. 'There ain't.' Then what do I do? 'Know it, and go on out the yard. Go on'" (244).

Denver's ability to act on this advice, to act responsibly, indicates one final thematic revision of *Huck Finn:* whereas Huck is left with no other choice than to "light" out for a world unaffected by the kind of civilization the slaveholding society on the shores of the Mississippi has created, Denver reenters the black community of Cincinnati. Morrison lets her overcome the difficulty of becoming a social individual. Her gradual integration into the community makes her realize that the complex reality outside 124 is characterized not only by an absence of safety, but also by the existence of a life-sustaining cultural tradition that informs communal practices and ways of thinking.

In her rewriting of the encounter between the black fugitive and the white, in her evocations of the characters, setting, and theme of *Adventures of Huckleberry Finn,* Toni Morrison confirms the significance of the concerns addressed by Twain and thus acknowledges the eminent position of the novel in American literature. At the same time, however, her formal and thematic alterations expose its limitations and demand the acknowledgment of the variety of perspectives from which the experience of slavery can be described. Morrison's revisionary writing implies a rejection of any claim to exclusive representation. Moreover, her emphasis on the fugitive slave woman Sethe's perceptions alters traditional readings of *Huck Finn.* It suggests a rereading based on an awareness of its omissions.

Morrison's intertextual engagement with *Huck Finn*—her shifts in thematic emphasis, her expanding repetitions, her critical additions and refusals—must, however, ultimately be regarded as a formal technique to support her central goal in *Beloved:* to make visible what has been absent. As she creates an awareness of the crucial absences in *Huck Finn*, Morrison heightens her readers' susceptibility to her exploration of these absences in her own novel, most notably her exploration of the black female perspective. Still, in the context of her revisionary writing Morrison leaves no doubt that both the story of Amy Denver and the story of Huck Finn are stories that have to be passed on.

*Hélène Christol*

# Reconstructing American History: Land and Genealogy in Gloria Naylor's *Mama Day*

iscussing the visions and revisions as well as the attempts at redefinition of the New World developed by African American writers implies discussing their reassessment of American history and their multioriented search for new forms, traditions, myths, legends, stories, and interpretations which, if they do not necessarily run counter to white experience, exist on its edges, sometimes uncovering an unknown continent. Such destructuring of white, traditional history remains the uniquely useful act that can reveal the meaning and the specificity of black experience. Trapped in white definitions, deprived of their culture, expropriated of their land, bound by what Ralph Ellison called "the familial past," alienated from self, black authors can recapture their language and their power by rejecting the India that Columbus thought he had found and by replacing white "official history" with their own stories. In his essay "The Topos of (Un)naming in Afro-American Literature," Kimberly W. Benston defines black literature as one vast genealogical revisionist poem "that attempts to restore continuity and meaning to the ruptures or discontinuities imposed by the history of black presence in America."[1]

Such attempts are even more necessary if the author is a black woman: doubly invisible in the eyes of history, she alone can reread her own story within a field of gender and ethnicity that implies both conflict and the

---

1. Kimberly W. Benston, "I Yam What I Am: the Topos of (Un)naming in Afro-American Literature," in *Black Literature and Literary Theory*, ed. Henry Louis Gates, Jr. (New York: Routledge, 1990), p. 152.

search for consensus and communality, transcribe or recreate her group's own "social dialect," thus resurrecting the distant silenced names that give shape to her experience and, more largely, to that of her community. "Under the recorded names," writes Toni Morrison, "were other names . . . recorded for all time in some dusty file, [hiding] from view the real name of people, places, and things. Names that had meaning . . . When you know your name, you should hang on to it, for unless it is noted and remembered, it will die when you do."[2] Such a "recorder of names" is Gloria Naylor in her two novels *Linden Hills* and *Mama Day*. Whether these names are found in old recipe books or discarded letters and papers forgotten in a cellar but finally brought to light by the last epiphany of *Linden Hills*, or in an old ledger kept in an attic and resurrected by the "genealogical revisionism" of *Mama Day*, they form the core of the narration. In *Mama Day*, especially, topography and genealogy are the two essential elements that determine the stance of the narrative voice and allow Naylor to reconstruct a parallel black history, to reinvent America by subverting its historical and mythical elements.

## Topography

> Our latitudes and longitudes have other names
> Fiction/Nonfiction.
>
> —NTOZAKE SHANGE, *A Daughter's Geography*

From the very start Naylor establishes the necessary relation that links people, history, and land. Blacks were originally taken from the land, and the journey back to origins has to start with the reappropriation of the land, in *Mama Day* the definition of a free territory, Willow Springs, an island that belongs to the blacks who live on it.

Ownership of the land is the first sign of independence. It has to be established legally by contract ("[deeded] all his slaves every inch of land").[3] *Linden Hills* starts with a long description of the dispute over the exact location of the place and with the history of the various deeds establishing the property rights of Luther Nedeed. In the same way *Mama Day* emphasizes the importance of the piece of paper, the "deed," that confirms the territory as "black territory," as if for a people defined as a piece of property the legal,

---

2. Toni Morrison, *Song of Solomon* (New York: Knopf, 1977), p. 329.

3. Gloria Naylor, *Mama Day* (1988; rpt. New York: Vintage, 1989), p. 3; subsequent references are cited by page in the text.

material deed making them masters of the land was the palimpsest of their freedom and autonomy. Moreover, the land is owned two generations down so that no one can sell it. It belongs to the blacks eternally ("Belongs to no one except the black people on it"; "It belongs to us, clean and simple" [5]). The reiteration of this motif throughout the novel stresses the stability gained by ownership of the piece of land where the Day family has built a house, a garden, and, more important, a graveyard. Each Day has his or her own grave with his or her own name engraved on it. Set in opposition to the disruptions of black family life, Willow Springs is the very symbol of continuity and permanence. When George, the black "outsider," visits the island, he marvels at the fact that Ophelia, his wife, knows all her ancestors, and he envies these "people who could be so self-contained. Who had redefined time. No totally disregarded it" (218).

Willow Springs's geographic situation also emphasizes its difference. Linked with the American continent by a bridge which is regularly destroyed by hurricanes, it cannot be inscribed in the American geography. It "ain't in no State," neither in Georgia nor in South Carolina; it appears on no official maps. Naylor even calls it "un-American ground" (5). In fact, the population reject any kind of American filiation by tracing their ancestors back to Wade, the first and last white master, who was Norwegian, and to Sapphira Day, his slave, who was African. If they still maintain political and commercial relations with the American continent, they do so on their own terms and do not depend on the American system of law and justice. Reminiscent of the Gullahs, the freed slaves who fled to the Sea Islands when the Civil War ended and kept their distinctive dialect and culture, the people of Willow Springs have in fact colonized and invested their own territory. Thus, Naylor creates a land on the edge of things, out of official charters, totally autonomous, a kind of nation in its own right whose existence cannot be negated since the first page of the novel offers a map, the iconographic evidence of this "New World" revisited.

The remote island of *Mama Day* inscribes itself on a piece of paper (like the deed that ensures its ownership), the visible charter establishing its existence. Yet, as in *Linden Hills*, whose circular structure reminds the reader of Dante's *Inferno*, Willow Springs also seems to spring from Shakespeare's "American fable" *The Tempest*, the topography of which, to quote Leo Marx, prefigured "the moral geography of the American imagination."[4] Naylor

4. Leo Marx, *The Machine in the Garden: Technology and the Pastoral Ideal in America* (Oxford: Oxford University Press, 1964), p. 72.

plays with the founding myths of America as a garden, but also as a howling desert, placing at the center of her imaginative construction the conflicting images of the pastoral Eden and the forces of death. The main character Miranda, the hurricane that echoes Prospero's tempest, allusions to magic and the Book of Spells all impart a mythical dimension to the story, as if the tale were reenacted with Miranda as the new Prospero of the island. Initially the New World was a utopia, and Willow Springs shares some of the characteristics of the primeval Paradise. The island seems to be outside of time: "Nothing changes here but the seasons" (160). It is compared to a still life, to a "picture postcard." George, taking a walk in the morning, notices that "it smelled like forever" (175); he is attracted by the "primal air," and admires the trees "which had to have been there for almost two hundred years" (175). The luxuriant, beautiful, untouched vegetation reminds the reader of other unspoiled worlds such as those seen by Captain John Smith or by Columbus himself. The small, preserved community with its quaint characters such as Dr. Buzzard, and its witches such as Ruby and Miranda, leads a simple rural life, protected from the "modern life of the cities," where blacks have become "honorary white folks" (38), to use Miranda's derogatory words. Such an isolated pastoral environment seems favorable to George's Adamic dream: "Let's play Adam and Eve" (222), he tells Ophelia, who wisely brings him back to earth by alluding to the hard work attached to rural existence.

Naylor clearly balances the mythical elements of this Paradise rediscovered with darker elements. Though it stands on the edges of the American continent, Willow Springs has been "infected" by some original sin and has not been spared suffering, losses, suicide. When George optimistically exclaims; "We could defy history!"(222), Miranda's next chapter opens with the word "Death." The roots of such pain have to be found in the familial past which reflects the racial past. Owning the territory is not enough; reappropriation of land has to go with the reappropriation of time and thus of history.

## Genealogy

> He had barely had a chance to live. He was just learning to write his name.
> —LINDEN HILLS

The history of the race and familial history are inextricably linked in *Mama Day*. The map of the island on the first page is followed by a genealogical tree. A woman named Sapphira Wade figures as the only founder of a family of seven sons (fathers unknown), who fathered seven sons, the seventh one siring three generations of women. As in the Bible, from which this genealogy is obviously drawn, Sapphira has "rested" after her seventh son and given the name Day to her family. This genealogy is immediately followed by the certificate of sale of a slave woman named Sapphira, age twenty, of pure African stock, to Bascombe Wade, on August 3, 1819. Thus the arresting, unusual first three pages of the novel offer a clue to the inner structure of the book, introducing what Barbara Christian has called a "creative dialogue"[5] between public and private life, history and biography, the past and the present. Genealogy, a search for filiation and lineage, finds itself at the intersection of these patterns as it concerns the individual private and family sphere, but also largely serves to remedy the failures of memory through its minute literal reconstitution of human history.

Any genesis of "black" history has to go back to the original trauma of slavery (here the sale of Sapphira in 1819) and to the sexual exploitation of black women. Any kind of filiation starts with a white master. *Mama Day* alludes to the different miscegenations that made one of Miranda's ancestors say, for instance: "Some of my brothers looked like me and some didn't . . . In them times, it was common to have a blue-eyed child playing next to his dark sister" (151). Ophelia herself constantly insists on the fact that she is black in spite of her "golden" skin: "You hated to think about the fact that you might be carrying a bit of him [Wade]," says George. "Even your shame was a privilege few of us had. We could only look at our skin tones and guess. At least you knew" (219). Thus, establishing one's filiation, or one's genealogy, even if it implies uncovering a story of violence and rape, is a structuring and ethical process which is emphasized by the very structure of the novel.

In fact, slavery and its history are "revisited" by Naylor: Sapphira is presented as an independent, active agent who was owned in body but not in mind, who may have killed her master or driven him to "deed his land" and to despair, who "took" her freedom—a genuine femme fatale. With her independence she freed her sons: "Her seven sons lived as free men, 'cause their mama willed it so" (151). Indeed, she was not herself a slave:

5. Barbara Christian, *Black Feminist Criticism: Perspectives in Black Women Writers* (New York: Pergamon, 1985), p. 209.

"He [Wade] had freed them all but her; 'cause, see, she'd never been a slave" (308). The real victim seems, finally, to have been Wade himself, who lost everything—his land, his love, and his life. Such an inversion of perspectives, a true rewriting of history, sheds a much more positive light on the woman who was sold in the original document, and who becomes the founding mother of a dynasty, for which she invents a symbolic name, the Days.

Uncovering the genealogy of the Day family involves the process of uncovering the names of its members. *Mama Day* could be viewed as an attempt to reconstruct the Book of Names of a black family who is the family of blacks. Bearing in mind the importance of naming and its specific symbolism in black history and literature, the reader immediately sees that the Days *own* their names, as they own their land. Every time their personal story is told—at least seven different times in the novel—it takes the form of a litany of names, Miranda, Ophelia, Abigail, Peace, which *are* the story. Moreover, the discovery of family names goes with the discovery of the self: the main character, first nicknamed Baby Girl, then Cocoa, recovers her real name, Ophelia, only after her aunt Miranda tells her the story of her grandmother Ophelia, who committed suicide in despair over losing one of her children: "It's her [Cocoa's] family and her history. And she'll have children one day . . . She ain't a baby. She's a grown woman and her real name is Ophelia" (116), a name that saved her life and "helped to hold her here" (267). Meaning grows from such genealogical archaeology; only this work of patient reconstitution (like the quilt sewn by Miranda which serves as a metaphor for the link between generations) can lead to knowledge and self-knowledge. In one of Miranda's dreams she "opens door upon door . . . She asks each door the same thing: 'Tell me your name'" (280). What she discovers is a string of women's names, Savannah, Samarinda, Sage, who are Sapphira's sisters, thus creating the large family of women slaves who had escaped, if not in body at least in mind, from slavery.

The Book of Names of *Mama Day* is essentially composed of women. In spite of two earlier generations of men, the word and the power have been given first to Miranda, then to Ophelia, following their original ancestor, Sapphira. In *Linden Hills* the voice and power of women had been hushed up until one of the Day women rose from the cellar and destroyed the Nedeed house. In *Mama Day* women are the source of power: born to the seventh son of a seventh son, Miranda is the central character of the story, the "little mother," the woman with a gift who understands the voices of history and can interpret them. As for Sapphira, various legends, all reported in one place or another in the book, show her as a "namer" ("a woman who brought a whole new meaning to words" [3]), the liberator of slaves, an African who "left by wind," the "great, great, grand, Mother" (218), which she is literally and figuratively, carrying the attributes of the goddess. She is also referred to as the one whose name nobody knows: she lives beyond words and, as the "unnamed," is close to the sublime, the stance of unchallenged authority. As the "greatest conjure woman on earth" (110), she even signed pacts with God, who has abandoned the island to her rule.

Woman's power, however, is viewed as both positive and negative. It can give life, as in the amazing scene of Little Caesar's conception by Miranda; it is also destructive, as embodied in the hurricane which "could only be the workings of Woman. And She has no name" (251), a statement that can be compared to George's: "That was power. But the winds coming around the corners of that house was God" (251). The other motif of the novel of "the man with the broken heart" (151; 308) is also indicative of the formidable power of women to inspire such passions that even the white master Wade perished, burned by the fire of Sapphira.

Yet this fire which ends *Linden Hills* and destroys the tainted kingdom of the Nedeeds is not the ultimate word of *Mama Day*. Unlike *Linden Hills*, *Mama Day*, though it speaks at times in dialogically racial and gendered voices, seems to enter what Mae Gwendolyn Henderson calls "a dialectic of identity," articulating "a relation of mutuality and reciprocity with the 'Thou'—or intimate other(s)."[6] The revival of the familial past and the reiteration of motifs which gradually uncover the story of the Days by questioning their genealogy develop a parallel, alternative history in which black experience is remodeled and transfigured, in which ruptures and tensions, pain, suffering, and death can be transcended and eventually stilled like the waters of the novel's last sentence. Language itself may be the ultimate medium for effecting this metamorphosis, language as the "archive" of history, a language forgotten but reinvented by the legends and tales, preserved in the conversations and dialogues between the dead and the living. One ritual of the island asks the living to put some moss in their shoes before they enter the graveyard so they may hear the voices of their ancestors. *Mama*

6. Mae Gwendolyn Henderson, "Speaking in Tongues: Dialogics, Dialectics, and the Black Woman Writer's Literary Tradition," in *Changing Our Own Words*, ed. Cheryl A. Wall (London: Routledge, 1990), p. 19.

*Day* resurrects these voices and, stressing the importance of the oral tradition in black culture, underlines the necessity of listening to all the voices, including the voices of the past.

## Voices

> So has the book been written
> So has your heart become perfect.
> —JAY WRIGHT, "Son"

*Mama Day* uses a great number of narrators, including the reader, to develop its central themes. "Think about it: ain't nobody really talking to you. We're sitting here in Willow Springs and you're God knows where. It's August 1999 . . . the only voice is your own" (10), says the first introductory narrator. First-person sections are written—or uttered—by George, Cocoa, Miranda, John Paul, and even Jonah Day, every narrator bringing a new clue to the story and adding meaning to it. Yet in spite (or because) of this polyphony of voices, this multivocality, the narrative "I" seems to fulfill the function ascribed by Benston to the primal name as central source, "a force which drives into history . . . as a poetic intelligence, a receptacle into which history flows in order to be carried by the vector of the poem into the present."[7]

Thus, a transcultural genealogical myth is created. Sapphira's legend does not live in "the part of our memory we can use to form words" (4). She belongs to some prelinguistic age, not yet in history but close to its edges. Miranda, as seer, *griot*, nurse, and doctor, with her prescience of things to come and knowledge of things past, has a voice that can be described as shamanistic. Considered together, the lineage of women going from Sapphira to Cocoa encompasses fire, air, land, and water, all elements unified in the vital logos, Jay Wright's Nommo, which they embody. "Speaking in tongues,"[8] these women are one with the forces of nature that surround them. The three essential elements are also found on their island; air (wind, hurricane), water (the Sound, waves, drowning or crossing the Sound in dream), and fire (lightning or the Candle Walk). Thus, the concrete objectification of the island's topography and the imaginative vision of the narrators combine to create a highly metaphorical space in which what is discovered

7. Benston, "I Yam What I Am," p. 167.
8. Henderson, "Speaking in Tongues," p. 22.

is not only Columbus's island or some New World revisited but a no-man's-land poised between chaos and form, the place where the original Word was uttered. The paradigmatic family of the Days becomes the paradigm of the human family, its genealogy the genealogy of the human race beyond color and history.

It is a primitive ritual, the Candle Walk, whose meaning had been lost, but has been rediscovered through the resurrection of the Days' history, which brings its epiphany to the novel: "It weren't about no candles, was about a light that burned in a man's heart" (308). Because of George, and because of the other voices, including male and even white voices, the story of hatred and sorrow has become a story of love. The motif of the man with a broken heart, which implied violence, revenge, enslavement, suffering, and death, has been replaced by the motif of the man with light in his heart. When Ophelia tries to describe George to her young son, she can describe only him as "a man who looked just like love" (310). In the same way, the words of the legal document selling Sapphira to Wade have been erased by age, and the only words left are "Law. Knowledge. Witness. Inflicted. Nurse. Conditions. Tender. Kind" (280)—terms that define the inheritance passed on to Ophelia. This inheritance sees the reconciliation of master and slave, and the reconciliation of black men and black women. The words of the message emphasize the new code (law reinforced by knowledge) whose key words are "tender" and "kind." Even though George does not understand Miranda's message ("Could it be that she wanted nothing but my hands?" [300]) and literally dies from a broken heart, meaning has been handed over to Ophelia, who has heard Miranda's voice: "She needs his hands in hers, his very hand. So she can connect it up with all the believing that had gone before . . . So together they could be the bridge for Baby Girl to walk over. Yes, in his very hands, he already held the missing piece she'd come looking for" (287). The terms used—"connect," "bridge"—underline the fact that knowledge and wisdom have been acquired and handed over to future generations, here embodied by Baby Girl/Ophelia, the first adventurer who crossed the bridge to go to the continent. In her next novel, *Bailey's Café*, Gloria Naylor takes us back to the mainland, for as one of the characters contends, "even though this planet is round, there are just too many spots where you can find yourself hanging onto the edge . . . and unless there's some space, some place, to take a breather for a while; the edge of the world—frightening as it is—could be the end of the world which would be quite a pity.'"[9] The journey back to the island of origins, this kind of Middle Passage revisited, the exploration of the interface between life and death have thus opened, "bridged," the way to some kind of reconciliation between the self, society, and history.

In *Linden Hills* Naylor uses sexual domination and the oppression of women by both white and black men as a model for all other exploitive systems. The original sin of Linden Hills is Luther's buying his land with the money he got from selling his octoroon wife and children into slavery. The Nedeed wives are granted neither value nor life. They have no recorded history: they do not exist in the twelve-volume history of the area written by Dr. Braithwaite, the professor from Fisk. Naylor calls attention to the fact that any kind of history that does not take into account black women's existence and voices is irresponsible and as sterile as Dr. Braithwaite's dead willows and bonsai trees. The awakening of the "last woman," a Day woman, finally gives a "face" to the thousands of black women who have been (literally in the novel, and figuratively in American history) kept in the netherworld, erased, blotted out of the Book of Names. Unlike *Linden Hills,* which stresses ruptures, crises, discontinuities, *Mama Day* tries to restore the lost unity of man and nature, of men and women. Owing to the special topography of Willow Springs and to genealogical archaeology, peace which had been lost (as expressed in the metaphorical story of the little girl, Peace, drowned in the well, whose suffering is finally freed by Miranda) has been regained. Thus, the book offers perfect proof of the centrality of African American women's shaping of a vision that overthrows the old white, male, elitist-centered view of the universe and becomes "an expressive site for a dialectics/dialogics of identity and difference."[10] Rejecting Columbus as founder of America and great father figure, it opens alternative, generous views of new communities, reinventing language and thus utopia, to connect the natural world and the possibilities of a more harmonious social order.

9. Gloria Naylor, *Bailey's Café* (London: Heinemann, 1992), p. 29.
10. Henderson, "Speaking in Tongues," p. 37.

*Justine Tally*

# History, Fiction, and Community in the Work of Black American Women Writers from the Ends of Two Centuries

We speak the truth as we know it. We say, I am a Black Woman, I cannot separate my race from my sex, cannot separate racism from sexism. They are rarely separate, never indivisible. So don't ask me to choose, I cannot; I am myself, I am not you. Nor will I let you choose for me. And I will not let you pretend that racism and sexism are not inseparable issues in *all* of our lives. And we speak in tongues.

—MARCIA ANN GILLESPIE

*S*peaking in tongues," the trope on which Mae Henderson centers her evaluation of African American women's writing, has taken on new significance since the Clarence Thomas—Anita Hill hearings, which Henderson eerily foreshadows in her analysis of Janie's courtroom hearing toward the end of *Their Eyes Were Watching God*.[1] The questions of who has access to the discourse, how, and when have become intertwined with the question of how historical discourse can be manipulated for personal gain.[2] Michel Foucault's observations as to who is allowed to speak with authority and the intimate relationship of discourse to power are especially pertinent for understanding the historical position of African American women, doubly silenced by race and by sex. If it is true that black people in the United States have traditionally been excluded from mainstream history, the Thomas hearings confirmed that women are still denied the veracity of their own experience.

1. Mae Gwendolyn Henderson, "Speaking in Tongues: Dialogics, Dialectics, and the Black Woman Writer's Literary Tradition," in *Changing Our Own Words,* ed. Cheryl A. Wall (London: Routledge, 1990), pp. 16–37.

2. Toni Morrison's introductory essay to her book *Race-ing Justice, En-gendering Power* (London: Chatto & Winus, 1993) is incisively perceptive on this subject; see "Introduction: Friday on the Potomac," pp. vii–xxx.

Literature is no less subject to these forces. Toni Morrison writes that "the languages [writers] use and the social and historical context in which these languages signify are indirect and direct revelations of that power and its limitations."[3] The narrative of (white) American literature, she argues, "is used in the construction of a history and a context for whites by positing history-lessness and context-lessness for blacks."[4] Creative black writers, therefore, have undertaken the reconstruction of both history and context for their people. The importance of this enterprise cannot be underestimated, for as James Baldwin writes, "History . . . is not merely something to be read. And it does not refer merely, or even principally, to the past. On the contrary, the great force of history comes from the fact that we carry it within us, are unconsciously controlled by it in many ways, and history is literally *present* in all that we do."[5]

Bring it down to basics: no history, no story, no culture, no identity, no present, and, therefore, what future? Pressing questions of the 1990s, these were no less fundamental to the 1890s. In fact, a look at the relationship between history and the literary texts of black women over the last hundred years reveals features that constitute a literary tradition ripened with the purpose of its authors. The task of literary creation is combined with and propelled by the task of social and cultural creation, for "words [do] not just reflect social and political reality; they [are] instruments for transforming reality."[6] These considerations are vital when we begin to examine texts from the end of the last century or look at fictional "revisions" of the slave experience written at the end of the present century. They also help to illustrate the different functions of fiction in the African American woman's literary tradition as it relates to historical consciousness: (1) literature as recording history; (2) literature as recovering history; (3) literature as writing/righting history; and (4) literature as shaping history.

Alice Walker remarked in the BBC program *Omnibus: Alice Walker and "The Color Purple"* that African American literature has always been involved with a great deal of recording. To this end her own novels *Meridian*

---

3. Toni Morrison, *Playing in the Dark: Whiteness and the Literary Imagination* (Cambridge, Mass.: Harvard University Press, 1992), p. 15.

4. Ibid., p. 53.

5. James Baldwin, "White Man's Guilt," in *The Price of the Ticket* (New York: St. Martin's 1985), p. 410.

6. Lynn Hunt, "Introduction," in *The New Cultural History*, ed. Lynn Hunt (Berkeley: University of California Press, 1989), p. 14.

and *The Third Life of Grange Copeland* record the South in transition both before and after the civil rights movement. In *The Salt Eaters* Toni Cade Bambara focuses on modern pressures brought to bear on the black community by racism, on black women by sexism within that community, and on the world at large by the white patriarchy's misuse of technology. In much the same way Frances Harper captures the era of the Civil War and Reconstruction from a black woman's point of view in her novel *Iola Leroy, or the Shadows Uplifted.*

Recovering an "invisible" history has been a task set out by many of these writers as well. Toni Morrison explicitly dedicates *Beloved* to the "60 million and more" whose story has never been told. She "reinvents" the Middle Passage, an experience so devastating that she speculates it has purposely been "disremembered" from the collective African American mind. Paule Marshall's character Avey also reenacts the Middle Passage in *Praisesong for the Widow* as she journeys from her status in the black middle class back to her African roots in the Caribbean. Alice Walker explores African history itself in *The Color Purple* and in *The Temple of My Familiar,* while Rosa Guy recreates high jinks in Harlem at its heyday in *A Measure of Time.* And while Marshall ostensibly records the progressive disaffinity of the black (particularly male) middle class with the larger black community (also the major theme of Gloria Naylor's *Linden Hills),* both in the United States and again in the Caribbean, her main character in *Daughters* desperately wants to write her senior research project, originally foiled by her white supervisor, to recover the history of male and female roles during slavery, using as her models Will Cudjoe and Congo Jane ("Coleaders, co-conspirators, consorts, lovers, friends. You couldn't call her name without calling his, and vice-versa, they had been that close").[7] Fiction calls on history as validation for its moral stance.

Not only is this literature dedicated to recovering a history which has been lost or to recording one that is in danger of being so, but also many times it finds itself in the difficult position of setting the record straight: writing/righting history. "The half was never told concerning this race that was in bondage nearly two hundred and fifty years," writes Mrs. Albert in *The House of Bondage, or Charlotte Brooks and Other Slaves,* and what was told was often misrepresented and distorted by white narrators. Frances Smith

7. Paule Marshall, *Daughters* (New York: Atheneum, 1991), p. 14.

Foster writes in her introduction to this novel that "Octavia Albert's depiction of slavery and its aftermath is in clear contrast to the two most popular nineteenth-century authorities, Harriet Beecher Stowe and Thomas Nelson Page."[8] This corrective dialogue has been continued with Margaret Walker's response to Margaret Mitchell's *Gone With the Wind* in an epic story based on her own family history, *Jubilee*. And Sherley Anne Williams contests William Styron's travestied memories of a black folk hero in *Nat Turner* with her creation of Nathan in *Dessa Rose*.

Yet, throughout all these texts there rings the moral imperative of literature as a molding force in history. Black women authors have always had a sense of themselves, whether unconscious or not, as keepers of the flame as well as of the hearth, with an enormous sense not only of history but of mission as well. Some one hundred years ago Anna Julia Cooper wrote, "Only the BLACK WOMAN can say when and where I enter, in the quiet, undisputed dignity of my womanhood, without violence and without suing or special patronage, then and there the whole . . . race enters with me,"[9] words which were reformulated by Paula Giddings in 1985: "For it is the historical concerns of the Black woman which are at the core of the Black and women's movements. When she is at her lowest ebb, the racial struggle flounders. When she is compelled to articulate her needs and becomes active in their behalf, the Black movement advances."[10] Exactly what this mission entails is subject to an evaluation of the sociocultural-historical context of each age, though in addition to differences attributable to the evolution of society, such an analysis reveals striking, sometimes devastating, similarities in spite of the passing of a whole century.

Just as "freed people" experienced the failure of Reconstruction and watched the severe curtailment of their newly won rights roughly thirty years after the "Day of Jubilee," so contemporary blacks are struggling against the loss of "consolidated gains" won during the civil rights movement, again thirty years after the passing of landmark legislation. Just as blacks were faced with a racist backlash exemplified by the exorbitant surge in the lynching

8. Frances Smith Foster, "Introduction," in Mrs. Albert, *The House of Bondage, or Charlotte Brooks and Other Slaves* (New York: Oxford University Press, 1988), p. xxxvii; see also p. 2.

9. Quoted in Paula Giddings, *When and Where I Enter: The Impact of Black Women on Race and Sex in America* (New York: Bantam Books, 1985), title page.

10. Ibid., p. 348.

of black men[11] and disenfranchisement, so the black community today confronts a renewed, and perhaps more insidious, backlash.

All these developments can indubitably be linked to the economic situation of the two eras: the 1890s witnessed a serious depression and the flight of black people to urban centers; in the 1990s blacks were confronted with another serious recession and the decay of urban areas. Both circumstances represent an attack on the black family and the black community and the values considered so fundamental for the survival of the race.[12] The scourge of the 1890s lay principally in alcohol, gambling, poverty, and violence from whites. In the 1990s the black family and community has been under assault from drugs, AIDS,[13] the "feminization of poverty,"[14] "the marginalization of black males by unemployment and incarceration—the one often leading to the other,"[15] and most, heart-rending of all, black-on-black violence. Paula Giddings writes of the "strangely quiet" black male leadership around the

11. "Between 1840 and 1860 there were three hundred recorded victims hanged or burned by mobs. Of that figure, only 10 percent were Black." Ibid., p. 79. "From 1865 to 1872, hundreds of colored men and women were mercilessly murdered and the almost invariable reason assigned was that they met their death by being alleged participants in an insurrection or riot. But this story at last wore itself out. No insurrection ever materialized; no Negro rioter was ever apprehended and proven guilty." Ida B. Wells Barnett, "A Red Record," in *Black Women in White America*, ed. Gerda Lerner (New York: Vintage, 1973), p. 200. Wells's campaign against lynching was as effective as it was vigorous: "The number of lynchings decreased in 1893—and continued to do so thereafter." Giddings, *When and Where I Enter*, p. 92.

12. Writes Paula Giddings: "Thriving Black communities were congealing into ghettos. Children had few recreational facilities and suffered neglect, as both parents were forced to work at labor that deadened the energies of the soul, as Maria Stewart would say. The situation worsened as Black communities became havens for drugs (cocaine was popular even then), crime, and prostitution—often with the complicity of White authorities. All these things added to the pressures on Black family life which were exacerbated by Black migration to the cities, both southern and northern. Between 1890 and 1910, as many as 200,000 blacks left the soil that had borne so much of their blood and tears. Blacks were beleaguered. The black family was under siege." Giddings, *When and Where I Enter*, pp. 79–80.

13. "Black teens comprise one of the fastest-growing groups of HIV-infected individuals. A study done at Children's National Medical Center in Washington, D.C. found that between 1987 and 1991, infection rates among teens rose 250 percent. The rates among black teens are much higher than among whites: black women age 21 have an HIV infection rate ten times higher than that of white women in the same age group; among black men it is three times higher." Angela Mitchell, "Risky Sex: Candid Talk about Responsible Behavior," *Emerge*, 3 (March 1992): 31.

14. "Age composition shifts in the black community are yeilding more and more young female-headed families whose members are disproportionately represented among the lowest earners." Playthell Benjamin, "The State of Black America, 1992," *Emerge*, 3 (March 1992): 36.

15. Ibid., p. 34.

turn of the last century, a vacuum that was amply filled by the dynamic black women of the era. She also documents the sexist attitudes of the end of the twentieth century in her discussion of the blatant lack of male support for the first black candidate for the presidency since Reconstruction—Shirley Chisholm.[16]

In both eras black women writers responded directly to these overriding sociopolitical concerns. Mary Church Terrell stated at the end of the last century that "we can build the foundation of the next generation upon such a rock of morality, intelligence and strength, that the floods of proscription, prejudice and persecution may descend upon it in torrents and yet it will not be moved," and to that end these writers have dedicated their efforts. Techniques, topics, concerns, and concepts may have varied, but the black female author still turns her creative ability to the moral development and solidarity of her community, literally writing to ensure its survival. The outstanding feature of these women's work both then and now is an exhortation to revive the community values that sustained blacks during slavery: a strong sense of race pride and self-worth, an egalitarian relationship between men and women, solidarity with the less fortunate, a common front against white racism, and the commitment to improved conditions for the whole race, not just the fortunate few. As Terrell declared, "Self-preservation demands that [black women] go among the lowly, illiterate and even the vicious, to whom they are bound by ties of race and sex . . . to reclaim them."[17] Certainly both of Mrs. Johnson's books, *The Hazeley Family* and *Clarence and Corinne,* make a point of reclaiming the prodigal members of the family who have been misled by alcohol and other vices of the "city."

Through Flora of *The Hazeley Family* and Iola Leroy, Mrs. Johnson and Frances Harper expound on the virtues of a proper education for women and their roles as moral examples for the family. Flora not only practices this role but "preaches" it to her Sunday school class. As Barbara Christian points out, the novel is "certainly based on the belief that 'a happy home is the acme of human bliss,' and that woman is central to the achievement of that acme." Although Flora and her mother must support themselves by sewing, "the emphasis is decidedly not on black women as wage earners . . .

16. Giddings, *When and Where I Enter,* pp. 337–340.
17. Mary Church Terrell, in Giddings, *When and Where I Enter,* pp. 100, 97.

but on the other important aspect of the homemaker, the capacity to create a nurturing and beneficial space within which the family might flourish."[18] Iola Leroy extols both the role of women in the home as caretakers and mothers of the race while insisting that the black woman must take her rightful place in the job market, thereby ensuring her economic independence, and improving the fortunes of her race as well.

In a very real sense all these considerations were tightly bound together. As Lucy C. Laney wrote, a good part of the philosophy of uplift had to do with alleviating the burdens of "ignorance and immorality," and was concerned "with true culture and character, linked with—cash."[19] The moral fabric of these stories, then, goes beyond the limited vision of life in the nuclear family to a concern for the whole race; the community is understood as the extended family. With its emphasis on the breakdown of the social order caused by alcohol and poverty, *Clarence and Corinne* offers "an extended exhortation to a new social order, now urged to bind up the wounds of its battered women, its broken children."[20] In her introduction Hortense Spillers finds the novel in this sense "astonishingly" similar to the contemporary situation, yet it is this sense of mission that is the outstanding constant in the writing of all black women. One of the messages in *The Hazeley Family*, according to Christian, is that "young girls are expected to take care of their older relatives, regardless of how they are treated."[21] But consider Ondine's reproach of Jadine in Toni Morrison's *Tarbaby:* "I'm just saying what a daughter is. A daughter is a woman that cares about where she come from and takes care of them that took care of her . . . What I want from you is what I want for you. I don't want you to care about me for my sake. I want you to care about me for yours."[22]

Flora, writes Christian, "effects not only the unity of her own family, but also that of other families. Thus she is not merely a homemaker but a social housekeeper, a role of increasing importance in black Northern communities

18. Barbara Christian, "Introduction," in Mrs. A. E. Johnson, *The Hazeley Family* (1894; rpt. New York: Oxford University Press, 1988), pp. xxviii, xxx.

19. Jeanne L. Noble, "The Negro Woman's College Education" (Ph.D. diss. Columbia University, 1956), p. 45; Giddings, *When and Where I Enter*, p. 102.

20. Hortense J. Spillers, "Introduction," in Mrs. A. E. Johnson, *Clarence and Corinne: or God's Way* (New York: Oxford University Press, 1988), p. xxxvii.

21. Christian, "Introduction," p. xxxi.

22. Toni Morrison, *Tarbaby* (London: Triad/Panther, 1984), p. 283.

. . . and one that women activists, black and white, undertook in their respective club movements of the 1890s."[23] True, but one is also tempted to use a "New Historicist" approach and read into the text a metaphor that extends beyond the black community to the society of the United States as a whole. As Christian astutely points out, the name of Ruth's half-sister, Jem, "provides the only hint of blackness in the novel"[24] (though perhaps her "saucy" comments might qualify as well). Jem is the daughter of Ruth's father by his second wife, an "invisible" woman about whom we are told nothing. If we can assume that this family is white and assign Jem's mother a "black" marker, then Jem becomes the metaphor for the unacknowledged but nevertheless "blood" kin of American whites; hence Ruth's mulatto half-sister. When the newly found grandfather (read: the white patriarchy) denies responsibility for the orphan, Ruth refuses to abandon her, thereby effecting the acceptance of this "child in distress" into the greater "family," perhaps an appeal to white women for "sisterhood."

Inextricably intertwined with this moral vision of family and community is the emphasis these writers place on the role of religion. Religion is a source of strength for the community and is basic to all three of the novels of the 1890s I have mentioned. Flora is stirred to her filial duty by a sermon and takes solace from religion throughout her trials. Her wayward brother, Harry, is rescued from moral and physical collapse by Joel Piper, who induces him to "accept Christ," and later becomes a minister himself. Corinne is ministered to by two religiously-minded sisters and also finds solace in a certain passage from the Bible when she is particularly distressed: "Casting all your care upon him; for he careth for you."[25] Readers, then, are exhorted not only to follow the moral guiding light of religion to prosperity but also to turn to religion for comfort in times of hardship and to proselytize. The moral tone of these writers, therefore, was decidedly directed toward the improvement of the black community at the turn of the last century. Although the circumstances of that same community have undoubtedly changed in the last hundred years, the moral imperative, the sense of mission, has not. It is a prime example of Eliseo Viva's theory of "subsistence,

23. Christian, "Introduction," p. xxxiii.
24. Ibid., p. xxxvi.
25. Johnson, *Clarence and Corinne*, p. 63.

insistence, and existence."[26] Communal values that subsist in the culture can be insisted upon by artists within that culture and brought into existence and acknowledged by all the members of the community. Or, in the words of Antonia S. Byatt: "In these readings, a sense that the text has appeared to be wholly new, never before seen, is followed, almost immediately, by the sense that it was *always there,* that we, the readers, knew it was always there, and have *always known* it was as it was, though we have now for the first time recognised, become fully cognisant of, our knowledge."[27]

Although contemporary discourse will now determine the criteria by which moral judgments are made, the objectives have remained unaltered: the traditional values of the black community must be revitalized if the race is to survive into the twenty-first century. And black women continue to believe that they have been "authorized" as speakers for that community. It is no coincidence that Paule Marshall has named the protagonists in her novel *Daughters* Estelle and Ursa-Beatriz; both "Estelle" and "Ursa" play on the idea of stars in the constellation Ursa Major, particularly as it contains the two stars that point to the ever-present North Star, so important to black people in times of slavery. And the name Beatriz is reminiscent of Dante's beloved, whom he came to see as the instrument of his spiritual salvation.

What, then, are the contemporary terms for "spiritual salvation" as seen by black women writers? The question of their morality as defined by their sexuality is now a moot point, the criteria for "ideal womanhood" in the twentieth century having been redefined as "active, attractive, ambitious, and ambivalent" rather than in the nineteenth century "pure, pious, domestic, and submissive."[28] Those novelistic "slave narratives" *Beloved* and *Dessa Rose* study questions of morality from a humanistic point of view. Apart from the more sexually explicit scenes, sexual and physical abuse is interpreted as abuse of power and an affront to humanity rather than an affront to femininity. Whereas Paul D is shocked to discover what School-

26. Eliseo Vivas, "The Object of the Poem," in *Creation and Discovery* (New York: Scribner, 1973), pp. 1069–77, discussed in Chester Fontenot, Jr., "Angelic Dance of Tug of War? The Humanistic Implications of Cultural Formalism," in *Black American Literature and Humanism,* ed. Baxter R. Miller (Louisville: University Press of Kentucky, 1981), p. 40.

27. Quoted in Morrison, "Preface," in *Playing,* p. xi–xii.

28. Patricia Graham, "Address upon the Installation of Sara Simmons Chapman as Dean of H. Sophie Newcomb Memorial College," *Under the Oaks,* 8 (Winter 1984): pp. 18–22.

teacher's nephews have done to Sethe's back, Sethe is still suffering from the horror of having her milk—her baby's sustenance—sucked from her breasts.

Dessa, by contrast, is not so much concerned about the morality of Nathan's having sex as with the morality of his having sex with a white woman, an act she sees as a betrayal of the race. Even though she comes to share a certain respect and even regard for Ruth by the end of the novel, Dessa is not prepared to share her future with a white woman, a far cry from the optimistic search for integration with whites at the end of the nineteenth century. Toni Morrison and Sherley Anne Williams have written (hi)stories with an eye to reclaiming what has been denied by the dominant culture. In *Dessa Rose* Nehemiah's "scribblings" and "blank pages" serve as testimony to the distortions and omissions of the black woman's story, while all traces of Beloved disappear, her footprints (historical marker) and even "the water too and what it is down there."[29]

What remains are individuals disposed to carry on a tradition and to pass down those values necessary for survival. Both Morrison and Williams emphasize not only "what it cost us to own ourselfs"[30] but also the human solidarity that was necessary to make the payment. The sisterhood required of Ruth to bring Jem into an integrated society in the 1890s is no less integral to Williams's novel, in which another white woman named Ruth orchestrates Dessa's and the others' escape to the West. In *Beloved* Sethe is assisted in giving birth to Denver by Amy, a white girl on her way east. Moreover, Sethe's liberation from the debilitating past is effectuated by the same community of women that had ostracized her to begin with. And it was perhaps the lack of that community during Sethe's youth that led her to slaughter her own child when faced with a crisis.

Missing almost entirely from the works of the end of this century, even in these "slave narratives," is the preoccupation with traditional religion so prevalent in the last century. Humanistic concerns, pride in and dependence on the self, contrast dramatically with abdication to God's will and the abiding faith in justice in the afterlife. Baby Suggs exhorts her listeners to love their bodies as the key to the celebration of the will to survive. Shug abandons the white man's God for a version of pantheism and encourages Celie to

29. Morrison, *Beloved*, p. 275.
30. Sherley Anne Williams, *Dessa Rose* (New York: Berkley, 1987), p. 260.

look for "it" everywhere, even in sex. More and more writers connect the rituals and interpretations of the Christian religion with remnants of African heritage. References to voodoo gods appear throughout the texts. Beloved is herself a "revenant," a soul in agony who returns to the scene of a terrible crime.

The abandonment of an all-powerful deity has placed responsibility for the race even more squarely on the shoulders of its women. The imperative of spiritual education has given way to institutional education[31] as a means for race improvement. College degrees for modern heroines are a given. But individual economic improvement never takes priority over the collective. In *Daughters* Estelle sends Ursa to school in the States to ready her for the struggle, not just for a job. Mae Ryland abandons her position at City Hall to defend the people in the South Ward once their newly elected black mayor has become deluded with grandiose projects beneficial only to whites in the suburbs; Ursa-Bea will betray her father in an agonizing decision to defend government lands from a plan that can only be detrimental to the Morlands, her father's people. Marshall's men, Mackenzie and Lawsen, are not evil, just misguided, and it is the women who must take it upon themselves to redirect their efforts.

Redirect, yes; abandon, no. The survival of the race depends on the solidarity of the community. Sethe is reunited with Paul D and integrated into the whole community; Dessa needs not only Nathan but Harper and the rest to make a collective effort to escape bondage and form a community in the West; Mr. Justin, having defeated Primus Mackenzie in the elections, calls on him to join in waging a battle against the incumbents, who want to sell out their people. And Marshall insists on the importance of the understanding and mutual support of black men and women: Estelle stands by her husband throughout all the years of disagreement and infidelity, "their two profiles like bas-relief heads on a medallion or a specially minted commemorative coin . . . Estelle's not going anyplace. She'll never leave." And Viney, who decided to rear a son all by herself, feels "this blank space, this hole next to me and Robeson." Even Ursa acknowledges the "hollowness" she feels having "definitively" quarreled with Lowell.[32] Marshall resurrects

---

31. Although the new crisis among black youths concerns precisely the loss of respect for education, a dramatic departure from traditional black values. Young blacks with a respect for education are accused of "acting white." *Time,* March 16, 1992, pp. 56–58.

32. Marshall, *Daughters,* pp. 356, 331.

Will Cudjoe and Congo Jane as models for forging a unified stance within the community in order to ensure survival in the face of continued assault.

Morrison, Williams, Marshall, and many other writers of fiction call on history to verify this moral position which is the strength of the community past and present. Just as women of the nineteenth century took pen in hand not only to document but also to mold the history of their people, so contemporary female writers combine fiction and history to reclaim the traditional values of the black community and forge a strong sense of moral purpose among its members. It is through this access to historical discourse, then, that the culture of the community is to be preserved. And it is this relationship of history to fiction that enables black women authors to turn their sense of mission into works of art that enrich us all.

*Abby Arthur Johnson*
*Ronald Johnson*

# Charting a New Course: African American Literary Politics since 1976

*T*he year 1976 was a major marker in African American culture, clearly signaling the end of the Black Arts movement and the emergence of a new literary period. The time represents a type of cultural "juncture," to borrow an expression used by Joe Weixlmann, editor of *Black American Literature Forum,* now called *African American Review.*[1] During the preceding decade spokespersons for the Black Arts movement had advocated the "black aesthetic," which meant art as propaganda and a literature exclusively by, about, and for blacks. In the mid-1970s African American writers began increasingly to explore a plurality of theoretical approaches. In so doing they set a new course for black literature. As in earlier decades, African American cultural and literary periodicals have both shaped and documented this change.

The shift in the cultural times marked by the year 1976 began several years earlier. As the Black Arts movement of the 1960s and early 1970s unraveled, the black revolutionary journals lost their constituency. Most of them—*Black Dialogue* (1964–1970), *Liberator* (1961–1971), and *Journal of Black Poetry* (1966–1973)—ceased publication at the turn of the decade.

Among those journals that had been powerful advocates of the black aesthetic in the 1960s, *Black World* (1970–1976), formerly *Negro Digest* (1942–1951, 1961–1970), survived the longest. Guided by Hoyt Fuller, the most influential journal editor of the Black Arts movement, *Black World*

1. Joe Weixlmann, "Black Literary Criticism at the Juncture," *Contemporary Literature,* 27 (Spring 1986): 48–62. *Black American Literature Forum* became *African American Review* in 1992.

recorded the demise of a cultural period. The examples range from poems, such as Jo-Ann Kelly's "Did I Dream Them Times? Or What Happened?," to summations of cultural events, including Carol Parks's observation that a number of participants at the first National Annual Conference of Afro-American Writers at Howard University in November 1974 thought that the preceding decade had been nothing but "jive."[2] Among the most notable essays was " 'Why I Changed My Ideology': Black Nationalism and Socialist Revolution," which was written by Amiri Baraka, once charismatic leader of the black cultural revolution. His turn toward Marxism seemed a final blow to the Black Arts movement. "It is fantasy," he wrote, "to think that we can struggle for our own liberation and be completely oblivious to all the other struggling and oppressed people in this land. Or throughout the world for that matter."[3]

The last two issues of *Black World,* dated January and February 1976, included statements that were highly critical of the black aesthetic and that went unanswered in the journal. In "Division and Confusion: What Happened to The Black Movement," published in the January number, Nathan Hare scorned the lack of substance he saw in the literature of the 1960s: "We soon arrived at an ultra-nationalism that was mystical, messianic, and hence dysfunctional. Our symbols, our dashikis (where, oh where, did they go?) and our bushy Afros became Black badges of militancy which required no acting out or actualizing." A parting word came from eighty-one-year-old George Schuyler, who had been managing editor of the *Messenger,* journal of the Brotherhood of Sleeping Car Porters, during the 1920s. In the transcript of an interview by Richard Long published in the February 1976 issue, he declared that much of the black literature produced in the preceding decade had been "crap" and "dribble."[4]

The death of *Black World* in February 1976 was a convincing sign that the Black Arts movement was no longer the dominant voice in African American literature.[5] Published statements by Larry Neal, once a prominent advocate

2. Jo-Ann Kelly, "Did I Dream Them Times? Or What Happened?," *Black World,* 21 (May 1972): 67; Carol Parks, "On Images and Control: The National Black Writers Convention," *Black World,* 24 (January 1975): 90–91.

3. Amiri Baraka, " 'Why I Changed My Ideology': Black Nationalism and Socialist Revolution," *Black World,* 24 (July 1975): 30.

4. Nathan Hare, "Division and Confusion: What Happened to The Black Movement," *Black World,* 25 (January 1976): 26; Richard Long, "Renaissance Personality: An Interview with George Schuyler," *Black World,* 25 (February 1976): 75–76.

5. Attempts to revive the movement in the late 1970s were largely unsuccessful, as is illustrated by *First World,* established by Hoyt Fuller in 1977. The opening issue of this journal, published in

of the black aesthetic, coincided with the end of *Black World* and underscored the shift in the cultural debate. In 1965, as arts editor of *Liberator,* he had declared that "the only goal" for black literature was "the psychological liberation" of black people across the globe, beginning with the United States. In an essay published a decade later in *The Black American Reference Book* (1976), he asserted the importance, even the primacy, of form in literature, substantiating his views with a quotation from Kenneth Burke, a white critic: "When the appeal of art as method is eliminated and the appeal of art as experience is stressed, art seems futile indeed." Neal no longer saw art as propaganda: "Literature can indeed make excellent propaganda, but through propaganda alone the black writer can never perform the highest function of his art: that of revealing to man his most enduring human possibilities and limitations." The black writer, he concluded, had to be open to universal concerns, to the "accumulated weight of the world's aesthetic, intellectual, and historical experience."[6]

Other persuasive indicators of cultural change appeared in 1976, particularly with the emergence of two literary-cultural journals that have served as major outlets for contemporary African American writers. One of these was *Black American Literature Forum,* which had been founded in 1967 but was reconfigured in 1976 when Joe Weixlmann became editor. The other periodical was *Callaloo,* established by Charles H. Rowell in 1976 as a southern black literary magazine. In the twentieth-anniversary issue (Spring–Summer 1986) Weixlmann recalled that *Black American Literature Forum* had "set out to help resituate the critical and theoretical planes of discourse about Afro-American literature and culture."[7] Both the *Black American Literature Forum* and *Callaloo* have met this goal, quickly emerging in the second half of the 1970s as primary platforms for a whole new look at the aesthetics of African American literature. They have been joined in this effort by *Hambone,* established in 1974 at Stanford University and edited by Nathaniel

---

Atlanta, featured Addison Gayle's "Blueprint for Black Criticism," which called for a return to the use of art for political and propagandistic purposes. Out of step with the times, the periodical failed to attract a wide readership and began a steady decline. Announced as a bimonthly in early 1977, *First World* finished the year as a quarterly and then appeared irregularly before ceasing publication in 1980, one year before Fuller's death.

6. Larry Neal, "The Black Writer's Role: Richard Wright," *Liberator,* 5 (December 1965): 20; Larry Neal, "The Black Contribution to American Letters, Part II: The Writer as Activist—1960 and After," in *The Black American Reference Book,* ed. Mabel M. Smythe (Englewood Cliffs, N.J.: Prentice-Hall, 1976), pp. 783–784.

7. Joe Weixlmann, "The Way We Were, the Way We Are, The Way We Hope to Be," *Black Literature Forum,* 20 (Spring–Summer 1986): 4.

Mackey; *Reconstruction*, founded in 1990 by Randall Kennedy, a law professor at Harvard University; and *Transition*, which had originated in Uganda in 1961 and then reappeared in 1991 under the editorship of Henry Louis Gates, Jr., and Kwame Anthony Appiah and with the imprint of Oxford University Press.

Wanting to restart the debate about African American literature and culture, Weixlmann encouraged and published a wide range of critical views, including a particularly influential series of essays and special issues in the early 1980s. The dialogue engaged the attention of the broader cultural community, and in 1983 the journal became the official publication of the Modern Language Association's Division on Black American Literature and Culture.

An immediate catalyst for the discussion in *Black American Literature Forum* was *Afro-American Literature: The Reconstruction of Instruction*, a volume of essays edited by Dexter Fisher and Robert Stepto and published by the Modern Language Association in 1979. This text, most notably the three essays by Gates, who emerged as a central figure in the ongoing critical dialogue, faulted the Black Arts movement for its overtly extraliterary positions.

Houston Baker, Jr., who resisted the preoccupation with theory he saw in Fisher and Stepto's volume, responded in the spring 1980 issue of the journal, which he guest-edited. He published writers who had been associated with the Black Arts movement, such as Amiri Baraka and Stephen Henderson, and who argued for the analysis of black literature within the historical and cultural context of "real life." Baraka directed his critique, given in "Afro-American Literature and Class Struggle," at the new generation of writers: "I know when I mention historical (and with that social, political, economic, etc.) context the structuralist and neo-new-critical types get their dander up. Good! This essay is meant to jump all over them."[8]

Baker addressed the new voices in "Generational Shifts and the Recent Criticism of Afro-American Literature," an essay featured in the spring 1981 issue of *Black American Literature Forum*. Using terms reminiscent of the labels once given Alain Locke's book *The New Negro* (1925), he acknowledged Fisher and Stepto's *Afro-American Literature* as "the handbook of the new generation." This "new group of intellectuals" was correct, he thought,

---

8. Amiri Baraka, "Afro-American Literature and Class Struggle," *Black American Literature Forum*, 14 (Spring 1980): 5–14.

in seeing a need for change in the critical direction of African American letters: "There were blatant weaknesses in the critical framework that actually accompanied the postulates of the Black Aesthetic." Baker also found weaknesses, however, in the new African American criticism, which he thought separated the study of black literature from the context of black life and depended unduly on the theories of white critics.[9]

Gates countered this critique in the winter 1981 and spring 1982 issues of *Black American Literature Forum,* which he guest-edited. He intended, with these issues, to "encourage a plurality of readings." Proceeding with this understanding, he opened the winter 1981 issue with his "Criticism in de Jungle," which insisted on the centrality of the text: "Close reading of any intellectual complexion is that which I advocate; there can be no compromise here."[10] Illustrating this approach, he assembled essays for the two special issues which represented a wide variety of readings, formalist, structuralist, and Marxist. The contributors were both black and white, from the United States and Europe, and included Anthony Appiah, Kimberly Benston, and Wole Soyinka.

The climax of the debate initiated in the special issues of *Black American Literature Forum* came in 1984, when Gates, Baker, and Baraka published books that advanced the views they had explored in the journal. Gates promoted theoretical pluralism in *Black Literature and Literary Theory,* which included eight articles originally published in *Black American Literature Forum* during 1981–82. Baker advocated the contextualizing of African American literature in *Blues, Ideology, and Afro-American Literature,* a volume comprising three essays, one of which was his "Generational Shifts and the Recent Criticism of Afro-American Literature." Baraka identified himself as "a Marxist-Leninist," in favor of a "complete social change," in *Daggers and Javelins,* a collection of essays including his "Afro-American Literature and Class Struggle." These books, all of which proceeded from key periodical essays, illustrate once again the important role of the journals, in this case *Black American Literature Forum,* in the ongoing dialogue about African American literature.

Sexual politics figured in the critical debate fostered by *Black American*

9. Houston A. Baker, Jr., "Generational Shifts and the Recent Criticism of Afro-American Literature," *Black American Literature Forum,* 15 (Spring 1981): 11, 9.

10. Henry Louis Gates, Jr., "Introduction: Criticism in de Jungle," *Black American Literature Forum,* 15 (Winter 1981): 124.

*Literature Forum* as well as the other African American periodicals. Women writers, who had spent a considerable amount of time backstage during the Black Arts movement, came center stage in the mid-1970s. Their very clear presence brought a host of new metaphors, with critics talking about "a black feminist aesthetic," "an era of black women's writing," "a major international movement."

*Black American Literature Forum* celebrated the contributions of black women writers in its winter 1984 issue, which included essays on the work of Toni Morrison and Alice Walker, an interview with Michele Wallace, author of the controversial *Black Macho and the Myth of the Superwoman* (1979), and reviews of *Black Women Writers at Work,* edited by Claudia Tate; *Home Girls,* edited by Barbara Smith: and *Black Women Writers, 1950–1980,* edited by Mari Evans. The lead article, "The Sexual Mountain and Black Women Writers," came from Calvin Herndon, author of *Sex and Racism in America* (1965). By its title the essay recalls the challenge proffered by Langston Hughes in "The Racial Mountain and the Negro Writer," published during 1926 in *Nation.* Herndon, who agreed with the feminist critics, faulted the sexism he saw during the Black Arts movement of the 1960s, when, he asserted, "the unequal recognition and treatment of women writers was enunciated more bigotedly than perhaps ever before." Working to right this imbalance, he identified four generations of active women writers: the "Old Timers" writing before the 1960s, such as Gwendolyn Brooks, Paule Marshall, and Margaret Walker; women emergent in the 1960s, including Maya Angelou, Toni Cade Bambara, June Jordan, Audre Lorde, Sonia Sanchez, and Alice Walker; the "Late Bloomers," who had been writing in the 1960s and 1970s but were first published in the 1980s, such as Hattie Gossett, Regina Williams, and Barbara Christian; and the "prodigious progeny of new black women authors"—Lorraine Bethel, Gloria Hull, Hillary Kay, Thylia Moss, and many others. Herndon has expanded his essay, in which he discerned a "vision of unfettered human possibility" in this roll call,[11] into a book, *The Sexual Mountain and Black Women Writers* (1992).

The winter 1984 issue of *Black American Literature Forum* presents a balanced, open endorsement of black women writers. The issue is in sharp contrast to the preceding controversy swirling about some of these authors,

---

11. Calvin Herndon, "The Sexual Mountain and Black Women Writers," *Black American Literature Forum,* 18 (Winter 1984): 139, 140, 145.

including Ntozake Shange, author of *For Colored Girls Who Have Considered Suicide/When the Rainbow is Enuf* (1977). Having felt left out of the Black Arts movement, some of the women writers drafted angry critiques of this cultural period. Underscoring a significant change in the politics of African American letters, they placed these critiques not in black literary periodicals but in magazines the revolutionary spokespersons of the 1960s and early 1970s had called "the white racist press."[12]

A case in point is Michele Wallace, who published the essays that eventually became *Invisibility Blues* (1990) in a wide variety of cultural and feminist magazines. Her work appeared in *Village Voice* (6 essays), *Zeta* (5), *Ms.* (2), *Art Forum International* (2), *Feminist Art Journal* (1), *Heresies* (1), *Women's Review of Books* (1), and *Nation* (1). In addition, Wallace placed a substantial part of *Black Macho* in *Ms.*, which featured her face on its cover when the book was published in full.

*Black Macho* fanned a heated controversy within the black community, particularly with statements such as: "Perhaps the single most important reason the Black Movement did not work was that black men did not realize they could not wage struggle without the full involvement of women . . . By negating the importance of their role, the efficiency of the Black Movement was obliterated. It was just a lot of black men strutting around with Afros." *Black Scholar* (1969 to present), a basically political and sociological journal edited by Robert Chrisman, responded to this challenge. The March–April 1979 issue featured a critique of *Black Macho* by the sociologist Robert Staples, who called Wallace's views "puzzling": "I found little . . . that related to my personal experience."[13]

The Staples essay stimulated such a volume of commentary that the next issue of *Black Scholar* (May–June 1979) published forty-six pages of responses by sixteen prominent black writers. The comments generally split along gender lines, with some of the critics claiming that the white press had embraced *Black Macho* because of its negative statements about black males. One such writer was Askia Toure, earlier an associate editor of *Black Dialogue* and an editor at large for the *Journal of Black Poetry:* "If one views

12. See, for example, Willard Pinn, "Towards a Black Communication System," *Soulbook,* 3 (Fall–Winter 1970): 43–44.

13. Michele Wallace, *Black Macho and the Myth of the Superwoman* (New York: Verso, 1990), p. 81; Robert Staples, "The Myth of Black Macho: A Response to Angry Black Feminists," *Black Scholar,* 10 (March–April 1979): 25.

the white, middleclass elitism of *Ms.* magazine, its basic values (procapitalist, 'liberal' white supremacist) . . . then naturally one is both suspicious and annoyed when a close-up of Michele Wallace's face becomes its front cover." He considered her book "one of the most vicious, slanderous attacks against both black men and women, and indeed against the Black Liberation movement, on record."[14] Others, including lecturer and poet Sarah Webster Fabio, welcomed the voice of a new generation of women.

The other African American journals of the period, those that had emerged at about the same time as Weixlmann's periodical, did not engage directly in the debate over sexual politics, at least not to the extent of *Black Scholar*. They agreed with the endorsement given by *Black American Literature Forum* in its winter 1984 issue and welcomed the work of the women writers. These journals included *Hambone,* which had appeared once in 1974, two years before Weixlmann became editor of *Black American Literature Forum,* but then did not resurface until 1982.

One particular controversy, publicized in the 1982 issue, illustrates the critical independence of *Hambone.* Both the topic—the function of black literature—and the combatants—Amiri Baraka and Ishmael Reed—were familiar. The stimulus for this discussion was an interview of the irascible George Schuyler by Reed and Steve Cannon, included in Reed's *Shrovetide in Old New Orleans* (1978). The published interview showed Reed and Cannon in apparent agreement with disparaging comments Schuyler made about Malcolm X. An indignant Baraka reacted in the spring 1980 issue of *Black American Literature Forum,* declaring that the comments represented "straight-out agentry, and in certain circumstances could easily get these dudes iced." Reed, interviewed in the fall 1982 issue of *Hambone,* had two objections: to the "threat" by Baraka and to Weixlmann's publication of the remark in his journal. With a statement carried in the fall 1983 number of *Hambone,* Weixlmann responded to Reed with a statement that essentially ended the discussion in the periodicals: "Let's keep our print media unfettered, uncensored; let's keep our journals open to radically differing views."[15]

14. Askia Toure, "Black Male/Female Relations: A Political Overview of the 1970s," *Black Scholar,* 10 (May–June 1979): 47.

15. Amiri Baraka, "Afro-American Literature and Class Struggle," pp. 5–14; Ishmael Reed, "Ishmael Reed Replies to Amiri Baraka," *Hambone,* 2 (Fall 1982): 125; Joe Weixlmann, "Amiri Baraka and *Black American Literature Forum:* An Epistolary Reply to Ishmael Reed," *Hambone,* 3 (Fall 1983): 143.

By airing the controversy proceeding from the Schuyler interview, the reemergent *Hambone* announced its own openness to divergent opinions. Issued annually in the fall, *Hambone* has maintained its independence from special interests, publishing poems and book reviews from a diverse group of contributors, including Michael Harper, David Henderson, bell hooks, Clarence Major, and Ishmael Reed.

*Callaloo,* initiated in December 1976, also meshes with the periodical tradition promoted by Joe Weixlmann. In the beginning, however, the publication appeared headed in a different direction. In the opening issue Tom Dent, who was initially a co-editor with founder Charles Rowell, stated that the readers of African American literature were "suffering the demise of *Black World* and many of the community-based literary magazines" of the late 1960s and early 1970s. This comment may have led readers to think that *Callaloo* had accepted the mantle of the Black Arts movement and would emerge as a revolutionary periodical. Steered primarily by Rowell, who emerged as editor in chief with the second issue, dated February 1978, the journal has taken a different course, securing a valued position within the new generation of African American writers.[16]

Identified originally as "a forum for Black South creative voices," *Callaloo* appeared as "A Journal of African-American and African Arts and Letters" in 1985, when Rowell brought the periodical to Charlottesville, where he had accepted a faculty position at the University of Virginia. This more generic description of *Callaloo* is appropriate, for the journal does not promote any particular critical theory or any school of literature, remaining open to new and established writers, white and black, including John Callahan, Michel Fabre, Ernest Gaines, Michael Harper, Stephen Henderson, and Charles Johnson. The individual numbers highlight a wide range of genres: poems, short stories, plays, critical essays, interviews, bibliographies, book reviews, and photographs. Special issues have featured the work of Aimé Césaire, Ernest Gaines, Gayl Jones, Paule Marshall, Larry Neal, Alice Walker, and Richard Wright, among others.

The spring 1991 issue of *Callaloo* headlined Charles Rowell's interview of Henry Louis Gates, Jr., who reasserted the critical openness he and others had enunciated in contemporary periodicals. He revealed a personal reaction

16. Tom Dent, "Preface," *Callaloo,* 1 (December 1976): v–vi; Charles H. Rowell, "Editor's Note," *Callaloo,* 2 (February 1978): 3.

against the insularity of the Black Arts movement: "One of the reasons I write and talk so much about intellectual intolerance on the cultural left is that I remember very painfully those days in the late '60s when if your Afro wasn't two feet high and your dashiki wasn't tri-colored, etc., etc., then you weren't colored enough." Echoing the militaristic language of the Black Aesthetic, he explained his emergence among the critical opposition: "As I say, the Black Aesthetic movement provided the immediate context of my first critical forays." Continuing his insistence on theoretical pluralism ("I just want people to be smart critics"), Gates endorsed the contributions of black women writers: "I don't know of any worthwhile work done in black literary criticism in the past decade that hasn't been profoundly informed by the perspectives of feminist criticism." His conclusion was optimistic: "No matter how narrowly you demarcate the field of study . . . the critical community doesn't fissure neatly along lines of race, gender or ethnicity."[17]

This statement provides a fitting backdrop for the emergence, or reemergence, of two additional periodicals: *Reconstruction* in January 1990 and *Transition* in January 1991. These journals, both of which reflect a commitment to diversity within African American literary circles, are part of group of new black periodicals, including *Catalyst,* established in 1986 by Pearl Cleage in Atlanta; *Shooting Star Review,* founded in 1986 by Jerry W. Ward and others in Pittsburgh; and *Konch,* founded in 1990 by Ishmael Reed in Berkeley.

Randall Kennedy established *Reconstruction* as a quarterly "journal of opinion" that would be "concerned with providing a forum for uninhibited commentary on African American politics, society, and culture." Envisioning a periodical modeled on George Schuyler's *Messenger* and W. E. B. DuBois's *Crisis* in the 1920s, he wanted "to create a vibrant, interactive community of readers and writers that is unafraid of robust, wide-open debate." Kennedy named the journal after the period of political reform following the Civil War. The title has, he declared, "a certain historical resonance."[18]

Since its founding *Reconstruction* has fostered debate on a number of fronts. The first issue, for example, included law professor Stephen Carter's article criticizing black dependence on affirmative action programs in educa-

---

17. Charles H. Rowell, "An Interview with Henry Louis Gates, Jr.," *Callaloo,* 14 (Spring 1981): 445, 447, 453.

18. *Reconstruction,* 1 (Spring 1990): title page; Denise K. Magnet, "Law Professor Creates a 'Forum for Open Debate' on Black Society," *Chronicle of Higher Education,* May 30, 1990, p. A3.

tion and the professions. In the same issue Kennedy reviewed *Succeeding against the Odds* (1989), the autobiography of magazine publisher John H. Johnson. Although he praised many of Johnson's achievements, Kennedy sharply reprimanded the founder of *Negro Digest/Black World, Ebony,* and *Jet* for his concentration on trying to "make money." He said Johnson failed to tell the whole story about the rise and fall of *Black World* or to give editor Hoyt Fuller due credit for the journal's success.[19] The Carter essay and the Kennedy review highlighted an issue that also featured photographs by Walker Evans and Robert G. O'Meally's appreciative profile of Johnny Hodges. Subsequent issues have included reader correspondence critical of the journal, along with Kennedy's rebuttals, articles on the King memorial in Atlanta, rap and censorship, Terry McMillan, Charles Davis, Billie Holiday, and multiculturalism.

*Transition* experienced a new beginning in 1991. Aptly named, this quarterly publication has experienced several passages. Founded in Uganda during 1961 by Rajat Neogy, an Indian intellectual, *Transition* functioned as a controversial outlet for political and cultural commentary during a period of Ugandan internal conflict, which ended with the rise of Idi Amin to power. When Neogy was imprisoned in 1968, *Transition* ceased publication. In 1971 the journal resurfaced in Ghana under the editorship of Wole Soyinka, who kept the publication going until issue 50, released in 1977. When the periodical reemerged in January 1991, with issue 51, the masthead identified Wole Soyinka as chairman of the editorial board and Kwame Anthony Appiah and Henry Louis Gates, Jr. as the editors. The editorial board included some well-known names: Houston Baker, Aimé Césaire, Carlos Fuentes, bell hooks, and Toni Morrison. By the end of the year, with issue 54, *Transition* was the official publication of the W. E. B. Du Bois Institute at Harvard University. Gates had become director of the institute that autumn.

The lead article for issue 51, appropriately called "A Time of Transition," was by Wole Soyinka, who noted this "third determined appearance" of the journal and then cited the greater significance of its intriguing past: "Since its sojourn on the African continent (Uganda) owed both birth and midwifery to an Indian, it is not too whimsical to suggest that *Transition* has actually (or, at the least, symbolically) circled the globe . . . materializing in the tradition of the phoenix." He envisioned a large mission for the reborn

19. Randall Kennedy, "Making It," *Reconstruction,* 1 (Spring 1990): 66–67.

journal—assisting in the passage to the next millennium, to a new, democratic world order: "*Transition* will provide yet another plank in the erection of a global platform for the debate on a new humanistic ordering, striving to remain at the forefront of that ultimate question in the unfettered realm of ideas and creativity."[20] As indicated by this comment, *Transition* has re-emerged with a global view. The January 1991 issue, for example, included articles titled "Beyond the Berlin Wall," "On Seeing England for the First Time," and "AIDS, Africa, and Cultural Theory." In addition, the journal has a particular concentration on African American culture.

Each issue of *Transition* coheres around three sections: "Positions" (essays on cultural and political topics), "Under Review" (commentary on recent books), and "In Focus" (interviews). All of the sections encourage the "unfettered" debate advanced by Soyinka. Film maker Spike Lee, interviewed by Gates for issue 52, provided a good example of this kind of discussion. In a wide-ranging dialogue about race, politics, and the black cinema, Lee rejected the notion that he was antifeminist in *Do the Right Thing*, particularly with Rosie's dance at the beginning of the film: "Fifty percent of the feminists hate the film, fifty percent of them like it: no one group is going to totally endorse anything." He went on to stress the diversity he saw within the black community, saying there was no "one monolithic black view": "If you get ten black people in a room, there can be ten different views."[21] This comment, which parallels statements by other spokespersons featured in *Transition*, provides a measure of the distance traveled by African American cultural critics since the 1970s—the journey from the black aesthetic toward greater acceptance of varied aesthetic approaches.

E. Ethelbert Miller has provided a fitting summation of this cultural passage. A poet and director of the African American Resource Center at Howard University, he is also a poetry editor for *African American Review* and a frequent contributor to both that magazine and *Callaloo*. His comments focus on the possible meanings of "The Black Columbiad: Reinventing America," the title of a workshop at the 1992 meeting of the European Association of American Studies in Seville. Placing the term "Black Columbiad" in the context of the previous two decades, Miller talked about the "exploration of uncharted waters," the rediscovery and expansion of African Ameri-

20. Wole Soyinka, "A Time of Transition," *Transition*, 51 (1991): 4–5.
21. Henry Louis Gates, Jr., "Final Cut," *Transition*, 52 (1991): 182.

can culture, the quest for more diversity in literary aesthetics, and the "find-ing" of a new generation of writers.[22] Beginning with *Black American Literature Forum* and *Callaloo* in 1976 and continuing into the present with *Reconstruction* and *Transition,* black periodicals have traced this movement into "uncharted waters," this new journey into African American literature and culture.

22. E. Ethelbert Miller, conversation with Ronald Johnson, March 3, 1992.

# Prospects?

Adrienne Kennedy

# Motherhood 2000

*Characters*
A writer and mother
Four actors in the miracle play

*I* finally found the policeman who beat my son that January night in 1991. He ran a theater on the steps of the Soldiers and Sailors Monument on Riverside Drive at 89th Street.

Homeless people who had lived in the park under the 89th Street overlook now lived on 89th Street on the sidewalks, in the hallways of apartment buildings at 173 and 145 Riverside Drive, as well as in the apartments with the legal tenants.

This policeman who had haunted me for nine years performed a play nightly; it was an ancient miracle play.

How amazing that this man should appear on the very street where I lived.

Evenings I could hear the actors, from the roof of my brownstone where I went to rest. The "Soldiers" spoke to "Christ."

Writer as a soldier:

And I have gone for gear good speed. Both hammers and nails large and long, then maybe boldly do this deed.

I walked to the edge of the roof and listened.

This man who I had thought of constantly since 1991 was playing Christ. The soldiers spoke again to him.

Writer quoting actors:
The foulest death of all shall he die for his deeds that means cross him we shall.

It was quite by accident that I had found him. I had come out of my brownstone one morning when I saw a band of disheveled men walking up Riverside Drive in the rain. They stopped when they came to the Soldiers and Sailors Monument. One stepped forward and climbed the steps to the doorway of the statue. I recognized him immediately.

I had seen Richard Fox only on videotape. The night of the beating my sister hid in the doorway of her house and photographed him: he handcuffed my son and kicked him again in the stomach.

I had wanted to find him. I wanted to find his house somewhere in the suburbs of Virginia, but the lawyers concealed any information about Fox from me.

"You're behaving like a mother," the lawyer said. "You could hurt your son's case. Don't interfere. We have a detective looking into this policeman's history. Anyway, we've heard he will no longer be with the force. He's going to work for the Secret Service at the White House. Mrs. Alexander, please go back to your classes. Don't interfere. You will hurt your son's case."

Now nine years later I sat on the grass at the monument and watched Fox: acting the role of the Savior. The name of the troupe was The Oliviers.

I recognized the other actors. They were the former district attorney, the county manager, the police chief, and two policemen who had been involved in my son's case. They had been at the hearing.

At that time I wrote to them as well as to the governor, congressmen, the NAACP, and friends.

"I am writing to you again. On Friday night, January 11, my son was knocked to the ground and beaten in the head and face, kicked in the chest and stomach, and dragged in the mud by a policeman."

"My son was stopped because he had a tail light out . . ."

I wrote again and again:

Congressmen
The Black Caucus
The County Manager
NAACP
Chief of Police

My beloved son was also a Rhodes scholar and traveled the country giving speeches for the causes of blacks.

Nine years had passed. It was 2000.

The sun and the ships on the Hudson were still wonderful. But I hadn't been to Broadway for more than a year. It was impossible to make my way through the men on the sidewalks fighting among themselves. Shootings occurred daily.

I remembered the lovely street fairs when I strolled and bought faded voile dresses and sweet oils in green bottles. The children and David and I gorged on ice cream and crimson ices and bought paperback books on trees and gardens—trees and shrubs, trees for shade and shelter on the lawn.

"Mom," the children said, "we want another ice."

Now I was often hungry. Food was at the market on Broadway and 91st, but unexpected shootings on the street kept me fearful. I saved sacks of potatoes so that in case of shootings I would always have something to eat.

It was then I daydreamed of old movies, *The Sound of Music,* Fellini's *Amarcord.* The old movie theaters, the Thalia, New Yorker, the Symphony, had closed long ago.

Refugees from New Jersey arrived every morning at the 79th Street boat basin where armies of people lived.

Riverside Park between 86th Street and 116th was dangerous, inhabited only by gangs.

I remembered when my baby sons and I had walked in the snow deep into this park down to the highway, across to the shore of the Hudson. The cruise ship *Circle Line* sailed past. We waved then walked to 116th Street and Broadway and stopped at Prexy's for chocolate. I dreamed of the beauty of Columbia University Mall, where civil unrest and chaos now never ceased.

Members of The Oliviers were all white. They seemed protected by the soldier costumes they wore. My neighbor, Judy, a casting director, said she thought The Oliviers were one of the groups who traveled from national monument to monument trying to find asylum.

Judy still delivered tapes of her clients to an agency on 47th and Sixth and said things in that area were sometimes pretty much as they had been in the past.

She said the most popular movie downtown was called *Suicide Mission* about a group of unhappy housewives from Davis, California. Sometimes she still went shopping at Saks and once bought me a straw hat. I wore it when I sat on the roof to read. Sometimes she had to stay downtown for the night. You never knew when bombings would occur. Still, she was younger than I was and less afraid.

Often people who made it across the Hudson lived in the PATH station for weeks. Civil strife had destroyed a great deal of New Jersey. Yet some suburbs remained intact.

In the brownstone I lived in it was impossible to tell friends from enemies: the five floors were occupied by Bosnians, Californians, Haitians, neo-Nazis; all were split into subgroups, and each group had their own agenda and language.

My sons were somewhere in Washington but I didn't know where.

I lived on money from the royalties of my plays, a very small but sufficient amount.

City officials were constantly drowned near the Statue of Liberty.

Nights I continued to watch the ancient miracle play from the roof.

One night I came into the park just as a scene began.

The soldiers spoke.

Although my asthma was very bad due to the conditions of the dirty streets, I tried to speak along with the actors.

And I never took my eyes off Richard Fox. His costume was very shabby; soldiers closed in upon him. I realized how agonized I still was by him.

I decided to join their company. I told them I had once been a playwright and had taught at Harvard. I was relieved to see they did not remember my name from my son's case.

I became their only black member. They said I could rewrite a section of the play.

That night as I sat on the roof writing I remembered my son screaming when the policeman kicked him in the stomach, my son who as a child laughed at his turtle and ate Pop Tarts and watched *Rawhide* with his cowboy hat on.

The next night I arrived at the monument early.

On that night The Oliviers allowed me to perform with them. I was to be one of the soldiers.

The play began.

(The play appears before her. Three soldiers and Jesus, Richard Fox, stand directly opposite her.)
Soldiers:

>*Soldier:*   We have them here even at our hand.

>*Soldier:*   Give me this wedge; I shall it in drive.

>*Soldier:*   Here is another yet ordand.

>*Soldier:*   Do take it me hither belive.

>*Soldier:*   Lay on then fast.

>*Soldier:*   Yes I warrant
>I thring them sam, so mote I thrive.
>Now will this cross full stably stand;
>All if he rave, they will not rive.

>*Soldier* [*to Christ*]:   Say, sir, how likes you now
>This work that we have wrought?

>*Soldier:*   We pray you say us how
>Ye feel, or faint ye aught.

[*Writer speaks with them*]

>*Soldier:*   We! Hark! He jangles like a jay.

>*Soldier:*   Methink he patters like a pie.

>*Soldier:*   He has been doing so all day,
>And made great moving of mercy.

>*Soldier:*   Is this the same that gan us say
>That he was God's Son almighty?

>*Soldier:*   Therefore he feels full fell affray,
>And deemed this day for to die.

>*Soldier:*   Vah! qui destruis templum . . .

>*Soldier:*   And, sirs, he said to some
>He might raise it again.

*Soldier:*   To muster that he had no might,
For all the cautels that he could cast;
As Pilate deemed, is done and dight;
Therefore I rede that we go rest.

*Soldier:*   This race mun be rehearsed right,
Through the world both east and west.

*Soldier:*   Yea, let him hang there still,
And make mows on the moon.

*Soldier:*   Then may we wend at will.

*Soldier:*   Nay, good sirs, not so soon.
For certes us needs another note:
This kirtle would I of you crave.

*Soldier:*   Nay, nay, sir, we will look by lot
Which of us four falls it to have.

*Soldier:*   I rede we draw cut for this coat—
Lo, see how soon—all sides to save.

*Soldier:*   The short cut shall win, that well ye wot,
Whether it fall to knight or knave.

*Soldier:*   Fellows, ye thar not flite,
For this mantle is mine.

*Soldier:*   Go we then hence tite;
This travail here we tine.

Writer: I spoke my lines coughing, wheezing . . . then found my place directly before Fox and struck him in the head with a hammer.
   [She does.]
   [He falls.]


END

# Contributors

ANNALUCIA ACCARDO, Università di Roma (Italy)

PAOLA BOI, Università di Cagliari (Italy)

HÉLÈNE CHRISTOL, Université Provence, Aix Marseille (France)

ROSEMARY F. CROCKETT, Pretoria (South Africa)

MARIA DIEDRICH, Universität Hannover (Germany)

ANN DUCILLE, Wesleyan University

GERALD EARLY, Washington University, St. Louis

GENEVIÈVE FABRE, Université Paris (France)

MICHEL FABRE, Université de la Sorbonne Nouvelle, Paris (France)

ROBERT GOODING-WILLIAMS, Amherst College

FRITZ GYSIN, Universität Bern (Switzerland)

FRIEDERIKE HAJEK, Berlin (Germany)

PHILLIP BRIAN HARPER, Harvard University

MAŁGORZATA IREK, Swiebodzin (Poland) and Freie Universität Berlin (Germany)

JOSEF JAŘAB, Palacky University, Olomouc (Czech Republic)

ABBY ARTHUR JOHNSON, Washington, D.C.

RONALD JOHNSON, Georgetown University

ADRIENNE KENNEDY, New York City